The Last
RABBI

NEW JEWISH PHILOSOPHY AND THOUGHT
Zachary J. Braiterman

The Last
RABBI

Joseph Soloveitchik and Talmudic Tradition

WILLIAM KOLBRENER

INDIANA UNIVERSITY PRESS

Bloomington and Indianapolis

This book is a publication of

Indiana University Press
Office of Scholarly Publishing
Herman B Wells Library 350
1320 East 10th Street
Bloomington, Indiana 47405 USA

iupress.indiana.edu

Manufactured in the United States of America

Library of Congress Cataloging-in-Publication Data

Names: Kolbrener, William, author.
Title: The last Rabbi : Joseph Soloveitchik and Talmudic tradition /
    William Kolbrener.
Description: Bloomington and Indianapolis : Indiana University
    Press, [2016] | Series: New Jewish philosophy and thought |
    Includes bibliographical references and index.
Identifiers: LCCN 2016017125 | ISBN 9780253022240
    (cloth : alk. paper) | ISBN 9780253022325 (ebook)
Subjects: LCSH: Soloveitchik, Joseph Dov. | Rabbis—United
    States—Biography. | Jewish scholars—United States—Biography.
Classification: LCC BM755.S6144 K66 2016 | DDC 296.8/32092aB—dc23
LC record available at https://lccn.loc.gov/2016017125

1 2 3 4 5 21 20 19 18 17 16

For my children

The main thing is to learn Torah with joy and excitement.
—Joseph Soloveitchik, *And from There Shall You Seek*

Contents

Abbreviations   *ix*

Preface   *xi*

Introduction: The Making of Joseph Soloveitchik
and the Unmaking of Talmudic Tradition   *1*

Part I. Talmudic Tradition: Mourning   **15**

1   Hermeneutics of Rabbinic Mourning   *17*

2   Pluralism, Rabbinic Poetry, and Dispute   *36*

Part II. Joseph Soloveitchik: Melancholy   **65**

Interlude: Primal Scene in Pruzhna   *67*

3   Love, Repentance, Sublimation   *76*

4   Joseph Soloveitchik: A Melancholy Modern   *101*

5   Beyond the Law: Repentance and Gendered Memory   *127*

6   From Interpretive Conquest to Antithetic Ethics   *152*

Conclusion: The Last Rabbi and Talmudic Irony   *184*

Notes   *203*

Index   *221*

Abbreviations

Abbreviations of Works by Joseph B. Soloveitchik

"Brisker" Jeffrey Saks, "Rabbi Joseph B. Soloveitchik on the Brisker Method," *Tradition* 33, no. 2 (1999): 50–60.

"Catharsis" "Catharsis," *Tradition* 17, no. 2 (1978): 38–54.

"Confrontation" "Confrontation," *Tradition* 6, no. 2 (1964): 5–29.

Family *Family Redeemed*, ed. David Shatz and Joel B. Wolowelsky (Hoboken, NJ: Ktav 2000).

LMF *The Lonely Man of Faith* (Northvale, NY: Jason Aronson, 1997).

"Majesty" "Majesty and Humility," *Tradition* 17, no. 2 (1978): 25–37.

Man *Halakhic Man*, trans. Lawrence Kaplan (Philadelphia: Jewish Publication Society, 1983).

Mind *The Halakhic Mind* (New York: Free Press, 1986).

Repentance *On Repentance: The Thought and Oral Discourses of Rabbi Joseph Dov Soloveitchik*, ed. Pinchas Peli (Jerusalem: Oroth, 1980).

"Sacred" "Sacred and Profane," *Jewish Thought* 3, no. 1 (1993): 55–82.

Seek *And from There Shall You Seek*, ed. David Shatz and Reuven Ziegler (Hoboken, NJ: Ktav, 2008).

Shiurim *Shiurim Le-Zecher Avi Mori* (Jerusalem: Mossad Ha-Rav Kook, 2002), 2 vols.

"Talne" "A Tribute to the Rebbetzin of Talne," *Tradition* 17, no. 2 (1978): 73–83.

Vision *Vision and Leadership*, ed. David Shatz, Joel B. Wolowelsky, and Reuven Ziegler (Hoboken, NJ: Ktav, 2012).

"Voice" "*Kol Dodi Dofek*: It Is the Voice of My Beloved That Knocketh," in *Theological and Halakhic Reflections on the Holocaust*, ed. Bernhard H. Rosenberg (Hoboken, NJ: Ktav, 1992), 51–117.

Whirl *Out of the Whirlwind: Essays on Mourning, Suffering and the Human Condition*, ed. David Shatz, Joel B. Wolowelsky, and Reuven Ziegler (Hoboken, NJ: Ktav, 2003).

Abbreviations of Other Works

Action	Jonathan Lear, *Therapeutic Action* (New Haven, CT: Yale University Press, 2003).
Desire	Jonathan Lear, *Aristotle: The Desire to Understand* (Cambridge: Cambridge University Press, 1988).
Loewald	Hans Loewald, *The Essential Loewald*, ed. Norman Quist (Hagerstown, MD: University Publishing Group, 2000).
Love	Jonathan Lear, *Love and Its Place in Nature* (New Haven, CT: Yale University Press, 1990).
Midrash	David Stern, *Midrash and Theory* (Evanston, IL: Northwestern University Press, 1996).
Religion	Dov Schwartz, *Religion or Halakha: The Philosophy of Rabbi Joseph B. Soloveitchik* (Leiden: Brill, 2007), vol. 1.
SE	Works by Sigmund Freud cited from *The Standard Edition of the Complete Psychological Works of Sigmund Freud*, trans. James Strachey and Anna Freud (London, 1967–1974), 24 vols.
Sun	Julia Kristeva, *Black Sun* (New York: Columbia University Press, 1992).

Preface

That is what the highest criticism really is, the record of one's own soul. It is the only civilized form of autobiography as it deals not with the events but with the thoughts of one's life . . . the spiritual moods and imaginative passions of the mind.

—Oscar Wilde, "The Critic as Artist"

THIS BOOK BEGAN in disillusionment.

That all scholarship is personal—that academic inquiry is never strictly "objective"—informs the argument of this book on Joseph Soloveitchik, namely that what philosophers and historians of science call the constraints of subjectivity and objectivity are always mutually defining, and the insistence on "objectivity" a fussy remnant of an older scholarship. Not only is the scholarly born out of the personal, indeed, as Wilde writes, even "the highest criticism" is born out of the "passions of the mind." The current work, which evolved from an earlier, in retrospect idealized, perspective on Soloveitchik, aspires to meet Wilde's criteria of "high criticism" while remaining a deeply personal work.

My first book, written nearly twenty years ago on the historiography of the English poet John Milton's critical reception, was informed by the disciplinary languages of early modern literary studies. But Milton, as I have told skeptical Israeli undergraduates in pedagogical efforts to license a critical encounter with the author of *Paradise Lost*, has never been a normative figure of authority for me; he is not, as I tell them, "a Rebbe." By contrast, the subject of this book, Joseph Soloveitchik, the scion of the Brisk dynasty of Talmudists, did occupy a version of that role for me, as he was for many others, though unlike them, I met him only through his writings. Prefacing the current work with an acknowledgment of a personal engagement with Soloveitchik serves neither as disclaimer nor confession but a disclosure of the personal investments that brought me to writing *The Last Rabbi*.

Indeed, my engagement with Soloveitchik's work over several decades reflects more than a conventional scholarly commitment. The composition of this book over those years spanned significant changes in my life, including a turn to Jewish observance and study in yeshiva, both enabled through institutions administered by *talmidim* (students) of Soloveitchik. That I refer to the subject of this book as Soloveitchik and not "the Rav," or even R. Soloveitchik, serves a double purpose, to relate to him from a more critical scholarly perspective, but also to accord him the status he deserves as a figure within the intellectual history of the past century, a religious philosopher of consequence, independent of his rabbinic title and the status derived from the institutional frameworks in which he thrived.

The Last Rabbi remains a work of reverence for a teacher, but also registers a distancing from the idealism that my earlier investment in Soloveitchik entailed. Consequently, the current work embraces what may seem like contradictory approaches, for it situates itself internally to the discourses and teachings of Soloveitchik and the traditions he represents while also looking at those discourses from an external perspective, employing the critical methodologies of literary theory, psychoanalysis, and gender studies. That Soloveitchik scholarship, much of it written by his students, has often embraced the former perspective may be a function of both Soloveitchik's brilliance, as well as his charismatic appeal as rabbi and teacher. This work's primary arguments, however, originate from a perspective that is external to that framework and its language, entailing for me bringing different, interdisciplinary methodological assumptions to reencounter works I had first met from within the hermeneutic circle. *The Last Rabbi* thus employs not only a principle of interpretive charity, reflecting an earlier engagement with "the Rav," even if then mediated by the academy's literary critical discourses, but also a critical hermeneutics, and even psychoanalytic suspicion, in relation to Soloveitchik's work as philosopher and theologian.

What has transformed into the current work had unexpected beginnings in my earlier study of Milton and seventeenth-century England. While in graduate school at Columbia University in the 1980s, I focused on the contested nature of authority in the seventeenth century—the ways in which the hermeneutics of Protestant Reformers at once licensed interpretive freedom while at the same time threatening the cohesiveness of community, leading England, in the end, to civil war. The literary careers of Milton, John Donne, and Ben Jonson might all be described as revolving around this tension. Milton's *Areopagitica*, a tract written in 1644 against state licensing of publications, was the most optimistic, even utopian, representation of pluralism—of a possible balance between the claims of individual and community. My book on Milton represents a meditation on multiplicity in interpretation, on the possibility of sustaining diversity—a multiplicity of perspectives—within a public sphere of interpreters. My abiding interest in pluralism and multiplicity—despite the distance between early modern England and rabbinic thought—always informed my interest in Soloveitchik, and continues to do so in *The Last Rabbi*.

Unlike many who embraced Jewish observance as part of a post-Holocaust third-generation desire for cultural authenticity and authority, it was neither the appeal of ritual nor cultural nostalgia that changed my life in dramatic personal and professional ways, but my encounter with rabbinic texts. Before moving to Israel to formally study Talmud, the first books I read on rabbinic Judaism—ones that resonated with me as more than clichéd apologetics—were Soloveitchik's *Halakhic Man* (1983) and *Halakhic Mind* (1986). I studied them as philosophical works, but also as methodological guides to the Talmudic texts that had been inaccessible to me, largely because of the arcane approaches of conventional yeshiva study, distant as they were from my academic pursuits, especially from my literary theoretical interests in interpretation and pluralism.

Soloveitchik's work opened up Talmudic texts while providing an unexpected framework to refocus questions urgent to me from graduate school—on sustaining possibilities for meaning under the pressure of the demands of pluralism. Those pressures were present in my study of multiplicity and authority in early modern England, but also in the poststructuralist and New Historicist literary criticism dominant during the multicultural moment at Columbia during the 1980s. Where Jewish studies had, since that decade, taken a theoretical turn, my early publications focusing on pluralism and multiplicity, driven by the interdisciplinary languages of the Humanities, took a *Jewish* turn. My first scholarly engagement with Soloveitchik's work on his conception of pluralism in its rabbinic framework came in the still-prevalent context of deconstruction's advocacy of unmediated polyvalence and intertextuality. Born out of the interdisciplinary methods of literary studies, my early work translated Soloveitchik's writings, especially the contours of his interpretive pluralism as I understood it then, as part of Emmanuel Levinas's project of translating "the Hebrew into the Greek." Turning to the language of contemporary theory to articulate the unstated epistemological and hermeneutic assumptions of rabbinic models of interpretation, I provided the contours of rabbinic pluralism as an alternative to the models elaborated by the poststructuralists, post-Marxists, and pragmatists I encountered in graduate school. The current work, however, followed the realization as I was first conceiving a book on Soloveitchik and what I call "Talmudic tradition," that the hermeneutic assumptions of the rabbis and Soloveitchik, perhaps their most influential twentieth-century expositor, exist in uneasy tension, and sometimes in outright conflict.

In contrast to the book I first imagined writing, the current work finds rupture—soliciting the psychoanalytic perspective often elaborated here—not only internal to Soloveitchik's corpus, but between his work and that of Talmudic tradition. *The Last Rabbi* began as a means to overcome an earlier wishful attempt to accommodate Soloveitchik's methods to my American pluralist and liberal aspirations, as well as to the pluralism present, however circumscribed, in his rabbinic antecedents of the Talmudic tradition. The book I imagined writing on Soloveitchik, emphasizing continuity between his various works as well as between him and his rabbinic antecedents, with "the Rav" as a normative figure for a contemporary theologically derived pluralism, will remain unwritten.

The current work, a product first of melancholy disillusionment not only in Soloveitchik but in the current institutions and practices of reading throughout the Jewish world that embody the hermeneutic of the figure of the "halakhic man," began as a kind of compensation for that lost ideal. *The Last Rabbi* aspires to provide a more complex critical assessment of Soloveitchik's work, one that is attentive to the voice that captivated his students (as well as myself), and also to those occluded, even repressed voices, to which scholars have given less attention. As an interdisciplinary and admittedly hybrid work, *The Last Rabbi* attempts, to adopt David Stern's method of *Midrash and Theory*, to be both "accessible and challenging" to readers in both Jewish studies and cultural theory, re-presenting Soloveitchik as a figure of interest to scholars in both fields. Although I do not perpetuate the idealized image of Soloveitchik still current among his students, *The Last Rabbi*, I hope, carries forth parts of his legacy, as both theologian and philosopher, into the twenty-first century.

I am grateful to those both inside and outside Soloveitchik's hermeneutic circle who have made the writing of this book possible: Aden Bar-Tura, Daniel Abrams, Avi Block, Harvey Belovski, Josh Eisen, Daniel Feldman, Shlomo Felberbaum, Richard Hidary, Michael Kramer, Yaakov Mascetti, Elliott Melamet, Jeffrey Perl, George Prochnick, Jeffrey Saks, Yael Shapira, and Smadar Wisper. I am especially grateful to Yonatan Brafman, reader for the Press, as well as to the other anonymous reader. I owe special thanks to Elie Jesner and Josh Weinstein for many conversations on psychoanalysis, philosophy, and Soloveitchik. I am grateful to the editorial staff at Indiana University Press, especially Dee Mortenson, who has guided the editorial process with wisdom and good cheer. My wife Leslie, my best editor, has not only tolerated but encouraged the pursuit of the hybrid interests expressed here. This book is dedicated to our children.

The Last
RABBI

Introduction

The Making of Joseph Soloveitchik and the Unmaking of Talmudic Tradition

Thus play I in one person many people,
And none contented.

—William Shakespeare, *Richard II*

B<small>OTH EMBODYING AND</small> departing from the heritage of the halakhic men his works often commemorate, Joseph Soloveitchik cultivated himself as the last true exemplar of his family heritage after the Shoah, and, at the same time, with regret but also evident pride, as the last rabbi of Brisk. Soloveitchik brought the provenance of his family, the Brisk "dynasty" of Torah scholars, to the New World, addressing the demands of America on its own terms and providing the theological and intellectual ballast for the creation of "Modern Orthodoxy."[1] This book's title phrase, "The Last Rabbi," attests to the story of Soloveitchik's self-construction implicit in his works, how through anxious engagement with his predecessors, he elicited an ambivalent path from Brisk to Modern Orthodoxy. *The Last Rabbi* not only charts the trajectory of Soloveitchik's philosophical and theological works but also his self-creation in the representations of personal and family history, as well as his focus on the psyche, as a means to distinguish himself from his ancestors. For Soloveitchik and his family tradition, the *hiddush*, or innovative interpretation, represents the apotheosis of the freedom associated with the type most associated with his work: the "halakhic man." Soloveitchik's greatest *hiddush* in the account given here is the innovation of the self in his proclaimed role as "self-fashioner" through a process, however fraught, that undermined the values and commitments of the precedent "halakhic men," whose legacy he continued to exemplify and also surpass (*Man*, 113).[2]

Soloveitchik's experience of personal defeat explains the tension in the subtitle of the work, between the interpretive traditions informed by his intense and idiosyncratic consciousness of loss and the radically different hermeneutics of what I call "Talmudic Tradition," presupposing a different conception of loss as well as its recuperation. The extent to which Soloveitchik shows himself, as

Julia Kristeva writes, as "not knowing how to lose," despite the persistent attention to loss and trauma (even catastrophe) of his later works, demonstrates how his conceptions of interpretation, tradition, and consequent attitudes toward pluralism, entail a departure from the models of the Talmudic rabbis (*Sun*, 4).

The Last Rabbi thus tells two mutually intertwining stories. The first emerges from the tension between the demands of Soloveitchik's Brisk family provenance and his self-fashioning through an ethical consciousness nurtured by loss; the second, also informed by Soloveitchik's acute sense of loss, arises from the tension between his representation of legal hermeneutics and that of Talmudic tradition. Both of these stories are constructed through a Freudian lens. The story of Soloveitchik's self-construction, the process through which, to adopt the title phrase of Adam Phillips's biography of Freud, Soloveitchik "becomes" himself, revolves around his representation of gender, the ambivalent embrace of the traditions of his father and the law, and the persistent pull of the maternal feminine and the emotional life it represents.[3] The story of Soloveitchik's departure from antecedent rabbinic models of pluralism shows him to be, following Freud, a "melancholy modern," in contrast to what I call the "mourning rabbis" of Talmudic tradition. That is, for this study, Soloveitchik's modernity has dual aspects, neither of the sort conventionally acknowledged in his traditions of reception, or to be associated with the principles of Modern Orthodoxy or its institutions. Indeed, Soloveitchik, as "the last rabbi," is both more conservative and more radical than his reputation as founder of Modern Orthodoxy suggests. The self-professed lonely man of faith is revealed, in the current work, as an exemplar of Freudian melancholy modernity, responding to the catastrophic trauma of personal and historical loss, underwriting an idiosyncratic and highly conservative conception of law and legal interpretation distinct from that of Talmudic tradition. The other side of Soloveitchik's ambivalent modernity, rooted in a post-Freudian attention to the psyche, leads from the methodological pluralism of his early work, *Halakhic Mind*, through his developing conceptions of repentance to his post-Holocaust ethical writings in the United States, charting an equally idiosyncratic path of philosophical radicalism.

Soloveitchik's "becoming," his turn inward to the psyche and cultivation of a complex dynamic between multiple agencies or perspectives in psychic as well as ethical realms, shows him to be consciously fashioning himself as the end of tradition of his fathers. Portraying himself, at least in some of the personae he adapts, as having exhausted the resources of Talmudic tradition—specifically that of his Brisk ancestors—Soloveitchik turns toward a psychic realm, often gendered for him as feminine, in which the conflicts banished in his idealized description of rabbinic legal hermeneutics express themselves fully. The realm of the psyche, and later that of ethics, paired because of their common accommodation of conflict and multiple agencies, become the contexts for Soloveitchik's realization of the imperative emanating from what he calls Judaism's primary innovation in the world—the affirmation that "man must create himself" (*Man*, 134). This story of Soloveitchik's self-making, based in part on the *unmaking* of Talmudic tradition, both enacts and anticipates a contemporary crisis in Jewish life, indeed in religious life in the twenty-first century—a crisis in religious authority, for Soloveitchik, the rabbinic authority he came to embody. In his biography of Freud, Phillips determines Freud's life to be "impossible," caught between "dogmatic narrow-minded knowingness" and "an absorbing and wide-ranging skepticism."[4] Although Soloveitchik's reference points are wildly different, in *The Last Rabbi*, Soloveitchik comes after Freud, another melancholy modern, for whom the conflicts between authority and tradition on the one side and skepticism and pluralism on the other are equally urgent—also remaining unresolved.

*　*　*

In a written memorial eulogy for Soloveitchik, Jonathan Sacks observes that "the impact of the Holocaust on the Rav was immense" and that he was "terrified by death and destruction," especially the "unprecedented destruction" of the Shoah. The Holocaust "left him," Sacks writes, "in a real sense not just a survivor, but *the* survivor." Sacks argues that through his teaching and writings, Soloveitchik "was engaged in nothing less than '*techiyyat hametim*,' bringing a dead world back to life."[5] For Sacks, Soloveitchik's work, inflected by an unremitting awareness of loss, performs the act of cultural *translatio*—literally carrying over the Brisk legacy of Torah study to an American context.[6] As a survivor, Soloveitchik fulfills the mission of guaranteeing continuity between Europe and America. From Sacks's perspective, Soloveitchik may be the last rabbi of Europe, but at the same time, he is an undeniable figure of transition, among the first rabbis in the New World.

Indeed, Soloveitchik gave rabbinical ordination to more than two thousand students, creating a legacy both personal and institutional (the latter through his relation to Yeshiva University) that changed the shape of Jewish orthodoxy, if not Judaism in the twentieth century. But Soloveitchik, for this work, becomes "the last rabbi" not as a reflection of his actual institutional achievements but rather in his own self-representations. "I have not," he writes in 1960, reflecting on his career as a rabbi, "fulfilled my obligation as a guide in Israel." While engaging his students intellectually, he was not able, he confesses, to solicit "growth on the experiential plane." "I have not," he continues, "succeeded in living in common with them and bestowing some of my personal warmth on them." This emotional inability to convey "the Torah of the heart" (those teachings both emanating from and allowing his own distinctive self-fashioning) leads him to conclude, "I seem to have lacked the ability required of a teacher and Rav." The "survivor" of Holocaust and the bearer of European tradition to America does not, by his own estimation, show the requisite powers of a teacher; rather, he portrays himself as isolated and disconnected from his students. Yet Soloveitchik's self-proclaimed "failure" may also by implication reflect a disavowal of those who showed themselves to be failed *talmidim*, unworthy of receiving their unclaimed inheritance, distinctive for its psychic and ethical complexity: Soloveitchik's "Torah of the heart."[7]

In a contemporary essay also in part a meditation on personal failure, Soloveitchik identifies with the biblical Moses, whom he depicts as "lonely and forlorn." Despite having reached the pinnacle of prophesy and achieving chosen status in the eyes of the divine, Moses remains, nonetheless, in a near-melancholy state of desolation and personal suffering. For Soloveitchik, however, failure is always ambivalent in psychic realms—a precondition in his psychic dialectic—for a preeminent form of success. Soloveitchik's failure, on the model of Moses as leader of the People of Israel, also nurtures the existential privilege that allows for his "becoming." As Soloveitchik writes, in unmistakably autobiographical terms, Moses lived out "the tragedy of the teacher who is too great for his disciples, the tragedy of the master who is too exalted for his generations" (*Vision*, 212). Failure becomes a distinctive part of Soloveitchik's self-fashioning, but also, by implication, the tragic undoing of the legacy as he imagines it. In Sacks's terms, he is "*the survivor*"—the lone survivor of Europe. In Soloveitchik's self-conceived individuation, he is doubly isolated—from both his Brisk ancestors *and* the bearers of the future, the students who fail to live up to the expectations of their teacher. Soloveitchik's idealized conception of a timeless Talmudic tradition, one that is almost Platonic in its perfection, emerges in *The Last Rabbi* from a sense of the failure of *mesora* in his generation, the fault lying with both himself as a failed figure of transmission as well as with his students, the failed inheritors of his legacy.

Returning to the lone figure of Moses, Soloveitchik puzzles over the rabbinic principle that a leader (he mentions, among others, Mordechai from the Book of Esther, Rabbi Akiva of the Talmud, and Moses) may personify the Jewish nation, adding a rhetorical and apparently skeptical flourish: "isn't it sheer absurd nonsense?" Yet Moses did, Soloveitchik continues more assuredly, personify six hundred thousand Jews, and somehow "the individual turned ... into a nation." Continuing, again in a revealingly personal register, he equates the "individual" with the "people," the "single" with "the many," and finally, the "lonely man" with "community." Soloveitchik imagines himself as Moses, but a Moses transformed into a "lonely man," standing as the exemplar of Soloveitchik's melancholy, in whom the many are encompassed.[8] Soloveitchik, the self-confessed lonely man of faith, may lament his failure as an "educator," but he also embraces the rabbinic synecdoche through which the part, the leader of Israel, stands in for the whole, the nation. The paradox of synecdoche allows Soloveitchik to identify with the people of Israel as an abstract entity without having to relate to them as individuals. Indeed, in a strange echo of *Leviathan* and Hobbes's political leader who encompasses in himself a "plurality of voices in one will," Soloveitchik expresses multiplicity internal to his own singular and representative psychic world, but only in that realm.[9] While Soloveitchik's interior psychic realm—first cultivated in early discussions of repentance—becomes increasingly complex, accommodating multiplicity in the form of different agencies (later expressing itself in his ethical writings as well), the interpretive traditions that he represents, remain absolutist and singular, devoid of tension or multiplicity. This story of Soloveitchik's self-making or "becoming" following the Mosaic model informs the second story rendered here: Soloveitchik's departure from the pluralism implicit in Talmudic tradition.

The current work, then, not only elaborates the increasing tensions between the psychic and interpretive realms in Soloveitchik's work, his eventual self-construction as a figure of ethical integrity and existential authenticity, distinct from his Brisk ancestors. *The Last Rabbi* also shows Soloveitchik to be an ambivalent figure of modernity, failing to live up to the promise of his early methodological pluralism as well as the pluralism of his rabbinic antecedents of Talmudic tradition. Unlike his more traditionalist contemporaries (including others bearing the Brisk mantle), Soloveitchik was a legal innovator for the community he led, embracing historical processes and contemporary political mechanisms with his support for Zionism, secular learning in his advocacy of university education, and gender equality in his advocacy for women's study of the oral law.[10] Yet for all the evident modernity of Soloveitchik's institutional and educational innovations in practice, *The Last Rabbi* shows him advocating a model of interpretation that departs from the more pluralistic hermeneutics of the Talmudic tradition.

My earlier work represents an example of the failure to discern the discontinuity between Soloveitchik's arguments for disciplinary pluralism and rabbinic hermeneutics, a failure consecrated by Soloveitchik's reputation as "the Rav," remaining in many circles, the privileged contemporary expositor of Talmudic tradition. In a 1996 article, I detailed Soloveitchik's use of the history of science as the basis for arguments on behalf of methodological pluralism, primarily the autonomy of religious philosophy, arguments based on a conviction in epistemological pluralism, itself founded on "ontological factors" (*Mind*, 15). Soloveitchik's modern physicist, the heroic (though unknowing) advocate of interdisciplinarity, confronts a world "beyond the range of man's intuitive faculty and sensibility," and thus acknowledges the need for a "philosophical interpretation" no longer in thrall to the "time hallowed myth of the insularity of the objective world" (*Mind*, 25). According to Soloveitchik, where even William James's pragmatism had surrendered to the epistemological monism of the scientist—the so-called objective world implied in his worldview—modern physics demonstrated the need for epistemological pluralism, affirming the validity, and even the necessity, of a multiplicity of interpretive perspectives (*Man*, 76).[11]

This earlier account of Soloveitchik's argument for methodological pluralism stands, but the extent of his arguments for pluralism remains circumscribed to the realm of interdisciplinary study, part of the philosophical justification of the independent authority of religious philosophy.[12] Even as Soloveitchik cultivates epistemological multiplicity in the realm of interdisciplinarity, mirroring an earlier rabbinic pluralism, an insistence on a singular conception of truth when it comes to hermeneutic models—following enlightenment paradigms otherwise aggressively rejected in *Halakhic Mind*—persists throughout his works.[13] My earlier conviction that Soloveitchik was "unencumbered by both the influences of Christian universalism and the enlightenment," and that for him, "transcendence" is produced locally through interpretation, while theology is rendered thoroughly "pragmatic," does reflect the strain of philosophical radicalism, and even skepticism, of his early work.[14] The arguments for the disciplinary multiplicity of *Halakhic Mind* and *Halakhic Man*'s updated language of the *Nefesh Ha-Hayyim*—with its privileging of the contingent and the this-worldly realm taking precedent over the transcendent—both undermine enlightenment universalism, with its denial and erasure of the particular. The assertion, however, that a post-enlightenment *legal* epistemology tied to the "shifting, contingent, and the partial" finds an antecedent in "the methodology of the Rabbis of the Talmud" *and* that of Soloveitchik conflates disparate perspectives. That is, the "halakhic" epistemology emerging from the Talmud, with its recognition of the contingency and multiplicity of interpretative frameworks, may be an antecedent for postmodern theologians, as I once wrote, acknowledging "the risk of interpretation," but not an antecedent for Soloveitchik.[15] Further, the tradition of the rabbis may, as Christine Hayes recently argued, through a "predominantly nominalist understanding of divine law," paradoxically mark the "divine status" of the law, but Soloveitchik's conception of rabbinic hermeneutics refuses the collapse of pragmatic and divine criteria within the legal realm. Hayes places the rabbis on the same continuum as literary and cultural theorists interrogating the nature of meaning and authority, but Soloveitchik's conception of truth *within rabbinic hermeneutics*, inflected by his Brisk pedigree and his own idiosyncratic philosophical provenance, falls outside of that continuum.[16]

As I discuss in relation to the reception of *Halakhic Man* in chapter 5, Soloveitchik is among those figures whose complexity of thought lends itself, as Steven Marcus and Charles Taylor write, to a fraught legacy and reception, eliciting a wide range of disparate and sometimes contradictory engagements and responses.[17] However, a reading that elides Soloveitchik's methodological pluralism with that of Talmudic argument is simply flawed.[18] Soloveitchik may embrace pluralism in the framework of arguments about interdisciplinary method, but does not do so in his representations of rabbinic legal interpretation. To be sure, Soloveitchik's pluralist tendencies are in evidence when engaged, in Wittgensteinian terms, in the "game" of legal hermeneutics (and to a lesser but still significant extent, as legal authority for the Modern Orthodox community), but his representation of that interpretive game, as well as the epistemological assumptions that underwrite it, are always uncompromisingly conservative. That the hermeneutics of the Talmud aggressively cultivates pluralism, embodied in the principle "these and these are the words of the living God" (Eruvin 13b), renders Soloveitchik's melancholy refusal to follow the trajectory of his own pluralism into the realm of legal hermeneutics all the more striking. Out of recognition of this latter uninterrogated conflation, the second story of the current work emerges, one that elaborates the distinction between Talmudic tradition and Soloveitchik—between what I call "mourning rabbis" and a "melancholy modern," respectively.

Soloveitchik's son, Haym, engaging with questions similar to the ones that preoccupied his father (though mediated, for him, in academic disciplines) asks, "Is the loss of creativity occasioned by death significant?"[19] *The Last Rabbi* answers that question both in relationship to the interpretive models of the rabbis of the Talmud and Haym's father. In the individual life, death and creativity must be opposed, but as I understand Talmudic tradition, not only in the rabbis' programmatic statements but in their hermeneutic praxis of dispute, death and loss are central to, and even, counterintuitively, enabling of the hermeneutic process. Death, for the "mourning rabbis" of Talmudic tradition in *The Last Rabbi*, is at once an obstacle to continuity, transmission, and creativity, but also their impetus. Understanding tradition as a response to temporality and death, this study begins with the "mourning rabbis" of the Talmud to foreground how their interpretive practices and those of Soloveitchik differ in attempts to overcome the challenges imposed by discontinuity and loss.

The first two chapters, which make up part 1 on "Mourning," elaborate the hermeneutics of the Talmudic sages, what I call following Freud, the rabbinic hermeneutics of mourning, in which death and loss are figured as essential to the process of *mesora*, or tradition, a motor for creativity, not its impediment. As Albert Baumgarten and Marina Rustow argue, the "relationship between rupture and tradition" need not be absolute, but rather should be understood as "merely oppositional."[20] That tradition involves, first and foremost, elaborating "strategies for underlining ... discontinuities," and then overcoming them, as Baumgarten and Rustow assert, informs the rabbinic hermeneutics of mourning in which death is the necessary precondition for *mesora*.

The principle of mourning I develop here emerges from Freud's "Mourning and Melancholy," but also *Moses and Monotheism*, the latter of which elaborates the insight that the discontinuities created by death and forgetting are central to the perpetuation of the tradition of Moses.[21] An antecedent rabbinic version of that insight emerges in the multiple Talmudic accounts of Moses's death in which mortality—particularly the death of Moses and the loss of privileged access to the divine—entails the beginning of legal transmission, a loss transformed into tradition through creativity. As I argue in chapter 1, "Hermeneutics of Rabbinic Mourning," in both Freudian and rabbinic renderings, the forgetting entailed by the loss of a singular absolute truth leads to an interpretive process that Dominick LaCapra, following Freud, refers to as only a *partial* leave taking of the past, not a complete repudiation, nor an attempt to recapture it entirely.[22] Indeed, in the mythography of the rabbis, only when the lawgiver Moses is dead can the hermeneutics of mourning—the creative appropriation and rearticulation of the past—be enacted. Further, forgetting, the generational reexperience of mortality, the result for the Talmudic sages of the breaking of the first Tablets of the Law, underpins conceptions of memory and a tradition based on epistemic humility, resulting necessarily in a multiplicity of perspectives.

Rabbinic mourning, as its Freudian counterpart, already presupposes its opposite: the inability to properly mourn, that is, melancholy. The failure to acknowledge mortality and the hypostatizing of a tradition outside of the realm of death leads, in Freudian terms, to melancholy repetition, tradition perverted into replication, or fundamentalism. From the rabbinic perspective, this failure—a refusal to confront the challenges of loss—entails an abandonment of obligations to the past, but more significantly to the future, specifically to the activities of interpretation upon which it is based. Indeed, the pluralism of Talmudic tradition guarantees such futurity, as against, what I describe in part 2 as the idealization of a timeless tradition presupposed on the epistemological certainty of Soloveitchik's melancholy model.

Where chapter 1 focuses on rabbinic representations of loss, chapter 2, "Pluralism, Rabbinic Poetry, and Dispute," anatomizes the legal multiplicity advocated in rabbinic thought, articulating the implicit hermeneutic and epistemological assumptions of Talmudic dispute. Moving on from scholarship in the last decades that focuses on midrash and theory, especially works by David Stern and Daniel Boyarin, the current work turns not only to the programmatic midrashic statements on rabbinic multiplicity but to the dynamics of legal dispute itself as a means to elaborate the contours of rabbinic legal pluralism. Starting, however, with midrashic multiplicity, I examine the rabbinic "poetry of dispute" and an unlikely parallel "aesthetic," that of the seventeenth-century English poet, John Donne. Through the trope of *discordia concors* pejoratively attributed to Donne's poetics by the eighteenth-century critic Dr. Samuel Johnson, I elaborate the Talmudic poetics of dispute. Donne's conception of wit—both a poetic and metaphysical principle—finds a parallel elaborated in the activity of rabbinic dispute in which differences, however discordant, are still mediated, and in some attenuated sense, made harmonious.

While previous literary critical accounts of rabbinic pluralism have turned to continental theory of the 1980s, *The Last Rabbi* moves from seventeenth-century poetics to the works of the Cambridge historian Quentin Skinner and the German philosopher Hans-Georg Gadamer. This admitted odd coupling shows how the subject–object distinction, prominent in some theoretical discourse, as well as in the often-invidious distinction between midrash and halakha, occludes the nature of rabbinic legal pluralism. In *Halakhic Mind*, Soloveitchik argues against the subject–object distinction, insisting on their always-reciprocal relation, thus making possible his arguments for the validity of multiple disciplinary perspectives. Employing the methods of Gadamerian hermeneutics and Cambridge School history, I show, in relationship to Hagiga 3a, how the epistemological and hermeneutic underpinnings of Talmudic discourse are distilled in an idealized Talmudic interpreter, for whom subject and object are mutually defining. The elaboration of the "poetry of dispute," in Skinner and Gadamer's sometimes irreconcilable languages, underlines the Talmudic presumption of multiple agencies of perspectives, in what must be alternatively figured as the understanding *and* production of truth, against what I argue in part 2 to be the certainty and "objectivity" of Soloveitchik's melancholy model.

The introductory chapters on mourning provide the background for part 2 on "Melancholy"—a reading of the major philosophical works of Joseph Soloveitchik. *The Last Rabbi* not only values Soloveitchik as a *Jewish* thinker but also claims his legacy—however fraught and conflicted—as significant for the development of theology in the twentieth century. As much as the current work embraces the disciplinary rigors of Jewish studies, *The Last Rabbi* takes its point of departure from other sets of discourses—philosophical, literary, and finally, psychoanalytic. Moving beyond the internal perspective and the sometimes hagiographical readings of Soloveitchik's work that it has produced, the current work examines representations of legal discourse through not only the lenses of, for example, Aristotelian and neo-Kantian philosophy and the history of science, but also psychoanalysis and gender. Although *The Last Rabbi*, with its reading of Soloveitchik as a "melancholy modern," adopts a psychoanalytic register, it also enacts an attitude of interpretive humility, where my question has been, what is this text intended to mean? To look at Soloveitchik's work through the lens of Freud's conception of melancholy, as I am proposing, does not mean eschewing a hermeneutics of empathy and rejecting its explicit registers and intentions. To read Soloveitchik against the grain—elaborating what I am suggesting are unconscious forces at work in his text—does not mean eschewing the "grain" altogether.

In this sense, *The Last Rabbi* enacts a Geertzian "thick description," which takes Soloveitchik at his word as a neo-Kantian when he articulates an epistemology insisting on the disjunction between language and the reality it represents.[23]

But it also looks to other contexts, such as, not so controversially, *Halakhic Man* enacting—though not explicitly—the epistemological assumptions of the antecedent *Nefesh Ha-Hayyim*. The neo-Kantian and Brisk frameworks acknowledged by Soloveitchik are brought here, however, with a Freudian one, in which I look at Soloveitchik's representation of his personal history, as fragments of a spiritual memoir that have yet to be fully investigated. The invocation of Freud in relation to Soloveitchik's representation of his family life is not merely to provide a voyeuristic and simplifying reading—to promote a vulgar psychoanalytic reading—but rather to examine Soloveitchik's conceptions of gender and how they are mediated in his representations of fatherhood and motherhood in the context of his work as a whole.

Although explicit references to Freud are almost entirely absent from Soloveitchik's work (and when present are mostly negative), his turn to family, marriage, and sexuality represents an attempt to provide a Jewish—or rather what he would term a "halakhic" or legal—response to the Freudian emphases on desire, and therefore indeed invite a psychoanalytic approach. One of the assumptions of *The Last Rabbi* is that much of Soloveitchik's work is inflected by an interest in Freud (however much Soloveitchik distances his "halakhic" project from psychoanalysis), and that the later work, especially, is informed, however implicitly, by questions emanating from psychoanalysis and the Freudian emphasis on the psyche. Indeed, I argue that Soloveitchik's self-creation as a thinker independent of the "halakhic men" of his past follows a trajectory into the psyche that shows parallels with the thought of the founder of psychoanalysis. In *The Last Rabbi*, Soloveitchik's "becoming" is dependent on the largely unacknowledged but precedent set of stories about desire and sexuality told in Freud's work. More than that, Soloveitchik may have sensed, however reluctantly, that Judaism, which for him introduced the ideal of self-creation, may have found in psychoanalysis a privileged inheritor and contemporary expositor of the distinctly Jewish imperative of creative selfhood.

From the psychoanalytic point of view articulated here, the oft-noted "split" in Soloveitchik's work between the emotions and the intellect reads as an ambivalence toward both love and law, paralleled by a never fully resolved ambivalence toward both masculine and feminine.[24] Distilling these contradictory attractions, part 2 begins with an "Interlude" in Pruzhna, one of those fragments of personal history, in the living room of Soloveitchik's grandfather, Elijah Feinstein. In the form of a narrative "diptych" recounted from the point of view of the young Joseph, Soloveitchik presents complementary accounts, showing both his father's hermeneutic triumph and defeat, as well as his mother's ambiguous relation to the father and the masculine realm he represents.

In what I understand as his hermeneutic version of the Freudian "primal scene," Soloveitchik shows a simultaneous attraction and resistance to the con-

quest of masculine law, as well as an ambivalent attraction to the feminine, anticipating a lifelong struggle with the figure of his father, the paradigmatic halakhic
man. Soloveitchik's "becoming" or "self-creation"—to employ Leo Bersani's revision of Freud's Oedipal terms—is enabled by the symbolic killing off of his father
in order to become him, but in the case of Soloveitchik, his new identity is, in the
end, inflected by the feminine. The cultivation of melancholy isolation in his
grandfather's living room already anticipates the later "becoming": his self-
construction through his post-Holocaust ethical works and the implicit and ambivalent repudiation of the masculine practitioners of Brisk.

Charting Soloveitchik's path from the realm of the psyche to the ethical
sphere, chapter 3, "Love, Repentance, Sublimation," begins with love, for Soloveitchik not merely an emotional category but central to an epistemology of love, with
its origins in Aristotle. I place Soloveitchik in dialogue with the contemporary
psychoanalyst Jonathan Lear to elicit the implications of Soloveitchik's emphasis
on individual autonomy and choice, itself based on the recognition of multiple
psychic agencies, unified by love in the process of *teshuva*, or repentance. In
seeking out a kinship between Soloveitchik's conception of repentance and the
Freudian notion of sublimation as articulated by Lear, I elaborate the grounds
for a strong counterbalance to the more monolithic conception of cognition and
the psyche of halakhic man. The intrapsychic dynamic of love, articulated in psychoanalytic terms, elaborates the basis for Soloveitchik's later emphasis on ethics, as well as for his creative individuation in relation to his predecessors.

Foregrounding the rupture in Soloveitchik's work, chapter 4, "Joseph Soloveitchik: A Melancholy Modern," focuses on the melancholy assertion of the
singularity of law against the tendency of love toward multiplicity, articulated in
chapter 3. Soloveitchik's longing for a metaphysical presence, never fully satisfied,
as well as the ambivalent compensations of law, are read retrospectively in relationship to his later-articulated conceptions of gender, family, and sexuality. Even
Soloveitchik's work in the 1940s, I argue, is informed, though in the terms of the
history of science and neo-Kantian philosophy, by an avoidance of love, producing a melancholy ambivalence toward a masculine law. Through the lens of
Freud's early essay, as well as the works of the post-Freudians Julia Kristeva, D. W.
Winnicott, and Hans Loewald, Soloveitchik emerges, like Freud himself, unable
finally to accommodate loss through mourning, a paradigmatic melancholy
modern.

The conceptions of gender elaborated in the essays collected in Soloveitchik's
Family Redeemed reveal the pull of the feminine, with its promise of absorption
and nondifferentiation, as well as the always-partial compensation of the masculine, promising differentiation and autonomy, but only through adherence to a
sometimes punishing law. Soloveitchik's tentative embrace of what Jacques Lacan
calls "the law of the Father" is simultaneous with his cultivation of the melancholy

and protected sphere of his own loneliness, which paradoxically, in his representations, is the means through which he claims autonomy from his father. The incomplete and always ambivalent identification with the Lacanian law of the Father manifests itself in the realm of hermeneutics, the chapter concludes, in Soloveitchik's adoption of an aggressive masculine persona and the forms of knowledge associated with it.

Chapter 5, "Beyond the Law: Repentance and Gendered Memory," situates Soloveitchik's conflicting epistemology of love and his melancholy hermeneutics in relation to the reception history of *Halakhic Man*. By providing a new account of the tensions in Soloveitchik's most canonical work, I show that the psychic energies of the man of repentance in the second part of *Halakhic Man* are at odds with the hermeneutic certainties of the figure of the work's title as well as the halakhic men celebrated in part 1. The continued Freudian pressure on the personal articulated in the second half of this chapter serves to further elaborate Soloveitchik's melancholy sensibility, showing how it produces gendered conceptions of memory and repentance, as well as an idealized, ahistorical, and masculine conception of tradition. Further, I show that the energies of desire that Soloveitchik means to bracket are, in the end, summoned through what Harold Bloom would call a "misprision" of a Talmudic proof text in a legal theodicy fashioned by Soloveitchik at the center of part 2 of *Halakhic Man*. The realms of otherness, desire, and the precedence of a form of feminine memory return in Soloveitchik's idiosyncratic renderings, providing the bridge to the exploration of ethics in his post-Holocaust writings.

Chapter 6, "From Interpretive Conquest to Antithetic Ethics," shows how Soloveitchik's simultaneous rejection and embrace of the assumptions of the halakhic man produces, in his later work, an emphasis on multiple agencies and difference, though not in the hermeneutic but rather ethical sphere. In these post-Holocaust writings, Soloveitchik, I argue, takes his most explicit Freudian turn, not only in the focus on sexuality but also in the turn to the psyche, with the true innovations of his work (and his full independence from his Brisk ancestors) emanating from bringing the *hiddush*, the creative interpretation from the sphere of hermeneutics, into psychic and ethical realms. Soloveitchik's melancholy sensibility persists—indeed finds its fullest philosophical articulation—in the writings collected in *Out of the Whirlwind*, in an ethics taking into account the otherness repressed in *Halakhic Man*. Even as Soloveitchik foregrounds epistemological humility, he does so only in these psychic and ethical realms, not in the masculine realms of interpretation, law, and tradition, where the knower may experience the oblivion of "defeat," but in the end, still rises to a form of knowledge based on conquest. That is, although Soloveitchik, like the rabbis, is focused on maintaining tradition in the face of loss, the result for the former in the realm of legal interpretation is singular and certain, not the pluralism, circumscribed though it may be, of his Talmudic ancestors. The masculinist "Brisk" conception of tradition—originating in his grandfather's living room in Pruzhna—which Soloveitchik continues to advocate throughout his works, does not so much rebel against enlightenment truth and certainty, but in its epistemological stance of masculine mastery, embraces them in the service of Halakha.

The conclusion to this work, "The Last Rabbi and Talmudic Irony" situates itself at the crossroads of Soloveitchik's self-avowed personal failure as the "last rabbi"—between the inexorable trajectory of his "becoming" and the demands of the Brisk tradition he inherited and always, however ambivalently, continued to embody. Although Soloveitchik may now be associated with institutions and sets of practices defined as "halakhic," the direction of his works, and especially his self-representation in them, leads from law to ethics. Following that direction, the current work concludes by elaborating what I call "Talmudic Irony," informed by a return to the hermeneutic pluralism of Talmudic tradition but rendered contemporary through an appeal to the dynamic sense of multiple agency in Soloveitchik's realm of the psyche. Talmudic irony—limned here in relation to the psychoanalytic irony of Jonathan Lear and the "liberal irony" of Richard Rorty—emerges from the rabbinic hermeneutics of mourning, presupposing a community of interpreters pursuing difference, in contrast to Soloveitchik's melancholy modernism alternating between epistemic humility and conquest. *The Last Rabbi*, finally, moves past the crossroads where Soloveitchik's work ends—and the choice between skeptical pluralism and absolute knowingness—with the hope that the post-traumatic twenty-first century will return to a conception of tradition based on a new appropriation of the rabbinic hermeneutics of mourning, as well as an embrace and further cultivation of Soloveitchik's antithetic ethics of love.

PART I
TALMUDIC TRADITION: MOURNING

Dissonance is the Truth about Harmony.
—T. W. Adorno, *Aesthetic Theory*

1   Hermeneutics of Rabbinic Mourning

Learning mourning may be the achievement of a lifetime.
—Stanley Cavell, *In Quest of the Ordinary*

LEARNING HOW TO mourn may take a lifetime to achieve, as Cavell writes, its challenges emanating from not knowing how to lose. Soloveitchik's sense of loss—both personal and historical—shows itself to be acute, cultivated in his later works to form the underpinnings of his radical conceptions of both ethics and the psyche. In programmatic midrashic statements, Talmudic tradition also figures loss, but does so at the center of its legal hermeneutics.

The "face to face" between the human and the divine in the biblical representation of the encounter between Moses and God in Exodus—"The Lord spoke with Moses face to face" (33:11)—depicts the fullness of presence, an historical manifestation of the Edenic ideal, but one that already anticipates its eventual loss.[1] This book on law—legal hermeneutics and epistemology—begins with midrashic readings of the "face to face," or, in an extension of the generic category to include the Christian midrash of Paul, the philosophical midrash of Spinoza, and Freud's extended set of psychoanalytic and anthropological midrashim on the life and death of Moses. Together, with rabbinic meditations on the death of Moses—an event that marks for the rabbis an end to the privileged encounter of the human with the divine, as well as its loss—they provide meditations on the nature of transmission and truth from out of which the parameters of the rabbinic hermeneutics of mourning emerge.

I begin, however, with the Rolling Stones' *Exile on Main Street* and the presentation of its own unlikely midrash of the "face to face" from Exodus, expressing an anxious response to lost presence and an impatience with language as compensation for that loss. The persona created in this 1972 portrayal of Main Street America laments, "Don't wanna talk about Jesus, just wanna see his face." The song thus expresses the desire to dispense with the trappings of language, the excrescence of the material that detract from—and veil—the unmediated truth. That is, in its expression of a craving for the revelation of the divine "face," *Exile* expresses the desire for the pure presence of an unmediated truth, or what Jean-Luc Nancy describes as the possibility of "penetrating into pure immanence."

This fantasy has been nurtured from the beginnings of early modern philosophy, tapping into a trend of thought that has an ancient theological pedigree as well, what Harold Fisch describes as a "Christian impatience with textuality."[2]

For the author of the second letter to the Corinthians, the veil that Moses puts over his face (Exodus 34:33) is a sign of the Jews' continued entanglement with language—specifically, the old dispensation of the law. As Paul's Christian midrash elaborates:

> But their minds were hardened; for to this day, when they read the old cove-
> nant, the same veil remains unlifted, because only through Christ is it taken
> away. Yes, to this day, whenever Moses is read, a veil lies over their minds; but
> when a man turns to the Lord, the veil is removed. Now the Lord is the Spirit,
> and where the Spirit of the Lord is, there is freedom. And we all, with unveiled
> face, behold the glory of the Lord. (2 Corinthians, 3:13–18)

As Fisch points out, Paul defines the veil of Moses "as an image of textuality it-self," the inability to translate the literalism of the Old Testament into the allegorical truth of the Christian redeemer—the "unveiled face" of the "glory of the Lord." Paul himself, however, "believes that the New Covenant, using great plainness of speech, can evoke actual *presence*." Against a tradition enmeshed in the carnality and contingency of language, Paul holds out the promise of an exoteric truth without mediation that is available to all—a "freedom" founded on the unmediated perception of the "unveiled face."[3] Paul dismisses the tradition of the "old covenant" on account of its historicity, and indeed, that as a tradition, it depends on language at all. For Paul, those of the prior covenant read and hear, while those of the second—in a purely visual register—simply "behold the Glory of the Lord."

Paul's project, Platonist in its roots, evidences the conviction that theological languages could better accomplish what philosophy had once claimed, eliciting the presence of the divine face. Where the "divided line" in Book 6 of *The Republic* diminishes the ontological validity of the phenomenal (in relation to the noumenal forms or ideas), the rejection of poetry in Book 10 echoes the allegory of the divided line by placing imagination and poetic representation on the lowest ontological and epistemological levels. As Plato's Socrates claims, the "art of representation is . . . a long way removed from truth, and it is able to reproduce everything because it has little grasp over anything, and that little is of a mere phenomenal appearance."[4] In Paul's articulation of the "face," the discourses of the law are not merely *phenomenal* but now fleshly sinful and dead, implicitly taking their place in the lower part of the divided line, the realm of representation. The sight of the "glory of the Lord" enacts in theological terms the accomplishment of the Platonic ideal—rejection of the phenomenal and achievement of an unmediated, nondiscursive realm of truth.

Paul may have translated Plato's philosophical categories into Christian terms; Spinoza, returning to Corinthians and its Old Testament antecedent, appropriates the "face to face" to assert the disciplinary priority of the early modern philosopher. For Spinoza, the philosopher would once again claim precedence, ascending to the highest rung of the disciplinary hierarchy through an unmediated access to truth. In his championing of a new modern philosophy based on what he calls "universally valid axioms" and the study of "Nature," Spinoza turns to Christ as providing a model of the privileged acquisition of knowledge. In the *Tractatus Theologico-Politicus*, Spinoza argues explicitly for an unmediated form of truth: "We may quite clearly understand that God can communicate with man without mediation, for he communicates his essence to our minds without employing corporeal means." Communication, in the Spinozan context, is not through the corporeal means of language, rather, immediate—"of the divine ontological essence." Spinoza continues, affirming: "a man who can perceive by pure intuition that which is not contained in the basic principles of our cognition and cannot be deduced therefrom must needs possess a mind whose excellence far surpasses the human mind." For Spinoza, the highest form of cognition is limited to a mind that, in Aristotelian terms, transcends the category of the discursive and understands through "intuition" only. No one, in his view, has attained "such a degree of perfection surpassing all others, except Jesus." To his Jesus, the privileged mediator, Spinoza continues:

> God's ordinances leading men to salvation were revealed not by words or by visions, but directly, so that God manifested himself to the Apostles through the mind of Jesus as he once did to Moses through an audible voice. . . . Therefore, if Moses spoke with God face to face as a man may do with his fellow (through the medium of their two bodies), then Jesus communed mind to mind.[5]

In asserting that God communicates with man without "mediation," Spinoza argues against forms of knowledge that rely on the intervention of language or images, taking the Pauline attack on the letter of the law and giving it philosophical force. Indeed, for Spinoza, the entirety of the Jewish tradition is compromised because of its self-avowed reliance on forms of mediation—language and images. From his perspective, such mediations, subject to time, place, and circumstance, are transcended for philosophical concepts of universal and eternal validity.

From the perspective of Spinoza's Christianized philosophy, even the prophecy of Moses is compromised because of its reliance on speech—for God speaks to Moses "in an audible voice." Spinoza's exemplary philosopher, Jesus, however, requires no such intervention, as he moves beyond all forms of mediation to a direct apprehension of God. There are neither "words" nor "visions," only the direct contact with the divine. While the Jews celebrate Moses, who spoke "face to face" with God, Spinoza himself heralds the Christian philosopher, who requires no intermediary but rather communes with God "mind to mind." For the Spinoza of the *Tractatus*, philosophical discourse achieves both truth and certainty, reaching axioms of universal and eternal validity. The Jewish tradition, however, comprised merely of "history and language," leads not to "truth," Spinoza writes, in anthropological terms, only "obedience." In Spinoza's view, the ideal figure of Jesus, replacing Moses in the face to face encounter (as Paul did before him) is not a figure of tradition, and certainly not one of historical transmission. Even when he communicates with the Apostles, it is nondiscursive—an abstraction—rendered through Jesus's mind.[6]

Along with other early modern philosophers, Spinoza set the ground for the emergence of modern conceptions of objectivity, tied to early modern scientific methodologies and assumptions of epistemological neutrality, as argued further in chapter 3.[7] In contrast to the theological culture from which they emerged, such early modern methodologies begin to assert, as Jonathan Lear writes, that "knowledge is available from no perspective at all" (*Love*, 120). Indeed, the situated nature of both knowledge and interpretation, tied to language and history, are from within Spinoza's early modern philosophical perspective impediments to a truth that is abstractly conceived and objective. Spinoza and his philosophical contemporaries were part of an early modern movement to initiate a split between subject and object (one maintained in an earlier poetic culture), through which the philosopher-scientist claimed objectivity and religious figures, humanists, and poets were relegated to an impoverished realm of subjective contingency.[8] In Spinoza's reading, "the face to face" celebrates an unmediated truth, one that emerges, as the philosopher Thomas Nagel puts it, "from nowhere at all."[9] Through his appropriation of Paul, Spinoza transforms a tradition based on transmission into a visual culture of imminence, based on a more literal reading of the Old Testament "face to face."

Focusing on the figure of Moses, Freud elaborates the psychological, historical, and anthropological underpinnings for what Spinoza understands as a Jewish culture grounded on "obedience." The priority of obedience leads to what Freud describes as a psychic phenomenon based on repetition and the necessary avoidance of the divine face. Freud, like the rabbis, focuses on Moses as a historical figure of transmission, but for him, the prophet fails at his task. In Freud's genealogy, the Jews reenact the primal murder of the father in the killing of Moses, and through the repression of its memory, fall prey, as Robert Paul explains Freud, to "a collective obsessional neurosis, namely Judaism itself." In Freudian terms inflected by Spinoza, the neurosis of Judaism is the refusal of an unmediated truth, the avoidance of the face (not only of God, but also Moses), and the subsequent fall into repetition. The inability to remember transforms into repetition, as Robert Paul writes, of "apparently trivial or pointless rules, ordinances, ceremonies, prohibitions and self-accusations." In the Judaism understood to be a religion of repetition, the "Torah" is merely an "instruction manual" to be "recited, copied, taught, studied, and infinitely replicated."[10] Taking themselves out of history, Freud's version of the ancient Hebrews consign themselves, as Hans Loewald, adopting Mircea Eliade, to an "atemporal realm" in which there is "no emphasis on individuality, nor on process with a direction either into the past or into the future, and no emphasis on actively establishing a relationship . . . between past and future, which activity would give dignity to the present." In their repressed guilt for the unacknowledged murder of Moses, Freud's Jews give up autonomy, which is itself a function of their abandonment of history. Relegated forever to the realm of Eliade's primitive "premodern," Moses's descendants, for Freud, inhabit a realm outside of history in which the conditions for a tradition—other than as mere repetition—never maintain (*Loewald*, 99–100). That is, Freud's Jews are distinctive for having lost the capacity to remember and for never achieving a state of "modernity," itself defined through memory, and the futurity and free will that rest upon it. For Freud, it is not a Christianized philosophy that redeems humanity from loss; rather, the endless repetition of the unacknowledged guilt of Judaism is replaced by a Christian memory that saves and, in the process, overcomes the obsessional repetitious neurosis associated with the law.[11]

Freud's figuration of Judaism is linked to his representation of Moses, particularly his death—his slaying, in the story Freud tells, at the hands of the people of Israel. The primal act of the murder of Moses emerges as a cultural, indeed a world-historical, principle through which the psychic configuration of guilt characteristic of Western culture (and especially, for Freud, Western religion) is traced to the original trauma enacted in the repressed rebellion of the people of Israel against their leader, itself a reenactment of the murder of the primal father by the horde. For Freud, the history of the Jews and religion itself begins with that repetition, and a failure of memory. The "shared obsessional neurosis" of guilt begins in the failure of transmission, part of the ambiguous Jewish legacy to the West, with its antecedent and cause in the forgotten murder of Moses. Without the activity of tradition, informed by the psychoanalytic self consciousness embodied in the process of "working through," the Israelites remain unredeemed from their tragic repetition. As Freud writes, the more one evidences "the compulsion to repeat," the less one experiences "the impulsion to remember" (*SE*, 1:151). For Freud, religion imagined as obsessional repetition and obedience—and the loss of memory—begins with the murder of Moses.

Without adhering to Freud's narrative of Jewish origins, however, *Moses and Monotheism*, remains important for its insights into what Richard Bernstein describes as "the meaning of a religious tradition," the nature of religious transmission, or what Freud describes as the ideal possibility of uniting "influences of the present and the past" (*SE*, 23:207).[12] Paul and Spinoza remove the "face to face" from history, assimilating it to a nonlinguistic conception of the "glory of the Lord," thus rendering tradition obsolete. Freud, however, focuses on Moses as the historical figure who, on account of his murder, shows himself to be a failed figure of transmission. This Freudian account of Moses's murder and its relationship to a tradition understood as repetition allows for an understanding of a different set of representations of Moses's death: those in rabbinic literature, that is, the *aggadic* figurations or interpretive stories of the Talmud.

In both rabbinic and Freudian narratives, Moses's death figures significantly in the respective conceptions of transmission, particularly of how the people of Israel perpetuate the law (though often despite themselves). In abandoning the genealogical narrative of *Moses and Monotheism*—Moses's death at the hands of Israel—the current account emphasizes what Lear describes as the volume's most significant insight, "that it is only when one kills off the messenger that the message gets installed."[13] For the rabbis, however, the "killing off" is not the literal event that it is for Freud, one that makes any future based on memory impossible.[14] To understand the rabbinic representation of Moses's death, or more figurative "killing off," I elaborate the insight of *Moses and Monotheism* that death as well as a certain kind of forgetting—Cavell's mourning—are critical to transmission and the recovery of loss in relation to rabbinic figurations of Moses's death.

The representations of Moses in the Talmud show the rabbis meditating on forgetting death (and even murder) in ways that foreground not so much guilt but rather anxiety in facing the demands of transmission, particularly mourning and the creative remembrance it entails. Further, what I call, in relation to Talmudic tradition, the hermeneutics of mourning does not elicit a singular absolute truth. Embracing loss and language produces a necessary pluralism, one which, read backward, reinforces the emphasis on textuality that Paul and Spinoza aggressively reject. Through the representation of Moses's death, the rabbis elaborate the anxiety of the people of Israel in facing a truth that no longer has its provenance in the privileged prophesy of Moses, and requires embracing a historical tradition based on loss and nurturing multiplicity.

Death of Moses: Mourning Becomes the Law

The Old Testament verse cultivates the possibility of unmediated access to the divine that Paul would later celebrate as uniquely Christian, the revelation of God in his ontological fullness and the possibility of complete knowledge, in a later philosophical language, of an objective truth. However, the passage that describes Moses's unmediated access to the divine—"So the Lord spoke to Moses face to face"—is followed at the end of the chapter by an apparently contradictory verse, the answer to Moses's request for the revelation of God's glory. God informs

Moses, "You shall not see My face and live," but he provides a consolation: "I will take away My hand, and you shall see My back, but My face shall not be seen" (Exodus 33:23).

The *Targum Onkelos* (the second-century Aramaic translation of the Five Books of Moses), whose translation habitually veers away from suggestions of imminence, provides a resolution of the contradiction between the two verses, translating the first of them against the grain of a literalism that attributes to Moses an unmediated knowledge of God. The *Targum* renders "face to face" (*panim el'panim* in Hebrew) in Aramaic as *m'lal l'm'lal*, or "words to words." In anticipation of Spinoza, Onkelos affirms that even the revelation to Moses was one mediated through "words." In the *Targum*, what Fisch calls the "veil of textuality," the insistent mediation of language, is aggressively professed. In the Spinozan account, the Apostles are portrayed as taking in the visual aura of the divine mind as it is transferred through Jesus. In the continuation of the rabbinic account, again reflected in the *Targum*, after his encounter with the divine, Moses takes off what Paul calls his "veil," worn to shield the people from the radiance of his face, in order to teach them. The residue of the experience of the encounter with the divine is temporarily put aside for the priority of the encounter with the human through language.[15]

Against a constellation of Western traditions that crave, as Hilary Putnam has written, access to the "God's-Eye View" (his version of Nagel's "view from nowhere"), the rabbinic tradition constitutes itself through the discursive. What Putnam argues in a paraphrase of J. L. Austin informs the principles of rabbinic epistemology and hermeneutics—"though enough isn't everything, enough is enough."[16] For Putnam, although language is not able to recuperate truth in its totality, even ordinary language can nonetheless get things "right." "Enough" may not be everything, but "enough" nevertheless suffices. Abandoning the dream of unmediated presence, even when the biblical verse elicits that fantasy, the rabbis affirm that language, notwithstanding its limitations, is *enough*. In contrast to Spinoza's Christian and philosophical midrash on the "face to face"—with its enlightenment optimism about the transparency of an unmediated truth—the rabbis emphasize the inherent frailty and contingency of interpretive traditions. Not the possibility of aspiring to the clarity of truth thematized in the Christian version of the "face to face," moving beyond language and history, but a truth always only partially recovered and reconstructed in the encounter with loss.

The *Seder MeKabblie Ha-Torah*, dating from the late Middle Ages, recounts a mythography of a Jewish past with a multitude of lost legal texts: "From the days of Moses until Hillel, there were six hundred orders of Mishna just as they were given unto Moses at Sinai." According to the *Seder*, however, from the time of the tannaitic sage Hillel, "the world became impoverished and the glory and power of Torah became diminished."[17] Tradition, in the present that the work occupies, is already impoverished and its continuation depends on a recuperation enabled through the processes of exegesis and recovery. Not only, for the rabbinic tradition, is the necessity of hermeneutics affirmed at Sinai, with the assertion of a dual Torah of written and oral traditions (Berakhot 5a), but the nature of historical experience itself—and the impoverishment intrinsic to it—leads, inevitably, to the hermeneutic moment, and the necessary diversity emerging from it. In this reading, the articulation of loss is not an apologetics for interpretive diversity but serves, from the rabbinic perspective, as a description of the hermeneutic situation.[18]

In a series of narratives in Tractate Temurah of the Talmud (15b–16a) centering around the death of Moses and the mourning period that followed, the rabbis meditate on death and loss and the beginnings of tradition, the latter made necessary when the privileged access to the divine ends with Moses's death: "Three thousand and seven hundred laws . . . were forgotten during the period of mourning for Moses. Rabbi Abbuha said, 'Nevertheless, Otniel the son of Kenaz restored the forgotten teachings as a result of his dialectics.'" The acknowledgement of loss, as that experienced in the mourning for Moses, becomes the precondition for the renewed activity of interpretation as embodied in the *pilpul*, or "dialectics," of Otniel, who emerges from the period of mourning to restore the lost teaching.

The "work of mourning" is rendered productive, providing the means, in Freud's terms, of distancing oneself from the object of loss, and, as Dominick LaCapra paraphrases Freud, moving toward the possibility of "critical judgment" as well as a "reinvestment in life." Against the model of a pathological mourning (one of the models of melancholy) that refuses to acknowledge the final loss of the mourned object, the "working through" achieved through normative mourning entails remembrance, as well as, writes LaCapra, taking a "partial leave" of the past (*SE*, 14:244).[19] The mourning thematized in the rabbis' paradigmatic account—Otniel's restorations—enacts this process. Taking "partial leave" of the past, through the recognition of Moses's death, permits a future of creative reconstruction informed by the remembrance of Moses and the law that Otniel continues—through the innovations of his "dialectic"—to represent. Yet, as multiplicity is affirmed, the rabbis, in their way anticipating Spinoza's anthropological insight, affirm the Jewish people's ambivalence about living in a post-Mosaic tradition of difference, for their preference is obedience and a singular truth. While the Freudian representation of transmission stresses the guilt of Israel, the rabbinic representations of Moses's death, as well as the transmission that follows, emphasize not guilt but anxiety over the loss of Moses and the fall into interpretation and diversity.[20]

A further meditation on the possibility of continuity—tradition after the death of Moses—begins with the same account of death and then loss: "R. Yehuda said in the name of Shmuel: 'three thousand laws were forgotten during the period of mourning for Moses'" (Temurah 16a). Again, in this representation, the trauma of Moses's death—and the loss of access to the divine—is represented in the loss of the law. Not only is Moses gone, but the clarity and singularity of his prophetic knowledge is as well. For this, the people of Israel turn to the newly-anointed leader of Israel, Joshua. "Ask!" they demand. The demand represents a desire to recapture the prophetic experience lost with Moses; it also represents an anxiety about inhabiting a world without prophetic certainty. The response of ambiguous origin in this narrative (either that of God or Joshua) is a verse from Deuteronomy (30:12)—"It is not in heaven"—emphasizing that the law had already been given, and, no longer in the province of the divine, has passed to the people of Israel. Notwithstanding the supplication of the Israelites and their desire to recover a transcendent truth, in the rabbinic narrative the divine response is that recourse to the certainty achieved through the initial revelation to Moses on Sinai is no longer available, with a verse from the Torah serving as proof text for rabbinic authority and power.

The Talmud provides accounts of similar stories, with the people each time making a similar demand upon a different version of the archetypal leader—to Phinehas, Eleazar, and Samuel, as they had earlier to Joshua. Although Moses is gone, the desire to return to the prophetic knowledge that he represents remains. The rabbis figure the people of Israel preferring a passive access to a transcendent truth, resisting active engagement in the processes of interpretation that God's rejoinder entails, as well as the subsequent multiplicity and uncertainty it entails. For the rabbis, the people of Israel prefer the return of Moses, or a version of the archetypal leader, to insulate them from death and the experience of history and tradition.[21] In Eliade's terms, the people prefer the atemporal archetype to the loss and multiplicity that genuine tradition entails.

In Moses's death, the people of Israel are represented as facing up to the consequences of loss, confronting both mortality and doubt: "R. Yehuda said in the name of Shmuel: 'Three thousand laws were lost during the period of mourning of Moses.'" "After the death of Moses," the narrative continues, "if those who pronounced a vessel impure were in the majority, they declared it impure, and if those who pronounced the vessel pure were in the majority, they declared it pure" (Temurah 15b). Lacking the clarity of insight available to the prophet, the rabbis enter the realm of disagreement. It is this realm, and the hermeneutic responsibility it entails, that the people of Israel, in the rabbinic representation, actively resist. For Moses, the law would have been clear and singular (and the object either pure or impure); for the rabbis, however, it becomes a subject for debate. Instead of a unitary law, the people of Israel, with the death of Moses, enter a world characterized by uncertainty and multiplicity.

Adopting Gillian Rose's argument in *Mourning Becomes the Law*, and through the appropriation of its title phrase as a hermeneutic principle, loss and "mourning," in this reading, serve as the preconditions for interpretation.[22] Whether over the loss of the orders of the Mishna, the loss of particular laws, or more generally, the experience of loss that precedes every hermeneutic engagement (for which the story of Otniel may stand as a metonymic instance), mourning thus "becomes" the law, that is, in the law's continual rearticulation and reinterpretation. For the rabbis, as in Rose's more general argument, mourning is rehabilitative, and even fruitful, leading to diverse rearticulations and reconstructions of lost or "impoverished" antecedents. Indeed, the commitment to something like Putnam's principle that "enough is enough" leads to recuperations and the acknowledgement of the sufficiency of these recuperations, even in their multiplicity.

The rabbis, however, show their awareness of the resistance to the hermeneutics of mourning in the people's preference for a tradition resembling Freudian replication and a truth approximating Spinoza's noncontingent absolute. The persistent demand—"Ask!"—expresses anxiety about occupying that realm of doubt, a desire to return to the transcendental truth of the Torah represented in the figure of Moses. The Freudian narrative focuses on the trauma entailed by the giving of the law, and the people's subsequent rebellion. The rabbinic account, by contrast, focuses on the loss of the singularity of the law that Moses's death represents, the refusal to face up to the challenges of transmission and multiplicity that his death entails. For the rabbis, the people are unable—or at least reluctant—to experience loss (and the attendant hermeneutic uncertainty) as an opportunity for recovery through creative interpretation.

The people of Israel show themselves to lack the characteristic that for Lear, appropriating Aristotle, represents as the primary "psychological virtue": "courage." Lear's conception of courage (a synthesis of Aristotle and Freud, with uncanny biblical resonances) entails facing the "rip in the fabric of life"—acknowledging and tolerating loss so that creative meaning becomes possible. The alternative to "the development of courage" in the face of loss is "traumatic neurosis."[23] Israel's failure, in Lear's terms, is their lack of courage, brought on by their neurotic fixation on the figure of Moses. But loss in the rabbinic narratives is presented not only as a consequence of death; indeed, the laws are lost during the period of mourning for Moses. With their continued demand for Moses's return (or the transcendent law that he represents), the people of Israel show that they do not know how to mourn properly—that they do not know how to lose. In Lear's Aristotelian terms, they do not have the courage to mourn.[24]

Without this courage, Israel is unable to inherit or transmit the law, the two integral aspects of *mesora*. In the Talmudic narrative of Moses's final moments before death, Joshua, the anointed leader of the people, is revealed to be an unfit figure for the law's transmission, for the younger prophet is in denial—about both death and loss. "When Moses was departing to enter *Gan Eden*"—to his death and the afterlife—he turned to Joshua and said, "Ask me to resolve any uncertainties you have" (Temurah 16a). Before his passing, Moses tried to mitigate the uncertainties and doubts that he knows would follow upon his death. Moses acknowledged the principle of *yeridat ha'dorot*—the decline in generations—as a hermeneutic principle, his appeal to Joshua an attempt to limit the inevitable consequences of that decline.[25] Joshua's response, however, reveals a failure to acknowledge the inevitability of loss and death—a failure, furthermore, to understand the conditions of transmission. "Did I ever for a minute," Joshua asks, "go to another place?"—"I was always by your side." That what Joshua said was true makes it, however, no less a denial. "Didn't you yourself write about me"—the younger prophet continues, citing chapter and verse—"and his attendant Joshua the son of Nun, a youth, would not stir from out of his tent" (Exodus 33:11; Temurah 16a). Joshua had served Moses faithfully, and in the simple reading of the biblical narrative that Joshua cites in his defense, had shown himself the consummate disciple, the natural inheritor of the Mosaic law. Yet from the perspective of the rabbis, Joshua fails to recognize the inevitability of death and loss, and in so doing, becomes a compromised figure for the law's transmission.

From the biblical account—in which God twice blesses Joshua with courage—the rabbis derive his *lack* of courage. That is, God, for the rabbis, understands the characteristic that Joshua lacks. In each of the blessings, at the time of his anointment in Deuteronomy (31:23) and then again in the first book of the prophets that bears his name, death is in the foreground. In the account in Deuteronomy, God first tells Moses that he will "lie" with his fathers (31:16); in Joshua, Moses's actual death is recounted (Joshua 1:1–2). When the fabric of life is ripped, as Lear writes, one needs courage. The divine injunction and blessing to Joshua follows the intimations and facticity of death: "be strong and of a good courage." In Lear's reading—an echo of the biblical account—courage entails a creative response to loss. For the rabbis, Joshua lacks courage, especially at the moment of Moses's death, revealing himself to be an unsuitable figure of transition into a history of transmission. He does not acknowledge loss, and as a result, in the rabbinic account, is debilitated by it. When Joshua asserts—"wasn't I always in your tent?"—in the Talmudic account, "he" falters: "At that moment, he became weak, and three hundred laws were forgotten, and seven hundred doubts entered his mind" (Temurah 16a). The ambiguous antecedent for "he" shows that either Moses as transmitter of the law or Joshua as inheritor has become unfit for his task. In either case, with Joshua's boast of his ability to pass on a tradition without loss, the tradition is impaired. Moses's death provokes loss and doubt; Joshua's boastful certainty, showing a lack of preparation for mourning and loss, disrupts *mesora*.

The continuation of the rabbinic narrative of Israel's experience of Moses's death has Freudian resonances—about Israel's murderous tendencies—but not as

Freud represents them. For the rabbis, so anxious are the people of Israel when faced with the doubts brought on by Moses's death that "they stand ready to kill Joshua"—unless he shows himself able to reclaim the missing laws (Temurah 16a). Here the rabbis represent Israel as preferring murder and obliterating the memory of Moses to facing up to loss and mourning, the responsibilities of transmission in a world of doubt. In this reading, Israel's murderous desires are expressed, but not, as in *Moses and Monotheism*, in relation to Moses for the giving of the law, but rather to Joshua for forgetting it. For Israel, it is either all or nothing: either the prophetic clarity represented in the law of Moses—which they had hoped Joshua to continue to embody—or nothing, the death of the law of Moses, figured in the threatened death of Joshua. To the principle articulated by Putnam: "enough isn't everything, but enough is enough," the people of Israel protest, in the rabbinic account, in their desire to kill Joshua upon his forgetting, "we want everything."[26] Without the certainty of the fullness of revelation, the people of Israel choose, in this narrative, to kill the messenger and the memory of the revelation that he embodies. Acceding to their demand, the story continues, Joshua asks for resolution of the doubts, but God's reply gives no satisfaction: "It is impossible to resolve your doubts and tell you the forgotten laws" (Temurah 16a). There is no return to the archetype and the mythological past. God thus tells both Joshua and Israel—against their respective resistances—to embrace their experience as historical beings and take up the demands imposed by a Torah not in heaven, but in their own hands. David Stern writes that the rabbis "happily embrace the stance of belatedness"; the people of Israel, by contrast, as the rabbis depict them, are reluctant, indeed unable, to adopt that stance (*Midrash*, 32). Belatedness nurtures pluralism, but the midrashic renderings of Moses's death emphasize both the necessity of multiplicity in history and the people's tendency to resist it.

Challenged to embrace loss, difference, and doubt, the people of Israel show themselves to lack courage, willing to be passive recipients of the Mosaic law, but not creative inheritors of it. They evidence the characteristics of Eliade's anthropological "primitive," able to live in a timeless realm of ahistorical repetition, but they do not embrace history with the loss it entails. The prerequisite for creative memory, both psychoanalytic and rabbinic, is courage—the courage to mourn. Mourning requires the recognition of death as well as an acknowledgment of the continued need for life, a simultaneous movement, as LaCapra suggests, toward past and future. In the rabbinic hermeneutics of mourning, the courageous acknowledgment of loss is the precondition for both interpretation and creative memory. In the narrative in Temurah, Joshua refuses to acknowledge the possibility of loss and inherits doubt, which he is unprepared to confront; the people of Israel, with their fixation on the memory of Moses, prefer death to mourning.

In the rabbinic account, God does not resolve the doubts of the people Israel, but he does offer another solution, ushering them into history as actors: "Go and occupy Israel with war!" To authorize this remedy, God turns Joshua's attention to the opening verses of the book that bears his name, which narrates first the death of Moses and then the divine command to conquer the land: "After the death of Moses the servant of the Lord, the Lord said to Joshua, son of Nun, Moses's attendant: 'My servant Moses is dead. Prepare to cross the Jordan, together with all this people, into the land I am giving to the Israelites'" (Joshua 1:1–2; Temurah 16a). For the rabbis, the prophet not only records the conquest of the land but also a more primary activity—one that is not military but rather hermeneutic. The war that requires supreme courage in facing up to loss—the real subject in the various rabbinic figurations of Moses's death—is the war of Torah, that is, the entry into history, interpretation, and the transmission of the law in the face of death. "My servant Moses is dead"; the war of Torah—of hermeneutic transmission—follows.

For the rabbis, the psalmist's "sharp arrows" are words of the Torah; the warring "enemies at the gate" who show hatred for one another are "Torah scholars" (Kiddushin 30b). "Go and occupy Israel with war" is God's response to the Israelites' passivity and their continued desire for a prophetic revelation that will free them from the obligations imposed by history—creative memory and the hermeneutics of mourning. In the rabbinic narrative, both the leader of Israel and the people fail to understand the nature of interpretation after Moses's death. The people waver between denial of the absence of their lost object—the wishful fantasy of Moses's continued presence as an "archetype" (to which they assimilate other biblical figures as potential substitutes)—and the denial that the lost object was ever present, enacted in the fantasy of Joshua's death. The only continued commitment they evidence is what Mark Edmundson calls a "fundamentalist" one, in which they entertain neither doubt nor complexity.[27] Joshua denies the necessity of remembering and the historicity of transmission, thus making creative memory impossible. Both positions entail passivity in the face of loss. To these complementary stances, God commands Joshua, "Be strong and of good courage," and "Go and occupy Israel with war."

Notwithstanding his primacy of place in the biblical narrative, in the rabbinic accounts in Temurah, Joshua's status is more ambiguous. He may be the first to carry on the tradition of Moses, ordained by God, but he is represented as a passive middle man, awaiting divine instruction before he lives up to the challenge of loss.[28] By contrast, Otniel ben Kanaz, the first of the Judges to lead Israel after Joshua's death, shows no hesitation to go to war, thus taking a central place in the rabbinic narrative of memory and recovery. In Judges, Otniel conquers *Kiryat Sefer*, literally the "Citadel of the Book" (1:11). In this conquest, the rabbis see him as evidencing the paradigmatic response to death and loss; indeed, he is the model figure for transmission, for he knows how to mourn. For the rabbis, his conquest of the Citadel of the Book is primarily interpretive. Otniel enacts the war of Torah—a battle that the people of Israel are represented as resisting through their refusal to acknowledge the final loss of the mourned object (Moses) and their equally problematic desire to obliterate the memory of the lost object in the threats to kill Joshua. The creative remembrance or "working through" of healthy mourning entails a forgetting placed in the service of remembrance, a re-membering without fixation.[29]

Otniel faces the pain of loss and provides a link between past and future through mourning, thus becoming the true representative of the rabbinic hermeneutics of mourning, recreating the lost laws through *pilpul*, or creative dialectics. His mother, the Talmudic account continues, gave him a second name, Yabetz, because she cried out at his birth, "I have borne him through pain"—pain, or *etzev*, containing the root letters of the name, Yabetz. Born of pain, Yabetz, the rabbis say, earned his name because "he gave counsel and multiplied Torah in Is-rael" (Temurah 16a). By confronting suffering and death—the encounter with pain—the restoration of the Mosaic law leads to multiplicity. Through Otniel's dialect, the creativity of *pilpul*, the law continues (Nedarim 38a).

This is what Loewald calls an act of recreation—"the moment of generating a new organization of something old," a "repetition with its face towards the future while aware of the past."[30] Living out the fate of his name, Otniel trans-forms the pain of loss into creative remembrance. Loss and creativity are tied to-gether, however, which underlines the paradox that, in rabbinic readings, the possibility of creative remembrance is presupposed first on the accommodation of loss. Joshua and the people of Israel evidence an unwillingness to acknowledge Moses's death, opting either for the full presence or total absence of his memory and the law that he represents. They are unsatisfied with what Lear, adopt-ing D. W. Winnicott, calls a merely "good enough interpretation" (*Love*, 213). Only through the acknowledgement of pain and loss is there creative memory and difference—the "good enough interpretations" in the plural—that allow for and indeed constitute tradition.

Foreshadowing Death: Forgetting

Memories become, writes Adam Phillips, "forms of forgetting."[31] The people of Israel's fixation on Moses represented in rabbinic accounts is a form of memory as forgetting. Otniel's war of Torah, by contrast, is made possible by mourning—a partial forgetting entailed in acknowledging and mourning Moses's death such that creative memory becomes possible. This is not to suggest that Otniel forgets Sinai or Moses, but that his mourning depends on distance from the memory of

Moses *as fixation* so that he can properly remember. Loss—Lear's ripped fabric—must first be acknowledged. Hence, the rabbinic paradox: Moses is dead, but the Torah of Moses lives on. This is the rabbinic version of Freud's insight paraphrased by Lear: "It is only when one kills off the messenger that the message finally gets installed." Only when Moses is dead can the hermeneutics of mourning—the creative appropriation of the past—be enacted. That such loss is integral to the continuity of tradition is enacted not only in the rabbinic representation of the death of Moses but in the representation of the precedent biblical event that also thematizes death and loss, the breaking of the Tablets of the Law.

After the divine pronouncement of the Ten Commandments on Mount Sinai, Moses ascends to the heavens to receive the law. Moses is presumed to be late, or rather the people, in the rabbinic account, miscalculate the forty days that Moses had told them he would be absent. Assuming Moses to be dead, the people seek out other gods (Shabbat 89a). In this other representation of Moses's death, the people of Israel abandon the law, thus providing a temporal antecedent for the rabbinic narratives about Moses's actual death, which provokes doubt and threats of violence.[32] Upon his descent from Mount Sinai, hearing the sounds from the camp and seeing the worship of the golden calf, Moses throws the tablets to the ground: "As soon as Moses came near the camp and saw the calf and the dancing, he became enraged, and he hurled the tablets from his hands and shattered them at the foot of the mountain" (Exodus 32:19). In Freud's reading, the biblical narrative is a Levitical cover-up:

> The people's defection from the new religion is also described in the text—only as an episode, it is true: namely in the story of the golden calf. In this, by an ingenious turn, the breaking of the tables of the law (which is to be understood symbolically: 'he has broken the law') is transposed on Moses himself, and his furious indignation is assigned as its motive (*SE*, 23:48).

For Freud, it is not Moses but the people who break the Tablets of the Law, repressed in the biblical narrative in the same way as Israel's murder of Moses, the source of their continued guilt. In the rabbis' homiletic reading, Moses not only breaks the tablets, as in the explicit biblical narrative, but receives divine approbation for his act: "*yashar ko'akh sh'barata!*"—translated idiomatically as "a job well done!" (Menakhot 99b). God does not condemn the breaking of the tablets, but he commends it. In the rabbinic mythography, the giving of the Torah made the people of Israel "immortal," placing them beyond the scope of death and history; with the sin of the golden calf, they lose that claim (Avoda Zara 5a). Moreover, with mortality comes the impairment of memory, or rather the beginning of its necessity, for had "it not been for the breaking of the first tablets," the rabbis say, "the Torah would never have been forgotten" (Eruvin 54a). In the rabbinic representation, Moses throws down the tablets with the result that the people of

Israel become mortal; memory is impaired and the Torah is forgotten. Paradoxically, after all this, God offers his praises—"a job well-done."

In the rabbinic account of history and tradition, the breaking of the first tablets represents a tragic reentrance into history for the people of Israel as well as the necessity of transmission of the law in the face of loss. Regarding this action inaugurating history, mortality, and memory, God proclaims, "well done!" The episode serves as an example of a principle of rabbinic interpretation, namely, that "sometimes, through negating the law, the law comes into being" (Menakhot 99b). On a simple narrative level, the divine utterance—"well done!"—stands as a pragmatic accommodation to a new reality, that the law cannot be nurtured in a culture of idolatry. Moses's breaking of the tablets allows for a new expression of the law, but within the rabbinic account, impoverished and distant from its original state. More radically, the acknowledgment of mortality after the sin of the golden calf—of the necessity of negating Torah—anticipates the principles that Otniel embodies when Moses, the privileged mediator of the law, dies. That is, for the law to be transmitted in a world of loss, mourning, with the forgetting it entails, is a necessary precondition. Joshua fails to acknowledge the possibility of loss; the people of Israel cannot endure it. Both fail to recognize that after the golden calf, in history, the hermeneutics of mourning is not merely an accommodation but provides the conditions for interpretation and tradition. The multiplicity of disputes and arguments that characterize the continued tradition—all of the disagreements that followed Moses's death and those that multiplied during later periods in the flourishing of the oral law—are the result of this forgetting. When the Talmud identifies the first dispute recorded among the early rabbis, or *tannaim*, it is attributed to their forgetting; when the minds of the rabbis became diminished, they started to forget.[33] For the Torah to show itself in its multiplicity and variety, there must first be, as Moses casts the tablets down, ushering the people of Israel into history, forgetting. Doubt may be experienced as traumatic and the conditions of forgetting as catastrophic—especially when imposed from outside, as in a later period, the Greek exile, figured by the rabbis as a period of darkness, with the subsequent forgetting it entailed.[34] Whatever the historical period, only forgetting and loss of the "face to face" (or the prophetic moment that stands in for it), leads to the multiplication of the law in Israel, for only in its negation does the law come into being.

Forgetting in the hermeneutics of mourning entails not a repudiation of the past (as in Israel's desire to kill Joshua), but as LaCapra stresses, a *partial* leave taking. The "shards" of the divinely-inscribed first tablets, the rabbis say, were preserved, transported with the second tablets in the ark (Bava Batra 14b).[35] The second tablets, written, as the Exodus narrative suggests, with Moses's human hand, stand as the rabbinic inauguration of a new more active relationship toward the law, resisted at first by the people, requiring argument, and producing and embracing diversity in the face of doubt (Exodus 34:1–4). The preservation of the first tablets, however, manifests the perpetuation of a theoretical ideal, the unity represented in the first set of tablets. Forgetting does not mean abandonment of the revelation at Sinai but rather a forgetting of a unified law of an earlier mythological era, when men were immortal and the law could not be forgotten.[36] As Phillips writes, creativity is made possible through "the gap we make by the act of forgetting," for the rabbis, the gap that leads away from paralyzed passivity to life.[37] In Freud's narrative, Israel, resisting the law, break the tablets; for the rabbis, it is Moses who allows for the perpetuation of the law after mortality and loss, the continued possibility of interpretation. The breaking of the tablets initiates history and tradition, the beginnings of the Israelites' entry into what Loewald calls a "modernity" based on memory. As Otniel is said to understand, only through acknowledging Moses's death does the law of Moses live. The rabbinic hermeneutics of mourning navigates between the two extremes, entailing both leave taking *and* remembrance, as a means of enabling the processes of creative recuperation.

The unity of the first tablets remains an ideal that is only accessible through the processes inaugurated by Moses with the second tablets—a hermeneutics of mourning that leads to multiplicity and differentiation:

> Rabbi Abba said in the name of Shmuel: "For three years, the House of Shammai and the House of Hillel debated each other. These said that the halakha [law] follows their view, and these said that the halakha follows their view. A heavenly voice went forth and declared: *These and these are the words of the living God*" (Eruvin 13b; emphasis added).

The Houses of Hillel and Shammai are themselves associated by the later *Seder* with that original "glory" of the Torah that had only later been diminished. Out of such forgetting comes dispute and the multiplicity and differentiation that caused the people of Israel, with their anxiety about creative memory, to clamor for Joshua's death.

Yet the disputes of Hillel and Shammai are proclaimed within the rabbinic tradition to be "very much beloved" by God.[38] Regarding the multiplication of the Torah that comes as a result of forgetting, the divine proclaims: "these and these are the words of the living God," even though they contradict one another— one says pure, one says impure; one says permitted, the other says forbidden. This rabbinic principle affirming the multiplicity of truth is a necessary corollary to God's expression of approval of Moses upon breaking the tablets: "a job well done."[39] In the realm of history and forgetting, where the tablets are broken and left as splintered shards, there must be disagreement, for there is no longer access to an unmediated primal unity of the divine.

That the divine approves of both Israel's entry into history ("a job well done") and difference ("these and these") shows the rabbis anticipating another of what

Lear calls Freud's "deepest insights": that "life can never be lived without remainder."[40] In the *Republic*, Plato's "allegory of the cave" presupposes, as Lear writes, an "outside." As Lear explains, the narrative of the cave and the escape from its limitations enacts a fantasy of breaking through "the restrictions of ordinary life" for "absolute knowledge and absolute happiness," a philosophical version of the biblical "face to face." The insights associated with that escape are so terrifying, however, that the messenger, Socrates, as Lear writes, must be killed. The fantasy of the remainder—of a truth outside of the limitations of language, convention, and interpretation (outside of the cave)—continue to haunt contemporary philosophical models. But that "remainder of life"—the dream of a world beyond the cave and an absolute truth to which Socrates aspires and for which he is killed—is acknowledged by the rabbis from the outset to be impossible to attain, evidenced in their refusal of the metaphysical implications of the "face to face" and their insistence on an interpretive tradition defined by loss. The interventions of Hillel and Shammai—as all the manifold and multiplying disputes of the generations—do not provide full compensation for loss. In claiming to do so, they would only produce an illusion of Moses's presence, a fantasy of his return. Although they are partial, these compensations are still, even in their inadequacy to the loss they come to address, "words of the living God" and beloved for their representation of a truth that, acknowledged from the outset, can never be fully recovered.

In presenting Moses as a figure who enacts loss through both the shattering of the tablets and his death, what Lear calls "the constitutive fantasy of 'outside'" is acknowledged but rendered impossible from its inception. It is as if Moses, in throwing down the tablets, enacts the equivalent of the Socratic taking of the hemlock as a means of showing that the Mosaic inheritance, from its beginnings, acknowledges death and loss. The divine revelation—the face to face—can never be confronted directly. In the midrashic representation, in which God acquiesces to Moses's desire for seeing the divine, he is seen only from "behind," donning a *tallit* and phylacteries (*tefillin*), the knot formed in the back of the latter in the shape of the letter *daleth*, emphasizing that divine revelation always takes place through language (Berakhot 6a). Similarly, in the image of the broken tablets, the sense of the "remainder of life" is acknowledged and deferred to the realm of interpretation—there can be no efforts to "construct an image of what lies outside." The rabbis' disputes are an acknowledgement that "the remainder" is always beyond history, that unity can only be achieved through interpretation and differentiation, through a remembering based on forgetting: "through negating the law, the law comes into being."

In the Talmudic representations of Moses's death, the people of Israel are anxious about the uncertainty they inherit, and the fear, as Putnam would gloss it, that "everything we say is false because everything we say falls short of being everything that could be said." For Putnam, this represents a particularly "adolescent" form of "error."[41] In Freudian terms, it is simply an inability—or unwillingness—to face up to the obligation to mourn, to live up to the interpretive creativity demanded in the face of loss. As I show in part 2, Joseph Soloveitchik's ethical psyche meets up to this demand, but his legal hermeneutics represents a departure from the hermeneutics of mourning, with its melancholy idealization of a tradition of archetypes and the certainty it produces. The implicit epistemological assumptions of Talmudic legal dispute that inform the circumscribed pluralism of the hermeneutics of mourning, from which Soloveitchik's melancholy modernism represents a deviation, is the subject of the next chapter.

2 Pluralism, Rabbinic Poetry, and Dispute

> One who proclaims, "I honor nothing but *Aggada*," is like the man who plucks the blossom, but is heedless of the fruit.
>
> —H. N. Bialik, *Law and Legend or Halakah and Aggadah*

RABBINIC PLURALISM BEGAN, in literary critical circles, with midrash. In the previous chapter, I focused on what Daniel Boyarin describes as those "narrative traditions" that "thematize dialectical argumentation and portray it as the highest form of Torah," that is, the programmatic midrashic texts describing rabbinic dispute.[1] In setting the grounds for understanding Soloveitchik's legal hermeneutics and his departure from Talmudic models, I start with midrash here as well—as a means to outline the implicit epistemological assumptions internal to rabbinic dispute. That is, the hermeneutics of legal dispute rest on the epistemological assumptions that inform them, particularly the relationship posited between subject and object, elaborated not in philosophical terms but instead rendered paradigmatic here in the narrative terms of a midrash from Hagiga 3a. Soloveitchik, as I claim in chapter 3, also argues against the subject–object distinction in his defense of methodological pluralism; however, those arguments, do not inform, as they do for the rabbis, a legal hermeneutics of pluralism.

The current chapter, after outlining a brief history of the flourishing of midrash in the literary academy in the 1980s, turns to a midrashic representation of legal difference where the "polysemy" of midrashic interpretation serves as a prelude to the parallel representation of multiplicity in legal dispute. The reference points to which I turn to elaborate what I call the "poetry of dispute" have their provenance in both literary criticism and philosophy, both disciplines admittedly foreign to conventional elaborations of rabbinic discourse. Understanding the Hebraic in the language of the Greek, as Levinas puts it, in this context means articulating the assumptions present in the Talmud that remain only implicit or are represented in complex but not completely transparent terms. The seventeenth-century poet John Donne elaborates a poetry of paradox that becomes, in my reading, a fit entry into midrashic homiletics. To this end, I invoke Donne's "metaphysical" poetics and his metaphoric conception of multiplicity—what

Dr. Samuel Johnson called pejoratively *discordia concors* (a discordant har-mony)—to elicit the poetics of midrashic commentary.[2]

As the current chapter positions itself in relation to the precedent conversations about rabbinic pluralism mapped out by Boyarin, David Stern, David Krae-mer, Steven Fraade, Christine Hayes, and Richard Hidary (among others), my aim is to elaborate the assumptions underlying rabbinic legal multiplic-ity, informed as they are by a complementary notion of midrashic polysemy.[3] The chapter then turns to the explicit languages of philosophy to unpack midrashic poetics and their consequences for understanding legal pluralism. That is, not-withstanding Wittgenstein's claim that "philosophy ought to be written only as a form of poetry," itself an apt description of midrash, I turn to philosophical models and languages to show the ways in which Talmudic dispute both refuses and transcends the subject–object distinction.[4] Where the poetry of Donne—in its cultivation of paradox—provides a later parallel for rabbinic poetry, the philosophers invoked here advocate contradictory models that, read together and in dialogue, help to articulate the epistemological assumptions of Talmudic argument. Moving from the midrashic poetry of commentary to the multiplicity of legal dispute entails the invocation of the seemingly opposed, but in my read-ing, complementary interpretive models of Hans-Georg Gadamer and Quentin Skinner. Gadamer's hermeneutic emphasis on "subjective constraints," along with Skinner's historicist stress on the recovery of objective "intention," informs a reading of the mechanisms of the hermeneutics of mourning, helping to elaborate the contours of the interpreting subject presupposed in Talmudic argument.

* * *

Meditations about conceptions of Talmudic difference and their implications for literary interpretation have largely entered the academy through the category of midrash. For literary theorists—and in the humanities in general—theological approaches to interpretation had been mostly dismissed in favor of hermeneutic models committed to the contingency, partiality, and historicity of interpretative practice. Starting in the 1980s, against the tendency to dismiss vestiges of the-ology from "postmodern" habits of reading and interpretation, scholars such as Boyarin and Stern began to recover the distinctly Jewish modes and dis-courses of reading and interpretation. In the process, they introduced, as Boya-rin stresses, a specifically Jewish mode of reading—that of "midrash"—into the literary theoretical canon.[5] In retrospect, the rehabilitation of midrash parallels the New Historicist moment in literary studies, which similarly entailed, in Foucauldian terms, the archaeology of suppressed discourses and knowledge.

For Geoffrey Hartman, whose volume *Midrash and Literature*, edited with Sanford Budick, marked the formal entry of midrash into literary studies, the suppression of rabbinic discourses remains embedded in a specific history of which his own work is a belated part:

> My motives in studying Midrash are not pure. I am a raider of the lost ark looking for treasure. It is not for the sake of heaven I study but to bring back voices and types of interpretations of which that ark is as full as Noah's was beasts. I cannot forget how these writings were slandered, and how public ignorance abetted such slander in the Nazi era.[6]

As a "raider of the lost ark," Hartman seeks to penetrate beneath the surface of "ignorance" and "prejudice," and in this "age of restitutions," he participates in the rescue of Jewish exegesis from Nazi "slander." Against the attribution of "a crass and stubborn literalism" to Jewish tradition, Hartman celebrates the "interpretive bounty" for which midrash becomes a symbol. Hartman responds to the Holocaust by turning to the intertextual "bounty" of midrash, releasing it from the "literalism" conventionally attributed to it.

This promise of "interpretive bounty" brought midrash as an interpretive mode into the precincts of literary criticism. Although the "Nazi era" and the "impact of the *hurban*" are never far from Hartman's mind, he also calls attention to the "shift in contemporary intellectual life from identity-philosophies to theories of difference based on an appreciation of the intertextual character of writing."[7] Midrash becomes both an example and expression of this kind of writing, made possible because of its avoidance of conceptual monovocality and its embrace of "difference." For Hartman, midrash emerges as a category of writing that is indeed possible—Adorno's well-known proclamation notwithstanding—after Auschwitz. Indeed, with the interest in "polyphony" and "intertextuality," midrash gained currency with a generation of literary critics schooled in Derridean *differánce*. Hartman and Budick find connections between midrash and a notion of the literary that, with the writing of their volume, was reaching its ascendancy: "What we are concerned with throughout this volume is a variety of 'open' modes of interpretation, a life in literature or in scripture that is experienced as in the shuttle space between the text." "Abiding in the same intermediary space is a whole universe of allusive textuality," they continue, "which lately goes by the name *intertextuality*."[8] The Derridean echoes are unmistakable, as the authors continue, celebrating midrash's production of "a continuum of intertextual supplements" offered "in a spirit of highly serious play."[9] Hartman further elaborates on the connection between midrash and the Derridean moment in his 1994 piece when he pronounced (if already belatedly), "Ask not what deconstruction may do for Midrash, ask what Midrash may do for deconstruction."[10]

Though not with the same urgency, Betty Rojtman pursues a similar argument when she asserts that "the mobility and indeterminacy of midrash . . . explains its attractiveness to present-day theoreticians who understand midrash in a way that feeds their faith in an infinite unfolding of textual signification." "The concept of the inherent polysemy of the literary text," one that "nullifies the possibility of a univocal interpretation," Myrna Solotorevsky echoes, "is one of the arch principles of midrash." For both Rojtman and Solotorevsky, the "infinite unfolding of textual signification" and the "inherent polysemy of the literary text" reveal the perceived conjunction between midrashic methodology and literary theory. Rojtman thus instantiates an opposition between midrashic reading, with its "responsiveness to elements of textual play," and a mode of reading wed to "a standard of truth," in the "logical and metaphysical sense."[11] Edith Wyschograd elaborates a similar dichotomy, for her, between a midrash "anticipating postmodern tendencies" and a rabbinic concern for law, which she describes as fundamentally "Platonic."[12] In these accounts, there is an articulation of the dichotomy in its barest terms. Midrash, associated with intertextuality, polyphony, and postmodernism (and an antifoundationalist ethos) stands against a tradition of interpretation tied to metaphysics and law (and a foundationalism affiliated with Plato).

Following on the postmodern appropriation of midrash, Stern has written vigorously on the importance of distinguishing the "polysemy" of the Talmud from the "indeterminacy" lauded by deconstructionists and poststructuralists, a form of "indeterminacy" associated for him with "sheer relativism" or the "negation of meaning" (*Midrash*, 15–16).[13] Stern does articulate the perspective on pluralism internal to rabbinic culture: "although the sages' opinions may contradict each other, they are all part of Torah, part of a single revelation" (*Midrash*, 20). Stern, however, also elaborates a different critical perspective for which the multiplication of meanings in midrash is "motivated by an anxiety about the loss of meaning or presence," a rabbinic response to "the textual fissures and continuities that exegesis discovers" (*Midrash*, 31, 30). As Stern continues, "the citation of multiple interpretations" stands as an "attempt to represent in textual terms an idealized academy of rabbinic tradition where all of the opinions of the sages are recorded equally as part of 'a single divine conversation'" (*Midrash*, 164). In this sense, the midrashic representations of dispute are examples of what Stern calls "a literary impression, something of an illusion created by the redaction of Rabbinic literature" (*Midrash*, 33). As an editorial creation, "the idealized portrait of interpretive pluralism" masks "an unhappy social reality" (*Midrash*, 37). The artificially created rabbinic "literary impression," as Stern calls it, raises "opinions that in human discourse may appear contradictory or mutually exclusive" to the status of "paradox," finally to be subsumed under the category of divine revelation (*Midrash*, 158, 164). The editorial representation and idealization of pluralism has become a "condition of meaning" and the "fantasy" resolution of "difference" is figured as an essentially "benign process."[14] Stern acknowledges, however, that the rabbis themselves "would have located" the "effective cause" of their disputes not "in their historical situation but in the act of Scriptural exegesis itself" (*Midrash*, 38).

Boyarin similarly distances rabbinic pluralism from those reading it as an expression of polysemic indeterminacy. While Stern hedges against the post-structuralist radicalizing of difference as indeterminacy (though he acknowledges his own reading as "nascently deconstructive" [*Midrash*, 39]), Boyarin claims that midrashic hermeneutics do not go far enough. Although there are those who claim that rabbinic Judaism—again focusing on midrash—encodes "either radical undecidability or radical pluralism," the Babylonian Talmud was founded, Boyarin argues, indeed was made possible, through "the most extreme acts of exclusion."[15] Stern sees midrashic representations of difference as enacting "a fantasy of social stability" of "human continuity in complete harmony" (*Midrash*, 33).[16] Boyarin goes further in asserting that the "possibility of pluralism was won by excluding any possibility of real dissent," and, for him, "even more 'successful' than the exclusionary practices of Christian orthodoxy."[17] In Boyarin's implicit appropriation of Stephen Greenblatt's New Historicist rhetoric, the representation of pluralism does not, in the end, amount to "subversion" but rather the "containment" of significant dissent.[18] In this reading, "these and these are the words of the living God" (Eruvin 13b) may be an expression of a highly circumcised pluralism, but primarily a technique for the "maintenance of absolute control." The Talmud, Boyarin adds, "seems to know this," suggesting that the rabbis themselves were complicit in the containment of difference, the wielding of what Stern calls "paradox" for the purpose of communal control by providing only a fiction of toleration.[19] That is, the Talmudic representation of difference in Boyarin's reading is the means by which difference is contained, even nullified, representing the "moment" when "real dissent was banished from Israel." The "Babylonian moment," he writes, "is a powerful technique for the maintenance of absolute control." In this representation, the rabbinic descriptions of pluralism, as in Stern's account, pursue the conscious editorial intent of keeping "the simulacrum of distinction alive, while defanging it of any power to make a difference."[20]

In contrast to the approach that focuses on the ideological work done by the literary representations of difference, I seek to elaborate the epistemological assumptions that are internal to Talmudic dispute, focusing on the mechanisms through which that difference emerges, especially in legal discourse. This is not to demur from the readings of the midrashic narratives elaborated above, but to focus on the conceptions of difference extrapolated from rabbinic disputes themselves. To do so is to provide a counterbalance to the literary critical and philosophical stress on midrash—as a means of further understanding rabbinic conceptions of pluralism.

The literary critical celebration of midrash as a mode of reading, on its own, has occluded the nature of legal discourse, often misrepresenting it. In Rojtman's

account, for example, while midrash is championed, halakha is either to be ignored or condemned as midrash's inferior handmaid—especially for its ostensible failure to embrace the pluralism implicit in its counterpart.[21] She laments, for
example, Jewish Law's supposition of a "standard of truth," both in the "metaphysical and logical sense" of the terms.[22] The invocation, however, of an ostensibly
metaphysical—even Platonically informed—realm of Jewish law (halakha) against
the polysemy of midrash unnecessarily bifurcates rabbinic thought, not only mis-
apprehending halakha but midrash as well. Indeed, the assertion that midrash is
"dialogic" and halakha "absolutist" entails a misreading of both. The failure to
show their interdependence reflects a reading of Jewish discourses according to a
vulgar simplification of Western philosophical categories where absolute truth and
a relativism informed by "polysemy" are the only reference points available.

That the starting point for many considerations of rabbinic hermeneutics has
been French poststructuralist thought has helped sustain the impression that
midrashic method does, in fact, provide a precedent for a postmodernist epistemological relativism. For this reason, I turn to the seemingly incommensurate
empirical and hermeneutic traditions of Britain and Germany, respectively, to
provide an account of rabbinic interpretation resisting dichotomies that have
emerged from the literary critical appropriation of French thought. By placing
Hans-Georg Gadamer's hermeneutics in dialogue with the Cambridge historian
Quentin Skinner's method of "intentionalist action" and reading a legal dispute
through the complementary lenses they offer, I employ philosophical languages
to show their limits, in the process elaborating the contours of the poetry of dispute. But first I turn to a reading of a particular midrash, one of Boyarin's narratives thematizing dispute.

Discordia Concors: Midrashic Poetry

The homiletic exercise attributed to Rabbi Elazar ben Azariah in Hagiga 3a, according to David Stern, is "an almost perfect illustration of midrashic reading"
(*Midrash*, 20). In Stern's reading of what he calls the "proem," he emphasizes
R. Elazar's "virtuoso" performance in the reading of Ecclesiastes 12:11. As Stern
writes, the multiplicity of different readings are ultimately assimilated, paradoxical as they may be, through the "literary image" at the end of the "proem" into
the "divine presence from which all contradictory interpretations derive" (*Midrash*, 20). Where Stern suggests, however, that this diversity is a literary artifact,
with the proem performing the cultural work of integration, I am interested here
in articulating the nature of diversity from within the rabbinic perspective, or as
Stern himself describes it, with the divine utterances themselves dictating the
"terms of polysemy" and the paradoxes they produce (*Midrash*, 38). To provide
this more normative account of rabbinic dispute, internal to its own discourses, I

turn now to an unconventional and unlikely parallel representation of difference in the work of the seventeenth-century English poet, John Donne.

Donne, the founder of what would later be called the "metaphysical school" of English poetry, was condemned by the eighteenth-century critic Dr. Johnson for yoking "the most heterogeneous ideas by violence together"—the bringing together of incompatible, indeed incommensurable, registers in his poetic images.[23] Donne's "metaphysical" conceits were, from Johnson's later philosophically informed perspective, merely fanciful combinations of dissimilar images, and therefore unjustified. Rather than elicit any intrinsic resemblance between things, Donne's inventions were, for Johnson, imaginative but arbitrary, producing a surprising, but ultimately unsatisfying, set of poetic effects. But Johnson also suggested, in an aside that goes against the grain of his canonical rejection of Donne, that the resultant *discordia concors* of Donne's poetry—the discordant harmony of multiple meanings—was not just an example of interpretive genius, an act of poetic invention (and thus to be dismissed by contemporary philosophers), but one of discovery.[24] In this reading, the relationship between Donne's images is not just fanciful—fantastic poetic virtuosity and wit on display—but justified through a set of counterintuitive similarities, though not immediately accessible. That is, Johnson senses an implicit logic or connection— "occult resemblances" in things only "apparently unlike"—in what the rest of his long essay on Donne and his school rejects as random and arbitrary associations of the poet, however ingenious. The resemblances of Donne's metaphysical conceits strain the merely visual imagination and demand a level of conceptualization that transcends the physical. In his "Valediction: Forbidding Mourning," for example, Donnean lovers are like "twin compasses"—Johnson sneers at the suggestion—not because of their outward physical appearances, but because of a conceptual link that connects the two. Similarly, Donne writes of sex in terms of divine love (and divine love in terms of sex), affronting readers like Johnson for his violent yoking of the temporal and the eternal.[25]

Following Johnson on Donne, I provide a set of readings that suggest that what Stern calls R. Elazar's "wit" is guided (indeed, both manifested and constrained) by the verse from Ecclesiastes; that the different and apparently contradictory interpretations that R. Elazar's commentary produces need not be viewed merely, as Stern suggests, as part of a "virtuoso" performance; and, finally, that the principle of *discordia concors* of R. Elazar's poetic practice informs the *discordia concors*, raised to a social principle, of legal opinions at the proem's end. My reading here thus elaborates, in anticipation of Soloveitchik's corresponding set of assumptions in part 2, the epistemological assumptions internal to the hermeneutic circle of Talmudic tradition, as well as the multiple perspectives it produces—however much that pluralism may fail by contemporary lights.

The proem begins with the citation of the verse from Ecclesiastes: "The words of the wise are like goads, and as well-planted nails are the words of the masters of the assemblies, given by one Shepherd." R. Elazar begins his midrashic inquiry: "Why are the words of Torah likened to a goad?" Changing the subject of the verse from "words of the wise" (*divrei hakhamim*) to "words of Torah" (*divrei Torah*) both announces and anticipates the strategy of the proem as a whole in which R. Elazar collapses the authority of Torah, the divine law, into that of rabbinic utterances. Here we find a corollary to Boyarin's claim that "God takes a fall into language," as R. Elazar aggressively equates the temporal and the eternal, human words with the divine.[26] At this stage in the interpretation of R. Elazar, these "words," now of both human and divine provenance—this reading does not erase or even "correct" the simple meaning of the verse—provide the power of guidance, renewal, and regeneration: "Just as goads direct the cow along its furrows to bring forth life into the world, so the words of Torah direct students from the paths of death to the paths of life." But R. Elazar further inquires, eliciting an alternate set of meanings: "If the words of Torah are likened to goads, then just as the goad is movable, so also are the words of Torah movable."

In R. Elazar's meditation on the nature of *divrei Torah*, these words, already attributed to wise men as "goads," have the status in the valence of the question as *mere* movables, that is, objects that are worldly and temporal, that in moving from place to place, compromise their status as divine and eternal. R. Elazar's homily proceeds, receptive to the developing metaphoric register of the verse, revising, as Stern writes, "the initial interpretation by interpreting Scripture through Scripture" (*Midrash*, 20). That the verse continues with "nails" allows permanence to be attributed to these "words." As in the Donnean conceit, however, contradictory images do not place each other under Derridean "erasure" but rather persist, complementing one another (in the language of the *beit midrash*, the *terutz*, or the answer, does not completely undermine the presuppositions of the *hava mina*, the supposition of the question). The words of Torah retain their movable status as goads—and the association with contingency and temporality—but are attributed permanence as well, thus reasserting the status of *divrei hakhamim* as *divrei Torah*. R. Elazar teases out the implications of the verse, transforming it through his commentary into something like a metaphysical poem, where words of Torah are both human and divine, eternal and contingent.

The internal logic of the verse compels the sage to continue his questioning: "Just as the nail diminishes and does not increase, so also the words of Torah diminish and do not increase." No longer associated with giving life, "nails" qualifies the original reading of goads that had associated the words of the sages with sustenance and renewal. The question itself implies an ambiguity, for nails may be said to "diminish" as they are employed, their size reduced with their usage (as they are pounded into the wood). In this reading, "nails" no longer serve as a proof text for the enduring permanence of the words of the sages but rather their finitude. Alternatively, R. Elazar can be read to suggest that the nails—as words of Torah—diminish the wood, and by extension, those who hear those words are diminished by them, a reading that undermines the original implication of goads as life-giving. As before, the different interpretations emerge in relationship to the constraints imposed by the verse, and their connotations are therefore both maintained.

R. Elazar answers by calling attention to the verse's mixed metaphor, noting that the "nails" are "well-planted"—turning the image of the nails into one combining inorganic and organic aspects. That is, just as they both grow and increase, so also the words of the wise grow and increase, or, according to the second way of phrasing the question, cause growth and increase. The proem then provides an instance of a rabbinic polysemy that is unified, indeed originates, through the verse in Ecclesiastes, distilled in the image—like a Donnean metaphysical conceit incapable of visualization—of "blooming nails." It also continues to be an extended meditation on the nature of words of Torah, which double as words of the wise. "These words" have the status, in R. Elazar's poetic rendering, of being simultaneously durable and eternal, organic and inorganic, fixed and bountiful. R. Elazar elicits the discordant harmony implicit within the verse—the paradoxical interpretations resulting in "blooming nails" emanating from the verse itself.

In R. Elazar's rendering, the multiplicity enacted in the *discordia concors* of his own commentary anticipates the social, and indeed legal manifestation of the principle that he elicits from the end of the verse, a rabbinic polysemy emerging from what Azzan Yadin-Israel calls a "scriptural polysemy," that is, an "inherent characteristic of divine language."[27] The multiplicity, however, inherent in the words of Torah, as R. Elazar continues, only comes into being through those who study Torah, the "masters of assemblies." The original ambiguity between "words of the sages" and "words of Torah" returns, suggesting now that only the sages, in their multiplicity, "who sit in various groups and study the Torah," are able to render "the words of Torah" in their multiplicity. Multiple subjects—the sages—produce, or reveal, the multiplicity inherent in Torah. In this reading, rabbinic polysemy both activates *and* depends on scriptural polysemy.[28] The subjects studying Torah, the masters of assemblies, through their engagement with words of Torah, effect the transformation by means of which "words of the wise" attain the status of "words of Torah" and by which, further, the distinction between human subjects and the divine words of revelation collapses.

The multiplicity enacted and produced in R. Elazar's reading of the verse now shows itself to be present in a broader legal context as well: "There are scholars who render clean, those who render unclean; those who prohibit and those who permit; those who disqualify and those who render fit." In response to the multiplicity that the proem both describes and enacts, R. Elazar imagines what Stern calls the "despair" and "anxiety" of an interpreting subject facing this apparent interpretive uncertainty, even anarchy: "Perhaps a man will say how shall I learn Torah?" (*Midrash*, 20, 33). Indeed, R. Elazar's elaboration of difference within the legal framework leads him to the end of the verse as a means to assimilate it: "All of them were given from one Shepherd" (ibid., 20). The shepherd is a paradigmatic figuration of Stern's literary artifact, assuaging the hermeneutic anxiety of the questioning student. The figure of the shepherd, with an ambiguous antecedent in both God and Moses (both are referred to as "shepherd" in the Old Testament, although this is more likely a reference to Moses in Numbers 27:12–23), reinstates the collapse of the divine and human suggested at the beginning of the proem. Further, the multiple rabbinic perspectives—the contradictory legal perspectives—emanate "from the mouth of the Master of all *ma'asim*," "all actions or matters," a divine name occurring only this once in the Bavli. The God who unifies activities (goading, planting, nailing, and blossoming) also brings together or unifies the words—the matters or sayings—of the sages in legal dispute, as midrashic polysemy becomes the precedent for, and informs, rabbinic legal multiplicity.

R. Elazar's biblical intertextuality ends with the citation of Exodus, unifying the different realms of the verse: "And God spoke all these words [or 'things']." The verse, "these words"—*kol ha'davarim ha'eleh*—now extends both to the words of Torah and the words of the sages, so that, again, they have become interchangeable, of the same divine origin. In R. Elazar's proem, the poetic principle that unifies the various interpretations of the verse also, by its own logic, informs the unity affirmed among the contradictory perspectives in legal argument. R. Elazar's homily, which in this reading is not a serendipitous multiplicity of unrelated interpretations but a poetry of midrashic commentary, provides a *discordia concors* of meanings unified through the verse, eliciting what Rojtman calls the verse's "deep structure."[29]

That the proem concludes with R. Elazar supplementing the "literary image" of the shepherd from Ecclesiastes with an image of his own making suggests that the transition from midrashic polysemy to legal multiplicity demands further elaboration and justification. That is, to accommodate the differences that are a product of midrashic interpretation within the legal realm of multiple subjects requires, for R. Elazar, a description of the proper attitude of the interpreting subject, one that requires an image of his own devising. So R. Elazar advises: "make your ears like a mill-hopper and acquire for yourself a discerning heart." The mill-hopper, an image extrinsic to the verse from Ecclesiastes, implies an epistemology, figuring the mind as a passive receiver but also asserting an injunction to be active in the acquisition of a discerning or understanding heart. Even the image of the mill-hopper depicts the mind in both ways, with its filtering mechanism condensing passive and active traits. Further, the understanding heart, associated with the active capacity of the mind "to understand one thing from another," implies creative, not merely passive, understanding.[30] As Rashi explains, the interpreting subject first needs to hear "the words of all" and then determine which side the law follows. Rashi's rendering gives R. Elazar's proem a thematic coherence, as the words of the anxious figure now determining the law for himself are themselves transformed into "words of Torah." The contingent judgment of the interpreter is raised to the status of Torah, in a process that both mirrors and repeats the process by which "words of the wise" transform into "words of Torah."

The mind as mill-hopper, R. Elazar's addition to the proem, as both attentive (passive) and attributive (active) agent, suggests a conception of legal multiplicity understood as more than just a literary artifact, that is, more than merely a fantasy of difference resolved. Stern's assertion that R. Elazar's midrashic interpretations are "virtuoso" informs the notion that the image of the shepherd performs only a figuration of resolution. In my reading, itself closer to the assumptions of rabbinic interpreters (as Stern himself defines them), for whom midrashic polysemy is dictated, constrained by the verse, the literary figure of the shepherd does more than represent a fictive resolution of inherently incommensurate legal interpretations. But what I am calling the *discordia concors* of legal multiplicity is presupposed upon the construction of an interpreting subject, thus requiring R. Elazar's addition of the mill-hopper.

Aristotle models the mechanism of the soul on what one commentator calls a "mirror-lens"; Donne calls the understanding soul a "potent receiver."[31] R. Elazar's more prosaic mill-hopper frames interpretation as informed by both passive and active aspects. In this model, different interpreting subjects elicit different aspects of the divine text to which they are receptive. The resultant diverse legal interpretations are, in this reading, held together by more than the literary fiat achieved by R. Elazar's virtuoso interpretations. The legal pluralism in the social context of "assemblies" does, however, require an articulation of the nature of the interpreting-subject, that is, R. Elazar's innovation of the mill-hopper. Donne's poetic sense of *discordia concors* is guaranteed both by a view of the subject as potent receiver and by an objective world, a cosmos integrated through medieval correspondences and signatures. As Fraade and Hidary argue, there are many midrashic representations of difference, but the *discordia concors* of Talmudic legal interpretation presupposes the mill-hopper as paradigmatic and an interpreting subject as both passive and active. Midrashic differences, however, unlike the Donnean correlate, emphasizes text not cosmos, a divine utterance redolent with multiple meanings.[32] To elaborate the complex relationship between the subject and the objective constraints condensed in the epistemology of R. Elazar's mill-hopper and presumed in legal multiplicity, I turn now to the works of Hans Georg Gadamer and Quentin Skinner.

Method and Meaning

On the surface, Skinner and Gadamer may seem to be not only an unlikely pairing but an impossible one. Skinner's meticulous focus on intention appears to be irreconcilable with Gadamer's insistence on hermeneutic contexts or "interpretive horizons," as he calls them, in which readings of texts are engendered, indeed produced. Gadamerian hermeneutics has been criticized for leading to an interpretive relativism and for engendering anarchy in interpretation. By contrast, Skinnerian intentionalism has been understood to be founded on a hopeless idealism (and naiveté) about the possibility of recovering the intentions that are meant to inform a text.[33] Rendering Gadamerian method schematically has him celebrating the paradigms, models, or subjective frameworks that produce the interpretations of texts. Skinner, by contrast, is seen to emphasize the objectively identifiable intentions that underlie the writing of a text. Such simplifications serve a heuristic function. There are, however, significant points of agreement between them, beginning with the acknowledgement of the failure of a theory of interpretation that depends uniquely on either subjective paradigms or objective intentions.

Articulating the hermeneutics of the rabbinic discourse of the Talmud demands a similar attempt, for neither subjective approaches, which celebrate "the polyphony" of rabbinic interpretation, nor objective approaches, which assert the self-evident objectivity of rabbinic interpretations, do justice to the multiplicity that follows on the hermeneutics of mourning. Independently, simplified versions of neither Gadamer nor Skinner provide an adequate model for approaching rabbinic multiplicity. From the bridge between them, and from their common acknowledgement of the reciprocal relationship between subject and object (the epistemological assumptions that underlie R. Elazar's "mill-hopper"), emerges a methodology suitable for elaborating multiplicity in Talmudic legal discourse.

To suggest the commensurability of Gadamerian hermeneutics with Skinnerian intentionalism raises problems, however—if not primarily from Skinner's attacks on Gadamer dating back to the 1980s. Writing in his introduction to the *Return of Grand Theory*, Skinner laments, "Gadamer has cast doubt on whether we can ever hope to reach the traditional goal of interpretation, that of grasping an alien action, utterance or text 'objectively' in its own terms." Because Gadamer had undermined the possibility of rendering the intentions of a text "objectively," Skinner warned that it would be just a "short step to the anarchistic conclusion that we ought not to think of interpretation as a method of attaining truths at all."[34] Here the historical empiricist Skinner invokes the dichotomy described above, arguing explicitly for objectivity in interpretation against the subjective—indeed anarchic—excesses of Gadamerian hermeneutics. Skinner suggests that once any subjective component is introduced into the hermeneutic enterprise, interpretive anarchy will reign.

Skinner's method, emerging from the twin strands of Austinian language philosophy and the historical traditions of R. G. Collingwood and Herbert Butterfield, stresses the importance of reconstructing authorial intentions. Before the methodological protest against the proponents of "Grand Theory," Skinner had different interpretive models in his sights—those of the New Criticism.[35] Writing in 1972 against W. K. Wimsatt's New Critical rejection of intention, Skinner fashioned a method that shifted emphasis "off the idea of the text as an autonomous object" toward an understanding of the text that would take into account "intentionalist action."[36] Rejecting New Critical principles, Skinner elaborates the "idea of the text as an object linked to its creator, and . . . what its creator may have been doing in creating it." Skinner emphasizes intention, but also Austin's "central insight" about the performative nature of language, distilled in the Wittgensteinian affirmation that "words are also deeds." Skinner's intentionalism does not entail a focus on the text in itself, but rather on what he terms, following Austin, the "particular force which with a given utterance . . . may have been issued on a particular occasion." Skinner thus invokes discursive contexts, or Wittgensteinian "language games," as a means for reconstructing the intentions of particular texts, or, as Skinner following Austin would have them, texts as performative utterances. While acknowledging that it is impossible "to step into the shoes of past agents" and "still less into their minds," Skinner nonetheless still holds out hope for recovery of the "intentions with which their utterances were issued, and hence what they meant by them."[37]

Against this hope, Skinner's critics have regularly invoked Gadamer. John Keane, for example, rejects Skinner's "dusty antiquarianism" and "old-fashioned positivism." Because language is always situated and interpreters always bear the unavoidable mark of Gadamerian "prejudice," Keane argues, interpretations are not discovered but produced as a function of present concerns. There are "no selfless researchers," Keane chides Skinner, who are "detached from their object." Similarly, Nancy Streuver finds Skinner's "pre-occupation with anachronism" a "fussy minor therapy"; she rejects both his interpretive model and what she sees as his relegation of past texts to the "status of antiques." "Presentism," that is, the process of taking into account the interpretive schemes, paradigms, and prejudices wielded by the contemporary subject encountering a text, is a "necessary element in good historiography."[38] Authorial intention—the category of the objective—is rejected as a chimera, with textual meanings understood as the result of the Gadamerian productive act of interpretation.

Notwithstanding the explicit attack of the *Grand Theory* volume, Skinner nonetheless moves in the direction of a rapprochement with Gadamerian hermeneutics. Indeed, Skinner refrains from a head-on attack on Gadamer, more often arguing against those who invoke his name.[39] Citing Kuhn, Skinner acknowledges that "whenever we report our beliefs, we inevitably employ some classificatory scheme," with the result that none of these different schemes can "ever be uncontentiously employed to report undisputable facts." This is not to deny, Skinner continues, always preserving the constraints imposed by the objective sphere, "that there are undisputable facts to be reported."[40] Yet Skinner acknowledges that different conceptual schemes reveal different aspects of the world.[41] That is, Skinner, an inheritor of the empirical assumptions of Francis Bacon, whose method implies an interpreting subject ideally functioning as a mere (nonactive) mirror of "objective" intentions, admits the role of the subject as active mediator. Skinner's concession to the reciprocal relationship between subjective and objective constraints in interpretation is even more evident with the claim that historians "inevitably approach the past in the light of contemporary paradigms and presuppositions, the influence of which may easily serve to mislead us at every turn."[42] In other words, the contemporary interpreter's presuppositions pose subjective constraints that not only influence but indeed shape the processes of interpretation.

Gadamer's hermeneutic model, by contrast, seems to rule out any possibility of an interpretive model based on objectively recoverable intentions. In his attempt to undercut the claims of a nineteenth-century "objectivist" epistemology, Gadamer associates the notion that interpreters "must transpose ourselves into the spirit of the age" with what he calls the "naive assumption" of an earlier positivist historicism. The "important thing" to recognize, he writes, is that "temporal distance" provides the "positive and productive condition enabling understanding." For Gadamer, there are no ahistorical, that is unsituated, interpretations. The "hermeneutical situation," irreducibly historical, is constitutive not only of the text but also of "what seems to us worth inquiring about and what will appear as an object of investigation." What follows from Gadamer's analysis of the constitutive act of understanding and from the appreciation of the "finitude of our historical existence" is what Skinner calls the "disturbing" consequence—"that there is something absurd about the whole idea of a unique correct interpretation."[43]

Gadamer's assertion that the inescapable historicity of interpretation renders "absurd" the possibility of "correct interpretation" leaves him open to the claims of anarchistic interpretation that Skinner had leveled against him. Yet just as Skinner's apparently objectivist emphasis on intention is qualified by a concession to the more subjectivist realm of "paradigms" and "presuppositions," so Gadamer's apparently subjectivist emphasis on the constitutive aspect of the hermeneutic situation is qualified by an acknowledgment of the demands exerted by the "object" of interpretation. Gadamer thus qualifies his argument about the absurdity of a "unique correct interpretation" by asserting that interpretation does not emerge only as a function of "mere subjective variety of conceptions" of the interpreter, but from the "work's own possibilities of being." The "subjective variety of conceptions" is limited by the "variety" of "aspects" located in the work itself, to which the interpreting subject must make himself receptive. "No matter," Gadamer writes, "how much the variety of the performances or realization of such a structure can be traced back to the conception of the players," "it also does not remain enclosed in the subjectivity of what they think, but it is embodied there."

For Gadamer, representation is not "mere imitation" or a copy, but a "genuine knowledge of the essence" of a thing. Further, Gadamer warns, seeming almost to migrate into the Skinnerian position, if "one regards the variations possible in the presentation as free and arbitrary," then "one fails to appreciate the obligatoriness" of the object under interpretation. All "subjective variations," Gadamer continues, are "subject to the supreme criterion of 'right representation.'" Although Gadamer's insistence on right representation acknowledges the impossibility of attaining unmediated access to the text (what Skinner calls more prosaically, "stepping into the author's shoes"), he does maintain a belief in the "true meaning of the object." As an interpreter of texts, Gadamer argues, one should "be aware of one's own bias, so that the text can present itself in all its otherness and thus assert its own truth against one's own fore-meaning." That is, Gadamer's much-vaunted "methodologically conscious understanding" makes prejudices "conscious," so "as to check them and thus acquire right understandings from the things themselves." Notwithstanding the primary role of the interpreter and his prejudices, Gadamer idealizes an interpreter who is "able to open" himself to the superior claim the text makes."[44]

Placing Gadamer and Skinner in dialogue with one another reveals that both recognize the necessity of the extreme against which they argue. Even the hermeneutist Gadamer turns to the constraints imposed by the object itself, while the intentionalist Skinner acknowledges the power of the paradigms and schemes that interpreters employ. Away from the scene of polemical appropriation and debate, there emerges common ground about the nature of the interpretive enterprise based on both subject and objective frames of reference, or more importantly, the inadequacy of either criterion independently. Indeed, the sense of the inadequacies produced through simplifications of their respective models reveals an implicit and unstated agreement about the problematic nature of the subject–object distinction. From that common acknowledgement emerges a hermeneutic removed from the binary between indeterminacy and absolute truth, suitable for encountering the hermeneutics of Talmudic legal dispute. Once the polemical debate shifts away from the invocation of subjectivity on the one hand (and the anarchy it is meant to entail), and objectivity on the other (and the naive idealism it is meant to presuppose), an opening emerges for an articulation of rabbinic dispute. Indeed, a method combining Skinner's injunction to be receptive to the text, with the Gadamerian emphasis on interpretation as a creative act provides a corollary to the assumptions distilled in R. Elazar's image of the mill-hopper, both passive and active, receptive and creative.

Temptation of Transcendence

Midrashic representations of dispute, as in the "mill-hopper," compress distinctions that are revealed—even as they become ossified as incommensurable opposites—in the language of later philosophical commentary. Just as philosophical disputes, as that between Gadamer and Skinner, can be read as emerging because of difference in emphases, so later rabbinic commentaries in their readings place stress—though in nonphilosophical language—on subjective or objective constraints. In the legal dispute between R. Eliezer and the sages about the ritual purity of an oven, for example, a *bat kol* (a voice) comes forth from the heavens, proclaiming that the law was to be determined like the single sage (Bava Metzia 59b).[45] Within the context of the oft-cited narrative, the heavenly voice is itself rejected (along with a number of preceding supernatural events), with R. Yehoshua citing the verse "it is not in heaven" as a means of supporting rejection of the divine intercession; indeed, the divine text is itself employed to support the authority of rabbinic interpreters (Deuteronomy 30:12). The Gaonic commentator, Nissim ben Jacob [Rabbenu Nissim], explains: "The intention of the voice from heaven was only to test the sages to see whether they would abandon the tradition in their hands and the teaching in their mouths. And this is what R. Yehoshua said, 'it is not in heaven'—meaning, the Torah of God is perfect, and has already been given to us at Sinai" (Berakhot 19b). The episode, as Rabbenu Nissim explains, not only thematizes the post-Sinaitic priority of human interpretation over divine command but also enacts the temptation of transcendence, that is, the temptation of aspiring toward a grasp of the absolute, what Jonathan Lear calls "the remainder," the fantasy of a truth no longer (or never) available. The narrative rejects the appeal, asserting, after the experience at Sinai, the priority of interpretation.

The rejection of divine intervention and the concomitant embrace of interpretation, entails, correspondingly, a rejection of the possibility of what Gadamer calls "a unique correct interpretation" or its theological correlate, the unmediated divine utterance, opening up to the realm of multiplicity, sanctioned by the principle "these and these are the words of the living God." In the later language of the medieval commentator R. Yom Tov ibn Asevilli [Ritba], the question that R. Elazar attributes to the interpreter in Hagiga is rephrased but here in relation to the philosophical standard of the Aristotelian principle of noncontradiction:

> The rabbis of France asked how is it possible that they are both the words of the living God, when this one says prohibited, and this one says permitted? And they answered: "When Moses went up to the above to receive the Torah, he was shown, on every matter, forty-nine ways to prohibit, and forty-nine ways to permit. And Moses asked the Holy One blessed-be-he about this, and he said that this will be passed to the sages of Israel of every generation, and it will be decided according to them."[46]

Ritba's answer affirms that a multiplicity of different legal perspectives were themselves already implicit in the original revelation to Moses at Sinai. Thus, the appearance of various opinions, even on the same matter, does not compromise the objectivist criteria of revelation. The judgments that emerge in particular situations, though contradictory, are nonetheless both, in Ritba's analysis, "the words of the living God." The Torah itself, and the experience at Sinai, are the guarantors of truth in multiplicity.

Whereas Ritba stressed the multiplicity grounded in the experience of revelation, later rabbinic commentators turn toward subjective variables in explaining multiplicity, that is, the role of the interpreter. Indeed, the principle articulated in tractate Needa 20b—"a judge can only decide by what appears to his eyes"—provides a Talmudic precedent for this subjectivist criterion. Transforming this principle into a broader interpretive principle, Solomon Luria [Maharshal] writes, in apparent disagreement with Ritba, that differences between the sages emerge not because of the multiplicity inherent in revelation, but rather because each of the sages "perceived the Torah from his own perspective in accordance with his intellectual capacity as well as the stature and unique character of his particular soul."[47] From the perspective of Maharshal, difference of perception—purely subjective criteria—constitutes an integral component of the Sinaitic revelation.

Ritba and Maharshal are therefore not so much disagreeing as articulating perspectives on "these and these are the words of the living God," their dispute coming under the aegis of the principle they explain.[48] Indeed, Ritba suggests the corollary and complementary interpretation of Maharshal—that scriptural polysemy depends on rabbinic interpretation—when he asserts that in addition to the explanation that he had already offered, and "according to the ways of truth," there is yet another "hidden explanation of the matter." The commentaries of Ritba and Maharshal are already inflected (though not explicitly) with binary philosophical categories—Ritba emphasizing objectivity and Maharshal, subjectivity. Even here the distinctions emerge as part of, to adopt Boyarin's phrase, the "logic of commentary," which necessarily produces opposed, apparently exclusive perspectives.[49] Together they presuppose the kind of subject distilled in the figure of the mill-hopper, which is at once receptive to an "objective" experience, but rendering that experience through "subjective" coordinates.

That the divine and human, and hence the subjective and objective, are mutually implicated receives further articulation in the account in tractate Gitten 6b that centers on another rabbinic disagreement, again resolved with different emphases according to the opposed but mutually informing languages of commentary. After describing a dispute between R. Avitar and R. Yonatan (on the correct interpretation of an episode in Judges), the Talmud provides an account of R. Avitar's encounter with Elijah the prophet: "R. Avitar went and found Elijah the prophet and asked, 'What is the Holy One blessed-be-he doing now?' The prophet answered: 'He is busy with the dispute between R. Yonatan and R. Avitar,' and He is saying the following, 'So says my son Yonatan, so says my son Avitar.'" The midrash demonstrates divine assent both to multiplicity in interpretation and to the entanglement of the divine and human. The nature of this dynamic remains ambiguous, however, and is again only fully brought out in the writings of later commentators, who necessarily, given the demands of commentary—the need to extrapolate from the *discordia concors* of poetic languages—stress only one side of the opposition.

A twentieth-century commentator, Hayyim Friedlander, in a predictably conservative account *Siftie Hayyim*, compares the disputants to Moses at the time of the revelation at Sinai: "Thus, when R. Avitar and R. Yonatan studied Torah, this was the Torah which was given at Sinai, and just as on Mount Sinai, the Holy One placed the words of Torah in the mouth of Moses, so at the time of their studying, they did not say their own words, but the words of the living God."[50] By referring back to the Sinaitic moment, *Siftie Hayyim* grounds the differences in opinions between R. Yonatan and R. Avitar in the original experience of revelation. Parallel to the way Ritba had done in his account of "these and these," this account stresses objectivist criteria in which the Talmudic rabbis merely repeat divine words, grounding human utterance in the divine. *Nefesh Ha-Hayyim*, however, provides a complementary and more radical explanation in which subjective rather than objective variables figure prominently: "Because R. Yonatan and R. Avitar were studying Torah, so the Holy One repeated their words in their entirety."[51] In this rendering, interpretation takes precedence, with God authorizing interpretive multiplicity as he repeats and validates the disputants' words only after the fact. In the *Nefesh Ha-Hayyim*'s version, unlike that of *Siftie Hayyim*, stress is placed not on God and Sinai but a present in which dispute is engendered. Focusing on one of the narrative's accounts (which accommodates, even dictates, both renderings), leads to a simplified version of a rabbinic interpretive model, as determined by either subjective or objective constraints only.

But the two commentaries presuppose one another, and are dictated—like the interpretations that produce "blooming nails"—by the text itself. The later renderings of the narrative, which are already responding, if only implicitly, to the Aristotelian demands of noncontradiction, provide necessarily simplified accounts of the nonphilosophical registers of midrash, rabbinic "poetry." In such poetry, the divinely sanctioned multiplicity of "these and these" mediates between the extremes of impoverished philosophical languages, the twin poles of the subjective and the objective. Between these poles emerges a notion of truth as well as a conception of disagreement—neither Platonist nor poststructuralist, neither absolute nor indeterminate.[52] To explore these notions, I turn now to the language of legal dispute, seen from a perspective informed by both Gadamerian hermeneutics and Skinnerian intentionalism.

Disagreement, Ditches, and Interpretive Charity

That "words of Torah" are only manifested through interpretation (understood as subjective elaborations of an objective truth) entails the application of what Moshe Halbertal calls, following Willard Quine, the "principle of charity." Such a principle, as Halbertal explains, demands adopting a stance such that "a speaker's words will make sense and the sentence that he utters can have meaning." This principle occupies a central place in rabbinic hermeneutics, as Halbertal argues, not only in the context of the interpretation of the canonical texts of the written Torah, but in the realm of disputes within the context of the oral law itself.[53]

Just as for Gadamer a symphony or even the game of tennis only exists by being "played" or performed, Torah is made manifest through the activity of interpretation.[54] As play or performance, interpretation produces multiplicity. In rabbinic terms, the persistent attribution of incoherence or falsehood to one's opponents (the rejection of alternate performances) amounts to a rejection of "the words of Torah." To be sure, the Talmud consists of and is defined by dispute, and hermeneutic effort is exerted to maintain the coherence of competing perspectives. Not only does this entail a practical acknowledgment of the necessity of multiplicity in the realm of the law; it also demands a constant application of the Quinean law of charity. To reject an opponent out of hand—to assume incoherence—entails a rejection of the interpretive activity that defines Torah; and by extension, to discount a subjectivity engaged in interpretation is to discount, indeed to misunderstand, Torah itself. However, to conceive of legal discourse as celebrating either an unbounded polysemy (or, for that matter, a Platonic standard of absolute truth) is to fail to acknowledge the distinctive conception of rabbinic disagreement and rabbinic truth. Whether or not what Menachem Fisch calls the rabbinic "second-order attempts at self-understandings" of midrash justify a defense of a genuine pluralism, the very form of Talmudic dispute itself presupposes multiplicity and process—both of which are qualified and even repressed, as I argue in part 2, in Soloveitchik's representations of legal hermeneutics.[55]

For this reading, rabbinic interpretation begins with an extreme version of the Skinnerian model, the rabbinic effort to understand the intentions of texts that precede them. In the case of the Talmud itself, this entails the efforts of *amoraim* (200–600 CE) to understand the utterances of their predecessors, the *tannaim* (0–200 CE). The conventional designations are not only historical, but entail primarily a historiography of interpretive periods.[56] The utterances of *tannaim* ("those who teach") form the basis of the oral law, or Mishna, which, once a strictly oral tradition, was codified by Rebbe Yehuda Ha-Nasi (or Rebbe) at the end of the *tannaitic* period. The *tannaitic* utterances of the Mishna provide the basis for all later articulations of the law, and within normative rabbinic contexts, are authoritative for all future generations. *Amoraim* (literally "those who say") derive legal principles and concepts from the earlier *tannaitic* sources (without, however, contesting the authority of those sources); indeed, the articulation of such principles almost always depends on both the acknowledgment and incorporation of those earlier texts.

Amoraim, who build their own diverse systems of halakha in *gemara* ("learning," or Talmud), debate the meaning of *tannaitic* sources as they argue for the authority of their own legal principles and interpretive systems. An *amoraic* statement, contradicted by a preceding *tannaitic* statement, is by definition subject to rejection. Yet *amoraic* statements that on a surface reading may seem to be contradicted by earlier *tannaitic* utterances are almost never rejected. Expressions such as "Rather say" ("this is what the text really means"), "This is what is meant," "With what are we really dealing?" abound throughout the Talmud, as *amoraim* attempt to demonstrate the integrity and authority of their own systems, as well as their responsiveness to the constraints imposed by the *tannaitic* text. Indeed, *tannaitic* sources are never merely *given*. The profusion of such formulaic Talmudic phrases testifies to that sense of impoverishment or loss—that is, the meaning of *tannaitic* utterances is never transparently or immediately available. Talmudic invocations of alternative conceptual and interpretive schemes become the means by which an apparently incoherent utterance—in my reading, the lost or impoverished text—is rendered coherent. This requires the application of the "principle of charity," moving out from the scrupulous Skinnerian emphasis on intention to the Gadamerian emphasis on interpretive horizons, that is, to interpretation as a form of creativity, reflected in R. Elazar's subject as mill-hopper.

* * *

The first mishna in the second chapter of tractate *Bava Batra* (17a) deals with the limitations imposed on a landowner's use of his property because of damage that may be incurred to a neighbor's property. The mishna begins with the precautions that a property owner must take, including the requirement that in digging a ditch, he must distance it from the wall of his neighbor's ditch by a distance, in the Talmud's measurement, of three arms-breadths. The mishna's proclamations are non-negotiable for future generations; what remains, however, is the extrapolation of principles from the mishna into other contexts and cases. The Talmud considers the case of one who wants to dig a ditch near the boundary of his own property: Can he do so if his neighbor has not yet dug on his property?[57]

On this question, the mishna does not offer an explicit ruling. For the *amoraim*, the question—the *aporia*—becomes a matter of dispute, that is, does the Torah permit someone to initiate digging on the edge of his property or not? In other words, does one have to take into account a neighbor's possible future actions when digging on one's own property? In the ensuing debate between *amoraim*, Abaye rules that one may place the ditch near the boundary, while Rava rules that one may not, and should distance his ditch appropriately. Both of these *amoraim*, however, claim that their ruling is in consonance with the intention of the author of the mishna. The Talmud goes on to "test" these *amoraic* utterances to show their adherence to this *tannaitic* antecedent of the mishna, as well as all the other *tannaitic* sources that reflect on the issue. In this instance, the mishna itself accommodates the perspectives of both Rava and Abaye; the questions on their respective perspectives emerge most strongly from other *tannaitic* sources.

Endeavoring to understand the *amoraic* discussion is further complicated because the dispute exists in two versions. The current discussion focuses on the second of the two versions and the Talmud's struggle to justify the positions adopted by Rava and Abaye against possible questions from other *tannaitic* texts. In this reading, the second account of the disagreement between Rava and Abaye, the two *amoraim*, are said to agree in the case of land where it is not customary to dig ditches. That is to say, even Rava agrees with Abaye in this set of cases that one can approach the boundary of one's property and dig. Even before the account of the disagreement begins, the point of dispute is narrowed to a particular set of cases. Indeed, rabbinic methodology almost always aims to maximize areas of agreement, finding disagreement in liminal cases, though ones that allow the extrapolation of further parameters or principles. In this instance, the Talmud constructs *amoraic* argument to show that the only place where the disputants disagree is on land where people are accustomed to dig ditches (in the other version, the dispute concerns land where people do not habitually dig). Here, Rava, against the more lenient ruling of Abaye, insists on the distancing of the ditch from the boundary to safeguard against possible damage to the neighboring property, especially since it is customary to dig on such property.

The text proceeds by citing *tannaitic* sources as a means of interrogating, if not openly questioning, the positions of Rava and Abaye. As part of the process, the Talmud invokes a mishna—and a dispute between the rabbis and R. Yose—that renders the positions of both Rava and Abaye incoherent (on the surface at least). Although the earlier dispute between the rabbis and R. Yose does not concern ditch digging, it implies principles about damages that explicitly contradict the rulings of the later disputants (Bava Batra 25b). To Abaye's claim that it is permissible to dig near a boundary, the Talmud cites the opinion of the rabbis who argue that one must distance a tree twenty-five cubits from the ditch of a neighbor lest its roots damage the ditch. R. Yose, by contrast, whose position is elaborated more fully below, articulates the seemingly more lenient position that licenses property owners to use their land as they see fit.

Here begins the Skinnerian analysis of intentions, as the Talmud invokes the rabbis' utterance as a means of rendering Abaye's position incoherent. For how can Abaye maintain the permissibility of digging near a boundary when the rabbis articulated a principle that offers protection against actions taken on adjoining properties? From the perspective of the questioner (adopting Rava's assumptions and arguing on behalf of his perspective), the intention of the rabbis was surely and clearly to prevent activity that would cause damage to adjoining property. Abaye, whose own utterance by definition needs to be consistent with the "language game" in which the rabbis participate, seems to have articulated a position that openly contradicts their position.

Yet rather than reject Abaye's opinion as incoherent, the Talmud goes on to elaborate a context in which Abaye's utterance emerges as coherent. Against the attack brought implicitly in Rava's name, Abaye's defenders elicit what Abaye would maintain are the rabbis' genuine intentions in their argument with R. Yose, and thus refine the sense of Abaye's intentions in his argument with Rava as well. The rabbis, Abaye would argue, did not intend to limit all forms of potentially damaging activity, but their intentions were, in fact, more specific. The questioner, the defenders of Abaye would argue, did not understand the precise nature of the rabbis' conversation with their interlocutor, and thus failed to understand their true intentions. Granted, the rabbis had required the distancing of the tree, but they had only made such a demand in a case where there had been a preexistent ditch. In the present case, however, of the *amoraic* discussion on the question of digging on boundaries, there is no ditch on the neighboring property, and Abaye's ruling is therefore not only correct but in accordance with the opinion that was meant to contradict him (as well as the apparently more libertarian opinion of R. Yose). Having re-elaborated the parameters of the rabbis' dispute with R. Yose, Abaye's opinion emerges as coherent and consistent with the views of all the relevant *tannaitic* antecedents.

If, as Wittgenstein puts it, the "sign (the sentence) gets its significance from the system of signs, from the language to which it belongs," then the *tannaitic* "sign" gets its significance first from the language to which it belongs, that of the

Mishna as a whole.[58] This "language," however, initially defined in terms of a synchronic relationship, is itself explained, refined, and recreated in the different languages of individual *amoraim*. In the current discussion, at the point of the attack leveled against Abaye, with its assumptions about the nature of the rabbis' intentions, Abaye's perspective seems without grounds. The shift of perspective, however, which entails a reconsideration of the intentions behind the rabbis' utterance, reveals the coherence—if not the actual complexity—of Abaye's view, as the rabbis' utterance is reconfigured within the context of Abaye's perspective. Rather than reject Abaye's utterance as incoherent, the Talmud elicits the intentions of the antecedent *tannaitic* text (the rabbis restrict the placement of a hazard only where the object liable to be damaged is already present) by re-elaborating the context for their utterance. The result of this Quinean reframing of contexts is to show that the rabbis themselves would, in fact, not argue against but countenance Abaye's legal ruling.

In the continuation of the discussion, Rava's position is subject to interrogation. While Rava had ruled that one who wants to dig a ditch must distance it from a property boundary, R. Yose had argued, against the rabbis, that "just as one may dig within his property, so one may plant within his property." Here the question, informed now by Abaye's perspective, understands R. Yose's intentions clearly. One is not required to distance potential harmful agents from a boundary (there is no prohibition against planting a tree, even where it is liable to damage the pit of one's neighbor). It is, in fact, incumbent upon the threatened party to protect his property. Again, from the perspective elaborated in the question, just as in the case of Abaye, the integrity of Rava's statement is contradicted by the preexistent (and authoritative) utterance of R. Yose. Rava might accede to the question and fall back on the opinion of the rabbis whose emphasis on precautionary distancing provides an obvious support for his position. The Talmud does not even attempt this, however, for its working assumption is that opinions of the *amoraim* should be accommodated with all previous *tannaitic* statements. In this case, some context must therefore be constructed allowing for the coherence of Rava's statement according to not only the rabbis' perspective but R. Yose's perspective as well. This approach is meant to both maximize agreement (such that Rava's statement will be consistent with the opinions of both *tannaitic* opinions, the rabbis and R. Yose) and to resist interpretive frameworks that bifurcate the tradition, with R. Yose and Abaye on one side and the rabbis and Rava on the other (with both sides remaining opaque, if not incoherent, to one another). Although there may be disagreement registered in the words of the *tannaim*, the later interpretive efforts of *amoraim* are meant to maximize points of agreement with *all* preceding texts and to see previous disagreements as informed and mediated by agreement. Not only do midrashic representations of legal argument figure "integrity" and harmony, as Boyarin and Stern argue, but in this reading, the Talmud's legal methodology is itself informed by a desire to achieve a harmony of difference. This legal version of *discordia concors* maintains a multiplicity of different perspectives, sustained by the *tannaitic* texts themselves.

In defense of Rava, the Talmud once again shifts conceptual perspectives and finds a new way of understanding R. Yose's intentions. The *tanna*, the Talmud argues, intended only a limited application of his less interventionist principle. Rava's ruling, this new perspective reveals, is in accord with R. Yose, who would have distinguished between the case of planting a tree, where the potentially damaging roots are not yet in existence, and the present case, where the ditch digging weakens the surrounding land, rendering it unsuitable for further ditches. That is, according to R. Yose, one need not anticipate future damages but should guard against the damaging consequences of present actions. Under pressure of the Talmud's question, R. Yose's intentions are refined, and consequently, those of Rava are as well. At the beginning of the discussion, Rava's statement, like that of Abaye, seemed to have merited rejection, but by the end, it is not only coherent but interpreted in such a way as to accord with all *tannaitic* predecessors—even R. Yose's opinion, which originally seemed to contradict his present utterance. In both cases, the shift in the analysis of the intentions of antecedent texts is motivated by the need to mount an appropriate defense for the position under attack. These defenses are only justified through elaborating discursive contexts responsive to the language—the Skinnerian intentions—of the texts themselves. Neither the defense of Rava nor that of Abaye would have been successful had the words of the *tannaim* been unable to accommodate the interpretations that the Talmud proposes—just as R. Elazar's midrashic conceit is, for him, unified through the constraints imposed by the scriptural verse.

The present process of the reconciliation of the utterances of *amoraim* against the attacks implicit in *tannaitic* texts is informed by a Skinnerian conception of intention elaborated through the construction of contexts. Yet the process also entails, necessarily, a rejection of a simplified version of Skinner's methodology. To be sure, the Talmud operates according to Skinnerian criteria in trying to draw out the parameters of *tannaitic* (and even *amoraic*) dispute, like that examined between R. Yose and the rabbis (as well as that of Abaye and Rava themselves). Only an intentional analysis—and the attempted recovery of the discursive context for their argument—adequately reveals what the rabbis intended in their ruling, and what R. Yose "was doing," to use the Austinian phrase, in his response to their statement. Yet even the simplified rendition of the dispute evidences how the discursive contexts of the argument between R. Yose and the rabbis undergo transformation, as do inevitably, the intentions that inform their utterances.

At this stage in the discussion of the text, there are two versions of the dispute between R. Yose and the rabbis, as their argument takes on a different aspect as the Talmud moves from the perspective that informed the question against

Abaye to the one that informed the answer offered in his defense (that is, from the perspective of Rava to Abaye). The shifting of perspectives, informed by the ever-present rabbinic invocation of the principle of charity, demands a move from a simple and monovocal view of intention to one where the intentions of individual agents transmute and multiply. In this reading, the Skinnerian attention to intention and language games is an indispensable means for understanding rabbinic disputes, provided, however, that it also accommodates the proliferation of frameworks and contexts that attend rabbinic interpretation. The different interpretive contexts for the same dispute provide, in this reading, two versions of the intentions of both the disputants, the rabbis and R. Yose.

All of this is to affirm the Gadamerian notion that interpretation is the means by which "the work explicates itself . . . in the variety of its aspects," as well as Skinner's concession that the existence of different classificatory schemes compromises the very notion of "undisputable facts." The demand for the shifting of perspectives in the Talmud requires not only a single analysis of a discursive context or language game, but the analysis of that language game from a multiplicity of perspectives. What R. Yose was 'doing' with his response to the rabbis, for example, will depend on the perspective one has, that of either Abaye or Rava. Further, it is not only the versions of the dispute between R. Yose and the rabbis that multiply, but the versions of the dispute between Abaye and Rava themselves multiply as the Talmud reports the two accounts of their argument. In the Talmudic rendering of the argument passed over here (where the dispute concerns land where people do not habitually dig), the context of Rava's disagreement with Abaye is different (as well as the intentions that inform their respective statements), as are the arguments of R. Yose and the rabbis whose opinions their arguments continue to accommodate. Gadamer's interpretive horizons (as well as the meanings engendered) continue to multiply, as the arguments of the *amoraim* are constructed, in later generations, in the works of medieval explicators, *rishonim*.[59] All of these commentaries, however, only claim their authority by eliciting the intentions of the texts they explain. The paradox of rabbinic dispute is that the unknowability of preceding texts—the ambivalence, or *aporias*, of *tannaitic* texts—leads to multiplicity of interpretation, the necessity, in my reading, of the hermeneutics of mourning.

The hermeneutic moment, characterized by indeterminacy shows an impoverishment of tradition in the face of loss and allows for—even dictates—a multiplicity of interpretive horizons. Those horizons reveal the fecundity of the words of the *tannaim*, which lend themselves to diverse and sometimes even contradictory explanations. But "these and these," as suggested in appropriations of the rabbis' words for a postmodern or liberal epistemology, does not function as a license for unrestrained subjectivity in interpretation, unqualified by receptivity to the object. The rabbis are not, as Stern rightly argues, deconstructionists *avant la lettre*, articulating a Derridian notion of open polysemy. Moreover, in the normative (even traditionalist) reading offered here, the representations of legal pluralism, following the practice of rabbinic dispute, need not be dismissed as editorial fantasies of social coherence, or in Boyarin's more minatory evaluation, instruments of social control. That is, when read from the perspective of Skinner and Gadamer, and the kind of subject they presume, both attentive and creative— R. Elazar's mill-hopper—a different kind of pluralism is made possible, revealing a tradition of what Adam Phillips calls in another context, "voices in the plural."[60]

There is, then, in legal dispute, as in R. Elazar's proem, a relationship between *divrei Torah* and *divrei hakhamim*, that is, between Torah and the sages who disseminate it. Subjective constraints, as Gadamer emphasizes, are indispensable to the production of meaning through a process that transforms "words of Torah" into "words of the wise," a reciprocal relation between scriptural and rabbinic polysemy. The borders of rabbinic community are maintained—Boyarin would say policed—through the criteria of learning *lishma*, that is, for its own sake. This is the articulation, as *Nefesh Ha-Hayyim* puts it, of the proper relationship between subject and object: "At every moment that a person is working and cleaving to the words of the Torah in the appropriate fashion, the words rejoice as if they were given from Sinai."[61] Translated into philosophical terms, when subject and object merge, the words of the sages—in their contingency—have the authority of Sinai. They are both planted and fixed, to adopt the metaphor of R. Elazar, grounded in Sinai, but also numerous, fruitful, and new.

* * *

The finitude of "historical existence," Gadamer writes, renders the singularity of "one correct interpretation" absurd. In rabbinic representations, the death of Moses initiates the historicity of interpretation; subjects, already at a loss, confront a universe of signs that are never transparent, always requiring interpretation. Otniel, the figure who recuperates loss does so with *pilpul*, dialectics, that which the rabbis define as an "active intelligence"—Boyarin's "logic of commentary." Elsewhere, the rabbis affirm that *pilpul* was given first to Moses and then bestowed by him to further generations, notably to Otniel (Nedarim 38a). *Pilpul*, as an early modern commentator explains, entails understanding a matter "incisively and with insight . . . like a person who is exacting in the law and chisels it from every side to clarify it."[62] Otniel's *pilpul* is the mechanism through which multiplicity is nurtured and the law is recovered, however partially. *Pilpul*, an indispensable part of the interpretive processes of the Talmud, enacts a dialectical awareness of the multiple hermeneutic perspectives and the need for diverse agencies, which reveal the intentions of antecedent texts in their fullness. This dialectical engagement, associated with a mind that is both receptive and active, is responsible, within the rabbinic tradition, for the multiplication of legal perspectives.

Rabbinic engagement presupposes training the mind (R. Elazar's mill-hopper remains a model) to see the picture of Wittgenstein's *Philosophical Investigations* as both a rabbit and a duck, a process requiring both receptivity and cognitive effort. From this point of view, the engagement entailed in rabbinic dispute becomes an exercise in attempting to inhabit perspectives that may not, at first, seem accessible. As Bernard Williams writes, adopting a Wittgensteinian framework, mental efforts may allow "those who had one picture . . . to see the point . . . of another picture, and also perhaps . . . to understand why those who had it, did so."[63] In this reading, in its various historiographical manifestations, rabbinic dispute presupposes an interpretive charity striving to elicit the coherence of differing perspectives, or hermeneutic horizons. The different "faces"—or aspects—of the Torah, to use a Talmudic idiom, are represented through the multiplicity of disciples from various "assemblies," who literally become, through their interpretive activity, different faces of the Torah.[64]

In a fallen world, the logic of commentary will always be necessary, the mechanism through which the text in its sometimes seemingly paradoxical multiplicity reveals itself. The contingency of different rabbinic interpretation—the words of a multiplicity of sages—are thus invested with the authority of Sinai in R. Elazar's proem as they become words of Torah through the process of interpretation. When mourning becomes the law, loss, the given of the historical process, is paradoxically transformed into Hartman's "bounty," and the resulting multiplicity of contingent perspectives partakes of the authority of the divine. Like R. Elazar's poetic conceit of goads transformed into nails—transformed again into blooming flowers—the words of Torah emerge from within a rabbinic perspective as both contingent and eternal, not only as a function of sociological necessity but internal to the poetics of dispute, the inclusive resonance of the divine utterance.

In the face of loss and contingency, the partial leave taking and creative remembrance enacted by Otniel's hermeneutics of mourning leads to continuity and multiplicity, that is, to a *discordia concors* of divergent legal perspectives that are unified from a rabbinic perspective through a divine revelation that not only authorizes but accommodates that diversity. Notably, in anticipation of part 2, for Soloveitchik, the poetically ambiguous and suggestive blooming nails of R. Elazar's interpretation of Ecclesiastes are rendered unqualified in the translation of *Halakhic Man* as "nails well-fastened," emphasizing singularity and stability—a form of certainty—not the multiplicity of the rabbinic model (*Man*, 57). "In Judaism," Soloveitchik writes, the "harmony of opposites is an impossibility" ("Majesty," 25). Soloveitchik refers here to ontological, not interpretive realms, but any form of mediated difference, however discordant, is absent from his hermeneutics as well. Like Dr. Johnson relating to Donne, Soloveitchik's "well-fastened nails" to R. Elazar's "blooming nails" enacts a rejection of *discor-*

dia concors. Indeed, for Soloveitchik, the poetry of blooming nails is flattened into the well-fastened nails that guard and protect a "halakhic" tradition founded on certainty. That conception of tradition and the melancholy hermeneutics that inform it, as well as Soloveitchik's attempts at self-creation independent of that hermeneutic tradition, are the subject of the chapters that follow.

PART II
JOSEPH SOLOVEITCHIK: MELANCHOLY

The temple lies in ruins . . .
  —Friedrich Nietzsche, *The Birth of Tragedy*

Interlude
Primal Scene in Pruzhna

We shall remain inconsolable.
—Sigmund Freud, Letter to Binswanger

JOSEPH SOLOVEITCHIK'S MELANCHOLY hermeneutics originate in the living room of R. Elijah Feinstein, his grandfather, in Pruzhna:

> I remember myself as a child, a lonely, forlorn boy. I was afraid of the world. It seemed cold and alien. I felt as if everyone were mocking me. But I had one friend, and he was—please don't laugh at me—Maimonides, the Rambam. How did we become friends? We simply met. (*Seek*, 143)

Soloveitchik looks at his past self in a register familiar to readers of his later work, where he announces the dilemma of identity in a "three-word sentence"—"I am lonely" (*LMF*, 3). This early memory already sets the scene for that solitary self-perception as a "lonely forlorn boy." In the cold and alien environment Soloveitchik describes, where he is the subject of mocking and anticipates the prospect of further scorn—"please don't laugh at me," he pleads—there is only, in this precocious fantasy, one comforting presence: Maimonides.

As the story unfolds, it turns out that "the Rambam" is present as a guest among his extended family: "Those were the days," he recounts, "when my father, my mentor, was still living in the home of my grandfather, the great and pious Rabbi Elijah Feinstein of Pruzhna." Although it is his grandfather's home, Soloveitchik's father "Rabbi Moses" is prominent in his father-in-law's living room, which is transformed into a study hall, a *beit midrash*: "Father sat and studied day and night" while a "small group of outstanding young Torah Scholars gathered around him and imbibed his words" (*Seek*, 143). The young Joseph, however, remains excluded from the group, his bed merely "placed" in the living room in which his father delivers his daily lectures. At the same time that he is an insider, part of the gathering of men and the dynastic joining of Soloveitchik and Feinstein families, the young Joseph on his bed also remains a spectator, recounting the encounter between his father, Rabbi Moses, and the Talmudic texts and its commentaries. Indeed, he would remain in that liminal space for the rest of his life, cultivating his ambivalent identity as both insider and outsider to the group that he calls "halakhic men" (*Man*, 137).

In the account based on his childhood memories, his father, Soloveitchik remembers, "would open up a volume of the Talmud and read a passage":

> Then he would say, "This is the interpretation of Rabbi Isaac [Rashi] and the [other] Tosafists; now let us see how the Rambam interpreted the passage." Father would always find that the Rambam had offered a different interpretation and had deviated from the simple way. My father would say, almost as a complaint against the Rambam, "We don't understand our Master's reasoning or the way he explains a passage." (*Seek*, 143)

To Joseph's father, Rabbi Moses, the explanations of the precedent Rabbi Moses, that is, the "Master" or Rambam, are opaque, diverting from the explication of the expositor of the simple meaning, Rashi. While "the members of the group would jump up and down and each of them would suggest an idea" as a response to the riddle presented by Rambam, their undisciplined gestures and suggestions are rejected. "Father would listen and rebut their ideas, and then repeat, 'Our Master's words are as hard to crack as iron'" (*Seek*, 144). Soloveitchik presents an image of his father as unruffled at the "still center" of this world, persistent in the face of the adversary, in this case, the uncertainty now threatening to overtake the group. The pointless activity of the others in the masculine assembly is set off by the focused concentration of his father, one Rabbi Moses on behalf of another: "But he would not despair; he would rest his head on his fist and sink into deep thought" (*Seek*, 144).

In Soloveitchik's recollection, the group accedes to the solitary quiet and presence of their teacher; they do "not disturb . . . his reflections" (the son intimating their fear in the presence of the Master; *Seek*, 144). After an interval, the silence is broken. His father "would lift his head very slowly and begin," and the young Joseph, still at a distance from the gathered assembly of men, would "strain" his "ears and listen to what he was saying" (*Seek*, 144). The despair that had threatened to overtake the gathered students is averted. Joseph's father "rescues" the Rambam, the precedent master, himself now dependent on the present Moses, Rabbi Moses Soloveitchik, the current agent of tradition.

In an act of double reflection, Soloveitchik remembers assessing the scene in his grandfather's living room:

> I did not understand anything at all about the issue under discussion, but two impressions were formed in my young, innocent mind: (1) the Rambam was surrounded by opponents and "enemies" who wanted to harm him; and (2) his only defender was my father. If not for my father, who knew what would hap-

pen to the Rambam? I felt that the Rambam was present in the living room, listening to what my father was saying. (*Seek*, 144)

In the psychic dynamics of the story, young Joseph's father, Rabbi Moses, stands as indispensable defender of the Rambam, staving off the "attack" of the latter's antagonist (the medieval commentator, Rabad), as well as the other "enemies" who want to cause him harm. Soloveitchik not only recalls the competition between interpreters but also his own pathos as a child, a witness to the encounter, on the brink of disaster: "if not for my father, who knew what would happen to the Rambam?" Rabbi Moses, however, is more than the Rambam's lone "defender." Through the implicit identification—the Rambam is present not only in the living room but also, as Soloveitchik remembers it, "sitting with me on my bed"—he becomes, at the same time, protector of the son. The two—Joseph and Rambam—are set on the bed passive together, dependent on the contemporary expositor of tradition, Joseph's heroic father.

The story figures as a contemporary midrash, an updated parallel to the Talmudic midrash in which Moses sits in the back of a classroom, listening in bewilderment to the interpretive innovations of Rabbi Akiva, who eventually, to Moses's astonishment, is claimed as the antecedent authority for the novel interpretations put forward by the Talmudic sage. In addition to the future's dependence on the past, the means through which R. Akiva's innovative readings find their authority in Moses and Sinai, in Soloveitchik's story, an identification between generations is also asserted (Menakhot 29b).[1] In Soloveitchik's rehearsal of what might be called—after Freud—his Talmudic primal scene, there is a physical resemblance, even an identification, between his father and Maimonides: "The Rambam was sitting on my bed. What did he look like? I didn't know exactly, but his countenance resembled my father's good and beautiful face. He had the same name as my father—Moses" (*Seek*, 144). The passage now elicits a triple identification between Joseph and Maimonides together on the bed, and also between the father, Rabbi Moses, and Rambam. In the blurring of identities, the story brings together past, present, and future in the figures of Rambam, Rabbi Moses, and the latter's son, Joseph. R. Akiva depends on Moses, in the midrashic representation, as a source and justification for his interpretive innovations; for Soloveitchik, the resemblance between the generations, paraphrasing Wallace Stevens, nearly transforms into identity between past, present, and future.

With that identity asserted, it is Joseph's father, Rabbi Moses, and his interpretive heroism that figures most prominently:

> Father would speak; their eyes fixed on him, they would listen intently to what he was saying. Slowly, slowly, the tension ebbed; Father strode boldly and bravely. New arguments emerged, halakhic rules were formulated and defined

with wondrous precision. A new light shone. The difficulties were resolved, the passage was explained. The Rambam emerged the winner. Father's face shone with joy. He had defended his "friend," Rabbenu Mosheh, the son of Maimon. A smile of satisfaction appeared on Rambam's lips. I too participated in this joy. (*Seek*, 144)

The father, depicted as a warrior, emerges triumphantly, the victorious herme-neut resolving the "'difficulties" encountered as the passage is finally and fully explained. In this masculine battle, interpretation figured as conquest, with Rambam declared to be the "winner" by virtue of the intervention of his "friend," Rabbi Moses. The generational identifications extend as the current Rabbi Moses's face "shone with joy," showing an affiliation not only to the medieval Moses, Rambam, but the lawgiver Moses, whose own face shines in the Book of Exodus (34:29–35). Rabbi Moses protects the Rambam for the sake of tradition, acting as the latter's agent, and thus, by extension, for the future, embodied in the young Joseph; indeed, the identification between past, present, and future en-acts the tradition it comes to affirm. Through the father's aggressive act of inter-pretive mastery, the younger Moses, acting in the service of the older one, enlight-enment—"a new light"—shines. As a version of modern midrash, Soloveitchik's recollection transfers the authority bestowed on Moses in the biblical story—his enlightened countenance shining from proximity to the divine—not to the Tal-mudic sage but to the modern sage: his father. In this account, the divine light, rendered new through Rabbi Moses's interpretive virtuosity, illuminates the Feinsteins' Pruzhna living room.

Joseph's father, the paradigmatic figure of the "halakhic man," provides an image of mastery, saving not only the Rambam from the threat of incoherence but also the tradition. The young Joseph, waiting expectantly, shows himself as a merely passive inheritor, anticipating the triumph of his father, enabling the tra-dition's perpetuation. Like a latter-day rabbinic Aeneas, carrying his father and clutching his son, Rabbi Moses rescues past and future, his own figurative father, Maimonides, and his son, Joseph. The survival of the young Joseph, himself iden-tifying with the Rambam under attack, and also, by extension, the brunt of mocking, remains dependent on the intervention of the heroic modern, his bold, brave, and triumphant father.

When the triumph is finally achieved and the collective joy expressed, Joseph imagines his inclusion in the celebration almost as an afterthought—"I *too* par-ticipated in the joy" (emphasis added). Not surprisingly, Joseph does not share his joy with those with whom from at the outset he imagined himself an outsider. In the presence of those gathered, only the Rambam "smiles," the smile of gratitude (and perhaps relief) that the self-conscious Joseph cannot express in their com-pany. Joseph does reveal his feelings, but not in the company of men. He leaves his grandfather's makeshift study to express his joy: "I was happy and excited. I would jump out of bed and run to my mother's room to tell her the joyful news: 'Mother, mother, the Rambam is right, he defeated the Rabad. Father came to his aid. How wonderful father is'" (*Seek*, 144). The young Joseph though excited by his father's triumph is nonetheless distant from the masculine cohort of legal mastery. Even with the definitive defeat of the Rambam's adversaries, Joseph does not participate in the celebration of his father and his gathered students. Instead, he runs to his mother's room; only there, in the province of the feminine, does he express his emotions. Although his father triumphs—even more steely and "hard" than the Rambam—it is the maternal feminine that allows the young Joseph to celebrate the victory on which he and the tradition remain dependent. In this recollection, Joseph represents the triumph of his father, with Talmudic knowledge resplendent and shining in its victory—the triumph of the law—but only for him in relation to the sequestered feminine. Joseph identifies with his father, but in something of a paradox, the only place he finds sympathy is in the presence of the feminine. This part of the story, focusing on the generations while inflected by gender, already intimates ambivalence toward the law and its champion, writ large in the story's second part.

The depiction of the law's success is paired in the other half of the narrative diptych with a representation of paternal failure, indeed a failure of the law itself, as the uncertainty and despair that had threatened in the first half of the story now emerge unchecked. This is not a story of hermeneutic triumph, but catastrophe:

> But occasionally the Rambam's luck did not hold—his "enemies" attacked him on all sides; the difficulties were as hard as iron. Father was unable to follow the logic of his position. He tried with all his might to defend him, but he was unsuccessful. Father would sink into his musing with his head leaning on his fist. The students and I, and even the Rambam himself, would tensely wait for Father's answer. But Father would pick up his head and say sadly, "The answer will have to wait for the prophet Elijah; what the Rambam says is extremely difficult. There is no expert that can explain it. The issues remain in need of clarification." The whole group, my father included, were sad to the point of tears. A silent agony expressed itself on each face. Tears came from my eyes, too. I would even see bright teardrops in the Rambam's eyes. (*Seek*, 144–45)

In contrast to the triumphant first half of the story, the second part shows the hermeneutic failure of the father, bewildered and unable to follow the logic of the teacher who came before him. Rather than the father's assured demeanor as in the first half of the story, he now confronts difficulties presented as "hard as iron," the curse from Deuteronomy (28:3) visited upon his grandfather's living room. The frustration of the father is rendered in the image of his clenched fist, with the overall mood sinking, the tension not ebbing, but intensifying. Faced with these difficulties, the young Soloveitchik's father is simply "unsuccessful." This failure weighs heavily not only on the boy, but on the father as well, as nearly tragic. Even with a lingering possibility of success, the now despondent Rabbi Moses concedes the difficulty: "there is no expert" able to offer the correct interpretation.

The young Joseph had already depicted himself in a "cold and alien" world; by the end of the story, the world of sadness, agony, and tears encompasses the living room and the generations of scholars. Instead of enacting *mesora*, or tradition, the figures represented participate, however unwillingly, in an intergenerational catastrophe of hermeneutic failure. The vulnerability of the Rambam, the "bright tears" in his eyes, distills young Joseph's distress. Indeed, Rabbi Moses, the Rambam, and the whole group remain silent, the agony experienced in the failure of the mastery that had once shown itself triumphant. This second half of the story concludes not only with the father's failure, but the failure of the mechanisms associated with the legal mastery and enlightenment aggressively fashioned in the preceding representation. The tradition is not triumphant, but rendered silent, offering no consolation. Rambam himself—the past waiting to be rehabilitated by the present master—looks on helplessly. In the absence of the heroic hermeneutics of the current expositor of Brisk, the tradition itself appears vulnerable, near collapse. Joseph, as potential inheritor of that tradition, is bereft, forlorn, melancholy.

Mirroring the first half of the story, Joseph's mother, the representation of the feminine, also figures prominently in the complementary second part. Following the lack of resolution and collective despair—indeed, the abject loss—with which the hermeneutic encounter ends, the young Joseph again turns to his mother. With the failure of his father and the masculine, the realm of the feminine serves now not as a place reserved for the praise of the father, but a refuge of solace. "Slowly I would go to Mother," he recounts, "and tell her with a broken heart, 'Mother, Father can't resolve the Rambam—what should we do?'" While the young Joseph situates himself outside of the realm of the masculine, he identifies with his mother during the time of Masoretic crisis: "what should *we* do?," he asks in the first person plural. To her son's imploring pleas, she responds with consoling words: "'Don't be sad . . . Father will find a solution for the Rambam'" (*Seek*, 145). Joseph reveals the secrets of his emotional life to his mother, opening up his "broken heart." In the face of his despair, indeed failure, the feminine maintains a belief in the adequacy of the masculine in defeat, reaffirming the idealized notion of Joseph's father in identification with her son. More important, however, in this second half of Soloveitchik's family midrash, the feminine allows for a future different from the one imagined by the masculine gathering, one in which there is a continuation of uncertainty without despair—a future in which there is the persistence of doubt, but also hope about finding a solution: "'And if he doesn't find one,'" she says of her husband, "'then maybe when you grow up, you'll resolve his words.'" It is Soloveitchik's mother who, teaching him to accommodate defeat, sends the young Joseph, by his own account, on the journey of self-creation. She acknowledges the sources for what will one day turn into his "Torah of the heart," anticipating that her son will not merely inherit his father's legacy, but one day surpass it.

Rabbi Moses had abandoned the possibility of resolution at least until messianic days: "The answer will have to await for the prophet Elijah." The feminine here, still sequestered away from the realm of masculine interpretation, offers a place where uncertainty is tolerated and accommodated, the possibility of a return to interpretation in history, a nonmessianic futurity. Rabbi Moses, however, is depicted in mutually exclusive and reinforcing extremes: as having achieved triumphant success, in which doubt is vanquished or, by contrast, having suffered devastating defeat, left with nothing. That is, the legal hermeneutics—and the conception of tradition—embodied in the figure of Rabbi Moses, the halakhic man, alternatively resolves all doubt or fails catastrophically. The feminine provides solace and the possibility of continuity, but the alliance with the feminine in the construction of the triumphant masculine comes, in this set of remembrances, at the price of Joseph's full identification with that masculine authority and the law, the halakha he represents. The uncertain relationship to a masculinity that Soloveitchik both reveres and questions informs a dynamic present in the rest of his work: the tension between the triumphant masculine and the lurking possibility of its catastrophic failure.

In the confrontation with lack of certainty, the maternal provides consolation and the possibility of continuation, an answer to his melancholy but not an antidote in the face of doubt. The masculine, as elaborated here, allows for the extremes of success or failure only, while the feminine permits for an alternative, a respite from melancholy, a momentary accommodation of loss. While the father provides the possibility of an idealized merging of past, present, and future, that fusion of generations comes together in a nontemporal realm, protected from contingency and loss. Soloveitchik's mother, however, both acknowledges loss and the possibility of a creative futurity—an attitude toward the future without certainty or triumph. In the realm of legal hermeneutics, however, Soloveitchik, as I argue in the following chapters, always chooses the masculine, but not without expressing ambivalence.

For the editors of the volume in which it appears, the narrative diptych "charmingly and vividly illustrates" the nature of tradition (*Seek*, xxxiii). The focus here on this Talmudic primal scene, with its emphasis on the relationships it depicts as well as the implicit conceptions of gender that underwrite it, emerges from the conviction that the recollection is more than just of passing interest—a "charming" biographical account. Indeed, I suggest that Soloveitchik's recollection of the paired memories—with its alternating emphasis on mastery and melancholy, the thematizing of loss, and the role of gender in mediating such loss—provides an opening to understand Soloveitchik's conception of legal hermeneutics throughout his life. The oscillation between triumph and melancholy, conquest and defeat (and the subsequent exclusion of the feminine from that hermeneutic dynamic), underlie the particularity of Soloveitchik's melancholy attitude toward interpretation and tradition.

Where the hermeneutics of mourning produces difference, for Soloveitchik, for all of the emphasis on loss in his later works (and the accompanying epistemological humility), the realm of legal hermeneutics remains a protected but continually circumscribed realm of certainty. To paraphrase Hilary Putnam's terms from chapter 1, for the hermeneutic traditions of Brisk for which Soloveitchik provides a philosophical apology, enough is never enough. Anything less than complete cognitive conquest—total certainty—is insufficient. In Soloveitchik's developing relationship to his antecedents, however, and his appropriation and transformation of the figure of the "halakhic man," he does pursue the contingency and otherness associated with the feminine, but not in the realm of legal hermeneutics, but in the realms of ethics and the psyche.

That the passage—the oscillation between hermeneutic triumph and catastrophe, and the way in which the relationship between memory and gender inform this movement—has not been seriously studied, mostly brushed over with the biographical gloss of the hagiographer, may suggest that previous analysis of Soloveitchik's work has also unknowingly conspired in the avoidance of elaborating the consequences of gender for reading his works. Further, that a current generation of scholars—many of them former students of Soloveitchik—have not provided an account of the epistemological and hermeneutic assumptions informing his work may be a function of their own investment in the Brisk traditions for which Soloveitchik still serves as a primary exemplar. To be sure, what David Singer and Moshe Sokol called in 1982 the "adulation" surrounding the reception of Soloveitchik's work has transformed, especially during the last decade, but the interrelationship between representations of gender, memory, and interpretation have yet to be critically assessed.[2]

My focus on family remembrance from *And from There Shall You Seek*, as well as on Soloveitchik's representations of gender throughout his work, is informed by the psychoanalytic insight that the seemingly "inconsequential" matters. What the psychotherapist Christopher Bollas calls the "shyness of the historian" in approaching "small" and even apparently inconsequential "details of the past" arises from the implicit knowledge that such attention may reveal things otherwise unknown. In Bollas's example, patients—or historical documents or memoirs—through their "trivial memories" register "secrets condensed." In the "intensities of a lifetime," there is the possibility of reviving a self that had been "consigned to oblivion," thus restoring meanings that through trauma have been repressed.[3]

The secrets present throughout Soloveitchik's often personal works, register traumas that are both personal and historical, and are here understood to inform his explicit arguments about tradition, epistemology, and interpretation.

Soloveitchik's primal scene reveals ambivalence toward the masculine—an obvious reverence for the halakhic man, but also profound reservations about the law that he represents. Although the maternal provides a locus of love and a possible accommodation of loss, the feminine for Soloveitchik also has an ambivalent valence. Indeed, it is also figured, most explicitly in his later writings, as an ideal of an always unattainable presence, or, inversely, an object of suspicion. This ambivalence toward both the masculine and the feminine informs what I call Soloveitchik's melancholy hermeneutics, and leads to the construction of a psychic space—in the realm of repentance and ethics—outside of the purview of the halakhic man. As a sign, in Adam Phillips's terms of "becoming" achieved, the once lonely, forlorn, and tentative young Joseph will proclaim himself to be, without apology, the lonely man of faith.

This second part begins, however, not with a psychoanalytic hermeneutics of suspicion, but a hermeneutics of empathy, placing Soloveitchik's work in relationship to that of the neo-Freudian Jonathan Lear. The focus on Soloveitchik's epistemology governed by love and a collapse in the realm of the subject–object distinction discussed in chapter 2 provide the foundations for a pluralism (however circumscribed) and the radical innovation in his conceptions of the psyche and Jewish repentance. While chapter 3 focuses on the epistemology of love present in Soloveitchik's conception of repentance (and in the parallel Freudian concept of sublimation), the remaining chapters focus on how the ambivalent conceptions of masculine and feminine amount to what Julia Kristeva refers to as a melancholy embrace of law. In my reading, the melancholy sensibility of Soloveitchik's childhood memories, as well as the conceptions of gender implicit within, inform his writings from *Halakhic Man* to his post-Holocaust writings on ethics, becoming the means through which he creates a different persona for himself: the last rabbi of Brisk. It is to the origin of that persona—in love and repentance—to which I now turn.

3 Love, Repentance, Sublimation

> Where id was, there ego shall be. It is a work of culture—not unlike the draining of the Zuider Zee.
>
> —Sigmund Freud, *New Introductory Lectures on Psychoanalysis*

THE PRINCIPLE UNDERLYING Soloveitchik's self-creation is not merely personal, but primarily a theological one. "The most fundamental principle of all," Soloveitchik writes in *Halakhic Man*, the "idea that Judaism introduced into the world" is that "man must create himself" (*Man*, 134). That Freud and the rabbis share an emphasis on the importance of individual creativity makes this chapter's pairing of Soloveitchik with the neo-Freudian thinker Jonathan Lear seem less improbable. For both, through seemingly incommensurate terms—the Jewish conception of repentance, or *teshuva*, and the psychoanalytic conception of sublimation, respectively—elaborate the possibilities for Soloveitchik's "self-fashioner," that is, the development of the individual psyche or soul (*Man*, 113). If psychoanalysis and religion since Freud's work have been seen to occupy separate and sometimes mutually exclusive (even hostile) disciplinary spaces, the works of Soloveitchik and Lear show how rabbinic and psychoanalytic discourses share a common emphasis on individuation. Further, by placing the two thinkers in dialogue, psychoanalytic discourse emerges as a means of understanding Soloveitchik's conceptions of *teshuva*, even a continuation of earlier rabbinic conceptions. The continued return to the language of repentance throughout Soloveitchik's work—in both his philosophical and more traditional writings—testifies to the centrality, for him, of the self-creation of *teshuva* in both theological and psychic terms.

Unlike other attempts among post-Freudians to find a space for religious discourse, the argument here does not focus on the reclamation of, as Lear himself puts it, the "infantile nature" of religious experience, or on how religion recaptures aspects of what Hans Loewald calls "archaic mind" or "primary process mentation" (*Loewald*, 196–98).[1] True, Soloveitchik and Lear both focus on the achievement of unity, but not one that derives from mysticism and the celebration of the nondiscursive, but rather an epistemological unity presupposed upon difference in the service of knowledge and the development of an autonomous self. Freud argued in *Moses and Monotheism* for a particular form of what he called the Jewish "phylogenetic inheritance." In an appropriation of the Freudian gesture, psychoanalysis may be seen, in the current reading, as a continuation, and even in some sense a fulfillment, of a rabbinic emphasis on individual autonomy and transformation.[2] Put in other terms, *teshuva* reaches a new form of expression—without its theological trappings—in psychoanalytic discourse. But more than that, given the presence of Freud, however mediated, in Soloveitchik's work (as I discuss in greater length in the following two chapters), Soloveitchik's accounts of *teshuva* may be inflected by his awareness of psychoanalysis and the parallel emphasis on psychic individuation. Reading Lear and Soloveitchik in dialogue enables an understanding of the psychoanalytic resonances of Soloveitchik's elaboration of *teshuva*, and further, the unacknowledged theological stakes implicit in Lear's articulation of the mechanism of sublimation—how both are presupposed upon a radical postulation of love. For both thinkers, love is presupposed upon a unity of subject and object, parallel to the unity assumed in relation to the Talmudic legal hermeneutics elaborated in chapter 2. For Soloveitchik, however, the unity presupposed between subject and object functions in the psychic realm of repentance, in his disciplinary apology for religious philosophy, but not in the realm of legal hermeneutics.[3]

If the story told here is one emphasizing Jewish reference points, there is another common and perhaps even more important figure in the stories that Lear and Soloveitchik both tell: Aristotle. In the current chapter, the common Aristotelian basis for Lear and Soloveitchik's thought are examined, showing how the two thinkers turned to an Aristotelian conception of knowledge to undermine early modern conceptions of objectivity, and further, to liberate their respective disciplines, psychoanalysis and Jewish philosophy, from the disciplinary constraints imposed by the truth criteria of the sciences. The dialogue enacted here between the works of Soloveitchik and Lear, in demonstrating the centrality of individuation enacted respectively through *teshuva* and sublimation, provides unexpected perspectives on the common reliance on, but in some sense more tellingly, the eventual abandonment of Aristotle. Although both thinkers depend on the Greek philosopher for their conceptions of knowledge, they both also reject him (or at least the Aristotle cited through their works), as they seek to elaborate a cosmic principle—of love—to inform their respective conceptions of personal development. For both Lear and Soloveitchik, love is primarily an activity, founded on an epistemological stance that presupposes both difference and unity, not just the mystical unity assumed from most Freudian perspectives to be the mainstay of religious experience. Indeed, the elaboration of a self in pursuit of "individuality, autonomy, uniqueness, and freedom" in Lear and Soloveitchik depends on an Aristotelian conception of knowledge, but also a conception of a universe and metaphysics informed by love for which the Greek philosopher, despite his significance to both of their works, fails to provide an adequate precedent (*Man*, 135).

For Soloveitchik and Lear, knowledge entails the unity of knower and known, an activity based on desire entailing an epistemological stance, and the self's active engagement with the world, or what amounts to, in both of their works, the knowing self's engagement with the "given." This unanalyzed matter of the given—whether psychic or worldly—only changes its character when taken up by a subject who *knows*. As Lear writes in his 1988 book on Aristotle, the "perceptible object has the capacity to be perceived," but the actualization of perception only takes place in the subject, and for both Soloveitchik and Lear, following Aristotle, a subject that *desires* (*Desire,* 103). The reintroduction of desire—and eventually for the two contemporary thinkers, love—into the process of cognition goes against the grain of early modern scientific and philosophical conceptions of knowledge, which, in giving priority to objectivity, threaten the disciplinary grounds of both psychoanalysis and religion. In an Aristotelian epistemology, transformed as it will be in the works of Lear and Soloveitchik, desire and love are not impediments, or even merely extrinsic to knowledge, but the means through which knowledge is enacted and attained. In this way, both thinkers, in contexts dominated by disciplinary models of the sciences and corresponding conceptions of objective truth, employ this epistemology of love to justify the autonomy of their respective disciplines, and even more than that, to redefine the nature of truth claims across the disciplinary spectrum. In Lear's psychoanalytic and Soloveitchik's "halakhic" or legal epistemology, the possibility of a disciplinary pluralism—with multiple and internally valid truth claims—emerges.

As much as serving as a disciplinary defense, the conception of love grounded in the Aristotelian unity of knower and known—the breaking down of the subject–object distinction as inherited from the seventeenth century—serves even more importantly in relation to Lear's and Soloveitchik's respective perspectives on self-knowledge. That is, the subject's knowledge of the "given" of the external world, as well as the conception of interpretation that flows from it, parallels the corresponding knowledge of the internal "given," the knowledge of the psyche or soul. The epistemology of the unity of subject and object, adopted from Aristotle but eventually transformed into an epistemology of love, is expressed in Lear and Soloveitchik in relation to the development of the individual, through the respective processes of sublimation and *teshuva*. Although psychoanalytic and rabbinic registers may presuppose opposing values, the psychic processes of *teshuva* and sublimation presume a possible unity of subject and object, and indeed are the primary means through which the subject acquires autonomy, or free will—the means by which individuation is achieved. Further, sublimation and *teshuva*, as distanced as they may seem from one another, assume, and indeed require, a world founded on love. In my reading, Lear's abandonment of Aristotle and his embrace (and perhaps even creation) of a Freudian world based on love helps underline the commitments expressed through Soloveitchik's correspond-ing abandonment of Aristotle and his parallel appropriation of a Maimonidean epistemology based on love. That is, Lear's idiosyncratic appropriation of Freud serves to elucidate Soloveitchik's self-consciously innovative reading of Maimon-idean epistemology.

The Desire to Know

In placing Soloveitchik's work in dialogue with that of Lear, the focus in the cur-rent chapter is on Soloveitchik's three major works of the 1940s: the articulation of the epistemological assumptions in *And from There Shall You Seek*; how those assumptions relate to the defense of the disciplinary sphere of the religious phi-losopher in *Halakhic Mind*; and finally, the conception of *teshuva* as articulated in *Halakhic Man*.[4]

And from There Shall You Seek provides a narrative meditation on God's presence, or more aptly, especially in the early stages of the often lyrical and some-times forlorn work, on the absence of God. For Soloveitchik, an abyss separates the creator and his creation, and the experience of divine presence is never achieved fully on an empirical or phenomenological level—but only through languages of revelation. Yet notwithstanding what amounts to a neo-Kantian framing of the "real"—its inaccessible distance from experience and immediate genuine knowledge—Soloveitchik represents knowledge in Aristotelian terms by means of a conceptual language he adopts from Maimonides, specifically in his emphasis on the relationship between subject and object, or the unity be-tween knower and known.[5]

"The secret of cleaving to God," Soloveitchik writes, citing the Maimonidean elaboration of Aristotelian knowledge, "involves the principle of the identity of the knower and the known" (*Seek*, 94). Divine knowledge does not allow for the duality of subject and object; indeed, God is unified with his creation in the act of knowing. "The world is the 'object' of God's knowledge, yet it is rooted in the subject," as the "known cleaves to the knower forever, without pause" (*Seek*, 102). Human knowledge, though informed by the model of divine knowledge, nonetheless presupposes a split not present in divine cognition. "It turns out," Soloveitchik writes, that "self-knowledge means splitting the personality and alienating itself from itself." Indeed, for Soloveitchik, knowledge is born out of a unity sundered, only to be reclaimed by means of the act of cognition. There are, Soloveitchik writes, "a plethora of strange figures within the soul," "half sub-ject" and "half object." Self-knowledge entails a confrontation between parts of the "I" that—addressed as separate entities and even agencies in the psyche—inevitably need to be overcome (*Seek*, 95). Although man lives with the never fully surmountable reality of the subject–object distinction, both internally and externally (in relationship to self and world respectively), cognition entails over-coming that separation. "Human cognition, limited and relative as it is, is rooted" in the "type of wondrous unity" associated with the instantaneous and eternal knowledge of the divine (*Seek*, 97). In the explicit borrowing of Aristotelian lan-guage, Soloveitchik writes that "conjoined with the active intellect," one "ascends to the level of a true knower" and "achieves the unity of the knower and the known" (*Seek*, 98). Through a mode of cognition that partakes of the same activ-ity and shares the same object of knowledge as the divine, "man and God are united in knowledge of the world" (*Seek*, 103).

What Soloveitchik cites as the Aristotelian/Maimonidean assertion of unity is not, however, merely a mystical attempt to elaborate a theological "cleaving"—a means to unify with the divine—but also represents the description of an episte-mological stance. It should not therefore be reduced or relegated to the realm of a theological experience only; it defines the nature of knowing itself. Indeed, in the absence of the unity that characterizes genuine knowledge, there is a fall into dualism. As Soloveitchik writes, when cognition no longer realizes its aim and degrades into mere "potentiality," the "dualism of subject and object emerges" (*Seek*, 98). Knowledge that is not based on activity merely receives "impressions" and is "passive," while the act of understanding leads to a "conjoining" with the world (*Seek*, 103). That is, for Soloveitchik, knowledge is achieved only through activity, while passivity, engendering "the dualism of man and world, of I and it" may yield impressions but not genuine knowledge (*Seek*, 101).

What Soloveitchik calls "the epistemological innovation" and the resultant "unity of knower and known" only maintains, however, in a cognition informed by both "love and desire" (*Seek*, 156). The introduction of love and desire as nec-essary components of the process of knowing articulated, for Soloveitchik, explic-itly by Maimonides—"one only loves God with the knowledge with which one knows Him; according to the knowledge will be the love"—may seem, according to some paradigms of knowledge, like a foreign presence in what should be an exclusively cognitive activity (*Seek*, 156). In Soloveitchik's Maimonidean appro-priation of Aristotle, however, desire and the subsequent pleasure are not addi-tions to the process of knowledge; they are fundamental defining parts. As Lear writes in his book on Aristotle, providing a useful gloss on Soloveitchik, "plea-sure is not an adventitious charm which accompanies thinking like a charming escort; the pleasure is *internal to the thinking itself*" (*Desire*, 297; emphasis added). The subject who desires is also the subject who knows. From an Aristotelian perspective, when subject and object are sundered—when the object appears as discreet, independent, and transparent, and the subject as without desire, disen-gaged, neutral, and objective—knowledge is not the consequence. Before elaborat-ing how desire and love function in the development of the psyche in both

Soloveitchik and Lear, I turn to the nature of their respective appropriations of Aristotelian epistemology, first as they relate to knowledge of the world and then to the redefining of disciplinary hierarchies.

Soloveitchik's Disciplinary Pluralism and Love

The reciprocity of subject and object, primary in the book on religious knowledge *And from There Shall You Seek,* also plays a significant role in Soloveitchik's elaboration of a disciplinary pluralism, his validation of the possibility of different kinds of truth claims, the rehabilitation of interpretation, and the defense of the disciplinary autonomy of religious philosophy. Although the arguments of *Halakhic Mind* are enmeshed in the language of philosophy and the history of science, they are also founded on the Aristotelian conception of knowledge—on the unity of knower and known.

To describe the sundering of subject and object, Soloveitchik traces Western intellectual history through the shifting fortunes of disciplines and changes in disciplinary hierarchies over the centuries. In the narrative Soloveitchik tells, both the humanist and the religious philosopher had been forced, after the advent of modern science, into the posture of apologists, defending religious experience in relation to the more authoritative truth claims of both science and a new empirical philosophy. Carrying the burden of objectivity as inherited through Newton, the humanist through the nineteenth and early twentieth centuries, as Soloveitchik defines him, had largely accepted the objectivist conclusions of the scientist. The humanist had acceded rationality, knowledge, and objectivity to the scientist, embracing for himself an increasingly romantic, subjectivist, and mystical worldview. If the scientist had claimed the realm of objectivity, then the humanist was left, though sometimes reluctantly, with an increasingly impoverished sense of subjectivity. In this narrative, subject and object are sundered not only in epistemological terms but also in disciplinary and historical terms, with the scientist inhabiting an objectivist realm of "truth," and the humanist, relegated to an increasingly mystical, emotional, and subjective sphere.

The social scientist and religious philosopher, however, acceded to the "scientifically purified world" available to the privileged perspective of the so-called neutral observer, accepting the epistemological assumptions bequeathed by the Newtonian scientist (*Mind, 7*). As a result, "the philosophy of religion could not progress" and was left to be a mere disciplinary apologist for the Newtonian scientist (*Mind, 39*). For the new avatars of the human and social sciences, the models and priorities of Newtonian science were adopted. These models emphasized the importance of objectivity and a nonsituated rationality that adjudicated cultural, religious, and social phenomena from an ostensibly external perspective.

In Soloveitchik's account, the quantum physicist, in some ways the hero of *Halakhic Mind*, mediating between the "subjectivity" of the humanist and the "objectivity" of the classical physicist, undermines the subject–object dichotomy instated by Newtonian science. The classical scientist maintained a belief in the so-called objective world in its autonomy, as well as the kind of disengaged observer it implied. The modern physicist, by contrast, acknowledged that the paradigms and structures of science were themselves constructs designed to elicit the truth of the "real." If the Newtonian philosopher had assumed a perspective of neutral objectivity, the quantum physicist acknowledged that the scientist and his experimental paradigms help to create the reality he surveys. The quantum acknowledgment of the "reciprocal relation of phenomenon and experiment" demands, Soloveitchik writes, that the relation "between subject and object must come up for reconsideration," and that the "claim of the natural sciences to absolute objectivity must undergo a thorough revision" (*Mind*, 25). Subjectivity and objectivity were not, as both the Newtonian scientist and "modern metaphysician" had agreed, independent realms, but reciprocally determining.

The reintroduction of the subject, and by extension, interpretation, reinstates, in quantum scientific terms, the Aristotelian emphasis on the interrelation of subject and object. Formulating what he conceives as a quantum update of Aristotelian thought, Soloveitchik writes, "contemporary epistemology has no ontological hierarchy and considers the direction between subjectivity and objectivity to be only directional" (*Mind*, 76). Pure subjectivity and pure objectivity are simply limiting abstract cases: "we do not find two different components, the subjective and the objective, but one unified phenomenon" (*Mind*, 66).[6] Quantum physics shows that aspects of "reality"—the as-yet unanalyzed "given"—are only revealed depending on the nature of the various subjective interventions. For Soloveitchik, the subjective component affirmed to be part of quantum observation allowed for the reintroduction of interpretation into the very discipline that had most denied its continued necessity. Even for the scientist, the world is affected by the "very act of observing" and the so-called pristine object becomes "transformed" through its "merger" with the "subject" (*Mind*, 25).

Indeed, for Soloveitchik, the quantum affirmation of the Aristotelian insight about the nature of knowledge allows the religious philosopher to free himself from the concepts of objectivity enshrined in classical Newtonian science. Causal or etiological explanations, borrowed from the sciences, which provide certain and singular explanations—dependent on an external perspective of objectivity—yield, in Soloveitchik's work, to a "thickness" of description and interpretation. Soloveitchik's use of the term "thickness" is felicitous, for his work, like that of the anthropologist Clifford Geertz after him, rejects the presumptive rationalizations of the traditional social sciences (from the ostensible external and neutral perspective), advocating instead multiple interpretations and descriptions (*Mind*, 34).[7] The methodology of the quantum physicist, translated for the religious philosopher, takes the latter out of the influence of the Newtonian realm and allows for "a multidimensional religious outlook" and the possibility of a pluralism of approaches (*Mind*, 88).

No longer "limited to causal designs" bequeathed by scientists advocating epistemologies of objectivity, the philosopher of religion engages in a process that always requires and encourages "further exploration." What Soloveitchik calls "our pluralistic cognitive approach" and his "methodological heterogeneity" is warranted by "ontological heterogeneity." The complexity and multiplicity of the "given" assures that the "philosopher may gain access to reality in a manner alien to the physicist and biologist" (*Mind*, 23, 16). Before the works of Thomas Kuhn and other revolutionary work in the history and philosophy of science, with their emphasis on changing and multiple paradigms, Soloveitchik argued for a religious knowledge, among other forms of knowledge, that is independent, autonomous, and internally validating.

For Soloveitchik, the realm of religious experience cannot be explained away through the causal analysis inherited from the so-called objectivist perspective of the sciences. The "profound religious mind" is "averse to the platitudes" that claim to "circumscribe"—indeed render transparent—"the religious act" from an external perspective (*Mind*, 97). As Soloveitchik writes, in the act of etiological explanation, "meaningful content" and "essential significance" are eschewed (*Mind*, 97). The etiological perspective provides functional explanations, as when, for example, Jewish dietary laws are reduced to "hygienic or sanitary considerations," or the Sabbath is reduced to a justification for priestly rest (*Mind*, 93).[8] For Soloveitchik, the elaboration of a singular external cause, the province of etiology, never exhausts the "given," nor does it allow for the kind of "penetrative" acts of interpretation that constitute religious acts beyond their merely "technical discipline." That is to say, the elaboration of religious acts from within an internal perspective—not the ostensibly disengaged and objectivist perspective that had been dominant in the social sciences and even the humanities—allows for autonomous sets of descriptions of the world of religious acts and texts. The religious personality, Soloveitchik affirms, and here again the Aristotelian resonances are clear, "finds delight in such interpretations" (*Mind*, 98). Released from passivity and inaction, the so-called neutral contemplation of the real that had been bequeathed by the Newtonian, Soloveitchik elaborates the grounds for an autonomous religious philosophy eliciting the "infinite" and "mysterious" spheres of interpretation (*Mind*, 97). The methodological pluralism that Soloveitchik cultivates presupposes undoing the subject–object distinction, allowing for a multiplicity of disciplinary approaches, including among them "religious philosophy."

Jonathan Lear's Psychoanalytic Pluralism

Jonathan Lear, University of Chicago classicist and psychoanalyst, similarly turns to Aristotelian conceptions of knowledge, but he does so to elaborate his Freudian conception of the psyche. Indeed, the subtitle of Lear's book on Aristotle, *The Desire to Understand* (1988), already suggests the Freudian turn toward "desire" that his work eventually takes. *Love and Its Place in Nature*, published just two years after *Desire*, consistently registers the presence of Aristotelian epistemology with consequences for an understanding of knowledge as unity with regard to both the self and the world. Although Lear's Freud is, in many ways, a creation in the image of Aristotle—a philosophical Freud—the Aristotelian framework fails to be a possible precedent for Lear's developmental conception of the psyche based on love. As we shall see, Soloveitchik embraces an Aristotle transformed by Maimonides for whom not only desire but divine love plays a role; Lear similarly elaborates a notion of reciprocal love, also through his transformation and eventual abandonment of Aristotle. The contours of Lear's epistemology of love, understood as Aristotelian action, provide a means to elucidate Soloveitchik's epistemology of love.

Lear's embrace of Aristotle, as well as his eventual dismissal of him, are equally important in what amounts to his idiosyncratic creation of Freud, a hybrid product of the appropriation and transformation of Freudian registers into Aristotelian philosophical language. As Lear describes it, in the knowledge of the self that takes place through sublimation, mind, in the process of active contemplation, is "at its highest level of activity," which Aristotle calls "divine" (*Love*, 215). "Humans," Lear writes, again alluding to Aristotle, "distinguish themselves from the rest of nature by the fact that they can participate in the divine act of understanding," thus bestowing a subjective form on the matter of the object world. In this Aristotelian rendering, the human partakes of the divine through imitation of the divine form of understanding. As Lear frames it, love is the process that works "actively" both "in and through mind" (*Love*, 215). In Lear's Freudian appropriation of Aristotle, however, it is the unconscious that takes the place of Aristotle's world of the "creaturely," the interpretations of the subject taking the place of divine understanding. Nevertheless, subject and object, modified for the Freudian context, are still framed by the ideal of the unity of knower and known. The subject at once distinguishes himself from the unconscious—the drives, dreams, and so forth—and unifies with them through sublimation in an act of knowing. The questioning of the subject–object distinction, primary for Lear's conception of psychic health, serves him as well in defense of the autonomous validity of psychoanalysis from attacks emanating from the sensibility inherited from seventeenth-century science. Like Soloveitchik, Lear views the epistemological models bequeathed by early modern science and philosophy as impinging on the "human." Indeed, from the latter's perspective, every sphere of knowledge, even the scientific, must answer to the criteria of love.

When one is "concerned with the human realm," Lear writes, "the objective use of objectivity closes down questions," and the "subjective use of objectivity opens them up" (*Action*, 90).[9] In Lear's lexicon, "the objective use of objectivity" refers to older scientific models and the presupposition and assumption of a nonsituated viewpoint, whereas the subjective use of objectivity, an attempt to undermine the subject–object distinction while employing its terms, already implies a relationship between knower and known. Lear cites Hans Loewald as an origin of the perspective in which subject and object are mutually defining but inflects his representation of the psychoanalytic conception with the precedent Aristotelian paradigm of unity of mind and world achieved through active thought (*Action*, 51). Soloveitchik, we have seen, questions Newtonian assumptions about objectivity in order to find a place for the religious philosopher within a disciplinary universe dominated by the sciences. Half a century later, Lear, who also questions the "scientific image" of "objectivity," redefines the disciplinary landscape, but does so not only for philosophers, instead giving priority to a general epistemology based on love (*Love*, 210).

Even "scientific detachment," Lear writes, "in its genuine form, far from excluding love is based on it" (*Action*, 44). "Scientific spirit" and "care for the object," with the former emphasizing an "objective" aspect and the latter a "subjective" one, are compatible. Lear affirms that "in our most dispassionate and objective moments we manifest our greatest love" (*Action*, 51).[10] In paradoxical language confounding both that of the traditional scientist and philosopher, Lear asserts that "there is a certain kind of passion in our dispassion," and that the object only reveals itself in its complexity—no singular perspective is exhaustive—through the right kind of subjective glance (*Action*, 51).

In the quantum terms that Soloveitchik espoused, different experimental frames reveal different aspects of an object, thus licensing interpretation in realms that had once been dominated by the sciences. Reading Soloveitchik through Lear's lexicon, it is only the right kind of experimental frame—which in itself can be understood as an expression of "care"—that will lead to revealing the variegated nature of the object and the taking up of the given. As Lear writes, "we shape ourselves into a certain kind of subject, a scientist, when we discipline ourselves into relating objectively to objects" (*Action*, 44). That is, the right kind of attention, whether an analytical attentiveness or a set of scientific hypothesis, allows for the "object" world to be known. Thus, the objectivity that is subjectively elicited is always just *such*, rendered present through the subjective care and "respect" with which one attends to the object, opening the way up, *pace* Soloveitchik, for disciplinary pluralism. So Lear writes, love not only "permits objectivity," but also, counter intuitively, "requires it" (*Action*, 55). Acknowledging the separateness and integrity of the object is itself an act of bestowing attention, therefore an act of love, entailing, in the end, a unity of knowledge.

Love, in parallel theological terms, is not merely derivative of mystical cleaving or an assumption of unity. Soloveitchik similarly avoids the epistemological error he attributes to the *homo religiosus*, where mystical unity is not preceded by differentiation (*Man*, 60). For Lear, respect for the object, the acknowledgement that it is "to a certain extent, self-standing," is not only the prerequisite, but itself a component of love (*Action*, 44). Only when one becomes the right kind of subject—one who desires to know, for him an act of love—will one see the world with "the appropriate objectivity" (*Action*, 86). This objectivity, on the other side of the paradox, is the prerequisite for an engaged interpretation, which for Lear is based on Aristotle's conception of unity of knower and known. That is, only with the right kind of "care"—a striving towards unity—will objects "reveal themselves in their many facets and dimensions" (*Action*, 44).

Turning to quantum physics to undermine the priority of scientific knowledge, Soloveitchik maps out a place for religious philosophy; even more aggressively, Lear proposes remapping the contours of science. For if love is, as Lear writes, "a basic force," there ought to be absolutely "no external vantage point from which a radical evaluation could occur" (*Love*, 207).[11] The general resistance to psychoanalysis in this way parallels the resistance to what Soloveitchik calls the activity of "subjective" interpretation (and the disciplinary pluralism it produces), both informed by the assumption that the "real" or "given" is transparent and unambiguously available to a "neutral" perspective. We are driven, Lear writes, by a "need for an Archimedean point, an absolutely objective perspective" and by the belief "that any 'internal' validation must be non-objective" (*Love*, 210). Indeed, like Soloveitchik, Lear locates in the seventeenth century the postulation of an "objective view of the world"—not from any particular perspective, but from "no perspective at all" (*Love*, 210). Because "psychoanalytic interpretation can only be validated within the context of a psychoanalytic therapy," that is, from its own internal perspective, "the objection," Lear writes, is that "psychoanalysis cannot be an 'objective science'" (*Love*, 216–17). Given, however, Lear's Aristotelian assertion of the interrelation of subject and object, neither a position of neutral observation nor the postulation of an unmediated objective reality are viable. The fantasy of an "Archimedean perspective," as well as that of a transparently knowable object world, give way to acknowledgment of the situated nature of all knowledge.

For Soloveitchik, the religious philosopher, the presumption of inert religious acts to be neatly organized and correlated, assimilated into the etiological schemes of the human scientist, not only eclipses the interpretive act but also obscures the variegated meanings implicit within them. For Lear as well, the "the external perspective" cannot and does not "give us the way things really are" (*Love*, 210). There are no external interpretive keys to psychic phenomenon, no lexicons of the psyche independent of the individual consciousness in which they are situated. The acknowledgement, however, of the importance of subjectivity does not mean, Lear warns, "that anything goes, but it does mean that we need to look at the various ways we live with a concept, rather than assume that a fixed meaning is forever imposed on us" (*Action*, 52). In therapeutic terms—and "therapeutic action" is an accommodation of the Aristotelian conception of knowledge as action into a psychoanalytic framework—"one cannot abstract from a person's subjective experience without making mysterious what it is for him to be" (*Love*, 220). For Lear, there is no perspective "outside of love"; for, as he writes, the perspective outside of love, understood as the engaged activity of knowledge, is one of "developmental failure and pathology" (*Love*, 211). In Soloveitchik's appropriation of Aristotle through Maimonides, the failure of knowledge as an activity of unification results in the split of subject and object, the fragmentation and alienation of the self. In Lear's work, that split, characterized by the denial of relationship, is construed in parallel terms as psychic illness. In this light, the argument for the disciplinary autonomy of psychoanalysis is not only a plea for the independence of a discipline, or even an affirmation of disciplinary pluralism and the validity of multiple internally validating interpretive frameworks, but for a return, through a reevaluation of the mechanisms of knowledge, to an epistemology of love, to psychic health, both in individual and cultural spheres.

Beyond Aristotle: The Necessity of Love

With its emphasis on desire and the unity of knower and known, Lear's epistemology is Aristotelian; though like Soloveitchik, he also abandons Aristotle. Lear's interrogation of the claims of Aristotle's *Metaphysics* and the critique of Aristotle's highest form of human life show a path leading to Freud. In *Love and Its Place in Nature*, Lear first remakes Freud in an Aristotelian image, but eventually turns to a Freud of his own creation to provide an element of love absent in the classical antecedent. Indeed, for all the emphasis on the unity of knower and known informed by desire in Aristotle, a notion of reciprocal love, crucial, as Lear writes, for the developing individual is absent. Love, for Lear, is the basis for personal autonomy, "the condition for the possibility of subjectivity" (*Love*, 173). That is, the active knowledge of the self and its developmental tendency must be nourished in a framework that encourages love. For Lear, in pragmatic terms, love is what is constitutive of the individual. The presence of "loving figures" help "constitute psychic structures sufficiently rich to enable a person to care about himself" (*Love*, 181). Only through the internalization of these external caring relations (note the importance of the relationship between external and internal worlds) does there emerge "a creature sufficiently reflective and self-aware to deserve the title of 'individual'" (*Love*, 181).

Although the desire for union is the engine of Aristotelian thought, eventually it is, as Lear explains in his earlier work, abandoned by Aristotle's ideal contemplative figure, who, emulating the divine, becomes a person who *had once desired*. For when engaged in that contemplative act of understanding, when the "understander" understands the world "that is meant to be understood," he reenacts a divine process in its self-sufficiency that itself transcends desire. Such "divine self-sufficiency" is, for Lear citing Aristotle, "the absolute identity of thought and object"—the "paradigm of metaphysical flourishing" (*Desire*, 313). Realizing his highest nature, the contemplative figure, Lear explains, achieves a metaphysical flourishing that is "perfectly general and *impersonal*." In this embrace of the contemplative life, "he leaves the nooks and crannies of his personality behind" (*Desire*, 316).

Read in hindsight and recognizing his later turn toward Freud, Lear can be seen to acknowledge, as Soloveitchik before him, the insufficiency of the Aristotelian philosopher. For Lear, neither Aristotle nor the universe that he inhabits can provide a model for love as a developmental process. For the Aristotelian divine, according to Lear, is such that man, at his highest level, aspiring to bridge the "gap between divine and natural world," will satisfy his desire to understand, but in so doing, will "transcend his own nature precisely at the point he finally realizes it" (*Desire*, 312). At the very moment that he most becomes human, realizing his species imperative and imitating the processes of divine knowledge, the contemplative figure abandons what had made him most human in his particularity: the *desire* to know. That is, when contemplative man attains this highest form of being, in doing so, he must "ultimately leave *himself* behind." Aristotelian contemplative man becomes himself—most human and divine—in abandoning his particularity, in choosing himself as "importantly *unmanly*" (*Desire*, 312; emphasis added). Where Lear's psychoanalytic turn emphasizes the importance of individuation and autonomy, the model of the Aristotelian philosopher of the *Metaphysics*, with its emphasis on the contemplative life, abandons the particularities of the individual life, the demands of the subject, for "the universal." Such a pursuit is, in imitation of the divine, a "deeply *impersonal* affair," as the contemplative philosopher comes to see "the human perspective" as "merely human," the adverb "merely," when it comes to qualifying the human, unthinkable from Lear's later Freudian perspective (*Desire*, 318). The final Aristotelian embrace of a form of knowledge, devoid of the particularities of the human—stripped, finally, of desire and devoid of love—is presupposed upon a notion of the divine as self-sufficient, with a demand to emulate this divine conception through transcendence of the personal.

In Lear's analytic prose, the unabashed praise of love—"Let us count the ways of love" (*Love*, 219)—is striking. Indeed, his positing of a source of love in the world, from his Aristotelian perspective, reads as a non sequitur, a metaphysical, if not a cosmological, even theological, innovation. From within the Aristotelian frame, the affirmation that "man is not just a donor of love" but also "a recipient" betrays a faith in love defying rational explanation, indeed a cosmos built on love. What I am calling a theological innovation in Lear's work as a way of moving on from Aristotelian assumptions—a belief in "love as a force permeating animate nature"—emerges more clearly in relationship to the parallel rejection of Aristotle in Soloveitchik's work (*Love*, 186). In this way, Soloveitchik's explicitly theological language helps elaborate the evolution of Lear's thought, in the same way that Soloveitchik's epistemological assumptions—the common assumption of the priority of love—emerge more clearly in relationship to Lear's psychoanalytic models.

Indeed, from the Maimonidean perspective that he advocates, Soloveitchik, as Lear, posits individual autonomy and agency, dependent on an active form of love in the world, in his framework, a God who loves. Soloveitchik's conception of individual agency and responsibility require, to use Lear's terms, a source of love in the world, but not of Lear's Spinozan variety. For Soloveitchik, it is what he understands as the Maimonidean departure from Aristotelian assumptions that shows the presence of love in the world. "Judaism," Soloveitchik writes, "rejects the passive tranquility of the Aristotelian *dianoetic* [i.e., intellectual] life, which is quiet, focused on itself, knowing what is to be known without creative action." The self-sufficiency of "contemplative cognition" without "dynamic initiative or practical action" has "no impact" (*Seek*, 104–5). The lack of a component of action in the Aristotelian contemplative man, Soloveitchik explains, has its origin in the absence of love in the world—the absence of a God who loves.

"Love in Aristotelian philosophy," Soloveitchik writes, "is one way: the world yearns for the Prime Mover, without experiencing reciprocal love." Aristotle's Prime Mover is "aloof from the world and does not long for it" (*Seek*, 153). Because there is no "directed Providence"—and the Aristotelian divine lacks "desire or intention"—knowledge and emotion are split (*Seek*, 154). As contemplation defines the divine exclusively, so the contemplative man who emulates the divine will aspire toward knowledge while rejecting the desire that makes him active. The Aristotelian god who, as Lear writes, is self-sufficient, solicits a parallel human ideal, a contemplative figure who is self-sufficient, not one who acknowledges desire as action, a form of connection and love.

As Soloveitchik explains, the Aristotelian divine is only a "teleological and necessary cause," a philosophical necessity born out of his system (*Seek*, 153). The Maimonidean innovation, however, which is an Aristotle who Soloveitchik both embraces and helps to construct (parallel to Lear in his relation to Freud), is a God who loves his creation such that man, in Lear's terms, is both donor *and* recipient of love. In such love, knowledge and desire are not only joined but given a divine imprimatur; they are rendered a metaphysical force in the universe. The God who loves his creation sets a model of cognition—a unity of knower and known—where the paradigm of divine love or love as a "cosmic metaphysical principle" is the basis of human activity. For Lear's Freud, "love permeates nature," and when love is said to "run through a person," he "becomes a locus of activity" (*Love*, 219). Soloveitchik's language avoids the pantheistic resonances of Lear's description, but for him, just as God is joined to the world through love as an active force, so man joins with the world actively through a cognition understood as an activity of love. "The unity of the knower and the known," Soloveitchik writes, "which is one of the main principles of Maimonides' theory, occurs only in a cognition imbued with love." When "affects blend with the intellect," both their natures change, Soloveitchik writes, "and they become less passive." The man who follows the paradigm of divine love, Soloveitchik writes, "rids himself of ethical indifference." The "concrete person," not a figure of abstract impersonality, remains committed to knowledge of the particularity of both himself and the world (*Man*, 141). This concrete person, like Lear's therapeutic investigator, does not abandon his subjectivity but raises it to a higher level through the processes of interpretation. Love is thus an active force through which knowledge, emulating the divine, transforms into choice of the particular. In place of the passivity bred through the aspiration for self-sufficiency and the experience "of involuntary impressions," desire, choice, and intention are cultivated such that "free activity blossoms" (*Seek*, 156).

So primary is the "metaphysical principle" of love to Soloveitchik's understanding of autonomy and free will—to man's ethical and psychological nature— that he underlines it as a fundamental principle of Jewish belief: "Anyone who says that Judaism commands the individual to love God but does not promise him reciprocal love is a heretic" (*Seek*, 154). Soloveitchik objects to "earlier scholars" who "suspected that Maimonides" may have "agreed with the teaching of Aristotelian philosophy that the yearnings of the world for God are one-way, without any reciprocal yearnings." Instead, he maintains that God cares "about maintaining a love relationship between Himself and His Creatures" (*Seek*, 154). As in Lear, whose implicit "theological" commitments become clearer in relationship to Soloveitchik's articulated theology, individual autonomy and creativity are dependent on a faith in a precedent, nonhuman source of love, allowing for reciprocal love as well as serving as the internal engine for transformation of the self through the activity of interpretation.

The focus on Soloveitchik's idiosyncratic appropriation of Maimonides highlights the extent to which Lear's psychoanalytic emphasis on love emerges as a radical innovation, as well as the extent to which Aristotle is an insufficient resource for both thinkers. Indeed, although Aristotle may provide the epistemological grounds for a unity of knower and known, only the metaphysical presence of a force of love in the universe turns knowledge into a means of development, for Lear, of psychic transformation. In the rhetorical terms of the argument Lear elaborates, the creative self requires not only the abandonment of Aristotle but the assumption of a force of cosmic love, which shows Lear evidencing unacknowledged theological affiliations, positing, as he does, a metaphysical force in the universe.

Further, reversing the terms of engagement, to the degree that Lear's positing of love, whether of genuine Freudian provenance or not, reads as a non sequitur shows the extent to which Soloveitchik's positing of a Jewish God who loves is an equally startling, indeed, radical innovation, itself an innovative appropriation of Maimonides. That is, the trajectory of Lear's work, from Aristotelian knowledge to Freudian love, has, when read in relationship to Soloveitchik's work, the effect of foregrounding the novelty of a philosophical perspective that posits an actively beneficent and loving God. Coming from the place of philosophy, whether the destination is psychoanalysis or Judaism, a cosmic force of love— Soloveitchik's Maimonidean God of the Torah or Lear's immanent divine force— reads as an innovation. The possibility of individuation depends on the parallel set of innovations in Lear and Soloveitchik, that is, through sublimation and *teshuva*, respectively.

Sublimation

Soloveitchik's stress on the Maimonidean transformation of Aristotelian epistemology permits an understanding of the stakes invested in Lear's metaphysics of love and how the philosophical trajectory of his own work parallels the shift in sensibility from the perspective of Athens to Jerusalem, that is, to a non-Aristotelian epistemology of reciprocal love. Yet more than that, articulating the language of sublimation and employing it to elaborate *teshuva* shows the extent to which the psychoanalytic perspective provides an explication of the Jewish concept, but also how, in some sense, it is a fulfillment of it. Turning toward psychoanalytic languages to understand *teshuva* is not, then, merely an example of translating the Hebrew into the language of the Greek. But in this reading, the psychoanalytic discourse articulated by Lear emerges as a privileged lens for allowing the complexities and nuances of *teshuva* to emerge.

Lear's conception of sublimation, what he describes as "a task of love," the "love manifest in psychological activity," has its origins in Loewald's precedent understanding of the Freudian concept. For Lear, like Loewald, the process of sublimation takes center stage. For the latter, as basis for self-creation, "the transformation" of "unconscious modes" entailed by sublimation is the "original and enduring quest of psychoanalysis" (*Loewald*, 545).[12] For both figures, sublimation entails first the acknowledgment of psychic differentiation, and only subsequently, unification (*Love*, 174, 181). The drives are first acknowledged as a part of the self, though constituted by forces of past psychic history outside of an individual's control. Because of the forces of repression, the drives are alienated, and therefore remain unacknowledged. "Repression," Lear writes in the first person, "is the archaic activity by which I deny that certain drives are part of me" (*Love,* 173). The process of individuation, or the activity of love, initially acknowledges the existence of those drives and psychic forces, desires that may appear at first as "aliens pounding at the gates," and then only later, integrates them into the self (*Love,* 174). The unity of subject and object, here the knowing self and the drives, is achieved through a knowledge based on love allowing, as Lear writes, for "a transformation of the relation" to "instinctual life" (*Love,* 165). The psychoanalytic love that Lear advocates first acknowledges the fundamental difference of the drives, and only then assimilates them into the self. Thus, the acknowledgment of difference precedes the psychic gesture of unification. As Jessica Benjamin writes, advancing on D. W. Winnicott's conceptions of early child development, there is a need for "mutual development." Lear, however, looks at this not as in Benjamin's adaptation of Winnicott's model, intersubjective between mother and infant, but rather intrasubjective between parts of the soul.[13]

Freud's principle, "where it was, there I shall become," is one in which the "given" of the past and the ideal self of the future transform into the self of the present. In other words, the "strangers at the gates"—Lear's metaphor is of the polis—are indeed part of the self and in fact provide the only means through which, to continue the metaphor, the future destiny of the city can be determined (*Love,* 173).[14] That is, the act of acknowledging those "strangers" is the integrative movement that allows the becoming self of ego and superego, or the ideal self, to find its origins in the givens of psychic life. What began in the act of differentiation of different psychic agencies—and cognizing the "aliens" is itself, as an act of recognition, an act of love—transforms into an act of identification, with acknowledgment of what had been construed as the merely "given" as part of one's own "active mind." In Loewald's terms, "unconscious forms of experiencing" are integrated into the "more lucid life of the adult mind" (*Loewald,* 545).

For Lear, this is the paradigm activity of interpretation, understood as internally validating. The "drives," taking the place of the world of living creatures in the Aristotelian world, are themselves agents "striving towards being understood" (*Love,* 215). In another transformation of Aristotelian language, the created world's striving toward intelligibility, the means through which matter acquires form, enabled for him by the particular human capacity to understand, transforms into a *psychic act of unification* through interpretation. With the Aristotelian cosmos internalized, the unconscious "standing" in for God's creation, the subject's "good interpretation . . . both relieves the pressure of an instinctual wish and informs its content." Here subject and object merge internally. The good interpretation, through the right kind of attention, allows the drives to speak, but it is precisely because the subject—or the interpretation—is oriented toward the drives in the right way such that they *can* speak. Indeed, for Lear, "the act of understanding of the wish is also an expression of the wish at its highest form of development" (*Love*, 213). Sublimation in this sense is not the "defensive" translation of the drives or wishes into a foreign register, as sometimes conventionally assumed, but, what Loewald calls "genuine appropriation," the means by which the interpretive act, informed by care or attention, brings unity to the psyche or re-elaborates a unity that, even in its denial, was always already present (*Loewald*, 578).

The human soul, as Lear writes, "is a psychological achievement," and thus the "fundamental issue cannot be merely internal harmony, but whether one has made one's soul one's own" (*Love*, 188). That is, harmony, for Lear, presupposes disparate psychic agencies in relationship, while the appropriation of the soul as one's own—the choosing of the self—also entails an act of unification. What had at first seemed foreign is now, "through the validation of a good interpretation," shown to have, paradoxically, both been given voice to by the activity of interpretation and provided the impetus for it (*Love*, 216). Lear transforms the Aristotelian conception of multiple psychic agencies, finding them unified not in abstract contemplation but rather in an interpretive activity based on love.

Lear's paradigm act of interpretation is also the paradigm activity of responsibility: "There is the relief in taking another step from passivity to activity, from a position in which one's life is lived by meanings over which one has little understanding or control to a position in which one actively lives according to meanings one has helped to shape" (*Love*, 216). Indeed, as Lear writes, it is the act of taking responsibility that defines the interpretive act: "accepting responsibility is an active love" (*Love*, 172). For Lear, this activity as interpretive engagement is rendered most forcefully in his figuration of Oedipus. From a conventional psychoanalytical point of view, Lear writes, Oedipus is viewed as determined by his fate. The "given," past history, is always already present in a way that makes one think—and Oedipus is the paradigm figure—that one's fate is already determined. In Lear's reading, however, whatever the gods ordained, Oedipus nonetheless acknowledges: "the fact is *that I did it*." In the claim at the end of *Oedipus Rex*—"I am Oedipus"—echoing the unconscious utterance of that same claim at the beginning of the play, Oedipus becomes, through the act of responsibility, a "locus of activity," and as a consequence, "demands to be distinguished from the rest of nature" (*Love*, 170–71). The failure of taking such responsibility leaves a person defined only, again in Aristotelian language, "as a potentiality, as something." Lear does not even accord this potentiality human agency: he is only something that *might* come into being (*Love*, 188). One who takes responsibility for the "given"—whether personal history, the drives, or dreams—engages in the active knowledge by which the self is transformed. Lear's Oedipus thus declares: "I am not just a passive sufferer of divine or cosmic forces, I am not just sunk in nature, I act" (*Love*, 171). So, for Lear, a creative relationship to the "given," a responsibility—this is the nature of love—to the drives, is the origin of genuine freedom and individuation. Only love, taking responsibility for the self, allows for the transcendence of potentiality and the possibility of free activity.

The Bonds of Love: *Teshuva*

"From Plato and Aristotle," Soloveitchik writes, to "the psychoanalytic school of Freud and his followers, who sought to probe the depth of man's subconscious, the problem of dualism keeps reappearing and demanding its resolution" (*Man*, 109).[15] In Soloveitchik's writing, this problem is addressed and resolved through the human imitation of divine activity, the act of creation. The creation to which Soloveitchik refers, however, is not Freud's sublimation, but *teshuva*, translated as "repentance," but meaning more literally in Hebrew "return," with a set of resonances rendered clearer in relation to Lear's psychoanalytic register.

Soloveitchik's conception of *teshuva* is one of creative self-fashioning that gives full recognition to the powers of a recondite and even apparently recalcitrant past, the unanalyzed given. In contrast to the normative religious figure, that of Soloveitchik's generic *homo religiosus,* who sees repentance as a function of atonement and of divine agency *alone,* in Soloveitchik's understanding, repentance is a creative act incumbent upon man, presupposing activity. The *homo religiosus,* Soloveitchik writes, "mourns for the yesterdays that are irretrievably past, the times that have long since sunk into the abyss of oblivion, the deeds that have vanished like shadows, facts that he will never be able to change" (*Man*, 113). Psychic history, from this perspective, which is fully part of the past, can only elicit regret. It is a dead mass, with the given never taken up, only in the end to be transmuted by divine fiat. Repentance achieved through atonement "is a wholly miraculous phenomenon made possible by the endless grace of God" (*Man*, 113). But Soloveitchik's true repentant does not "fight the shadows of a dead past, nor does he grapple with deeds that have fallen into the distance" (*Man*, 113). For him, the past is not "irretrievably lost," but rather an intrinsic part of his psychic identity. Indeed, the very idea of *teshuva* argued in *Halakhic Man* (and elaborated in Soloveitchik's essays later collected in *Repentance*) is presupposed on a past that is still in some sense "alive"—for "it is impossible to regret a past that is already dead, lost in the abyss of oblivion" (*Man*, 114). Here the dualism presupposed in conventional conceptions of repentance—including, for Soloveitchik, psychoanalysis—is transformed as the parts of the psyche, associated with aspects of time, merge together.

Freud saw the id as corresponding to the past, the ego as an agent of the present, and the superego as a possible image of an ideal future.[16] As Loewald expresses it, psychic unity is presupposed upon the "interpenetration and mutual determination of the three temporal modes," as well as the psychic agencies with which they are associated (*Loewald,* 546).[17] For Soloveitchik, past, present, and future are separate, but also mutually intertwining. A "person," Soloveitchik writes, "may . . . abide in the shadow of a simultaneous past, present and future" (*Man,* 114). In the conventional temporal model of the relationship between past and future, as Soloveitchik explains it, the past tyrannizes over the future and determines the shape that the future will take. In this reading, the "given determines," through a "causal lawfulness," what the future will be (*Man,* 116). Where past and future remain "living," however, the possibility of the relationship between them creates the dynamic from which *teshuva* and self-creation emerge.

For Soloveitchik, the model of a narrative about the self is borrowed from Jewish national history in which past, present, and future are interrelated, part of a divinely ordained plan. Just as there is an *"eschaton"*—an ideal toward which history tends on the national level, a collective redemption—so the individual elaborates his own *eschaton,* his ideal of a future to which to aspire (*Man,* 118). Through the forward-looking glance in sacred history for the "covenantal community," the moment is altered: "the fleeting evanescent moment is transformed into eternity" (*Man,* 119). In the terms of the literary critic Frank Kermode, chronometric time, *chronos,* is infused with "a sense of an ending," and thus becomes *kairos,* "a significant season."[18] So also, in Soloveitchik's telling of his own story through the activity of *teshuva,* by means of the image of an ideal future, the past is chosen and comes to life, in the process undoing the conventional causal relationship in which past determines future.

The "cause," Soloveitchik writes, "is located in the past, but the direction of its development is determined by the future" (*Man,* 115). Past and future selves relate one to another as interacting psychic agencies. As in Lear's Freudian conception, the Aristotelian conceptions of multiple cognitive agencies are adopted for the working and transformation of the psyche. Both "cause" and "effect" appear in what Soloveitchik calls "active-passive 'garb'"; each influences and is influenced by the other in his version of "intrasubjective" recognition (*Man,* 115). Indeed, past and future, the given of one's personal life and the ideal future image, are attributed agency. The "given" of the past, as Lear would call it, takes its shape from the future—"the future imprints its stamp on the past and determines its image" (*Man,* 115). More than that, however, the past itself determines the future self that will come through the gesture of repentance to shape it. The unifying act of *teshuva* described here does not simply obliterate or flee from the past—in psychoanalytic terms, that would be an "empty hysterical gesture"—but cultivates the resources inherent in the past through which the future, and in turn, a new past are created (*Love,* 179). *Teshuva,* from this perspective, is the art of storytelling, the choosing and re-elaboration of the past, an imperative for narration—the creation and recreation of the self.

Whereas for Lear the right kind of interpretation simultaneously allows the drives to be understood and emerges as a consequence of those drives, Soloveitchik cultivates a similar paradox in which the past self contributes to making the future ideal self, through which a new past and self, as it were, come into being. Past and future are no longer opposed, but there is, in Soloveitchik's conception of repentance in *Halakhic Man*, "a true symbiotic, synergistic relationship" (*Man*, 115). The past is not held at a distant or renounced, as in the more conventional dualist notions of atonement attributed to the *homo religiosus*, but rather cultivated for the possibilities it has within it. To be sure, there are, as Soloveitchik argues in *And from There Shall You Seek*, different "agencies," or parts of the soul that are split one from the other. The prerequisite for psychic unity, what Soloveitchik calls "the bonds of love," is the recognition of that precedent dualism (*Repentance*, 256). In Lear's terms, the "strangers at the gate" cannot be reintegrated into the city without the precedent recognition of their separateness. Unity, in Aristotelian thinking, is always presupposed first upon difference, that is, on granting the "given" autonomous integrity before the act of unification.

This psychic synergy of past and future selves for Soloveitchik has origins in the Talmudic sage Reish Lakish: "Great is repentance for deliberate sins are accounted to him as meritorious deeds" (*Man*, 116). The Talmud goes on to explain that the repentance through which the valence of past activities are reversed and changed from transgression to merit is performed out of "love," allowing the past to be transformed under the interpretive gaze of an ideal future (Yoma 86b). A repentance performed out of "fear," by contrast, may have the effect of neutralizing past transgressions, transforming them into actions that are considered retrospectively to be mere accidents to the soul, not integral to it. But this model of repentance is closer to Soloveitchik's conception of "atonement," where the past ceases to have any living force and is simply rendered null. Repentance out of "love," however, in the Talmud's conception, takes the "given" (or here "transgression") and transforms it into something new. The force of the interpretation tending toward development—the ideal image of the self that is projected by the repenting self—allows for a form of unification, and eventually a change in status of the person: "Man, through repentance, creates himself, his own 'I'" (*Man*, 113).

In the strange causality of *teshuva*, past actions do not bring about future events, but rather the ideal of an unrealized future helps to re-create the past, though attributing to it a trajectory that is *already* implicit within it. As Soloveitchik writes, instead of "event *a* leading to event *b*, event *b* leads to *a*"; a life narrative is not always already determined by past events but is subject to change, even retroactively (*Man*, 115). "Man cancels the law of identity" with *teshuva*. In repentance, the self becomes nonidentical to the self it once was. In other words, *teshuva* activates an aspect of the self, even a self that had once been dormant, "as much as to say," here Soloveitchik writes in the first-person singular, "I am another person and am not the same man who committed these deeds" (*Man*, 112–13). Yet this activity is not a mere assertion—the forced adoption of a new persona independent of recognition of the forces implicit in the self—but rather an achievement of psychic unity, based on not only divine love but also the internal mechanism of love that mirrors it. Indeed, the force of love in the world, so crucial to Lear, present for Soloveitchik simply in the God who loves and chooses his creation, makes it possible for man to manifest a loving relationship to himself. In this sense, man, in imitation of the God who chooses a particular nation (Israel), chooses to choose himself. "A person is creative," Soloveitchik writes, "endowed with the power to create at his very inception" (*Man*, 113).

The "cause" under direction of the "future" can take many paths. The creation of a new "I" occurs by eliciting, and indeed choosing, the "causes" in the past that are already present and that the right notion of futurity retroactively elicits. In this, one hears an echo of Freud's "where id was, ego shall be." For when man, as Soloveitchik writes, "molds the image of the past by infusing it with the future, the 'was' is subordinated to 'the will be'" (*Man*, 117), and the resultant self—the psyche or soul—becomes integrated. This becomes, again to use Lear's psychoanalytic terms, a "re-drawing of the boundaries of the mental" (*Love*, 192). What had appeared to be forces conspiring against the integration of the soul and the creation of a new identity are, in fact, the agents of that internal harmony, resulting in, to adopt the terms of chapter 2, a *discordia concors* of the psyche. The past, as Loewald writes, is "acquired" through the "creative development of the future" (547).

Soloveitchik describes this self as cultivating both psychic and temporal continuity. The integration between past, present, and future in the psyche is made possible by "the never-ending process of self-creation." Without that continuity and the persistent bifurcation between an unredeemable past and an idealized future, there is only the determination by the causality that leads to passivity. "When today and tomorrow are dominated and controlled by yesterday," the "spiritual constancy and continuity" of that "never-ending process," the prerequisite for narrative self-creation, simply "disappears" (*Man*, 122), becoming the equivalent of Macbeth's "tomorrow and tomorrow and tomorrow." In Soloveitchik's model, what amounts to, in Lear's terms, a loving accommodation of the past—its integration with an ideal future—is the beginning of an individuation based on creativity, but also engendering responsibility. "The primary mode of man's existence," Soloveitchik writes, "is the particular existence of the individual, who is both liable and responsible for his acts" (*Man*, 125). In Lear's framework, the achievement of individuation, "determining the shape of the soul," is through overcoming the forces that encourage the individual to abdicate "his conscience to the external world," and to attribute agency to forces beyond him (*Love*, 173, 200). For Soloveitchik, the man who has a "particular existence of his own is not merely a passive, receptive creature" but one who "acts and creates" (*Man*, 125). He is not, as Soloveitchik calls him, a passive "man of fate," subject to forces over which he has no control, but the active "man of destiny" ("Voice," 51). Indeed, the argument for the latter figure in "The Voice of My Beloved That Knocketh" is presupposed on the activity of interpretation, on the transformation of the seemingly recalcitrant "given" into meaning, with the repenting self, Soloveitchik's version of Lear's Oedipus, emerging as an agent of choice and unification. The interpretive powers of the subject are engaged to transform the "given" even, or especially, in "The Voice of My Beloved," the most recalcitrant of the "given": evil and suffering ("Voice," 51–54).[19]

Finally, Soloveitchik's conception of *teshuva* depends, as in Lear's account of sublimation, on rejecting the Aristotelian antecedent, even while embracing it. "The process of development from possibility to entelechy [or actuality] is the fundamental principle of reality" (*Man*, 133). For the Aristotelian, however, the fruition of the contemplative life, the celebration of the "theoretical life," does not entail the realization of "one's own individuality, the potentiality that is latent in matter," but rather "the abstracting of form *from* matter" (*Man*, 133; emphasis added). In Aristotle, according to both Lear and Soloveitchik, there is a movement out of the particular to the abstract form. By contrast, creative action, for Soloveitchik, as for Lear, entails embracing the material given, which is an action presupposed upon love, not its abandonment. For Soloveitchik, the assertion of the importance of activity is reflected not only in the realm of the psyche, the province of Lear's therapeutic action, but also the "concrete normative action" demanded by halakha. Soloveitchik elaborates this identity in the figure of the halakhic man who emulates the divine not only through cognition but love, and for whom emulation of the divine permits the expression of the human—in all of its material particularity and creative activity.

Though the soul, Soloveitchik writes, is grounded, citing a verse in Deuteronomy in "days past" (4:32), the individual "looks behind him and sees a hylic matter that awaits the reception of its form from the creative future" (*Man*, 122). The individual self was shaped by the past, but that self, in its hylic materiality, awaits further direction, a psychic transformation allowed, in Soloveitchik's reading, through the divine precedent of love. In this way, for Soloveitchik, the Aristotelian giving of form is not one-directional: one does not ignore the psychic reality and pull of "days past." The creaturely, in its potentiality a mere Aristotelian factum, something to be acted upon, becomes active. "The hyle in this process of creation, must," Soloveitchik writes, "ultimately be able to act, drawing upon its *own resources*" (*Man*, 131; emphasis added). The self, even as it is transformed, maintains its integrity and particularity; it is not to be assimilated by the universal. Through the image of the future projected back, the self finds, as it were, *within itself*, its own resources. "The individual," as Lear writes, "develops not by abolishing the drives, but by taking them up and incorporating them into the life of the emerging person" (*Love,* 203). So, in Soloveitchik's conception of *teshuva,* the imagined future is generated by the very desires—in his register borrowed from the Talmudic sage, the transgressions—that may have caused a failure of development or the distancing from God in the first place. Those transgressions are not pushed away, but are taken up as, and acknowledged to be, the energies that bring the penitent close to the divine.

As for Lear, Aristotle remains a primary reference point for Soloveitchik, even as his worldview is abandoned. "The dream of the Attic sage is the obliteration of particularity which is rooted in matter" (*Man,* 133). The ideal Aristotelian life—the contemplative one—abandons the particular and the creativity that attends to it for the contemplation of the universal. "The pure, first form does not create," writes Soloveitchik, "therefore, man is not obliged to create" (*Man,* 133). For Soloveitchik, as Lear writes in a different language, "man is a response to love," both a recipient and donor of love (*Love,* 219). Emulating the divine who loves is the beginning of an individuation based on embracing the human, the creative self in all his sometimes recalcitrant particularity. In a similar reversal of Aristotelian conceptions of human fulfillment, for Soloveitchik, it is through *particularity* that man most realizes himself. "With reference to all other creatures," Soloveitchik writes, "only the universal has a true continual existence . . . but with respect to man, individual existence attains the height of true eternal being" (*Man,* 125). Indeed, the universal man, in the continued inversion of the Aristotelian model, is "passive to the extreme" and "creates nothing" (*Man,* 125).

The divine love shown to the prophet, the apotheosis of the creative man, is, for Soloveitchik, not just an ontological privilege, a divine gift, but "dependent on man himself" (*Man,* 134). In an overturning of Aristotle, man realizes his species imperative through the activity of individuation. The prophet, defined as the man who most loves God, employing the cognitive resources of love to unify the soul, becomes, because of these efforts, most beloved by God. In this sense, individuation, as in Lear, is not only a response to love but also elicits divine love. The creature becomes a creator, the "object who is acted upon a subject who acts" (*Man,* 131). A precedent for what Lear calls Freud's innovation of love is, for Soloveitchik and the Talmudic conception his work distills, *teshuva* and a life not only of "cognition and profound understanding," but "creation" and "renewal" (*Man,* 131). That is, the internalization of an epistemology based on love raises the particular as an ideal, with the prophet an individuated agent of choice rather than a figure of the universal. For Aristotle, man's fate as an always "enmattered" being testifies to the extent to which the contemplative ideal, for men of "action" like Lear and Soloveitchik, will always, in some sense, be a failure (*Desire,* 318). Soloveitchik's appropriation and personal transformation of the "halakhic man," starting with *teshuva,* registers a desire for individuation. Against the

Aristotelian precedent, for Soloveitchik, the "life that is best *for man*" is how to best live as "an individual" (*Desire*, 318). The drive for individuation describes the figure of repentance in *Halakhic Man*, but also the trajectory, mapped out in his writings, of Soloveitchik himself.

Reading Soloveitchik through Lear's perspective not only provides a psychoanalytic explanation of a theological mechanism but also serves as an interpretation, using Lear's own hermeneutic model, allowing Soloveitchik's sense of *teshuva* to better speak, rendering his epistemological commitments "understood." Lear's psychoanalytic sensibility based on love emerges, in this reading, as a "fulfillment"—Freud's "phylogenetic inheritance" as a metaphor may not be out of place—of the antecedent rabbinic sensibility that Soloveitchik elaborates. Love as an epistemological category, as well as the embrace of multiple psychic agencies, makes itself present again in Soloveitchik's later works on ethics. In his early works, however, the epistemological category of love and the drive for psychic individuation are in competition with the legal hermeneutics of the halakhic man for whom not love, but rather a melancholy avoidance of love, with its repression of multiplicity, takes priority.

4 Joseph Soloveitchik
A Melancholy Modern

My depression points to my not knowing how to lose.

—Julia Kristeva, *Black Sun*

SOLOVEITCHIK'S DECLARATION IN *The Lonely Man of Faith*, "I am lonely," reads as the culmination of the story begun in the "cold and alien" living room of his grandfather in Pruzhna. The father's hermeneutic triumph may allow for a tenuous and temporary victory of the law, but it leaves the young Joseph vulnerable and agonized, with lingering doubts about the law's efficacy, as well as that of its agent and embodiment, his father, Rabbi Moses. The current chapter first examines Soloveitchik's metaphysical yearning for presence, that is, his desire for the "face to face," with the philosophical acknowledgment that it cannot be fulfilled, in the language he employs—that of Kantian epistemology and quantum physics. The chapter turns back to Soloveitchik's representation of that primal scene, and then forward to his later observations on sexuality, and especially gender as a way of understanding halakha as what Freud calls a form of "compensation." That is, the current argument charts the ways in which the longing for presence that Soloveitchik expressed in his early work (even as he recognizes its impossibility, even undesirability) comes to light in relation to his later explicit writings on sexuality and gender. Soloveitchik's melancholic ambivalence about the figure of law leads to his emerging, always fraught, sense of identity, one that he represents as both distinct from and continuous with the heritage of his ancestors.

Soloveitchik's "melancholy," in my reading, has a double function. His self-professed melancholy serves him in the process of individuation in distinguishing himself from his father and other "halakhic men," while at the same time, as part of the Oedipal rivalry with his father, adumbrating a never fully articulated ambivalence about the law. The previous chapter focused on love and the unity of internal psychic agents; the remaining chapters in part 2 look at Soloveitchik's work from the perspective of not love, but melancholy ambivalence. In the avoidance of love, Soloveitchik's figure of the halakhic man, with whom he ambivalently identifies, deviates from the hermeneutics of the rabbis in part 1 and emerges as a persona embodying the characteristics of the Freudian figure of melancholy. After looking at Soloveitchik's philosophical and theological accounts of presence and loss, I return to the language of Freud's 1915 "Mourning and Melancholy," as well as the post-Freudian commentaries of Julia Kristeva, Hans Loewald, and Jonathan Lear, to more fully understand Soloveitchik as a melancholy modern. The chapter concludes by examining Soloveitchik's melancholy sensibility through the lens of his ambivalent representations of gender. The maternal feminine provides warmth, but threatens the dissolution of the self; the paternal masculine promises autonomy and differentiation through the never-complete compensation of law, but also engenders loneliness.

Convulsions of the Spirit

In *And from There Shall You Seek*, recounting the progress of the type whom the volume editors call "cleaving man," Soloveitchik laments that although the "creation craves her Creator, she nevertheless refuses to open the doors of her dwelling" (*Seek*, xxxvii). The feminine-gendered "creation"—the *Shekhina*—tempts with a fullness of revelation, an opening of her dwelling that is never, and given the epistemological assumptions that inform the work, can never, be fulfilled. Dismissing the efficacy of philosophy in resolving ontological problems, Soloveitchik writes that the "question of whether the Deity's connection with the world is transcendent or immanent is irrelevant." "It all depends," he continues, "on the viewpoint of the individual who searches." Soloveitchik displaces the ontological urgency—is God present in the world or not?—to the epistemological standpoint of the percipient. For Soloveitchik, the question of God's presence is given expression in the contradictory perspectives of the *kedusha* of Jewish liturgy in which God fills the world but also remains distant from it. The liturgical moment provides, for Soloveitchik, a glimpse of how the "eschatological 'tomorrow'" might be linked with the "dismal today" (*Seek*, 83).

Soloveitchik, however, finds a different voice, one that is neither philosophical nor theological, in describing his search for the divine: "The splendor of his majesty breaks forth from every blossoming and every ray of light, from the shadows of twilight and the peacefulness of a clear evening filled with expectation and suspense, from the soft breezes of the spring and the howling of a storm on a weary night, from the silence of the hills and the quietness of the plain" (*Seek*, 22). The nineteenth-century aesthetic idealization of divine presence is qualified: "God reveals himself to His creation, but also eludes it." Following the assertion of divine proximity, Soloveitchik offers a more guarded assessment: "despite his closeness to us, He is boundlessly far from us." "He wraps himself in a cloud," Soloveitchik continues, "and retires to the recesses of eternity." "The Halakha," Soloveitchik affirms, "knows of the *Shekhina* revealed, but also of the *Shekhina* removed." The realization of the inaccessibility of the divine in creation and the sense that man is unable, accordingly, to be "redeemed from his pollution and contamination" means that he cannot come "close to God through creation alone" (*Mind*, 22–23). The openness seemingly promised through contact with the *Shekhina* is never fully realized. Not only does the divine seem to tease Soloveitchik with its presence, but Soloveitchik's own account to the reader does likewise, first invoking the *Shekhina*'s presence, but finally conceding its inaccessible distance.

For Soloveitchik, the divine presence remains subordinate to the legal framework, halakha. It is the "sober, realistic Halakha" that "leads the camp, but also brings up the rear, gathering up the fears of the religious consciousness." Ontology, as Soloveitchik renders it, is subordinated to law, for only within legal discourse is *Shekhina* ever revealed. As in the memory from his grandfather's living room, the divine countenance, when it is present, shines through the mediation of the law, the shining face of the father, the agent of law. The feminine divine presence never made fully present—*Shekhina*—depends for its revelation on that masculine figure of law. In this representation, halakha takes precedence, but also comes as a response—almost as a second thought—to the nearly overwhelming fears of the religious consciousness facing the ontological abyss.

Although there is a compensation provided through revelation, the language of Torah, or halakha, never overcomes the sense of loss or the gap separating creature and creator: the "distance that separates man from the Creator is infinite." "The absolute is totally different from the contingent world," Soloveitchik concedes, "and there is nothing in common between the Creator and anything in his creation." Although there is still the dream of a "living world that sings songs to its Creator," it is covered by a "fixed husk of mechanistic consciousness." The immanence of the divine—the lyricism of creation—is hidden by a "husk" of Hobbesian mechanism (*Seek*, 26). There is, from an elusive perspective, "an unrealized hint" of the divine—a mechanism somehow infused with a living inwardness—but "at the present time," "God is hiding Himself from us because of sin." All "human efforts to reveal God within the creation," must consequently, "end in failure and frustration." Any genuine knowledge of the divine, of an openness promised by an encounter with the *Shekhina* remains unrealized (*Seek*, 22, 26).

As an attack on the subjectivist excesses of the *homo religiosus*, *Halakhic Man* figures as a twentieth-century rewriting of Hayyim of Volozhin's *Nefesh Ha-Hayyim*, the early nineteenth-century Lithuanian attack on Hasidic contemporaries. But more than that, Soloveitchik's thoughts on the question of the immanence of the divine provide a fraught, even anxious, update of the precedent work that holds out a kabbalistic ideal of union with the divine, but in the end affirms the impossibility (and probable prohibition) of such a union. As Shaul Magid writes of the work by Volozhin, the student of the Gaon of Vilna, "the kabbalistic ontology of divine immanence" yields to "the epistemological claim that direct (or even indirect) experience of that divinity is not possible or even permitted." That is, Volozhin, who accepts the kabbalistic mechanisms of *sephirot* and the immanentist ontology that they imply, nonetheless asserts and provides the foundation of the Brisk sensibility that Soloveitchik himself articulates—that such an ontological viewpoint holds "no epistemological implications."[1] In Magid's reading, Volozhin accepts kabbalistic conceptions of the ontological mechanisms of the universe, while dispensing with any putative identification between creator and created that such mechanisms might imply (and did imply to his Hasidic contemporaries). Further, as Allan Nadler writes, the framing of the ontological identification of creator and creation and of spiritual and the material served Volozhin's insistence that "study alone . . . provides for all man's religious needs," and thus "frustrated any more immediate encounter with God in this life."[2] In this reading, Volozhin relies on, and indeed appropriates, the cultural authority of kabbalah, while rejecting Hasidic immanentism and the nondiscursive form of worship, *devekut*, or cleaving, on which it was based. As Magid affirms, *Nefesh Ha-Hayyim*, for all of its apparent accommodation of kabbalistic ontology, turns away from ontological questions, and in giving priority to epistemology, provides a "vehement defense of the discursive view of knowledge," as well as mediated knowledge of the divine.[3]

That discursive view of knowledge and an antipathy to unmediated subjectivity (intent on accessing either nature or the divine) is articulated in Soloveitchik's aggressive philosophical appropriation of Avot 3.8: "He who walks by the way and studies and breaks off his study and says, 'How beautiful is this tree, how beautiful is this fallow,' Scripture counts it to him as if he committed a mortal sin" (*Man*, 85). To the injunction that demands attention to linguistic texts before natural phenomena, Soloveitchik writes, "cognition should precede rapture." Soloveitchik provides a further gloss: "He who reaches a peak of enthusiasm prior to his having cognized, prior to his having completed his study, it as if he has committed a mortal sin" (*Man*, 85). For Soloveitchik, the "mortal sin" belies an epistemological error of hubris, that is, belief in a nonmediated relation, what he calls a "super-noetic" access to reality. The experience of mystical "rapture" involves a betrayal of the belief that there can be no relationship to the physical world outside of the constructs that presuppose only a correlation to the real. In Soloveitchik's reading, "rapture" must be postponed indefinitely because there is no foreseeable end to study. The "study of the Torah is not a means to another end, but is the end point of all desires," the "most fundamental principle of all" (*Man*, 87). The ongoing processes of study and interpretation preclude absorption in a divinely informed reality, indeed postpone ontological longings indefinitely. Although there is the "hint" of divine presence, ontological longings yield to the limitations imposed by epistemology and the priority of law over being. The mystics, Soloveitchik writes, seek "the silence of absolute unity" (*Seek*, 87); the rabbis, by contrast, Soloveitchik emphasizes, affirm that "one should cleave to Torah scholars and those who know God's name" (*Seek*, 88). Against the possibilities of mystical union, Soloveitchik stresses the primacy of the discursive, an always-mediated knowledge.

As Aviezer Ravitzky has written, the *Nefesh Ha-Hayyim* elaborates an epistemology that anticipates and parallels a Kantian one. In Kant's teachings, Ravitzky writes, "knowledge does not penetrate into an independent substance, into the thing-in-itself, but comprehends reality through the intermediacy of *a priori* concepts and forms." According to Ravitzky, human thought in this system is accorded a "creative role," but it is through that creativity, also present in the *Nefesh Ha-Hayyim*, that the "capacity of uniting with the thing-in-itself" and of therefore having the capacity to know "a divine intelligible" is lost. The ideal of unity achieved by Soloveitchik remains in the realm of revelation and the discursive, law alone: there is no merging with the real. In Ravitzky's formulation, "a Kantian revolution" took place in "the world of halakha . . . from its very inception" with Jewish law, through a combination of divine revelation and human creativity, elaborating its own independent and autonomous set of truth claims.[4] Soloveitchik, however, at once celebrates that Kantian revolution while also expressing reservations and ambivalence not present in the antecedent *Nefesh Ha-Hayyim*.

For Soloveitchik, the quantum physicist of *Halakhic Mind* provides a justification for methodological pluralism, but also attests to the break between language and reality asserted in neo-Kantian thought. Likewise, in *And from There Shall You Seek*, the hybrid philosopher-scientist—the "cognitive-scientific man"—produces only "a formal correlative" to the real. "Scientific man is aware of the mutual interconnections of the correlatives," Soloveitchik writes, and he may, at best, expect "the structures of the mind and the sequence of concrete phenomenon" to overlap. Quantum physics, Soloveitchik writes, led to the abandonment of the earlier "copy-realism" of classical physics and began "to regard itself as a postulated discipline of pure constructs and symbols only correlated with the given" (*Mind*, 31–32). The classical scientist had maintained faith in an objective world knowable, indeed accessible, through human constructs; the modern physicist acknowledged that the paradigms and structures of science were themselves merely constructs, artifacts that A. S. Eddington, for example, described as "purely symbolic forms." Soloveitchik cites Max Plank's *Philosophy of Physics*: the physicist, Plank affirms, "merely creates intellectual structures" that are "to a certain extent arbitrary" (*Mind*, 111). The Newtonian philosopher had assumed a perspective of objectivity and a corresponding knowledge of the real; the quantum physicist acknowledges that the scientist and his experimental paradigms create the reality to be perceived. For Soloveitchik, the idealized figure of cognition who brings together subject and object does so only in conceptual or discursive realms. Through Soloveitchik's work, the extreme nominalism initiated by

Hobbes, now filtered through quantum physics, illustrates the break between language and reality.

While his Lithuanian ancestor brackets the possibility of knowledge of an ontological fullness that is acknowledged nonetheless to exist (though beyond the epistemological limitations imposed on man), Soloveitchik less confidently proclaims the inaccessibility of a divine-infused reality. For Volozhin, the concession to epistemological limitations requires living "as if" God, in a reversal of the Hasidic maxim, is *not* immanent. Although Volozhin "believes" in an ontological reality, he acknowledges, to paraphrase John Searle, that ontological reality does not have a point of view.[5] Volozhin's epistemological humility, combined as it was with an almost Romantic confidence in the powers of the creative self, both competed with and tempered the optimism of Hasidic contemporaries who were asserting the identity between conceptual (and linguistic) constructs and a reality infused with the divine. But, for Soloveitchik, even as he eventually celebrates (at the end of the path traveled by his "cleaving man") the mediation of the divine that occurs through law, an undercurrent of lament for the loss of unmediated knowledge of the divine persists.

Despite the "unceasing hope" for the experience of immanence, Soloveitchik also warns of, for those in pursuit of presence, "the clear knowledge of the disappointment that is sure to come" (*Seek*, 78). The achievements of quantum physicists came at a cost, a result of having "despaired" of the efficacy "of any scientific achievements" to reveal the true nature of things, the sad revelation of science's inadequacy. The "deeper truth" has been "revealed to them" that they must "give up the vain attempts of the ancients to understand the essence of phenomena" (*Seek*, 10). The quantum revolution brings with it the traumatic revelation that the real can never be revealed. What remains is only the injunction to "concentrate . . . on creating abstract constructions composed of mathematical formulas," merely "corresponding to concrete objects" (*Seek*, 10). In the perspective of the quantum scientists, Soloveitchik found a contemporary correlate for the theological principle that *Shekhina* is subordinated to halakha, his version of Levinas's parallel principle that ontology is subordinated to ethics.[6] The "sober, realistic Halakha"—a characterization in which echoes of the "sober" Rabbi Moses are present—gathers up those "fears of the religious consciousness," establishing "concepts" that "reflect ways of actualizing the idea of cleaving to God" (*Seek*, 83). The desire for cleaving, the "vain attempt" to achieve unity with creation, is finally abandoned to push off the "despair" that finds compensation, for Soloveitchik, in the law (*Seek*, 10).

Echoing the "despair" expressed in the arbitrary formula of the quantum physicist, Soloveitchik admits a parallel despair in the presence of a creation refusing to yield its secrets. Soloveitchik's questing religious individual enacts a final "surrender" to revelational law, after having abandoned the now-acknowledged "crazy" insistence on believing that man "has the power to come close to God and cleave to Him" (*Seek*, 77).[7] The turn to *imitatio Deo* (imitation of the divine) comes about only as a compensation for the inability to merge with the divine. The "bereft human being," Soloveitchik writes, only "makes do with imitation," an activity that is "intended to compensate . . . for the failure of his aspiration to join together." The imitation of God, the "compensation" for the distance from the promise of union, Soloveitchik writes, entails "an intense effort to overcome the tragedy involved in these convulsions of the spirit" (*Seek*, 78). The answer to the tragedy of divine absence and the consequent fears of abandonment must be the acceptance and internalization of the revelational ideal, through which the questing religious figure in *And from There Shall You Seek* is finally "redeemed." While *Nefesh Ha-Hayyim* revels in the creativity afforded by the "creation of worlds"—the independent innovations afforded through study—the celebration of the creative powers of halakha in Soloveitchik's work of the 1940s remains qualified by a strain of melancholy. The residual despair of the "natural consciousness" that fails in search of concepts adequate to reality renders the experience of taking on the revelational law of the fathers—in Soloveitchik's case, "halakhic men"—as *mere* "compensation," in Soloveitchik's own terms, and in Freud's.

Melancholy Compensations

The story leading from a neo-Kantian (and parallel Brisk) rejection of a connection between concepts or language and the "real" comes to fruition in the quantum physicist's acknowledgment—they are bearers of a sad truth—of the distance between scientific symbols and their correlates. The intellectual history of the concept and the despair over its lack of anything but pragmatic efficacy parallels the personal story mediated in Soloveitchik's philosophical writings and embodied later in what becomes the proud confessional: "I am lonely." For Soloveitchik, after the uncertain and only partial compensation of law, the possibility for self-creation remains his primary consolation. Before the self-consciously theatrical assertion in the *Lonely Man of Faith*, however, Soloveitchik's works register a set of crises that are philosophical, historical, and self-confessedly personal in which loss and melancholy figure prominently. Soloveitchik's story of loss and its compensations—in both personal and historical dimensions—parallels that of the Freudian melancholic.

In "Mourning and Melancholy," Freud elaborates his conception of melancholy through the precedent concept of mourning. Profound mourning for Freud entails "the reaction of the loss to someone that is loved" and a consequent loss of interest in the world, with an inability "to adopt any new object of love" (*SE*, 14:244). For Freud, overcoming the mourning of the lost "object" and the desolation of the world that comes with it entails an acknowledgement of the past and a loss that allows for a partial forgetting and a "working through" such that the ego becomes "free and uninhibited again" (*SE*, 14:245). What Dominick LaCapra calls "a partial leave taking," the simultaneous acknowledgment of loss and movement into the future, are the components of Freud's ideal for healthy mourning, the conceptual underpinnings of what I referred to in part 1 as the hermeneutics of mourning.

Where Freud's notion of mourning, or at least its idealized version, allows for accommodation of an external loss—what Jonathan Lear describes as "the rip in the fabric of life"—in melancholy, the loss is internal, conflicted, and irredeemable.[8] "In mourning," Freud writes, "it is the world which has become poor and empty; in melancholia it is the ego itself" (*SE*, 14:246). As Lear glosses Freud, "melancholia is mourning directed inward," without the benefit of the externalized ritual or psychic processes that allow for productive mourning (*Love*, 159). The melancholic feels absence, but often, almost always, fails to acknowledge the external source for what he experiences as an internal lack.

For Freud, melancholy has its provenance in what he calls an "object loss"— not in the actual death of a figure—but the loss of an "object," most often a parent, through having been slighted, neglected, or disappointed. Thus, the child is abandoned in a prehistory of which he is no longer fully conscious. The child had once had "an attachment . . . to a particular person," but "owing to a real slight or disappointment coming from this loved person, the object-relationship was shattered." In the strange psychic tendency for identification, the ego identifies and internalizes the very "object" that had abandoned him, and in Freud's famous formulation, "the shadow of the object fell upon the ego" (*SE*, 14:249).[9] With this internalization of the other, one aspect of the I "sets itself over against the other, judges it critically, and, as it were, takes it as its object" (*SE*, 14:247). In the complex and ambivalent melancholy psyche, the internalized object, once loved, is now both loved *and* hated; the formally loved object is now hated for having abandoned the self.

In Freud's description of psychic development, the object has been internalized: the hatred for the "object" that has been "lost," as well as the ego's shame for being somehow worthy of abandonment, transform into self-hatred and recrimination. "Reproaches," as Lear explains, "that would have accurately been directed against a loved one" are instead "redirected onto the accuser," that is, upon the self (*Love*, 159). The feelings of loss and anger are internalized, the object casting its ambivalent shadow, but in self-recrimination, manifesting itself in what Freud calls "the circuitous path of self-punishment." The internal drama enacts a strange revenge upon the other by means of punishing the self, manifesting itself in feelings of "shame" and "depression" (*SE*, 14:251). The melancholic, however, evidences a paradoxically strong sense of self, even if it is one that thrives by cataloging his own shortcomings in self-recrimination. He nurtures his ego as an agent of the accusations against himself, but even more powerfully, in his sense of isolated individuality, as testimony to his lonely sense of abandonment and his feeling that the world has both disappointed and betrayed him.

Julia Kristeva, in her version of the primal scene leading to the birth of the melancholy psyche, foregrounds gender; for her, the Freudian lost object is feminine. For Kristeva, like Freud, the "disenchantment" experienced by the melancholy figure in the "here and now" awakens "echoes of old traumas" to which the self has never fully resigned himself, and which, unlike mourning, he has never adequately acknowledged or "worked through." "I can thus," Kristeva writes in the first person, "discover antecedents to my current breakdown in a loss, death or grief over someone or something that I once loved" (*Sun*, 4). This loss is constitutive, for Kristeva, of melancholy subjectivity. The "disappearance of that essential being," or what Freud calls the "object," is, for Kristeva, "the archaic feminine." "The inaugural loss of the mother," as Sara Beardsworth explains Kristeva, remains an absent presence, a lack that "continues to deprive" the subject of "what is most worthwhile" to his identity.[10] The loss of the essential being, or Freud's loved "object," is experienced as "a wound or deprivation." For Kristeva, the state of melancholy entails being in a continual state of loss, or of "not knowing how to lose," resulting from the failure to "find a valid compensation for loss" (*Sun*, 4). This heightened sense of loss and the persistent desire for the archaic feminine constitute, for Kristeva reading Freud, a particularly modern kind of consciousness, with a yearning for the fullness of presence that it intimates but to which it feels itself no longer privileged.

In Kristeva's framework, while the "lost object" is feminine, the masculine, in the figure of the father, provides compensation for loss. Identification with the father is the means, Kristeva writes, "that might enable one to become reconciled with loss" (*Sun*, 4). The mother figure, forever lost as a source of original and primary union, can only be regained as an idealized memory, though compensation is available in the figure of the father and the world of discourse he represents. Identification with the father allows for an imaginary adherence to "another dimension" restoring a bond, though not one of immediacy through the lost object, but through culture—language, art, or law. While the melancholic figure threatens to become "a radical sullen atheist," having lost his belief in the one connection that had sustained him, the compensation of the father—a new bond based on discourse—reminds him of the "bonds of faith" (*Sun*, 4, 13). That is, with the "primary narcissistic identification with the mother sundered," the child enters into the "universe of signs and creation" (*Sun*, 23). The association with this imaginary father as form, schema, symbol, or discourse provides the beginning of a new bond, not to the lost object, but through the mediation of culture and language.

The entry into the "realm of signs" begins with separation and the sense of "lack." The child, Kristeva explains, uses language as a way of providing "symbolic equivalents of what is lacking" (*Sun*, 23). In the melancholic, however, this attempt is always inflected by a sadness that verges on feelings of catastrophic hopelessness. Although there is a "joy" that "settles the melancholic in the universe of artifice and symbol," Kristeva writes, such symbols self-consciously proclaim *their distance* from reality (*Sun*, 23). Like Walter Benjamin's "baroque allegory," the realm of signs—initiating Kristeva's conceptions of the modern—self-consciously proclaims its distance from the reality it is meant to represent.[11] The symbolic realm merely "corresponds" to a "lost or shifted outerness" such that, Kristeva writes, "we are faced with *symbols* properly speaking, no longer with equivalencies" (*Sun*, 23). The move into language—"the artifice of signs"—provides compensation for loss, but, in announcing itself as such, can never be a full substitute for the lost object.

As Marcus Bullock writes, the resources of Kristeva's melancholic to repair "the crumbling and collapsing meanings of the world" into a "nameable melancholia" may help to withstand catastrophe but not to recover the significance and meaning experienced before the original loss.[12] Indeed, the consolations provided by the melancholic's escape into language may displace despair, but they do not provide a way back to the archaic experience of "the real." That is, though the discursive realms associated with the father provide solace, the artifice, for all its consolation, never recuperates the loss of the presence once felt. In some sense, the memory remains residual, always desired. For Kristeva, however, melancholy is not only the province of the therapist who uses it as a diagnostic term to describe the psyche, but also the cultural historian. For melancholy describes a historical subject suffering from a modern form of desolation, not the figure of Hayyim of Volozhin still celebrating creativity in the realm of discourse (law), but certainly his descendant. Notwithstanding the compensations of language, culture, and law, there is a strain of nihilism threatening Kristeva's melancholy modernists—and I place Soloveitchik among them—that emerges from their inability to forget the arbitrariness of the sign in which they have put their faith.[13] Although the faith in the sign is a protection against the despair of disbelief (for Soloveitchik, the power of the consolation of the revelational command), the knowledge that the sign is only arbitrary, an incomplete compensation, remains ever-present and haunting.

Freud's reflections on melancholy might be read—against their grain—as recording not so much the psychic results of personal trauma, but a collective cultural trauma resulting from the catastrophe of World War I. That is, Freud may be projecting his own experience of historical trauma onto the psyche. In this reading, Soloveitchik's three major works of the early 1940s, written during World War II, as well as Freud's "Mourning and Melancholy," written fifteen months after the start of the Great War, share a different and yet in some ways common provenance, with their melancholic meditations centering not on the decimation of the psyche but on Western civilization in general. Indeed, Freud's other works from the period, "Thoughts for the Times on War and Death" and "On Transience" show him, as Peter Gay writes, providing "an elegy for a civilization destroying itself" and facing up to the loss of "so much that is precious in the common possessions of humanity."[14] That is, Freud's works are informed by a sense of cultural upheaval and loss, so much so that the despondency of melancholy rather than the rehabilitative possibilities of mourning becomes, even for Freud himself, the dominant personal and cultural trope. Although Freud writes hopefully that, after trauma, "an acute state of mourning will subside," he also acknowledges that "we shall remain inconsolable and will never find a substitute."[15] In this reading, Freud's "Mourning and Melancholy" itself performs only an incomplete—and melancholic—form of mourning, with Freud himself figuring as one of Kristeva's melancholy modernists.

Notwithstanding the importance of maintaining broader cultural and historical frames, and reading Soloveitchik through the explicit historical and cultural lenses that he raises in his work (in his foregrounding of the Shoah), Soloveitchik's self-representations correspond with the Freudian model of the melancholy psyche. From this perspective, the works of the 1940s are generically works of philosophy, but they also present, as Christopher Bollas might suggest, a kind of memoir, with the explicit family reminiscences, especially of Soloveitchik's father, revealing the paradigmatic tendencies of the Freudian melancholic. The profound sense of loss, the assertion of cold loneliness, and Soloveitchik's self-representation as occupying an alien place show the young Joseph of the story as bereft, with a confused and already ambivalent relationship to his father and the law. In this self-figuration, Soloveitchik emerges as a type of the melancholic Kristeva describes, attracted to the feminine (and the possibility of ontological fullness she offers), but straining to the imaginary father for the compensations and satisfaction of the law. The imaginary associated with the father—for Soloveitchik, the revelational command—may afford such satisfactions, but the melancholy psyche always experiences them as lacking, advertising their insufficiency. Even when the agent of the law triumphs in the central childhood memory, when the countenance of Soloveitchik's father shines, the young Joseph avoids a full identification with the masculine, escaping into the protected and protective realm of the feminine. Although the father is the source of salvation, he remains both threatening and distant. The love of the mother, through both her consolation and admiration, as in Kristeva's account, allows the father's authority to come into being (her space guarantees that authority), but the always precedent identification with the feminine, for Soloveitchik, shows the compensations of the masculine to be precarious (*Sun*, 13).

True, Soloveitchik, in one of the few places he writes explicitly about Freud, emphatically distances himself from psychoanalysis, specifically the ambivalence Freud attributes to the melancholy personality. In emphasizing the distance between the Jewish and Freudian conceptions of the emotions, Soloveitchik writes that Judaism's conception of "emotional experience" belongs to the "interpretive" realm, and thus "has nothing in common with the Freudian concept of ambivalence, the interpenetration of love and hate." While the melancholy personality is confused by a simultaneous love and hatred for his parents, what Soloveitchik calls the "ethecized emotions" do not allow for such a mixture. Freud's notion of "ambivalence," Soloveitchik continues, is "immediate, primordial, direct," and finally, he says of the father of psychoanalysis, "unanalyzed." For Freud, as Soloveitchik reads him, "in the very essence of the feeling of love, there is a hidden resentment and hate" such that one "loves and hates at the same time." On this very point, he distances his own Jewish or halakhic view. "We must not," Soloveitchik warns, "speak of ambivalence in a Freudian manner—since the emotions themselves do not interpenetrate" (*Whirl*, 188–89). There may be, for Soloveitchik, a dialectical and interpretive conception of the emotions, but they must never mix or remain unresolved in relation one to another. In the text of 1915, Freud writes "hate and love contend with each other," but these contrary emotions are to be assimilated, according to Soloveitchik, to his category of the unreflective "mood," uninterpreted and therefore unredeemed.

Although neither Soloveitchik nor his contemporary editors note the place of this engagement with Freud, Soloveitchik shows both his engagement and explicit distancing from Freud in the encounter with "Mourning and Melancholy." Although Freud is rarely mentioned in his works, Soloveitchik's essays collected in *Family Redeemed* show a persistent interest in sexuality, gender, and the relationship between parents and children, and show him trying to redeem those categories from their vulgar, unredeemed, Freudian inflection. Indeed, the title for the collection of essays might well have been modified to be *Family Redeemed from Freud*. That is, despite Soloveitchik's explicit rejection of Freud, his later essays, including the figuration of his identity in them, emerges from Freudian coordinates. Soloveitchik's anatomy of gender in the late works provides a means by which to unpack the unstated ambivalences of his early work, as well as to understand his progressive self-creation as a figure who, through his own Freudian-inflected self-fashioning, both fulfills and undermines the legacy of the halakhic man.

For Freud, from his beginnings in the trauma of felt abandonment, the melancholy self simultaneously experiences "opposed feelings of love and hate" that either instigate or reinforce "an already existing ambivalence." Soloveitchik's explicit rejection of the emotional complex of the Freudian melancholic and such "ambivalence" demonstrates resistance to a model with which he identifies as he distances himself from it, an example perhaps, paraphrasing Hamlet's mother, of Soloveitchik "protesting too much." That ambivalence—to the maternal, which tempts with its presence but never fully reveals itself, and to the paternal whose compensations are insufficient, and even sometimes punishing—shows itself implicitly within the narrative of *And from There Shall You Seek* and more explicitly in the later works about sexuality and gender.

To affirm this argument about Soloveitchik is not to reject the ideal model of the emotions that Soloveitchik proposes but to explore the way his relationship to the masculine and feminine inform his conceptions of language and interpretation. Indeed, I am suggesting that the model of the "dialectics of the emotional experience" and the common emphasis seen in the previous chapter in processes of both *teshuva* and sublimation on "attention to opposites" is accompanied in Soloveitchik's work by an unarticulated ambivalence, in which the "harmony of opposites" remains "impossible" ("Majesty," 25). In other words, though Talmudic conceptions of interpretation are best understood through the mourning—partial leave taking—of Freud's early essay, Soloveitchik's conceptions of tradition and interpretation, as they are both explicitly rendered and "idealized" in narratives about family and gender, are better approached through Freud's complementary notion of melancholy.[16]

Masculine/Feminine

Soloveitchik's ambivalence expresses itself in relationship to the halakhic man—the figure of mastery whose strong compensations are a cause for joy, as in the first part of Soloveitchik's youthful memory where his father triumphs, but also self-avowedly affirming their inefficacy, indeed their inadequacy to fully summon presence. Indeed, the feminine provides solace, recalling a fantasy of presence, understood here as the residue of Freud's primary object or Kristeva's archaic mother, for which the mechanisms of law provide, in Soloveitchik's writing, their celebrated but always uncertain "consolation." In this way, Soloveitchik's later writings on gender can be read as retroactive glosses on the story in *And from There Shall You Seek*.

In the *hesped*, or eulogy, for the Talne Rebbetzin of 1977, Soloveitchik turns to the language of gender to re-elaborate the problem of divine presence, already suggested in his more philosophical earlier work.[17] For Soloveitchik, the idealized feminine figure offers a shadow of a primal unity once felt, a memory of immediacy now only nostalgically recalled. The eulogy, though focusing on the feminine, provides a typology both of the feminine and masculine, the former associated with the presence of the *Shekhina*. The feminine of which the "Rebbetzin" becomes an embodied type is associated for Soloveitchik with the "presence of God" ("Talne," 78). "I learned from her," he writes, "the most important thing in life—to feel the presence of the Almighty and the gentle pressure of his Hand upon my frail shoulders" ("Talne," 77). Dwarfed by the divine, here figured as masculine, the feminine is remembered, or idealized unambiguously, as a figure of "warmth"—the provenance of Soloveitchik's self-conceived "Torah of the heart" of which he confesses himself to be an inadequate transmitter ("Talne," 77). Like his "own mother," Soloveitchik writes, she taught him "how to feel the presence of God" ("Talne," 78). In the account, the typology of the feminine extends from the Talne Rebbetzin to his mother, to the biblical matriarchs:

> Consciously or unconsciously, I greeted not only her, but her mother and mother's mother, the entire community of mothers who kept our tradition alive. I felt as if all of them had been assembled in the dining room of the Rebbetzin, as if Shabbat ha-Malka herself had been present there. The room looked the way I imagined Sarah's tent must have looked. I was enveloped in a cloud, and there was the burning candle, there was the *Shekhina* . . ." ("Talne," 82–83).

Soloveitchik's summoning of the Talne Rebbetzin extends to generations of mothers: the congregation of the feminine transforms from the Talne Rebbetzin's dining room to the matriarch Sarah's tent, and from there to the enveloping cloud of the divine feminine, the *Shekhina*. The early memory in *And from There Shall You Seek* describes an intergenerational gathering of fathers and sons. In the eulogy, however, there is no corresponding community of women but a community of mothers, abstracted into the presence of the pure feminine, the divine presence. In Freudian terms, the description summons the fantasy of feminine presence, Kristeva's archaic mother, distilled into idealized images that are both personal and biblical.

For Soloveitchik, the construction of the feminine is not independent from that of the masculine; that is, masculine and feminine are complementary opposites, as in his childhood recollection, in which mother and father, in narrative terms, occupy different, but complementary spaces. Though for Soloveitchik, as he writes in another context, masculine and feminine ideally merge, for every person partakes of characteristics associated with the male and female.[18] Without, he confesses, the teachings of his own mother, "quite often transmitted to me in silence, I would have grown up a soulless being, dry and insensitive" ("Talne," 77). In contrast to the welcoming and nondiscursive warmth of the feminine, the masculine is, by implication, not only "dry and insensitive," but "soulless." The father is associated in Soloveitchik's eulogy—in some ways mourning not only the Talne Rebbetzin but the feminine itself—as the origin of "an intellectual moral tradition." "One learns much from the father," writes Soloveitchik, for he is responsible for entry into literacy, "how to read a text—the Bible or the Talmud—how to comprehend, how to analyze, how to conceptualize, how to classify" ("Talne," 76). The father initiates the son into Kristeva's imaginary, the languages of law, but also analysis, conceptualization, and classification, which serve, in Freudian terms, as "compensation" for the nonpresence of the idealized and therefore never fully accessible feminine.

As Soloveitchik continues, the father initiates the child into the realm of the "moral." "One also learns from father what to do and what not to do," Soloveit-chik writes, "what is morally right and what is morally wrong" ("Talne," 76). The compensation of signs—here, language, morality, and law—is also a tradition of discipline. Identifying, in Jacques Lacan's term, with the *nom-du-père* (the name-of-the-father) and the compensations it offers entails also accepting, in the in-tended Lacanian pun, the *non-du-père*, that is, the "no" of the father.[19] The father "teaches the son discipline of thought as well as the discipline of action" ("Talne," 76). There is, accordingly, a price to the identification with the compensation the father offers, for Soloveitchik, the law as Halakha. Literacy, the prerequisite for moral and legal education, comes with the implicit cost of distinguishing oneself from the feminine—perhaps renouncing the feminine—even, Soloveitchik im-plies, with the consequent risk of becoming soulless, dry, and insensitive. The entry into the realm of the masculine, the discursive sphere, has its rewards, but also implies a renunciation, paradoxically, for Soloveitchik, enacted in the ideal-ization of the feminine.

In a parallel typology of gender in the essays collected in *Family Redeemed*, Soloveitchik provides an explicit meditation on motherhood and fatherhood.[20] "The spiritual essence of man differs from that of the woman," Soloveitchik writes, and "the divergence in metaphysical spirituality finds its expression in the incom-mensurability of the motherhood and fatherhood experiences" (*Family*, 160–61). "Father and mother should each act," he writes prescriptively, "in singular fash-ion." "I cannot help associating," he writes, as he elaborates on the feminine, "the Talmudic phrase *meshadalto bi-devarim* with the import of the Biblical phrase *yeled sha'shu'im* (Jer. 31:19), a child with whom one plays, with whom one laughs, jumps, dances, sings and cries" (*Family*, 161). For Soloveitchik, the Talmudic em-phasis on play is associated with the feminine love of the mother bestowed upon her son. In contrast to that maternal love, Soloveitchik writes, which "consists of *shiddul*, embracing, dandling, playing—the father is engaged in a different activ-ity, teaching him Torah" (*Family*, 161).

Although Soloveitchik anchors his types in both Talmudic and biblical sources, the inflection of what he considers to be a traditional Jewish anatomy of gender is no less significant, revealing more than just a normative account of gender differences but a sense of the particular (and personal) nature of his gen-der "archetypes." In his reading, "the father disciplines the child while the mother affectionately plays with him." Initiation into Talmudic knowledge involves discipline; the mother's activity with the child cultivates the realm of play. That is, the "stern father" stands in contrast to the mother figure who both provides affection—her "outpouring of love"—and cultivates play (*Family*, 161). "Father," Soloveitchik writes in his typical typological language, "despises weakness, hates cowardiceness" (*Family*, 169). "The eye of the father," he writes, "is focused upon the objective expression of faith, the eye of the mother upon affection and love" (*Family*, 180).

The contrast, however, between the different relationship that the mother and father evidence toward the child, Soloveitchik writes, is not "*prima facie* a contrast at all." In Soloveitchik's account, as in the Freudian one in parallel ways, the mother and father take central roles in relation to the child's life at different times: "The mother dandles and plays when the child is very young, whereas father enters the scene as educator and disciplinarian at a much later stage, when the child begins to mature" (*Family*, 161). Upon reaching boyhood maturity, "the mother discontinues playing with the child and most probably restrains herself from showing her affection." The child, normatively masculine, Soloveitchik matter-of-factly affirms, "simply outgrows all this" (*Family*, 161). From a Freudian perspective, it is not that the child has outgrown these affections but has already identified with the father and embraced the discipline, the Lacanian nay-saying that necessarily entails renouncing the presence and pleasures—the play—that the mother affords. In Soloveitchik's rendering, however, though the child has given up the pleasures of the mother, the mother herself *has not*.

The mother "never stops dandling her child" and "never ceases to be affectionate and loving even though the child is a full-grown person" (*Family*, 161). In Soloveitchik's depiction of the mother–child relationship, the latter becomes indifferent; indeed, one can read him as evidencing annoyance at the continuing attentions of the mother. Even when the mother restrains herself and "does not engage" in such behavior physically, "she is preoccupied with all this inwardly, in thought" (*Family*, 161). Preoccupied, even longing for her adult child, she bears a state of mind that contrasts with that of the young man whose indifference threatens to render the continued affection irrelevant. Paralleling the gender antithesis outlined in the eulogy, "father and mother move in two opposite directions"; the father "keeps on moving away from the child," while the "mother continuously moves towards him" (*Family*, 162). Further, the mother and father occupy and enact opposed, if not mutually exclusive, principles. The father is "preoccupied with disengaging himself from" his son; the mother, by contrast, in a striking formulation, "with attracting herself to her child." The mother is represented as "refusing to let go," unable to "perform an act of withdrawal" (*Family*, 162). The mother and father thus have opposed projects: the father moves toward a planned and determined separation from the child, while the mother shows the need for further identification, achieved by an even unconscious desire to keep her son in her sphere of influence.

In Soloveitchik's gender anatomy, the father's emphasis on differentiation cultivates autonomy. As educator, he initiates the child into language, while also distancing himself, allowing, even promoting, "independence and maturity." The father's act of self-distancing, however, is insufficient. He must also help the child distance himself from the always-present, however repressed, designs of the maternal. "The mother holds onto the child"; "her desire," Soloveitchik writes, "is always to be a part of him." She thus "surges steadily towards her child," for "she can never forget the biological fact that her child was once a part of her, that she gave him her blood" (*Family*, 162). She actually "resents" the efforts of the father to nurture "her child's adulthood and the independence that education is supposed to promote and foster" (*Family*, 165). The fantasy of unity between mother and child attributed in Soloveitchik's account of the mother is expressed by an internal voice that Soloveitchik both recounts and translates: "When she says: 'My baby,' she means to say: 'Once we were one body. I gave you life. We together were involved in the same organic process'" (*Family*, 162). In *Halakhic Man*, Soloveitchik had already written of the relationship between mother and child as "an ontic community . . . which spells the oneness of existence" (*Man*, 81). In the latter work, the bond between mother and child takes on greater urgency with the memory of their organic unity together in "one body." In Soloveitchik's construction, the mother nostalgically recalls the former nondifferentiation between mother and child: "we . . . had a wonderful time, playing, laughing, jumping, running, and he was then so innocent, so pure, so babyish" (*Family*, 165). The father represents differentiation, the mother a remembered identity that, from the point of view of the "indifferent" adult son, may be a risk to his further development. The organic unity of mother and child is based on the mother's recollection of her experience of the child's prehistory; that memory, however, makes no claim on the developed child, represented only as a possible impediment to his proper development. There is, in Soloveitchik's rendering of Freud's Oedipal triangle, to adopt the Sophoclean personae, only a Jocasta who continues to long for her son.

D. W. Winnicott has argued that an infant's first experiences are indeed of mythic wholeness, of unity with the mother, but with their origin not in a prebirth biological union, but rather early infantile experience. Winnicott, following the Freudian precedent, focuses on the subjective position of the child, not the mother. With the sundering of the union once experienced by the child comes the beginning of his sense of an independent world, with the mother emerging as the child's first "object." But for Winnicott, it is the "good-enough mother" who is the primary agent in the early psychic processes that cultivates the beginning of selfhood.[21] That is, the maternal, unlike in Soloveitchik's account, is an agent of psychic differentiation for the child. She achieves this by being present to and identifying with her child, as well as by becoming a reliable separate, differentiated entity, responsive to the infant. The "good-enough mother" guides a process of development in which the child starts by feeling merged (a paradoxical preidentity before the child has any sense of "I"), and then leads into separateness and the beginnings of autonomy, the formation of which is presupposed upon play.

In Soloveitchik's genealogy of the child, however, the archetypal feminine is associated only with primal merging, that original organic unity that remains, as Soloveitchik represents it, a *maternal* fantasy, not a lingering fantasy, as Winnicott has it, of the child. Unlike Winnicott's "good-enough mother," for Soloveitchik, the mother figure is alternatively both too good (in the promises she offers) and also therefore never good enough. The father, emphatically, in Soloveitchik's account, educates his children for independence, expecting them "to learn to act on their own, to utilize the counsel they are given gratuitously, to take advantage of the opportunities and finally to attain complete independence and maturity" (*Family*, 162). The mother solicits, indeed encourages, a return to an infantile, if not primal, unity. The father's gifts, by contrast, seem almost begrudging—those gifts are given "gratuitously"—for his fundamental attitude, though described as "love" is really one of "recoil" (*Family*, 162). While "faith and belief satisfy the father," they "do not make mother happy." She only wants her child to "be near"—here familial and theological languages overlap—and "welcome her presence" (*Family*, 180).

The opposition between father and mother is continued in their respective attitudes to the marriage of their (male) child. The father encourages the autonomy required for matrimony: "He works hard to liquidate the very community which he formed." The mother, by contrast, never having "reconciled" with the biblical decree of marriage, "resists any effort aiming at the dissolution of the parent-child community" (*Family*, 165). In Winnicott's elaboration, in contrast to Soloveitchik's account of childhood development, though mother and father occupy different places, both parents—the feminine and the masculine—participate in the processes that lead to differentiation and autonomy. That is, the cultivation of the subject is not only the province of the masculine, but begins with the feminine and the capacities for creativity and independence she cultivates. Notwithstanding her dual role in Winnicott's account, the memory of the original merger between subject and object—between child and mother—lingers, though, again, not in the mind of the mother but in that of the developing child.

The memory of the identification with the feminine, as Evelyn Fox Keller writes, explaining Winnicott's provenance of early subjectivity, may be threatening to the developing and still "fragile ego." As recourse against the power of primary identification the masculine child feels in relation to the feminine, he turns "toward the father" for "protection" from that "fear of re-engulfment." The father, as Keller relates, stands for "individuation and differentiation," warding off the seduction of an earlier identification with the archetypal feminine, thus removing the danger of returning to a psychic prehistory before the emergence of the child's identity.[22] Freud referred to "the primary narcissistic unity of the infant-mother matrix" as providing, explaining the mystical religious experience of his friend Romain Rolland, "an oceanic feeling" to which the child both wishes to return, and at the same time, in the name of personal identity and autonomy, escape (*SE*, 21:68). In Keller's reading of Winnicott, the child retains agency in this developmental drama. The lingering power of the mother–child relationship emanates from the child with his desire to overcome the boundaries of identity that separate him from his mother. In Soloveitchik, perhaps as an indirect response to the Freudian model of the Oedipus complex (or simply its repression), the drama is played out one-sidedly among the parents, with the child merely reactive to the alternating tendencies of paternal recoil and maternal desire for union.

For Hans Loewald, similarly, the child's "primary narcissistic identity with the mother," a name for the desire for union attributed by Soloveitchik to the mother in early childhood, emerges later in life, but as both seduction and threat. The child's desire to return to that primary identity—to reexperience the "oceanic feeling" of connectedness and unity—"is also the source of the deepest dread." That dread of being subsumed through a regression back to infantile union leads the child to seek protection through the identification with the father, bringing about, in the end, "the ego's progressive differentiation."[23] In all these Freudian accounts, the father figure and the compensations of language and culture present the child with an alternative to being engulfed in the feminine. In Soloveitchik's account, the father's command—his moral insistence—also requires a renunciation of the feminine, perhaps already enacted in the assertion of adolescent indifference.

From this psychoanalytic point of view, the idealizations of Soloveitchik's eulogy for the Talne Rebbetzin may be read as showing the son's desire for the archetypal feminine (and for the community mother and son maintain against the father's desire to liquidate it), but, at the same time, the son's ambivalent renunciation of that fantasy union of "warmth" in favor of the discipline of the father. Soloveitchik's description of the persistence of maternal longings—her continuing occupation with attempts of attracting herself to her child—might be read, from this psychoanalytic perspective, as enacting a displacement of Soloveitchik's continued attachment to the feminine (his desire for presence), reinforcing, albeit unintentionally, aspects of Winnicott's story of childhood development, as well as the Freudian emphasis on ambivalence. That is, the representation of the apparent indifference of Soloveitchik's developing child toward the maternal—"the child simply outgrows all this"—may indicate the already precedent identification with the language of the father, the renunciation the masculine requires. But the consolation of the masculine has its price, affiliating oneself with the *nom-du-père* means saying a decisive "no"—in this case, to a feminine unity that remains both a temptation and an obstacle to the differentiation required for individuation. So Soloveitchik remembers his father teaching him "self-control," citing the prohibition of adultery in Exodus 20:14 as simply

"You shall not desire" (*Vision*, 65). In this reading, it is not the mother, who represents an already irrelevant threat to the normative developing child as in Soloveitchik's explicit account, but the repressed desire for the feminine providing the reason for its necessary bracketing. Soloveitchik writes elsewhere, providing his own Freudian gloss on the ostensible indifference of the maturing child: A "man desiring a woman is overcome by fear," which is based on an "implicit feeling of blameworthiness" because the "sexual experience is a guilt experience, a lust experience." "This explains," he continues, "the unnatural behavior exhibited by adolescents when their sexual instincts begin to awaken"—one of which may be the indifference Soloveitchik attributes to the developing child (*Family*, 85).

While the father seeks dissolution of the family unit, even its "liquidation," the heroic feminine for Soloveitchik is the woman who "clings courageously and tenaciously to that community whose liquidation would spell disaster." She further "refuses to accept her destiny and to surrender her baby to another woman," heroically preserving the relationship to the child: she "clings to it." At the prospect of her male child's marriage, she feels a resentment bordering "on enmity towards her daughter-in-law, since the latter is the one who is blamed for destroying the community" (*Family*, 165–66). In this version of the family drama, the relationship between mother and son is primary—with their partners, the father and the intended spouse and daughter-in-law, threatening that privileged primal unity. Soloveitchik thus represents the masculine and feminine as opposites, with allegiance to the feminine impossible for the developing (male) individual and allegiance to the soulless masculine, equally problematic, thus recapitulating the dilemmas of Freud's melancholy psyche, played out first, for Soloveitchik, in Pruzhna. The eulogy's idealization of the feminine may well reveal Soloveitchik's ambivalent desires for a unity that the fantasy of a community of mothers absorbed into a mythic biblical past already acknowledges as impossible. That is, the fully fledged fantasy of the feminine, in a paradoxical way, neutralizes what Loewald describes as the child's dread of being subsumed by the feminine.

For Soloveitchik, himself, however ambivalently, insofar as he sees himself as living out the legacy of halakhic man, there can be no full return to the feminine; its continued presence only serves as a reminder of a desire never to be fulfilled, a presence never fully encountered. In this way, Soloveitchik's representation of gender encourages an oscillation between two polar sets of associations, what Keller calls the "pleasures and dangers of merging" with the feminine and "the comfort and loneliness of separateness" of the masculine, the beginnings of melancholy.[24] Identification with the masculine puts an end to the painful dynamic of apparent revelation and concealment produced by the continued pull of the feminine. Yet for Soloveitchik, the differentiation tending to individuation never leads to full identification with the masculine but rather to loneliness and melancholy. As in Kristeva's account, the consolations that the father offers are never fully satisfying; indeed, for Soloveitchik, they are sometimes even punishing.

The unresolved anxieties about the relationship to the feminine leads the melancholy male, not fully consoled by the compensations of the father, Keller writes, into "postures of exaggerated and rigified autonomy and masculinity" so as to counteract "the anxiety and the longing that generates it."[25] That is, anxiety about the feminine, based on a continued longing for presence that remains unsatisfied, leads to the eventual identification with the father and adoption of an aggressive masculine pose, and what follows, exaggerated assertions about the power of forms of knowledge identified with the masculine. With this comes both new confidence (even, as in Kristeva, a new faith), but also, in the realization and despair of the imaginary father's inevitable insufficiency to capture the real (associated with the presence of the archaic mother), melancholy. This melancholy informs Soloveitchik's confession of failure to pass on the "Torah of the heart" and the implicit acknowledgment that with the identification, however incomplete, with the father, he was perhaps not feminine *enough* to convey the "personal warmth" associated with a community of mothers. Alternatively, in a paradoxical appropriation of the authority of the father, Soloveitchik disavows—and indeed recoils from—his followers for failing to live up to that legacy of the heart. For Soloveitchik, the aggressive assertion of the knowledge of the masculine—the continued assertion and even adoption of the prowess of the halakha man as a man of cognitive conquest—is accompanied by a conscious appropriation of melancholy, which becomes a means by which he distinguishes himself from the inheritance of his father.

Lonely Man, Unapologetic

The later works on family demarcate Soloveitchik's conceptions of gender, allowing, as I have been arguing, for a retroactive reading, eliciting the melancholy ambivalences already present in his works from the 1940s. This is not only to understand Soloveitchik's assertion of the impossibility of gaining access to an "impenetrable reality" in terms of the gender distinctions articulated in the later works. But even in the early works, Soloveitchik's identification with the divine law and the figure of his agent halakhic man is presented ambivalently. In response to the figure described as the one who recoils from his son, family, and the feminine, Soloveitchik begins to cultivate a space for himself presupposed upon the melancholy rejection of the stringencies and inflexibilities of the father.

One who "does not feel," Soloveitchik confesses in the narrative account of *And from There Shall You Seek*, "the pincers of the revelational distress compelling him to adapt to the laws and statues imposed on him by a separate authority is liable to disgrace himself in public" (*Seek*, 54). Affiliation with law entails an almost masochistic relationship to a fear-inducing authority that causes both "distress" and "shame." What I have been calling, after Kristeva, the compensation of revelation and the affiliation with the imaginary father and the law is tied to avoidance of the continued identification with the feminine, but it also initiates a process of affiliation in which shame and a sense of inadequacy emerges in relationship to the masculine. In Soloveitchik's account of the stages that lead to the internalization of the revelational compensation, he writes: "At first it seems to him that the response does not fit the question." "Man," Soloveitchik continues, "wants to understand the real world, and he is given knowledge of a revelational, supramundane command" (*Seek*, 126).

The prayer for "intellectual enlightenment," the desire for access to the "real," is refused, accompanied by the rebuke, "as if," Soloveitchik writes, "God were laughing at him" (*Seek*, 126). The divine laughter mocks the "natural consciousness," which seeks solace in the natural world, or, in the gendered terms of Soloveitchik's later works, the figure who continues to seek satisfaction from the feminine. God's laughter also echoes that heard by the young Joseph, always ready to seek the solace of the maternal, when he imagines that those in his grandfather's house are mocking him and he entreats the masculine assembly (and perhaps his reader as well): "please don't laugh at me." Beneath the acceptance of revelation and its eventual celebration lies the fear of not being equal to the masculine community of the law and its moral imperatives.

The shame present in *And from There Shall You Seek*, with its anticipation of public disgrace as echoed in the primal scene, has a further iteration in the 1959 essay "The Redemption of Sexual Life." Offering another implicit response to Freudian attitudes toward sexuality, in this essay, Soloveitchik, self-professed "lonely man," describes shame, but now from a perspective external to the father, as a cultivated defense mechanism protecting him "against intrusion from the outside" (*Family*, 80). Shame here transforms into a mark of distinction that "prompts him to withdraw into seclusion," a protection against the "state of insecurity'" (*Family*, 80). Such insecurity arises from external forces, as the expectation of the law and the potentially punishing father, the guardian of the revelational command, are once again invoked. This shame, Soloveitchik writes in the first person, brings him "to an awareness of culpability, to the knowledge that I am not the one I should have been, that I failed to realize what was expected of me, that I lead a disappointing existence" (*Family*, 80). Shame, Soloveitchik continues, owing much to the Freudian superego, is the expression of the moral consciousness that condemns man because of an "unfulfilled norm, an unrealized ideal, an aspiration which did not come true, or a wrong of which one is guilty" (*Family*, 80). Soloveitchik expresses a sense of "culpability" for not living up to a moral norm, to the law bequeathed by the father, "to the knowledge that I am not the one I should have been, that I failed to realize what I was" (*Family*, 80).

Soloveitchik reveals a consciousness of his inadequacy in relation to the external masculine norm. His feeling of shame stems, further, "from the realization that people [are] reading my thoughts, which ruminate on the fantastic and illusory" (*Family*, 82). Outsiders either intuit an internal "self-disapproval," an "apostasy or lapse from a higher existence" or "disapprove," as Soloveitchik writes, of his "daydreaming," that is, his "identification with an imaginary self" (*Family*, 83, 82). One form of disapproval is the knowledge of the self's recognition that it has failed to meet the ideal, the other the external disapproval of his pretension and presumption to have already met them. The latter functions as a gloss of the depiction of the youthful Soloveitchik on his bed, daydreaming of the Rambam, not risking the revelation of his fantasies with his father, who might reject his "musings" as both "childish and unrealistic" (*Family*, 82). In other words, the young Joseph fantasizes the disapproval of his father at the pretense of his belief that he is part of the masculine community of interpreters, part of the chain of tradition in which his father and Rambam participate. In this light, Soloveitchik's rush to his mother reveals his sense of inadequacy in relationship to that imagined judgment. The praise for the father, voiced from within this feminine context, represents an identification with the masculine, but as voiced from the province of the feminine, already shows Soloveitchik's implicit sense of failure to live up to paternal expectations.

The inchoate sense of shame, however, registered in the early memory later becomes an enabling form of self-identification. The young Joseph fantasizes that he is part of the tradition of the Rambam, but he will eventually adapt an identity different from those available in his grandfather's living room, one inflected by the feminine. For the model of the halakhic man is one of epistemological certainty, conquest, confidence, gendered as masculine, but also dispassionate, disinterested, and "soulless." The cultivation of the private, a defense against intrusion from the outside in the later work, spells out a partial refusal of this masculine realm, already adumbrated in the representation of the makeshift study in Pruzhna. The lonely man, Soloveitchik confides, "wants to retain his spiritual aloneness and meticulously watches out against the inquisitive eye which tries to disturb his privacy" (*Family*, 83). That figure thus proclaims, "I am lonely," nurturing his privacy and solitude (albeit in a very public manner)—a secluded place associated, for him, with "the tragic note in the feminine," serving as protection from the father and the shame the paternal identification induces (*Family*, 120). "I am lonely," from a psychoanalytic perspective, stands as part of Soloveitchik's assertion of individuation, an emphatic proclamation: "I am not my father."

Soloveitchik expresses not only the loneliness that he felt on his bed in his grandfather's living room but also his "embarrassment," which is later transformed into a positive mark of distinction—his own mark of Cain: "The man who has overcome all doubts concerning his self-worth and has found meaningfulness and purposiveness in his life is not as subject to embarrassment as is the person who is still locked in the moral struggle with life's problematics, perplexed and interwoven in the fabric of his existence" (*Family*, 80). Embarrassment, no longer a sign of shame, a function of the father's intrusive judgment, becomes a mark of distinction—of moral struggle and existential authenticity. The emphasis on a distinctly feminine interiority embodied in a struggle with life's "problematics" is not just evidence of an existentialist turn, but a turn away from the masculine triumphalism that rejects interiority as shameful, unmanly, and fantastic. Sometimes associated with the feminine (his and Rambam's shared tears), or simply unsuitable for the masculine sphere of cognition, this realm is one that Soloveitchik embraces as a means of distinguishing himself from the certainty embodied in the father. Representing himself as "perplexed," Soloveitchik declares publicly that he is not like his bold and brave father and the tradition of halakhic men that the latter represents.

By *The Lonely Man of Faith*, this perplexity has been transformed into a spiritual authenticity that leads to a divine service, both superior and more distinguished, than that of the father: "I despair because I am lonely and, hence, feel frustrated." "On the other hand," Soloveitchik continues, "I also feel invigorated because this very experience of loneliness presses everything in me into the service of God" (*LMF*, 3). Shame, a function of the father's recoil from the son, imposed from outside, has been internally transformed, thus invigorating a new service of God. Soloveitchik, asserting an identity between man and God as lonely figures, transforms them both into figures of existential solitude in extremis. So Soloveitchik compares himself to the Adam of Genesis: "In my desolate, howling solitude, I experience a growing awareness that . . . this service to which I, a lonely, solitary individual, am committed is wanted and gracefully accepted by God in his transcendental loneliness" (*LMF*, 4). *Imitatio Deo*, for Soloveitchik, means a cultivation of loneliness in the divine image. He thus pursues loneliness as a form of self-creation, as an ideal that brings him closer to God, in contrast to the "majestic man," but also, by implication, his father and those Brisk ancestors whose experiences are foreign to the existential authenticity he alone cultivates. Shame transformed into "self-reserve and hesitancy" is, in Soloveitchik's new persona, "connected with the experience of reverence" that "brings home the smallness of man facing the great incomprehensible, exalted and mysterious." Shame internalized becomes the precondition for an epistemological "humility" expressing itself in the very unmasculine trait of "shyness" (*Family*, 80). To adopt Shira Wolosky's terms, Soloveitchik's feminine "break and interruption within the self" as a form of "self-limitation" becomes a condition for a new kind of self, for Soloveitchik's own self-creation.[26]

The lack of full satisfaction with the "compensation" of the father, or what might be described as Soloveitchik's "recoil" from his father, is writ large already in *And from There Shall You Seek* in the strategy of transforming distance from "the real" into a virtue. True, Soloveitchik writes of the eventual unity that is achieved by the acceptance of the law, that "the wonders of the creation and the command from Sinai begin to gleam" and "illuminate man's entire being" (*Seek*, 126–27). But the "absolute imperative" does not always live up to the precedent claims of unity and the emphasis on "total compulsion" emphasizes a severe arbitrariness of the law, betraying a "despair" similar to that experienced by quantum scientists in their reluctant acceptance of the merely symbolic nature of their equations. Soloveitchik acknowledges that the law's "subordination to a priori postulates" is "bounded by a categorical restraint" that both "begins and ends with the system" (*Seek*, 108–9). Although the halakha evidences "systematic consistency, at least the equal," Soloveitchik adds, "of the other abstract and precise intellectual disciplines," that consistency is qualified by acknowledgment of its arbitrariness. Indeed, while there is "marvelous freedom" in halakhic thought, Soloveitchik already laments in the 1940s, it cannot "control its own postulates" (*Seek*, 108). The arbitrariness of the sign and the remembrance of the "pincers" of "revelational distress," announces, in Kristeva's terms, the always-partial satisfactions in the compensation of the law of the father.

Soloveitchik claims that the fulfillment of the arbitrariness of the law's commands is itself a source of pleasure; indeed, his praise of the arbitrary nature of the halakhic system presupposes that the greater the gap experienced between God and creation, the greater the service of the divine. In *And from There Shall You Seek*, he writes that "the heavy weight of laws and regulations" are themselves "an intensely attractive force that raises the individual from the mire of impenetrable reality" (*Seek*, 128). The pleasures associated with union with "the real," which are also associated with the "deepest dread," are now relinquished in favor of an allegiance to the law and the form of individuation that such affiliation permits. The "attractive force" of the law supplanting the pleasure of ontological union, now rendered as the "mire," a minatory corollary of Rolland's "oceanic feeling," takes precedence. For Soloveitchik, after the disappointment that follows the failure of union, the "revelational statutes are the individual's pleasures and sole comfort," no matter how threatening. The residual longing for that reality, however, whether in the language of "natural consciousness" or in the gendered terms of *Family Redeemed*, make Soloveitchik's affirmation that "the more salient the 'pointlessness' of the law, the more heartening the experience" seem to lack full conviction, or, in the Freudian term he rejects, ambivalent (*Seek*, 129). Indeed, the rejection of this "mire," which parallels the rejection of a sexuality associated with "anomalies," "guilt," "lust," and "crime," entails embracing the compensations of the law, now described in Soloveitchik's strangely refined aesthetic register as "heartening" and "delightful" (*Seek*, 129). For all of the Kantian trappings to Soloveitchik's celebration of the autonomy of the law, he continues to grapple with its arbitrary nature—the Brisk embrace of *hukkim*—as a form of what Kristeva calls a *mere* sign that fails to deliver a lost presence. That the compensations are described in the highly refined language of the "beautiful" may, as we shall see in the following chapter, help mask their inefficacy, as well as a melancholy shame in not fully embracing them.

Before the giving of the law, man is Soloveitchik writes, "unafraid and unworried that God may dictate, demand, force, reprove and punish" (*Seek*, 48).[27] But the law associated with the uncompromising father—and the distress, even the "fear of annihilation," he incites (*Seek*, 49)—finds Soloveitchik cultivating the personal space of the melancholic, advertising his existential authenticity in distinction to the punishing and "soulless" sensibility of the father. Indeed, there is a parallel, for Soloveitchik, between the God capable of annihilating his creation, and the father wanting to liquidate the relationship with his son, explaining, in Soloveitchik's works, the persistence of that protected personal space, often gendered as feminine, the provenance of a different form of individuation. The ideals that inform that melancholy personal space are fully articulated in discursive terms in Soloveitchik's elaboration of ethics; they are the means through which he reframes halakhic men in his own image, the subject of chapter 6. But it is to the origins of Soloveitchik's ambivalence about the law, expressed in *Halakhic Man*, and the reception history of that work, to which I now turn.

5   Beyond the Law

Repentance and Gendered Memory

> I am going to tell you what I am not;
> pay attention, that is exactly what I am.
>
> —Jean Hyppolite, "A Spoken Commentary on Freud's *Verneinung*"

THE TWO PREVIOUS chapters informed by different methodologies—from inside and outside the hermeneutic circle—present Soloveitchik as a figure driven toward the unity of love with regard to epistemology and the psyche, while also expressing ambivalence to love in relationship to the law. In the current chapter, I focus on Soloveitchik's most canonical work, *Halakhic Man*, which reproduces this split, with its articulation of a repentance based on love and its simultaneous affiliation with the figure of law, the latter guided by principles antithetical to the creative psyche. The reception history of that work—with its first publication in English in 1983—reflects, in fact also reproduces, that tension. In the reading put forward here, *Halakhic Man* provides both a memorial and testimony to the older worldview of the "halakhic men" of Europe (as well as Soloveitchik's ambivalent allegiance to it), but also strongly resists the categories his Brisk ancestors bequeathed to him.[1] The ruptures in that text—not to be assimilated to the category of dialectical tension—elicits its fraught reception and shows Soloveitchik's (not always successful) attempts to appropriate and transform the history, as well as the hermeneutic methods, that he inherited.

Reception

In a 1996 retrospective on Soloveitchik's works, Shalom Carmy writes that among the most significant of Soloveitchik's legacies is his "keen awareness of the complexity inherent in moral and religious existence," as well as his own "tireless commitment to make that complexity real."[2] In actuality, however, as Lawrence Kaplan observes, the attempts of various students and followers to embody Soloveitchik's ideals—to manifest that vision in cultural or institutional form—has been the compromise of complexity. As Kaplan writes, "different elements of the modern Orthodox community" have focused on aspects of Soloveitchik's teachings they find "intellectually or religiously congenial and gloss over those aspects they find uncongenial." Commentators on Soloveitchik, Kaplan writes, break down into "opposing camps," and each, he writes, not surprisingly, "dismisses those features stressed by the other as secondary."[3] In Alan Yuter's more recent formulation, Soloveitchik has become "a culturally validating icon," though for various groups—Kaplan's "'camps'"—often with radically different agendas.[4] For Kaplan, the "real task" of contemporary inheritors of Soloveitchik's legacy is to "avoid the oversimplifications of both left and right and to arrive at a portrait of him that will do justice to the complexity and multi-faceted nature of his teachings." Those who emphasize only the figure associated with the Brisk dynasty and the language of the traditional yeshiva world, for example, are actually the "mirror image," Kaplan claims, of the revisionists on the left who emphasize Soloveitchik's modernity and, among other things, his commitment to the languages of Western philosophy.[5] These polemical opposites, in Kaplan's reading, do not qualify each other, but reinforce one another in their extremes.

From Kaplan's point of view, Soloveitchik should be classed with that group of thinkers, as I write in the introduction, who, as Stephen Marcus and Charles Taylor affirm, acquire a "dichotomous image" in their reception history. John Milton is paradigmatic among such figures who, long before Kaplan writing about Soloveitchik, acquired a dual reputation based on the warring "camps" of critics that followed him, who claim his epic poem *Paradise Lost* either for orthodox Christianity, or, as the poet William Blake would later have it, for "the Devil's party."[6] To pursue the parallel, Soloveitchik is variously celebrated as both an apotheosis of the teachings of the more traditional Brisk dynasty, and on the other, as departing from traditionalist and conventional orthodox agendas.[7]

Through the course of his career, David Hartman enacted this phenomenon in his work, describing two versions of Soloveitchik—first, the innovating advocate of modernity, and then later, the staunch, even recidivist, defender of an inflexible traditionalism. In a 1990 work, Hartman constructed a contemporary Judaism in relation to a decidedly nontraditionalist Soloveitchik, a figure described favorably as "the poet of the Law," able to integrate the "modern values of creativity and autonomy" within "a halakhic culture," likely the figure whose energies stood behind the flourishing of the institutions in Jerusalem under Hartman's name.[8] Two decades later, however, this modernist figure of creativity had devolved for Hartman into a traditionalist whose "God of Halakhic Permanence" does not sanction "human 'empowerment'" but only "surrender and self-sacrifice."[9] Hartman reading Soloveitchik gives voice to the alternative, mutually exclusive visions of his teacher, usually enacted in the critical agon between critics.

Underlying Kaplan's analysis of Soloveitchik's split legacy, however, is the conviction that, from some perspective, Soloveitchik's works are in fact unified.

Kaplan's approach, traditional among Soloveitchik's students, is one in which the term "dialectic" is said to govern over, and ultimately unify, Soloveitchik's wide-ranging, and in his reading, only *seemingly* contradictory concerns. As Alex Sztuden, the most recent apologist for Kaplan and this approach, writes, "for Kaplan, the inconsistency in Soloveitchik's writings is due to the dialectical, tension-riddled nature" of his thought and the "various conflicting ways in which the religious personality experiences the world."[10] For Sztuden, the complexity of Soloveitchik's thought has been rendered by various followers into parallel and equally unsatisfying shorthand versions, reducing an original complexity into opposed often polemical perspectives, all claiming Soloveitchik as their origin.

By contrast, David Singer and Moshe Sokol, already in 1982, emphasized not the unified but bifurcated nature of Soloveitchik's work, underlining the disparity between the rationalist legal language of his works from the 1940s and the more emotional aspects of *The Lonely Man of Faith*. As Singer and Sokol write, "the Litvak" (or Lithuanian rationalist) in Soloveitchik "is determined to make things as difficult as possible for his non-Litvak," that is, the more emotional "side." For this early pair of critics, Soloveitchik's work evidences a continuing battle between the rationalist agenda of the Lithuanian master of Brisk and the emotional side that, for them, comes to fruition in the *Lonely Man of Faith*. Rebelling against a critical reception of "adulation" already in place, Singer and Sokol identify the gap between what they call Soloveitchik the "Talmudist" and Soloveitchik the "existentialist." For them, Soloveitchik's theological concerns are not only "characterized by tensions and polarities," but also "outright contradictions."[11] Marvin Fox, perhaps predictably, provides the normative response of Soloveitchik's students at Yeshiva University to Singer and Sokol (as Kaplan does later) by affirming the unquestionable "unity" of Soloveitchik's work, preserving a traditional version of "the Rav," the persona governing over the dialectic always said to be present in his work.[12]

Placing himself outside of the circle of conventional interpreters of "the Rav," Dov Schwartz, in his comprehensive recent work on Soloveitchik, identifies contradictions in *Halakhic Man* itself and not just the oeuvre as a whole. Anticipating Schwartz, already in 1993, Allan Nadler had attributed a bifurcated rhetoric if not sensibility to the work, pointing to the gap between its "theological originality and modernity" and the "ascetic and pessimistic spirit of the *Mithnagged* Man," the latter the type for Soloveitchik's often-invoked Lithuanian rabbinic ancestors. For Nadler, the anecdotes from both the earlier sages, but especially the "family's repository of oral history," primarily serve as a rhetorical function: "to lend precedent and authority" to Soloveitchik's "original construct of the halakhic personality." In Nadler's reading, Soloveitchik's gesture toward his Brisk ancestors gives authority and credibility to his innovations.[13] The dissonances present in *Halakhic Man* are merely instrumental, indicative not of substantive contradictions in the work, but rather Soloveitchik's deliberate rhetorical strategy.[14] Against those who have "casually accepted" Soloveitchik's representation of his ancestors as faithful, Nadler maintains a vision of Soloveitchik's originality as a modern thinker, assuming cultural authority through the figures of Brisk he invokes. For Nadler, as for Fox, Soloveitchik, outside of the rhetorical imperatives informing his work, remains a "pristine practitioner" of what William James calls "the religion of healthy mindedness," with Soloveitchik himself an "exemplar of the united self."[15]

Schwartz's reading of Soloveitchik, following that of Nadler, also foregrounds contradictions internal to *Halakhic Man*, not just in the incommensurability between Soloveitchik's own philosophy and those of his Brisk ancestors, but in the gap between the figuration of halakhic man and his more emotive antitype *homo religiosus*. Schwartz rejects Kaplan's strategies in resolving Soloveitchik's "incongruities and contradictions," and indeed the critical consensus and "accepted convention" in accepting the "harmonic model" dominating Soloveitchik studies (*Religion*, 13). While Nadler argues for the invocation of the Brisk world to give credibility to Soloveitchik's contemporary innovation, Schwartz argues that any presence of *homo religiosus* (and the emotional life with which that type is associated) comes only as a concession to a "modern religious world" that "perceives subjective religious feelings as constitutive of religious existence" (*Religion*, 18). Soloveitchik, Schwartz affirms, wrote for an audience of Americans at midcentury for whom religion was best, if not only, understood in emotional terms, and *Halakhic Man*'s sympathetic portrayal of the emotional life serves as a concession, an attempt to "market" religion as "an attractive alternative" to a possibly recalcitrant New World audience (*Religion*, 32).

Schwartz reads Soloveitchik through a Straussian lens, as writing to his own version of John Milton's "fit audience though few," including the "discerning reader" who will understand that "no essential relationship exists between halakhic man and *homo religiosus*" (*Religion*, 5).[16] "My central assumption," Schwartz writes, "is that this penchant for apologetics moved R. Soloveitchik to adopt an esoteric style, and the authentic messages intimated in his words can only be understood by reading between the lines" (*Religion*, 8). Schwartz's strategy in understanding a text that he concedes *appears* to be contradictory is to argue that the incongruities are intended, that the essay is itself "pervaded by deliberate contradiction" (*Religion*, 30).[17] Soloveitchik "*wishes to create an impression* of synthesis out of a dialectic and harmony of opposites" (*Religion*, 13). Although Soloveitchik's writings "*openly* strive to attain a balance," the balance achieved is a function of "an apologetic writing style," demanding "at times . . . departures from the absolute truth" (*Religion*, 34). The dialectic, Schwartz concedes, may be present in the rest of his work, but in *Halakhic Man*, the "dialectic" is "set aside" to present the "one-dimensional figure of halakhic man" (*Religion*, 228).

Schwartz at once acknowledges a bifurcated text, as had Singer and Sokol decades earlier, illustrating through his readings a surface text fraught with more profound discontinuities than encountered by previous readers of Soloveitchik's work. Like Nadler, however, Schwartz affirms the unity of intention, albeit an intention manifested and sometimes occluded by a rhetoric only to be understood by the rare discerning reader with ties to Soloveitchik's European heritage of learning. As Schwartz notes, "the outstanding scholars and *yeshivah* heads of the Brisk dynasty are a minority" (*Religion*, 30). Although Schwartz introduces a Freudian language—"the features of *homo religiosus* persist in repressed fashion in halakhic man and threaten to erupt at all times"—his Soloveitchik, as Straussian author of *Halakhic Man*, retains supreme rhetorical control (*Religion*, 13). More so than the authorial figure hypothesized by Kaplan whose "dialectical, tension-riddled" writings, according to Sztuden, reveal different "experiential modes of being," Schwartz's Straussian Soloveitchik deploys contradiction as part of a deliberate strategy of apologetics.[18] The Freudian language of repression employed by Schwartz is not one presupposing unconscious agency but rather a hyperconscious sensibility aware of tensions, resolved to repress them.

Reading what Alan Yuter calls "ambiguities" as Freudian ambivalences, I suggest that Soloveitchik is not always the figure mastering and conquering, as he claims, the existential rift. The very predominance of metaphors of conquest—in Soloveitchik (as well as among his followers)—suggests ambivalence about the final achievement of such conquest and the "synthesis" it is meant to entail. This is not to suggest, as Blake said of Milton, that Soloveitchik is of "the Devil's party without knowing it," but rather that ambivalence about the figure of halakhic man (and the law) characterizes the work that bears his name. The argument I make here elicits that ambivalence not only through the family stories that have been marshalled to show the halakhic man in an ambivalent (even negative) light, nor because of the sometimes ambiguous status of the *homo religiosus*, but rather because of the resistance *within the work itself* to the halakhic norm. Even as Soloveitchik argues for the priority of the norm, or what he calls the internalized "revelational statutes," his works register the persistence of the very forces of otherness that the norm is meant to hold in check. The figure of the halakhic man, in textual cruxes of the work, shows itself to be an insufficient power to control the forces Soloveitchik himself acknowledges as foreign to the halakhic norm.

In *Halakhic Man*, Soloveitchik evidences melancholy ambivalence about the law similar to that articulated in *And from There Shall You Seek*, with his canonical work emerging, in this reading, as an unintentionally bifurcated work. I am suggesting here that the gap that Singer and Sokol find in Soloveitchik's oeuvre, is present in *Halakhic Man*, not a function of rhetoric or apologetics, but reflecting a sense of ambivalence about a version of the law centered on what Soloveitchik calls *hok*, or arbitrary decree. Most important for this reading, the principle of repentance that he develops in the second part of the work, I argue, is not in consonance with the sensibility of the "halakhic men" he invokes throughout the first part of the work, but is, in fact, radically discontinuous with them. It is true that creativity, the autonomy Soloveitchik locates as central to the principle of *teshuva*, also informs, indeed defines, the typological halakhic man. Soloveitchik's innovation of creative repentance, however, discussed at length in chapter 3, appropriates the Brisk *hiddush*, understood as a hermeneutic principle, but for the life of the psyche. As I argue in the next chapter, Soloveitchik's post-Holocaust writings on ethics, also centered on the psyche, are presupposed on the same assumptions that enable the innovative conception of repentance, which also resist, and even stand in opposition to, the halakhic man's cognitive and legal certainties.

Indeed, the halakhic man of Soloveitchik's typology in the first part of *Halakhic Man* does not have the psychic resources required of the man of repentance described in the book's second part, with its noteworthy title, "His Creative Capacity." In this second part, Soloveitchik delineates a halakhic theodicy in which the authority of law is undermined by the summoning of foreign agencies, even though eventually, at least formally, the law is affirmed.[19] Through Soloveitchik's selective reading of the Talmudic accounts of the founding of the Temple in Jerusalem, his ambivalence toward a law not fully able to accommodate the psychic forces opposed to it once more comes to the fore. In other words, Soloveitchik shows himself struggling with the incongruities (and in so doing, manifesting the Freudian ambivalence he denies) between the sensibilities of the halakhic men of part 1 and the creativity he himself advocates in part 2 of the work.[20] Even as Soloveitchik expresses an unconditional allegiance to the law, there are undercurrents in his work suggesting the law's inefficacy, or at least the law as imagined by his forbearers. The chapter concludes by returning to repentance, which emerges, for Soloveitchik, as the apotheosis of creativity for a transformed version of the halakhic man. Not only, as Nadler suggests, does Soloveitchik abandon the theological imperatives of his Brisk predecessors, but in creating his conception of repentance, he forges a personality whose psychic resources are radically different from those of the ancestors he describes in the first half of the work. The current chapter concludes by elaborating *teshuva* through the Bergsonian conceptions of time invoked in *Halakhic Man*, and retrospectively through the gendered conceptions of time and memory of his later work. Soloveitchik's creative repentance emerges in this reading as presupposed upon the feminine and the assumptions about time, memory, and narrative that inform it—distinct as they are from those of halakhic men.

Dark Back Streets

In Soloveitchik's 1944 work, he refers consistently to the prowess of the halakhic man, the masculine figure of conquest "who knows no fear or dread"; it is rather the *homo religiosus* who is poised between "desire and dread" (*Man*, 67, 72). When the halakhic man "approaches the world, he is armed with weapons—i.e., his laws—and the consciousness of the lawfulness and order that is implanted within him serves to ward off the fear that springs upon him" (*Man*, 72). The figure of the law takes on a position that is confident, assured, even aggressive, though the aggressiveness is itself put in the service of pushing off the always-lurking threat of existential fear. Soloveitchik's primal scene—its dual nature—suggests that fear, dread, and even catastrophe are never far off from the aggressive masculine stance of the triumphant Brisk interpreter. Armed with his laws, the figure of halakhic man, however, encounters a world that is rendered devoid of mystery, for it is already subsumed to the conceptual categories at his disposal: "Halakhic man does not enter a strange, alien, mysterious world, but a world with which he is already familiar through the a priori which he carries within his consciousness" (*Man*, 72). The masculine law—the language is of aggressive conquest—commands over the very "alien" world in which Soloveitchik remembers to have suffered as a boy. Here, what Kristeva calls the consolations of law are substantive, as the alien world is rendered knowable, able to be domesticated through interpretation. For all of its avowed emphasis on contingency, however, "the gritty realia" that the halakhic man is said to encounter, are themselves subordinated to the "practical halakha," not of the world itself (*Man*, 85). Like mathematicians who "pay no attention to concrete correlatives," so the halakhic man seeks "only to establish a relationship of parallelism and analogy" (*Man*, 19). The world is merely the correlate of those a priori conceptions—in Soloveitchik, transformed into revelational statues—that preexist the moment of perception. This figure, like that of his father in the Feinstein home, is neither known for his "modesty" nor his "humility"; indeed, his "most characteristic feature is strength of mind" (*Man*, 79). There is no doubt, only the certainty of his categories. Certainty makes him one who "reigns over all," and moreover, one who is "esteemed by all" (*Man*, 81).

When the halakhic man "comes to the real world," he has created his ideal, "a priori image, which shines with the radiance of the norm." Embodying the Kantian philosophical correlate of the shining face of his father, the halakhic man undermines the dualisms of Christianity through the encounter with the "empirical world," and in the explicit register of *Halakhic Man*, the sanctification of that world. But that encounter does not, avowedly, "impose upon him anything new" (*Man*, 81–82). The halakhic man's encounter with the contingency of the empirical is paradoxically also an escape from contingency—or the "mire," as he calls it—and that which is alien or mysterious (*Seek*, 128). The resistance to the particularity of the world is reflected in the halakhic man's similar resistance to internal complexity, that is, to a sense of otherness within. The halakhic man of this description does not "waste time" with "spiritual self-appraisal or on probing introspection," for he is not concerned with the intricacies of the psyche, but dedicated only to "knowledge and cognition" (*Man*, 74). The figure of the halakhic man is not in the class of people Soloveitchik writes about in *And from There Shall You Seek*, those who deal with life's "problematics." Although the *hiddush*, or creative originality, is present in the interpretive realm, there is no genuine encounter with the new, either empirically or psychically.

Cognition—and here again the description of his father in his grandfather's living room-turned-study emerges retrospectively as being paradigmatic and precedent—is a matter of mastery. "The mysterious relationship in effect between the cognizing subject and object that is comprehended . . . results in man deeming himself lord and master with respect to the thing that is about to be comprehended" (*Man*, 73). The subject constructed in the antecedent *Nefesh Ha-Hayyim* is a maker and master of worlds; the halakhic man reaches these heights through the processes of cognition defined as mastery, as the kabbalistic powers of the knower are given a philosophical—a neo-Kantian—force. "Knowledge by definition," Soloveitchik writes, "is the subjugation of the object and the domination of the subject" (*Man*, 73). This conquest leaves the halakhic man triumphant, "adorned with the crown of absolute royalty" (*Man*, 71). The inheritor of the worldview of the *Nefesh Ha-Hayyim* is the halakhic man, Soloveitchik writes, with his triumphant powers: "the whole of transcendental existence is subjugate to him and under his sway" (*Man*, 82).

With his cognitive prowess and the law at his disposal, the halakhic man professes himself "unfamiliar with the dark back streets of defilement," never finding himself "astray in the blind alleys and narrow pathways of the world's emptiness and chaos" (*Man*, 72). Soloveitchik imagines contemporary Jewish life, as Ken Koltun-Fromm writes, through the image of the "depraved, primitive city," and the halakhic man creates a "religious cartography" that both confines and subdues terror. The alien world, "the urban dross," is exiled; Soloveitchik's "mire" rendered habitable; and the world that is alien to the strictly rationalist vision of the cognitive man renounced. But Soloveitchik's halakhic man—unlike his predecessors for which the work is a testimony—acknowledges that emptiness even in its denial, for the terrors of the urban landscape still remain beyond the boundaries set. The "structures of containment" serve only "to limit fear and anomy," but do not eliminate them.[21] In the 1944 work, the assertiveness with which the halakhic man claims to be distant from the "world's emptiness and chaos" suggests a consciousness of the world that may not be so readily subjugated.

To be sure, in the normative argument of the text, as in *And from There Shall You Seek*, something like a halakhic alchemy "sanctifies the profane, purifies it of the pollution it has absorbed, and refines being of the dross and baseness that human calculation have introduced into it" (*Seek*, 132). Indeed, the triumph of the norm—rendered through the metaphor of alchemy—transforms the world into something "beautiful, finished, and adorned" (*Man*, 72–73). Notwithstanding the confidence of the halakhic man in this transcendent triumph of the revelational statues and his ability to absorb and sanctify the empirical world, the residual presence of emptiness and chaos remains. In Soloveitchik's rendition, that is, the norm only incompletely assimilates the "baseness and dross." Thus, even in the early works of the 1940s, there are two voices: the normative voice of the halakhic man, associated with Soloveitchik's uncle, Velvel, and his father, Moses, and another voice resisting the authority and worldview of the halakhic man that the book celebrates and memorializes.

Those two voices are present in the paragraph that ends the work in which Soloveitchik, writing in a confessional mode, admits that his account of the halakhic man is unfinished and that his "essay" "is but a patchwork of scattered reflections, a haphazard collection of fragmentary observations, an incomplete sketch of but a few of halakhic man's features" (*Man*, 137). Soloveitchik goes beyond conventional tropes of humility in describing the book as one that is "devoid of scientific precision, or substantive and stylistic clarity" (*Man*, 137). Indeed, Soloveitchik ends the work that celebrates the cognitive exactitude and precision of his ancestors by foregrounding his own ostensible lack of clarity, his failure to live up to their ideals. The admission may be more than just a conventional rhetorical trope, evidencing his feelings of inadequacy and anxiety in relationship to the task of presenting halakhic men, as well as a self-conscious hesitation to define himself in their terms. It is true that Soloveitchik's professed "sole intention" is to "defend the honor of the Halakha and halakhic men," not just as an abstract type but as particular men (*Man*, 137). Schwartz reads this as a straightforward assertion of Soloveitchik's aim for the book—to preserve the name and reputation of his Brisk ancestry for a postwar American context (*Religion*, 32). The rhetoric and argument of the text, however, suggest Soloveitchik's less-than-straightforward embrace of the sensibility of the halakhic men of his past, even a distancing from them, perhaps an acknowledgment that that the book bearing their name would likely disappoint them.

Like the Joseph of the biblical story, mentioned in the book's epigraph from the Talmudic tractate Sotah, Soloveitchik sees himself as failing to live up to his father's expectations: "at that moment the image of the father came to him and appeared before him in the window."[22] When the biblical Joseph is tempted by Potiphar's wife, he envisions his father, and thus wards off the temptation of desire. In a book that begins and ends with fathers, it is not only a matter of upholding the Brisk tradition, as Singer and Sokol claim, but with the epigraph, Soloveitchik upholds the continuity of the Brisk tradition against the temptations associated with excesses—the "dross" and "baseness" of desire—not to mention the feminine, which elicits them. The Talmudic epigraph thus renders a rabbinic version of the Lacanian father's "no," with Soloveitchik, emulating the Joseph of the biblical story, identifying with his father, whom, as another midrash claims, he resembles—though Soloveitchik's rhetoric at the end of the book suggests perhaps not enough.[23] *Halakhic Man* shows Soloveitchik both struggling to live up to his father's image, and, at the same time, evidencing only an ambivalent identification with that image.

Soloveitchik's early works reflect the persistence of "dross," even as they assert the primacy of the Kantian a priori. That is, the halakhic man may be a creator of worlds, but there are constant reminders that the a priori categories do not assimilate, and at times, do not even take into account the "real": "Physico-mathematical science encounters the living, qualitative reality; metaphysics encounters the blind and impenetrable substance, mechanical nature; morality encounters sin and evil; art encounters the ugly and repulsive, *and so on*" (*Seek*, 127; emphasis added). Even as Soloveitchik asserts the triumph of the revelational norm, his prose shows the extent to which the phenomenal—the real, evil, the repulsive—exist independently, and are even "indifferent" to that norm. Soloveitchik's halakhic man faces a world unknown to the *Nefesh Ha-Hayyim*, and perhaps even unknown to the "halakhic men" of his immediate past, rendering his idealizations and symbolic correlates less assured. That is, he represents the halakhic man as a master of classification, but also shows an awareness of resistance to his classificatory schemes. The "and so on" serves as a marker of that excess, testimony to the refusal of the norms he insists on asserting and thus an acknowledgment of their precariousness. The inheritor of the worldview of the *Nefesh Ha-Hayyim* may affirm the unambiguous triumph of the halakha, even as his representations of the law attempt to assimilate a reality that shows itself distant from it.

Soloveitchik's modernist contemporaries embraced the primitive and primal—the "ugly," as Soloveitchik would likely gloss it—as sources for the imagination; one cannot, however, imagine the halakhic man looking at Picasso's *Demoiselles d'Avignon* as a positive development. Indeed, desire is acknowledged, but only in a form that has already been fully refined by a rationalist perspective, circumscribed and mediated by the law where all that is alien has been domesticated. It is true that in his early work, Soloveitchik situates himself as providing a counterimage to a life- and body-denying Christianity, anticipating his postwar Freudian explicit turn to sexuality. "The Halakha," he writes, "is a doctrine of the body," proclaiming further, "therein lies its greatness" (*Seek*, 117). In a normative formulation, Soloveitchik writes, "Halakha aims to sanctify man's body, refine the bestial aspects of human life with all their lusts and drives, and raise them to the level of divine service." Soloveitchik again expresses a consciousness of not only Christianity but Freud, showing how Judaism also confronts lusts and drives, yet raises them to the level of divine service. The "savage lusts" and "untamed instincts" of man are transformed by the "halakhic factor," bestowing "the glory of the *Shekhina* on human life." An implicit response to Freud: the halakha does not shy away from desire, but does so in the service of theology and ethics, while rendering desire "beautiful" (*Seek*, 111).

Nevertheless, the residual energies of a more dangerous desire for Soloveitchik's halakhic man are taken into account, even as they are held at a safe distance. "The pleasure of halakhic man," he writes, is "refined, measured, and purified" in "the one who has penetrated the furnace of lust and understood its nature," for Jewish law "abhors the chaos in pleasure." The one in search of pleasure, Soloveitchik goes on, is akin to "a body enslaved to nature, seized with panic before the gathering of mighty forces of desire." Soloveitchik thus acknowledges pleasure's presence—even presenting himself as one who has "penetrated the furnace of lust," but in the end domesticating that pleasure. There is an emphatic difference, Soloveitchik continues, between "the hysteria of desire and madness" and the pleasure advocated by halakhic man, which "has the beauty and refinement of life's aesthetic elements." In contrast to the "excessive intensity, stimulation of the nerves, and intoxication of the sense," Soloveitchik advocates a "pleasure" that is "modest and delicate," a form of enjoyment that avoids what he calls "the mania of sexual desire and gluttony" (*Seek*, 111).

Soloveitchik's explicit views of both pleasure and beauty are far removed from the "dross" of sexuality and desire. In *Family Redeemed*, in which Soloveitchik more directly confronts sexuality, offering an approving nod to psychoanalysis for giving "sexual experience" its "most radical scientific formulation," he claims that for Freud, the "libido" is "identified with sinful complexes, with a desire for rape and murder." Freud sees "sexuality in various guises," but for Soloveitchik, sexuality is associated with the "illegitimate and sinful anomalies" and "secret guilt." In Soloveitchik's rendering of Freudian psychoanalysis, "crime and sex are so frequently interwoven with each other that the line of demarcation is blurred" (*Family*, 85). *Halakhic Man* instead espouses a form of beauty and pleasure, dominant in the eighteenth century and distant from Soloveitchik's version of Freudian sexuality, associated with Kant—disinterested, universal, and in consonance with "an aesthetically grounded logical judgment."[24] The beautiful pushes off what is threatening in the aesthetic experience and renders it safe, as it did in eighteenth-century circles—safe for the drawing room, or perhaps in this case, the study hall. As Soloveitchik later writes in *Lonely Man of Faith* with regard to the "majestic man," with whom the halakhic man bears many similarities: his conscience is "energized" by "the beautiful" and by "the pleasant and functional" (*LMF*, 19). The pursuit of "aesthetic enjoyment," however, he writes almost a decade earlier, "always ends in the encounter with satanic gluttony, ugliness and vulgarity" (*Whirl*, 158). For Soloveitchik, the beautiful acts as a means of domesticating desire into a nonthreatening strictly aesthetic category. More than that, however, in the terms of Evelyn Scott Keller of the previous chapter, the "mire" of desire associated with a certain version of the feminine must be domesticated because it threatens the autonomous agency of the masculine figure of halakhic man. Indeed, the priority of a Kantian ego cultivating knowledge through conquest does so through rigid categories that bracket desire, rendering it pleasant and functional, and finally, harmless.

The Soloveitchik of *Halakhic Man* admits that "we may tend to look askance upon that religiosity which follows cognition" as "somewhat pallid, overly refined and indeed fastidious," but the refinement and beauty of the halakhic man in this work are also determined to be "highly auspicious," "modest" and "retiring," indeed, "very delicate" (*Man*, 85). Unlike the "great" figure in the Talmud who is depicted as dealing with powerful desires (Sukka 52a), the halakhic man is one who "does not struggle with the evil impulses, nor does he clash with the tempter who seeks to deprive him of his senses."[25] Halakhic men "are not subject to the whispered proffer of desire, and they need not exert themselves or resist this pull" (*Man*, 65). Yet the presence of the seduction of desire—the "whispered proffer"—remains present in *Halakhic Man*, even as the explicit languages of the work renounce it. That power of desire is manifest, rendered almost as a theological challenge to the halakhic man's worldview, as well as to his self-consciously presented "refined" image. As revealed in part 2 of the work, there are some forces that show themselves unable to be assimilated to law.

Misprision

Soloveitchik provides an account of creation in the second part of *Halakhic Man*. In the form of a halakhic theodicy, the presence of desire is expressed even as it is, in explicit ways, shown to be exiled by the law. Although the God of Soloveitchik's rendering of legal theodicy is the divine agent of legal decree, Soloveitchik's idiosyncratic reading of the Talmudic stories on which the sources are based— what Harold Bloom would call a misprision of those sources—foregrounds the presence of desire, even as desire is repressed.[26] The mechanisms of the poetic misprision described below are encapsulated in another of Soloveitchik's (mis-) readings, the verse from Ecclesiastes (11:12), the subject of R. Elazar's interpretive homily discussed in chapter 2.

In R. Elazar's reading, as I argued earlier, the well-planted nails are an ambiguous and even paradoxical image that combines inorganic and organic, at once solid and stable, but also blooming and fertile, thus encompassing a discordant harmony of images. In Soloveitchik's argument, however, the "nails well fastened" serve the function of transforming the "qualitative subjective energies of religious subjectivity" into "well-established [legal] quantities" (*Man*, 57). For

Soloveitchik, these "nails," in their unqualified translation, are stripped of their multiple Talmudic resonances and now stand as firm boundaries against the surge of the excess of religious subjectivity. In R. Elazar's reading, the nails may function as "fasteners," but they are also associated with organic metaphors of growth and blooming, excised in Soloveitchik's one-dimensional "halakhic" account. Soloveitchik thus intentionally reads against the grain of the Talmudic interpretation, though the repressed conventional rabbinic reading summons the repressed meanings—in their multiplicity. Indeed, Lawrence Kaplan's mistranslation of the verses' organic "planted" as the flattened and inorganic "fastened" is faithful to Soloveitchik's overall approach, but not to the biblical text or the rabbinic interpretation of that text.[27] Soloveitchik employs the rabbinic text—a marker of rabbinic multiplicity—to assert the singularity of the law. In Soloveitchik's legal or "halakhic" theodicy, a parallel misprision (here in his occlusion of important details of the Talmudic account) also leaves a residual impression of the energies his representation aims to occlude.

When God "engraved and carved out the world," Soloveitchik writes in his own midrashic language, he did not entirely "eradicate the chaos and the void, the deep, the darkness, from the domain of His creation" (*Man*, 102). Soloveitchik acknowledges the aboriginal forces of chaos and void, and deems their provenance divine. Soloveitchik's creator is one who creates through law—through what he calls *hok*, or decree. This act of creation is an act of separation or severance, one that enacts a breach between "the chaos and the void, the deep, the darkness, and relativeness" and "orderly, majestic, beautiful world." Even while affirming the separation from the biblical forces of the chaos and the void, Soloveitchik assents to their divine provenance and necessity. "All of these 'primordial' materials," he continues, "were created in order that they subsist and be located in the world itself" (*Man*, 102).

The narrative aspect to the theodicy, however, follows a different trajectory, not one of integration but of separation. Those forces that are part of the creation—as Soloveitchik renders his theodicy in narrative form, seeming to give these forces autonomy—exceed their bounds. Although these elements wish to "burst forth out of the chains of obedience" imposed by the divine "to plunge the earth back into chaos and the voice," the creator as lawgiver restrains them (*Man*, 102–3). "It is only the law," Soloveitchik writes, "that holds them back and bars the path before them" (*Man*, 103). Law understood as *hok*, Soloveitchik explains, comes from the three-letter Hebrew root that means to carve or engrave. The law "carves out a boundary," and thus "sets up markers, establishes special domains" for the purpose of "separating existence from 'nothingness,' the ordered cosmos from the void, and creation from naught." The lawmaker carves, engraves, and separates, as Soloveitchik illustrates, citing Proverbs 8:27, "When He carved [*hok*] a circle [*hug*] upon the face of the deep" (*Man*, 103). As the narrative account of separation continues, the circle provides "an all encompassing boundary" to the persistently present "deep, chaos and the void, darkness, and the 'nothingness,'" devoid of "image and form" (*Man*, 103). The hybrid biblical void and Aristotelian hyle are thus constrained and contained by law.

Theodicy requires dramatic tension, and in Soloveitchik's version, the relative "nothingness," Soloveitchik's satanic agent, plots evil: "the deep is devising iniquity, and the chaos and void lie in wait in the dark alleyways of reality and seek to undermine the absolute being, to profane the lustrous image of creation" (*Man*, 103). In part 1, Soloveitchik had written of the halakhic man's "unfamiliarity with the dark back streets of defilement," but now those "dark alleyways" threaten the cosmos itself. The halakhic man's "boundary construction" falls short, as Kulton-Fromm writes, and the "terrors remain beyond."[28] The lustrous image of creation, the cosmic corollary of the beauty of the halakhic man, comes under attack from the demonic forces of chaos. The confrontation the halakhic man avoids in the microcosmic realm of the psyche is now enacted in the cosmic macrocosm, the universe. Against the cosmic forces of law and order, the powers of chaos present themselves as a rebellious, seemingly self-moving creation: "the deep wishes to cast off the yoke of the law, to pass beyond the boundary and limit that the Creator set up and carved out" (*Man*, 103). Beyond the limits set up by *hok* is the "tempestuous sea" with its "raging waves" and their aim to "inundate the world." In this confrontation, Soloveitchik stages "the quarrel of the deep with the principles of order and the battle of confusion with the law." It is "as though," Soloveitchik writes, "the sea at high tide, rushing to meet the shore, desires to destroy the boundary and the law, as though the disorder of the primordial forces of chaos and confusion desire to cleave asunder the perfect and exquisitely chiseled creation and lay it waste" (*Man*, 103). The twice-mentioned "as though" already pulls back from the attribution of autonomy to the negative forces in creation. As in any formally successful theodicy in which divine providence triumphs, the forces of evil—here associated with desire—can only have *apparent* agency and effect. That the forces of nothing are only "relative" prepares for the resolution of the conflict: the assertion of the absolute authority of the law against the twice-repeated "desire" for destruction.

To elaborate the reassertion of the law's authority and complement his midrashic account with a rabbinic one, Soloveitchik turns from his representation of the cosmos to the Talmudic representations of King David's founding of the Temple in Jerusalem:

> When David began to dig the foundations of the Temple, he dug 15 cubits and did not reach the deep. Finally he found one potsherd and sought to lift it up. Said [the potsherd] unto him: You may not. Said [David] unto it: And why not? Said [the potsherd] unto him: Since the Almighty proclaimed on Mount Sinai 'I am the Lord thy God.' At that moment the earth trembled and began to sink

and I was placed here to restrain the deep. David, nevertheless, did not listen to it. As soon as he lifted it, the waters of the deep arose and sought to inundate the world. (Cited in *Man*, 104)

The forces from which the halakhic man claimed immunity now threaten the entire creation; in the absence of law, the waters of the deep seek "to inundate the world." Soloveitchik's theodicy of law gains its power in David's decisive gesture to "restrain the deep" by means of the shard engraved with the divine name. The threats of "nothingness," "desolation," and "ontic emptiness" are restrained through the assertion of the law, the shard with the verse asserting divine lordship and mastery: "I am the Lord thy God." After Soloveitchik attributes separate agency and even power to the cosmos, that agency is qualified and controlled by both law and lawgiver.

David's use of the shard with the divine name, that is, the original *hok* establishing divine authority, quells the rebellious forces in the universe. The divine name, as well as the halakhic man who internalizes the authority of the law, are able to push away the aleatory forces of the deep—darkness, desire, and evil. The revelational statutes become unified with reason in the figure of the halakhic man, and the internal statutes hold off the forces that threaten, but then are finally suppressed. Indeed, the founding of the Temple, in Soloveitchik's account, provides a parallel and precedent for the internal workings of the halakhic man, whose a priori strictures provide the boundaries that keep the potentially catastrophic forces of desire at bay. In *Paradise Lost*, Milton defined theodicy as "justifying the ways of God to men" (1.26).[29] Soloveitchik's Brisk theodicy based as it is on a decree (and not thereby constrained by rationality) does not justify or explain God's mysterious ways or the presence of evil in the world but creates the boundaries through which the forces of evil are contained. Indeed, in this theodicy, we find the origins of Soloveitchik's dismissal—in relation to questions of evil and suffering—of the "why" question; evil is, at best, bracketed and constrained.[30]

Although Soloveitchik cites part of the narrative from tractates Makkot and Sukkot, he neglects the full elaboration of the narrative in the latter tractate. In this version, David inscribes the shard with the divine name to restrain the waters from flooding the world (52a). That is, acting proactively, David takes the shard, the fragment that stands in for both law and lawgiver, and hurls it onto the deep. But when "David sees the waters descend sixteen thousand cubits," he resolves to compose the "15 songs of ascent" (Psalms 120–34) so that "the waters" will "ascend to a level a thousand cubits below the earth." In the rendering of the rabbis, when David sees the forces of the deep descend too far—to sixteen thousand cubits—he endeavors, through song, to raise them up again. When the waters do rise, in the passage not cited by Soloveitchik, David intones, "the closer the waters are, the more they will water the earth." The relationship asserted here between the law and the deep, as well as that between the forces of otherness and desire, qualify the argument implicit in Soloveitchik's idiosyncratic representation of the Talmudic narrative.

In this rendition, the divine name holds the waters back—but too far. The forces of otherness in the Talmudic narrative are necessary to the world's sustenance, and the divine songs of David elicit those forces to nurture the earth. The energies, associated with the deep, are necessary not only to David the individual—the figure in biblical history who reveals the complexity and depth of interiority—but also for the place of divine service, the Temple. Left unrestrained, the "waters" will destroy the earth, yet only when they are close is the earth sustained: "the closer the waters are, the more they will water the earth." The rabbinic representation of the Temple in its corollary to R. Elazar's "blooming nails" also requires the combination of both restraint and vitality, the latter of which is repressed in both of Soloveitchik's accounts. David, whom Soloveitchik calls "the sweet singer," wants access to the deep, and in fact he removes the shard with the divine name in order to come into contact with the forces—both cosmic and psychic—with which the deep is associated (*Man*, 105).

In Soloveitchik's representation and in the select rabbinic sources he does cite, the law's absolute triumph over the deep is necessary and unequivocal. This is not to suggest, pace Schwartz, that Soloveitchik knowingly "set aside the dialectic" in his representation of the halakhic man, but rather that the dialectic is occluded—and not through the act of a Straussian author in supreme control—in order to obscure any relationship to the persistently beckoning "back alleys of desire." Soloveitchik's cosmos depends on the decreed separation between law and desire; no less does the figure of the modest, retiring, and delicate halakhic man require a distance from the minatory powers of the deep—both cosmic and psychic—and the dangers they entail. "Man himself symbolizes," Soloveitchik writes, both "the most perfect and complete type of existence, the image of God" and "the most terrible chaos and void" (*Man*, 109). But the dualism so insistently affirmed by Soloveitchik, that between law and desire, is undermined in the uncited proof text in which the interplay between the two realms is more fluid than that represented in his depiction of a God who *only* separates—and makes distinctions— through the engraving of the law. Soloveitchik's omission shows an anxious disavowal of otherness, not a conscious suspension of the dialectic, but an avoidance of the forces of desire, remaining present even in their ostensible erasure.

While contemporary modernists such as Picasso, Joyce, and most of all, Freud, saw the encounter with the other (the primitive, the underworld, the unconscious) as potentially life affirming, Soloveitchik's representation of the Temple's founding keeps these forces at a distance. The Davidic founding of the Temple might have stood in *Halakhic Man* as an underworld journey of Soloveitchik's own, after Joyce's Bloom in *Ulysses*, or even Eliot of *The Waste Land* (both latter texts providing explorations of what Kulton-Fromm calls the "urban holy").[31] Instead of eliciting an encounter with that underworld—which David in the Talmudic account initiates—Soloveitchik's halakhic man and the lawgiver of his account foreclose that possibility. That Soloveitchik should be judged alongside modernist poets might seem an unlikely suggestion, as pushing to the limits the possible relationship between the traditions of Athens and Jerusalem, even for a figure as radically innovative as he was in that regard. Although the Nietzschean Dionysian may never find a place in a rabbinic context—certainly not one guided by halakha—the Apollonian urgency of Soloveitchik's representation of theodicy shows a need to repress forces that are acknowledged to be, however implicitly, beyond the law's control.

The persistence of a desire repressed in *Halakhic Man*, encapsulated in Soloveitchik's halakhic theodicy, is symptomatic of a more significant rupture present in the text: that between the principles associated with psychic change and transformation and the hermeneutic attitude and sensibility of the halakhic man. Indeed, Soloveitchik's elaboration of *teshuva* depends on the very psychic forces repressed in his account of the Temple, his conception of repentance understood through the lens of the Davidic maxim in the Talmudic account: "the closer the waters are, the more they will water the earth." In this sense, Soloveitchik's omission of the story's continuation does not so much show a polemical appropriation of the sages as it does the extent to which the forces associated with chaos and desire find only an ambivalent association within the halakhic man's personality. What Nietzsche refers to as the "cheerfulness" of "theoretical man," with his aesthetic of the beautiful and an optimistic faith in the progressive spirit of science, has its cost, the dissolution of and subordination of "the instincts."[32] But the fissure in *Halakhic Man*, which is both a testament to halakhic men and their legacy (indeed, a conscious affiliation with that legacy) and the articulation of a radical conception of psychic integrity foreign to their sensibility, leads back to repentance, memory, and gender.

Repentance Redux

The creativity that comes to fruition in relation to repentance is discontinuous with the halakhic man's creativity, and thus, the second part of *Halakhic Man* presents a radical break from that which preceded it.[33] To be sure, creativity is celebrated in the first part of the work. But the Brisk celebration of the *hiddush* is always internal to its own system: the so-called creator of worlds always does so within his a priori contexts and constructs. The halakhic man does not, as I have noted, "waste time" on reflection or introspection, as Soloveitchik observes, nor on emotive life. This is represented with the greatest pathos in the story of

Soloveitchik's grandfather, R. Elijah Feinstein, described as "hard like flint," hastening to put on tefillin before the anticipated death of his daughter (*Man*, 78). The halakhic man, the microcosm of the cosmos described in the ontological set piece that opens up the second part of the work, creates clear boundaries, pushing off the forces of chaos and desire, which for Soloveitchik includes the emotional world itself. But the work of repentance that Soloveitchik describes shares with psychoanalysis, as we have seen, an emphasis on transforming alien parts of the psyche. The halakhic man, by contrast, does not risk that encounter. The man of repentance encounters that which is alien, even that which is in excess of the constructs at his disposal.

The alien itself for Soloveitchik's repentant is, as discussed in chapter 3, paradoxically, a living force. Even nonassimilated materiality, the "hyle," as Soloveitchik writes in *Halakhic Man*, "must ultimately be able to act" (*Man*, 131). What had seemed to be unassimilable forces—maybe even violent and destructive—are brought, through the process of repentance, within the province of the psyche. The power of repentance is such that even "historical crimes, past aberrations" can "descend upon the bones like life-giving dew of resurrection" (*Man*, 117). Repentance is transformative of the past, not only historical traumas but aberrations and transgressions are to be assimilated through repentance into the human personality. As Soloveitchik observes later, in Pinchas Peli's rendering of his lectures between 1962 and 1974, "sin is the generating force," the "springboard" that pushes the penitent "higher and higher" (*Repentance*, 261). Repentance through which sins are "wiped away," Soloveitchik continues, is inferior to that through which sins are "elevated and exalted" (*Repentance*, 256). Indeed, in the ideal kind of repentance, "the very same hunger and zest" that drove a person to "do evil and sin can be utilized to do good and observe the precepts" (*Repentance*, 262).

To be sure, Soloveitchik accommodates different kinds of repentance, including those in which sins are erased, "wiped away." In *Halakhic Man*, metaphors implying transformation of evil contend with metaphors of "cutting off" and "severing" (*Man*, 112). In the latter, in concord with the act of creation represented in the halakhic theodicy as one of severance, the recognition of otherness—transgression—serves merely as a prompt to repentance. In this account, the recognition of sin has merely an instrumental purpose, and the sinner, Soloveitchik writes, feeling repulsed by his sins, turns to God. "Knowledge of past sins becomes a motivating factor," as Yitzchak Blau explains, in producing a "remorse" that drives the penitent "to perform better in the future, to make up for wasted years."[34] In this model of repentance, the past functions only as an extrinsic spur to modify future behavior.

Soloveitchik's more innovative formulation of repentance, however, is one in which the relationship to evil or sin is not merely extrinsic and formal but transformative. As Soloveitchik elaborates on the creative aspect of repentance, the

penitent "now has the capacity to sanctify these forces and to direct them up-
wards." The forces are not incidental or extrinsic motivators to repentance, but
they become the engines themselves to repentance. Soloveitchik elaborates this
perspective, declaring in the voice of the penitent: "I am not a different person,
I am not starting anew; I am continuing onward, I am sanctifying evil and raising it to new heights" (*Repentance*, 263). Soloveitchik articulates what is at stake
in the conception of *teshuva* already present in *Halakhic Man*—where repentance does not entail severing with the past or obliterating it, but rather appropriating and transforming it.

To return to the Talmudic terms of my earlier discussion, the two forms of
repentance articulated by Soloveitchik reflect "fear" and "love." The Talmud considers two contradictory utterances of Reish Lakish—one that through repentance "willful sins are turned into merits," and the other that "willful sins are
rendered into actions only committed accidentally or without intention." The first
is attributed to a repentance based on love, the second to a repentance based on
fear (Yoma 86a).[35] The latter—something like the feeling of aesthetic repulsion
at the abomination of past actions—has the effect of severing the past actions
from the agent who committed them. Presupposing the possibility of a discontinuity of selfhood, in the repentance based on fear, "premeditated sins are accounted
as errors" (*Repentance*, 256). It is only *teshuva* based on love, given philosophical
articulation at the end of *Halakhic Man*, that leads to transformation of the past
and continuity of the self. "Man is not required to cover-up and conceal the bad
years, the years of sin; rather he has the capacity to sanctify and purify them"
(*Repentance*, 264). It is not only that the penitent loves God, and is therefore re-
warded, but through this experience of love, he is able to draw closer to himself
(a self modeled on the Davidic interiority both summoned and repressed in the
legal theodicy). Reish Lakish's *teshuva* based on love of which Soloveitchik writes
in *Halakhic Man*, and continues to cultivate in later works, is not based on divine
fiat but on a creative act of love of not only God, but the self, with its retrograde
past now thoroughly transformed: "the bonds of love pull man up to great and
exalted heights" (*Repentance*, 256).[36]

In his willful avoidance of introspection and the purposive repulsion of all
sin, the halakhic man described by Soloveitchik in the first part of the 1944 work
does not have the psychic resources for this form of repentance based on love.[37]
Indeed, given the resources and ontological outlook of the halakhic men, such
an approach would be impossible. The figure of halakhic man remains one of
mastery *only*, akin to the divine figure of mastery, and the impediments to that
mastery—whether in the form of desire, evil, or sin—are always expunged, held
back by the boundaries of the law. The halakhic man does not appropriate personal loss; rather, he severs himself from it and triumphs over it. Indeed, in part 2
of *Halakhic Man*, Soloveitchik only cites the Reish Lakish who provides a source

for a repentance based on love, suggesting perhaps by implication that for the "halakhic men" of part 1, only a repentance out of fear is possible, and that further, their sensibilities are unable to produce the narrative *hiddush* most important to the individual psyche (*Man*, 116). To be sure, Soloveitchik emphasizes the halakhic man's prowess in the realm of interpretation and tradition, but the second part of the work appropriates their principle of creativity for a realm from which their psychic temperaments exclude them.

Gender and Memory

Informing the distinct notions of repentance, based on fear and love, there are, for Soloveitchik, two contending experiences of memory: one that is rehabilitative and transforms the experience of transgression, desire, and loss, and another that is one-dimensional, to which the notion of the creative concept of repentance is foreign. Soloveitchik articulates this dual conception of memory in relation to the work of Henri Bergson and what he calls the "dualism bound up with the concept of time" (*Man*, 120). The distinctive forms of memory implicit in Soloveitchik's two conceptions of repentance have their correlates in Bergson's dual conception of time.

In the conventional mechanisms of memory, Bergson writes, time is a process by which "learned recollection" abstracts from the moment, rendering the resultant memory "more and more impersonal, more and more foreign" to the actual moments of "our past life." The process of this form of memory abstracts from particularity into the realm of the conceptual. "Repetition," in Bergson's phrase, effects the "conversion" of raw memories into a realm of quantifiable abstraction that makes the experience of time habitual, utilitarian, and mechanical. Abstract "learned" memory, also associated with "repetition" and "habit," competes with a form of memory founded on the activity of "consciousness," one that "retains the image of the situations through which it has successively traveled, and lays them side by side in the order in which they took place." The latter, which are distinctly "personal" memory images, "picture all past events with their outline, their color and their place in time." In contrast to the schematic abstraction of the first form of memory, Bergson's more personal memory elaborates both color and depth, images in their particular specificity. From the perspective of the utilitarian consciousness, habituated to abstract memory, the second form of memory, with its qualitative richness, has a paradoxical nonreality, a "dream-like" aspect, potentially disruptive of the repetitions of quantified time. Because these latter "qualitative" recollections "are akin to dreams," Bergson writes, their "intrusion into the life of the mind" may "seriously disturb intellectual equilibrium." For the personality immersed in, even defined by, quantitative time, the eruption of qualitative memory disturbs the experience of a habitual and regularized time.[38]

The concept of "mathematical time," for Soloveitchik following Bergson, is "frozen in geometrical space and entirely quantifiable." By contrast, "the perception of time as pure, qualitative duration" forms "the very essence of and content of consciousness" (*Man*, 120). For Soloveitchik, repentance depends on the experience of the latter, with access to time's "quality," and the subsequent possible continuity between aspects of past, present, and future. Soloveitchik later writes that this form of "fleeting time, living and immeasurable," with its provenance in Bergsonian qualitative time, is "beyond the scientist's mesh." "No clock can be applied," Soloveitchik continues, "to this qualitative time, which is transient, intangible, and evanescent." Some live within the bounds of a "quantitative dead time"; indeed, one may "live an entire life span quantitatively." There are those, however, who are able to immerse themselves in a temporal frame characterized by "pure quality"—one that elicits "creativity and accomplishment." The "multidimensional" nature of this form of time, which permits the "co-penetrating" of past, present, and future, is "creative, dynamic, and self-emerging." While "Bergson limited himself to a philosophical and metaphysical analysis of time," Soloveitchik understands the "dualistic time concept" as the "prime norm of human life," carrying with it "practical implications and ethical aspects" as well ("Sacred," 64–65).

In *Halakhic Man*, repentance, conceived as both "practical and ethical" in nature, is dependent on the understanding of time, whether to mold "time in a quantitative or qualitative pattern" (*Man*, 121; "Sacred," 65). For Soloveitchik, full freedom and creativity, achieved through *teshuva*, are only granted to those who cultivate the experience of qualitative time and who understand the opportunity inherent in the "'fleeting moment" in the context of the creative interrelation between past, present, and future. Such an interrelationship is guaranteed through memory, for only it "can enable one to grasp hold of this rushing stream." Consciousness of different temporal modes remains important, but for the penitent, the particularity of "the fleeing moment," the basis of qualitative time, is the foundation for creative repentance. By contrast, "the individual," who experiences time in terms of Bergsonian repetition, "measures time in purely quantitative terms," and as such, remains "an essentially passive personality." For "pure chronometry," Frank Kermode's *chronos*, he writes, is "empty, uniform and noncreative" ("Sacred," 65). For Freud, repetition is opposed to creative memory, so for Soloveitchik, following Bergson, the creative memory of repentance is opposed to the repetition entailed by the "learned abstraction" of chronometric time. In Soloveitchik's own terms, qualitative time is associated with the creativity of the "man of destiny," chronometric time, with the passive man of faith.

For Soloveitchik, these different forms of time and memory, from the retrospective standpoint of his later writings, are gendered. Reading the *teshuva* of *Halakhic Man* from the perspective of the articulated conceptions of gender of the later work, the two Bergsonian conceptions of time (qualitative and quantitative), as well as the forms of memory with which they are associated, are correlated with the feminine and masculine, respectively. Father and Mother—as generic types—evidence different kinds of memory, shown through the different ways they relate to the memory of their child. There is, Soloveitchik writes, "a basic divergence in the act of remembering" between mother and father (*Family*, 163). The "progressive image memory" that is "basically a technical reproduction of knowledge" is the province of "Father" (*Family*, 163–64). Such a reproduction, Soloveitchik writes disparagingly, is consistent with the representation of quantified time in *Halakhic Man* and "limited to the projection of a pale image, a still picture, a lifeless copy of what transpired in the past" (*Family*, 164). The learned memory of the father is restricted to the inert reproductions of quantitative memory.

The alternative, Bergson's correlate to the quantitative memory of repetition, is a "non-progressive and timeless event memory." Unlike the mechanisms of quantifying memory placed in the service of habit and utility, this form of memory is faithful to "the experiences themselves and quickens bygones with new life." One endowed with this kind of memory is able not only to remember the past but relive it. The qualitative memories accessible to this personality "strike with enormous force, infusing images with life," converting old lifeless "pictures" into realities (*Family*, 164). As Bergson admits to the destabilizing characteristics of this form of memory, so Soloveitchik acknowledges its potentially disruptive nature: "This memory makes man retreat either into the dark night of loneliness or into the bright daylight of affection and love" (*Family*, 163). Qualitative memory, or what Freud might call creative memory, escapes the quantitative mechanisms of abstraction and allows for the feeling of both loss and love.

There are those who, Soloveitchik confides, "are fortunate not to possess such a capacity for re-living, for re-experiencing" (*Family*, 164). As Bergson writes, these memories are not controlled by the "will" as quantifiable memory is, but are spontaneous. Qualitative memory, like the forms of embarrassment and shame that Soloveitchik consciously cultivated, is another mark of Cain. Those with this memory, he continues, should be considered either "blessed or cursed by Providence" for having the ability to confront "the past as if it were the living present" (*Family*, 164). They who share this ambivalent gift, the existential awareness of time, "know," Soloveitchik writes in the first person, "what I mean" (*Family*, 164). Just as tortured loneliness emerges as a sign of chosenness, a means for Soloveitchik to show his distance from his father, so repentance—and the form of memory associated with it—emerges as a characteristic that distinguishes him from the halakhic men who preceded him. Soloveitchik admits to being both blessed and cursed—for being both like *and* unlike his father. For the memory that takes into account the "living present" is both an onerous burden and a mark of distinction, one that is associated, for Soloveitchik, with creative memory, *teshuva*, and the feminine.

For Soloveitchik, the archetypal "Mother" is endowed with an appreciation of Bergsonian qualitative time, that is, "timeless event-memory." Her memory takes into account the various stages of her child's development; she has the "capacity of living through a seemingly forgotten past, of restating and reenacting"—what amounts to the "great drama of motherhood" (*Family*, 165). In contrast, the "father belongs to the people whom Providence has spared progressive photo memory" (*Family*, 164). The father may have memories of his child, even as Soloveitchik writes suggestively, "a pleasant one," but it is just a "recollection"—a one-dimensional snapshot of the past. Like Freud's screen memory, the father's memory is a form of forgetting, providing an image of the past that is occluded even at it is revealed.[39] The mother's memory of the developmental phases of the child and her presence to both the moment and the continuum of memories in which they occur is the prerequisite for narrative, as well as for the self-creation of *teshuva* on which it is based. Soloveitchik's sense of an identity independent of his father begins in the province of the feminine with his mother in Pruzhna; the beginning of Soloveitchik's narrative self-creation begins in another feminine realm, that of *teshuva*.

Soloveitchik's adaptation of Bergson's conception of time and memory also allies him (again) with Freud and the belief in a form of nonquantifiable memory that allows for an encounter with the past. Within the typologies of *Halakhic Man*, it is the halakhic man, like the "physicist with his mathematical formula," who is associated with the realm of quantification, and by implication, the dead time anathema to the possibility of creative memory required for a repentance informed by love (*Man*, 83). The halakhic man, acting as a neo-Kantian cultivating novelties within the systems he acknowledges to be closed, is not only insulated from the real, but from the memories of existential moments (the "hyle" of personal history) that allow for a repentance based on love. For Soloveitchik, the "fleeting moment" and repentance, as well as the form of memory associated with them, are associated only with the feminine and her sensitivity to the present. Similarly, "Adam the second" of *Lonely Man of Faith*, who unlike "majestic Adam," has the possibility of entering into a community of sympathy with the feminine, also experiences the "evanescence of a 'now'-existence" (*LMF*, 69). Although it is "frightening," this conception of time, beginning in "insecurity," is the prerequisite for the experience of the "continuum of time and responsibility," experienced "in its endless totality" (*LMF*, 72). Only this Adam, in whom, as Shira Wolosky writes, "it is hard not to discern a certain feminization," experiences "the tragic and paradoxical" conception of time on which "the full eschatological realization of the covenant" and repentance depend (*LMF*, 70–71).[40]

What Soloveitchik later describes as the limits of masculine memory is tied, again in a retrospective reading, to other attributes of the halakhic man. The "cognitively framed solutions" of the halakhic man have no need for the kind of memory entailed in qualitative memory associated with the feminine, but also by extension, with the temporal norm associated with creative repentance (*Seek*, 125). While it is true that the halakhic man is a master of tradition, that mastery insulates him from the loss intrinsic to it. Talmudic hermeneutics is imagined as a distinctly masculine form of mastery (again as typified in the story from his grandfather's living room), and so for the halakhic man, the theoretical representation of tradition remains idealized. It occurs in what Soloveitchik imagines as "the beautiful and resplendent phenomenon of time." The "wondrous chain" of *mesora*, or tradition, Soloveitchik writes, "floats upon the stormy waters of time." There is no separation through time—no breach or loss created through time's passage. For the "consciousness of the halakhic man, that master of the received tradition, embraces the entire company of the sages of the *masorah*." The master of the tradition understands no meaningful periods of time, and thus "walks alongside Maimonides, listens to R. Akiva, senses the presence of Abaye and Raba" (*Man*, 120).[41] Although that past and future in the project of *mesora* become "ever-present realities," the project of memory confronting or overcoming loss is absent. Whereas the experience of loss is essential to the Talmudic representations of tradition (what I call the hermeneutics of mourning), there is no corollary emphasis in Soloveitchik's work. There is "no death and expiration," Soloveitchik affirms, "among the company of the sages of the tradition" (*Man*, 120), for the halakhic man dwells in an idealized form of time *without loss*. Indeed, there is no memory, for there is no loss, but only the representation of a seamless tradition, accessible to that master of tradition for whom the sciences, and not the humanities with their subjective Bergsonian emphasis on experiential time and memory, offer the correlates.

The "memory" Soloveitchik defines as "the greatest blessing of man *qua* man," which constitutes the "entire awareness of the human 'I,'" need not be present in the halakhic man. Indeed, Soloveitchik writes that halakha's relationship to time is of the quantifiable variety; it is bound up with measurable and objectified time periods, established time, and time periods that "are fixed and determined" (*Repentance*, 196). Further, Soloveitchik affirms that the Halakha "is not particularly concerned with the metaphysics of time," and that the Bergsonian conception of qualitative time, which is responsible, as he writes, for the rebellion of the human sciences against the methodology of mathematical science, is not the realm of the halakhic man (*Man*, 121). Indeed, this figure is later aligned with the more masculine figure of "majestic man" in *Lonely Man of Faith*, who lives in a similar realm, that is, in "micro-units of clock time," "quantified, spatialized, and measured" (*LMF*, 70). Although the underlying rhetoric of *Halakhic Man* suggests a continuity between the hermeneutic *hiddush* of part 1 and the psychic *hiddush* of part 2, the two figures that emerge from the distinct parts have antithetical commitments arising from their different conceptions of time and memory. Only the latter has the experience of time and historicity, which is the prerequisite for narrative, for *teshuva*, for, finally, self-creation.

Halakhic Man reveals a gap between a legal hermeneutics based on masculine conquest and a repentance based on the acknowledgment of multiple (internal) agencies, the foundation of the ethics of Soloveitchik's later works. Despite the unresolved ambivalences of the *Halakhic Man*, this most canonical work already charts a path away from the conventions of Soloveitchik's ancestors, anticipating his more aggressive transformation of the figure of halakhic man and the Brisk tradition. As the melancholy ambivalence in his work intensifies, the process of Soloveitchik's self-fashioning comes to fruition in his articulation of an ethics emphasizing otherness, following from the commitments of the second part of the 1944 work. Soloveitchik's articulation of his antithetic ethics and the concomitant reassertion of the hermeneutics of conquest and masculine mastery are the subjects of the following chapter.

6 From Interpretive Conquest
to Antithetic Ethics

Gradually it has become clear to me what every great philosophy has so far
been: namely the personal confession of its author and a kind of involuntary
and unconscious memoir.

—Nietzsche, *Beyond Good and Evil*

"THE TENSION BETWEEN the subjective and objective," writes Aharon Lichtenstein, was for Soloveitchik, "a major life-long concern."[1] That tension, in my reading, straining to be a dialectic, attenuates into an irreconcilable opposition, as in
the rupture between hermeneutic and psychic sensibilities described in the previous chapter. With that acknowledged, Soloveitchik's works of the 1940s stress
the "objective"; the essays collected in *Out of the Whirlwind* by contrast, the focus
of the current chapter, have their provenance in the sensibility of the second part
of *Halakhic Man*: the subjective sphere. Soloveitchik's later works embrace the
claims of the individual subject, and in so doing mark off his self-construction
and the more emphatic making of his distinctive identity—a self-creation
pursued in fraught relation to his Brisk antecedents. For Soloveitchik, through
acknowledging the cultural catastrophe of Holocaust, as well as the American
response to it, he continues to delineate an identity independent from the halakhic man. Yet even as Soloveitchik constructs a self that is independent of the
purview of tradition of his father by elaborating an epistemological humility,
even pessimism, he nonetheless maintains the assumptions about cognition and
hermeneutics that inform the halakhic man.

Acknowledgment of the failure of the cognition celebrated in his works of the
1940s gives rise to a new consciousness of subjectivity—Soloveitchik's new sense
of self—and, more important, a corresponding ethical attitude that emerges from
it, consistent with his conception of repentance. At the same time, however, Soloveitchik's later work shows the persistence of the epistemological categories of
the 1940s, specifically his representation of knowledge as conquest. In the same
way that *Halakhic Man* splits into two parts, with their corresponding sensibilities, so Soloveitchik's later works manifest a conflict between an epistemology
(and hermeneutics) that acknowledges otherness, and one that represses it.

This split is re-elaborated in Soloveitchik's reading of the biblical creation stories in *The Lonely Man of Faith* in the corresponding distinction between "majestic man" tied to knowledge as conquest and "covenantal man" tied to what Shira Wolosky calls "otherness" and a "break" from "instrumental selfhood," as well as the forms of knowledge associated with it.[2] In Wolosky's gendered reading, majestic man serves as the masculine counterpart to not only the "feminized," but the more "feminist" figure of second Adam. Wolosky is even "tempted to say," she writes, "that Rav Soloveitchik's lonely man of faith is in many ways a woman."[3] In my reading, Soloveitchik's loneliness—the break from the self first figured as a knowledge of a break from the men of Brisk—begins in the realm of the feminine, outside the gathering of male scholars in Pruzhna.

In Soloveitchik's idealized representation, as Lawrence Kaplan points out (in response to Wolosky), masculine and feminine may complement one another, creating the demand not for Soloveitchik's "lonely man" or Wolosky's "lonely woman," but rather the "lonely androgynous person of faith," neither exclusively male or female, embodying both conquest and otherness.[4] Soloveitchik himself glosses the relationship between the two figures that Wolosky sees as masculine and feminine as entailing a "complementary movement" rather than a "dialectical" one (*LMF*, 83). But Soloveitchik's continued ambivalence to both masculine and feminine renders this idealized androgynous version of the "two-faced creation" an artificial construct, occluding the continued tensions between what I map out in this chapter: a decidedly masculine realm of interpretation as conquest, and the realms of repentance and ethics, the latter, characterized by multiple agencies, and inflected by what Wolosky calls feminine "otherness." What Kaplan attributes to the "dialectical, tension-riddled nature" of Soloveitchik's works and what Wolosky calls the "reciprocal dialectic" between Soloveitchik's masculine and feminine types in *Lonely Man* remains, in my reading, fractured and anxious, leaving a split between ethical and hermeneutic realms.[5] In the essays of *Out of the Whirlwind*, as well as the contemporary essays "Catharsis" and "Confrontation," two attitudes emerge: one is genuinely dialectical, paralleling the languages of repentance in which otherness is acknowledged and transformed; the other is linked to the epistemological assumptions of the 1940s, in which otherness is exiled through knowledge as conquest. In the later works, loss and desolation are actively cultivated, but rather than undermining the conception of knowledge as conquest, the two inform one another, perpetuating each other as oscillating and mutually exclusive poles.

The experience of catastrophe and loss leads both to the radical qualification of the modes of cognition of *Halakhic Man*, but also, paradoxically, to the continuation of its paradigms. That is, the ideal of complete cognitive mastery embodied in the image of Soloveitchik's father in his grandfather's living room, and rendered as type in the figure of the halakhic man, produces its alternate and inverse image of cognitive desolation and loss. Rabbi Moses, as father figure, is not only the figure of triumph, but also—the earlier story remains a precedent for both triumph and defeat—the one who verges on despair. That alternation, never a dialectic, continues to inform the epistemological assumptions of Soloveitchik's later work. Although Soloveitchik is insistent upon showing, in Kristeva's terms, that he knows how to lose, the loss Soloveitchik experiences, and indeed cultivates, remains the devastating loss suffered by the Freudian melancholic, not a loss rehabilitated by mourning.

Where Soloveitchik's ethics, elaborated in the later essays, is based on the acknowledgment of multiple agencies and difference, as well as their dialectical relation, Soloveitchik's legal hermeneutics, informed by the continued conception of knowledge as conquest, remain uninflected by loss or difference. Although he attributes cathartic powers to loss and cultivates it in his well-known celebration of defeat, it remains ultimately separate from the cognitive act and from the act of legal interpretation itself. This experience of cognition as loss—the subject's desolation in the face of a reality he cannot hope to understand—is the flip side of the total presence romanticized in the epistemological capacity of the halakhic man. The oscillation between triumph and desolation experienced by the one who Soloveitchik refers to as "the knower" shows the persistence of the melancholy embrace of the law of the 1940s, the enlightenment idealization of full knowledge, and the consequent desolation and desperation at the loss of that ideal ("Catharsis," 51). Soloveitchik shows himself, in his own terms, to be "caught like a pendulum between two poles," between "victory and triumph" and "withdrawal and retreat" ("Majesty," 26, 31). The continuation of this model of cognitive triumph and defeat, along with the genuinely dialectical antithetic ethics that emerges in the essays of the late 1950s and early 1960s, shows Soloveitchik's work to be consistently conflicted, if not ruptured. The epistemological pluralism, perspectivism, and embrace of multiple agencies in conceptions of *teshuva* and ethics remain in conflict with—despite the emphasis on loss—conceptions of legal or halakhic cognition. In this sense, Soloveitchik's legal conceptions of cognition, married as they are to the model of conquest, never catch up to the pluralism and openness to difference of Soloveitchik's ethics. For at the very same time that Soloveitchik shows himself rebelling against the cognitive paradigms of his ancestors, he also, in the emphasis on loss and catastrophe, paradoxically reaffirms them, asserting a model of epistemological certainty, as well as a conception of transmission from which death and loss are absent.

To Lichtenstein's question, "Does Jewish tradition recognize an ethic independent of Halakha?" this chapter answers, by turning to his teacher's work, an emphatic yes, and suggests that Soloveitchik resorts to the ethical realm as a refuge from the epistemological certainty of the halakhic man with whom he identifies and, at the same time, resists.[6] Soloveitchik's later works enact the Freudian insight that the ego at once pursues its own aggrandizement and destruction—the *ergo sum*, Soloveitchik writes, "contains the moment of nihility"—but only in relation to an ethical realm independent from the realm of legal hermeneutics, outside of the study hall (*Whirl*, 156). The Brisk emphasis on Torah as decree, paradoxically, helps to open up the separate sphere of ethical consideration in which the undermining of the cognitive ambitions of the ego becomes possible.

The current chapter proceeds first by articulating the ways in which Soloveitchik's postwar emphasis on subjectivity qualifies earlier conceptions of cognition and helps lay the ground for a new ethics, one that situates itself as undermining the one-dimensionality of the post-Holocaust American man. The chapter continues in showing the persistence of the epistemological and hermeneutic categories of the halakhic man in Soloveitchik's work—even after the experience of catastrophe. In the 1959 *hesped*, or eulogy, for his uncle, Soloveitchik delineates the new type of the halakhic man, even as the lineaments of the old figure remain visible. For the halakhic man, even after the experience of epistemological humility brought on by the Holocaust, the singularity of an absolute truth, that is, a knowledge based on conquest, remains the ideal.

The Trace

The works on which Soloveitchik's reputation as a philosopher rest, *Halakhic Man* and *Halakhic Mind*, emphasize the priority of the objective realm, and the denial and even repression of subjectivity. Mayer Twersky elicits the parallels between the two texts of the 1940s, showing how their philosophical arguments presuppose an antipathy to religious subjectivity. The "three-pronged critique of religious subjectivism in *The Halakhic Man*," Twersky writes, "is essentially the same as the halakhic critique of subjectivism in *Halakhic Mind*."[7] Notwithstanding Soloveitchik's Marburg neo-Kantian emphasis on reconstruction—and the reciprocity between subject and object idealized in the epistemological realm—Soloveitchik's starting point in his texts of the 1940s are those "objective forms and principles" that must "supplement subjectivity." The "given," in the terms of Soloveitchik's philosophical account, takes priority, and not merely temporally, over the subject. The "exoteric objective series," Soloveitchik argues, "is far more universal than recondite subjectivity" (*Mind*, 80).

The attack on religious subjectivism not only focuses on the degraded forms of ethics and religious experience entailed by "recondite subjectivity," but also alludes to a framework in which philosophies founded on subjectivist intuitionism had been historically embodied. Soloveitchik's attack on religious subjectivity may deploy a Brisk tradition to inveigh against a modern strand of individualism, but the attack on the "subjective intuitive attitudes" of his contemporaries, Husserl's disciples "the most celebrated philosophers of the Third Reich" (Heidegger among them), shows the extent to which *Halakhic Mind*, among other things, is a meditation on contemporary events in Europe. Both works allude to the minatory potential of subjectivist philosophical tendencies unqualified by objectivist constraints as not so mediated responses to the Shoah (*Mind*, 53).[8] The Kantian "principle of the spontaneity of spirit" had, Soloveitchik writes, many manifestations. It was transformed by Schopenhauer into "blind will," by Nietzsche into the will of the "superman," and, finally, "perverted" by contemporaries "into the desire for brutal and murderous domination." Such views, Soloveitchik concludes, "have brought chaos and disaster to our world, which is drowning in its blood" (*Man*, 164n147). For Soloveitchik, religious subjectivism may have later attenuated (primarily in the United States) into sentimentalism and needless esotericism, but in Europe it provided the philosophical underpinnings for the "barbaric and deleterious" forces of the Nazi regime (*Mind*, 80).

David Weiss Halivni's work, his meditations on his personal experience of the Holocaust, serve as an instructive parallel to Soloveitchik's. After the Shoah, Halivni resorts to the consolations of prayer and the ostensible objectivity of the "literal meaning" of Talmudic texts. Soloveitchik, by contrast, turns away from what he understands as the "subjective excesses" that informed Nazi ideology, turning instead to an emphasis on the legal objectification of the halakhic system. Halivni abandons the hermeneutic enterprise of the subjective realm altogether (no longer possible in the absence of the divine), as the "plain meaning" occupies the center of his system. For Halivni, "the legacy of subjective rabbinic opinion," increased by the temporal distance from revelation, is an irreversible phenomenon. Given the divine abandonment of subjects acting—and interpreting—in history leads to the concession, Halivni laments, that "we are guided by the plain sense alone."[9] For Soloveitchik, however, it is the assimilation of meaning and experience within the hermeneutics of the objectively defined halakha that fends off a catastrophe associated with a degraded and dangerous subjectivity. Both Halivni and Soloveitchik of his early work retreat from the subjective realm, the former regretting the failure of "subjective" hermeneutics, and the latter emphasizing the necessary subordination of the subject within objective constraints. Halivni embraces the hermeneutics of plain meaning; Soloveitchik, the priority of an objectification within what he calls the *Deus dixit*, or "the canonized scriptures," for him, the most "reliable standard reference for objectivity" (*Mind*, 81).

The construct of "halakhic man" and Soloveitchik's emphasis on objectification not only serve as a response to contemporary historical tragedy but also to the family consciousness of death, which is rendered paradigmatic in the account of his grandfather, R. Hayyim. In the normative registers of *Halakhic Man*, the outpouring of emotion associated with death—both historical and personal—finds containment through the halakha, which sets the "objectivity" of halakhic man against the "highly subjective" tendencies of the *homo religiosus*. The latter finds himself immersed in the emotive realm of a subjectivity that leads toward the "blurring of forms and boundaries" associated not only with raw emotion and sentimentalism, but with fascism. By contrast, the ideal of the halakhic man evidences a "psychic equilibrium," characterized by his "thrust towards objectivity and lawfulness," which is an antidote and response to the excesses of religious subjectivity and contemporary events (*Man*, 66).

In this sense, Soloveitchik can be compared to T. S. Eliot, who anxiously disassociates himself from the individualism of Romantic and Victorian antecedents, subordinating what he calls in the canonical essay of 1923 "the individual talent" to a reified conception of "Tradition."[10] Like Eliot, who called for the "extinction of personality," *Halakhic Man*, evidencing antipathy toward the figure of subjectivity, *homo religiosus*, attempts to subordinate his energies to objective realms. But Soloveitchik, like Eliot, had a strong sense of the excesses his work attempted to contain. As the latter wrote, "only those who have a personality . . . know what it means to escape from it."[11] The objectifications of the halakha serve as a corrective to the dangerous excesses of subjectivity, with which Soloveitchik, like his earlier contemporary, likely identified. Only in the later works is that will toward the expression of subjectivity—rendered ethical—fully realized.

Although the halakhic man "draws upon the same psychic resources as does *homo religiosus*," Soloveitchik admits, he does not, in the end, strain "against the reign of the norm and accepts them against his will." Death may be "frightening," "menacing," and "dreadful," but when the cognitive mechanisms of halakhic man succeed in transforming death into an "object" of cognition, the "horror is gone" (*Man*, 73). Cognition, understood as mastery, transforms the emotions associated with the *homo religiosus*, as the "inner will," in this rendering, becomes identical with "outside command." Soloveitchik's grandfather, R. Hayyim, overcomes his fear of death in a paradigm moment of the "halakhic man" through the processes of cognition while studying the laws of ritual defilement. The account of his Brisk ancestor provides a primary instance of how "objectification triumphs over the subjective terror of death," not one so much based on Soloveitchik's explicit metaphors of "blending," but rather upon subjugation and conquest. In the cognitive gesture of the halakhic man, "law and principle" govern over the object, and the "person over the thing" (*Man*, 73). Mastery of the objective realm over the subjective rather than the dialectic dominates Soloveitchik's epistemological and hermeneutic conceptions.

For Soloveitchik, as presented in the previous chapter, the cognitive act is first akin to an act of acquisition, and then, conquest. It is through cognition that he "acquires" the object that "'strikes such alarm into him"; through the cognitive act, "he brings it into his domain and obtains title to it." As a result, the "terrifying abyss disappears, the strangeness fades from sight and leaves no trace behind" (*Man*, 73–74). The source of the most profound of *homo religiosus*'s subjective excesses—death—is confronted by the figure of halakhic man and domesticated through the objectifying act of cognition. In this account, the objectifying rationality of halakha emerges as an antidote not only to the historical manifestations of an unbridled subjectivity and intuitionism manifested in the events played on the contemporary historical stage but also to the outpouring of emotional life— the experience of otherness and death. As both "lord and master," the powers of cognition of the halakhic man triumph over the surging emotional forces to which the *homo religiosus* remains vulnerable (*Man*, 73).

The halakhic man's confidence in the efficacy of the objectifying forces of cognition does undergo explicit qualification in *Halakhic Man*, but in a footnote where Soloveitchik identifies an exception to the otherwise dominating powers of cognition, that is, "the cognition of God." When "man cognizes the Creator of the cosmos, he submits himself more and more to His infinite will," Soloveitchik writes, stressing here the emphasis on infinity and the "aura of mystery" (*Man*, 154n87). The acknowledgment of the inadequacy of the cognitive gesture in relation to the divine, relegated to a footnote in the earlier work, leads in the post-Holocaust writing to an encounter with the experience of that mystery and to the elaboration of the "crisis of human finitude." The essays collected in *Out of the Whirlwind* anatomize Soloveitchik's experience of that crisis, rendered in the confessional account of his illness and subsequent operation in 1959, which, he writes, initiated him "into the secret of non-being" (*Whirl*, 131) resulting in an epistemological humility absent in his works of the 1940s.

Soloveitchik's later writing return to the "trace" of the "horrifying abyss" of death, excised in the earlier work, and also to the subjective sphere that is able to register that trace. In this sense, Soloveitchik's personal encounter with "non-being" contributes to his resolve to reconfront, in the realm of cognition, the "*tertium quid* of being and nothingness" that was ostensibly overcome in *Halakhic Man* (*Man*, 72). In *Out of the Whirlwind*, particularly the four most philosophically substantive essays of the volume (written between 1957 and 1961), Soloveitchik explores the limits of the cognitive gesture alluded to in the note to *Halakhic Man*. From the acknowledgment of the limits of the powers of cognition and rationality, and the corresponding acknowledgment of the finitude of human existence, the "world's emptiness and chaos" reappears—and as more than a mere "trace" (*Man*, 72).

Indeed, consciousness of human finitude, the limits of the cognitive gesture, and an emphasis on epistemological humility emerging from a consciousness of defeat are the central philosophical emphases of Soloveitchik's post-Holocaust writing. With the focus on loss and catastrophe, these essays reflect an ongoing engagement with the legacy of the Shoah but also resonate with Soloveitchik's personal history, thus producing an even more emphatic version of the melancholy opposition between presence and loss. Soloveitchik's newly articulated epistemological humility does not lead to a qualification of the cognitive gesture but rather a retreat from it, followed, however, by a return to the model of knowledge as domination. Through the critique of American Jewish life, and the instrumental, utilitarian, reason that informs it, Soloveitchik argues that the prospect of an unbridled subjectivity no longer poses the greatest threat. Instead, the processes of rationalization, cognition, and objectification, which, unqualified by immersion in the "experiential," undermine, if not render impossible, in the normative registers of the text, what Soloveitchik calls the "full adventure" of man (*Whirl*, 176). Part of that "adventure" leads Soloveitchik to cultivate the subjective realm of the ethical, and consequently, an identity that is independent from the legacy of halakhic men.

Traumatic Chosenness

"A Halakhic Approach to Suffering" returns to the cognition of God, employing a language consonant with that of *Halakhic Man* in which the metaphor for cognition is one of subjugation and conquest. The "scientific adventure," Soloveitchik writes, represents the "human desire for conquest." The "crowning victory," however, of cognitive man is not knowledge of the natural world but rather "finding God" (*Whirl*, 106). In the approach to the divine, man is not only "a warrior" but also a "conqueror, an aggressive, bold courageous adventurer, yearning and longing for self-vastness, for self-explanation, for the infinite" (*Whirl*, 107). The energies of conquest and expansion that resolve in the "peace and tranquility" in *Halakhic Man* are undermined by the cognizance through which the "incessant drive for self-enlargement" necessarily "comes to a halt" (*Man*, 73). The man who had amassed "victory upon victory" and triumphed in "conquest upon conquest" now returns to his "point of departure and is defeated" (*Whirl*, 107). This acceptance of defeat is the most distinguishing characteristic of Soloveitchik's later work: what once had been anathema to him, that is, the terrifying loss conveyed in the story of his father, is now aggressively asserted as a sign of psychic as well as ethical well-being.

Defeat in *Out of the Whirlwind* comes into being as the experience of "cosmic man" gives way to the "crisis" of "covenantal man." Cosmic man is governed by the "logos"; his "world is replete with orderliness and beauty, serenity and peace." The move from cosmic man's "natural-historical" perspective (in which the logos enables man to domesticate the world) to that of "metaphysical-covenantal" man is engendered by the realization of the *failure* of the cognitive act. Imagined as totalizing in *Halakhic Man*, cognition is acknowledged as halting in its efforts to "reach the endless fringes of reality" (*Whirl*, 120, 107). The cognitive gesture, as Soloveitchik writes in "The Crisis of Human Finitude," remains insufficient in the face of what he calls "the *mysterium magnum*"—that which necessarily escapes human comprehension (*Whirl*, 156). While man's knowledge rests, in echoes of the language of *Halakhic Man*, upon "substitution of the known for the unknown, the comprehensible quantity for the qualitative phenomenon," the mystery of being remains allusive, outside of the grasp of cognition. Cognition attempts to expand its realm of conquest, but the "wider the areas" the intellect explores, "the greater and more challenging becomes the mystery of being as a whole" ("*Whirl*," 156). The mystery—eliciting the experience of human finitude—renders absurd cognitive man's desire for absolute intellectual conquest. For Soloveitchik, Kohelet (or Ecclesiastes) becomes the normative biblical text, as he asks in the contemporaneous essay "Catharsis": "Is man indeed a knower?" (51). Recognition of the "unknown quantity in the cognitive performance" leads to an awareness associated with man as a "creature" who, as "part of finite reality," acknowledges his condition as "incomplete, deficient and impregnated with paradoxes and absurdities" ("*Whirl*," 157). Cognition transforms "the knower" from an agent of certainty into an agent of only limited cognitive power.

The seamless efficacy of cognition as acquisition or conquest yields to a form of knowing that reveals its inadequacy in the presence of a reality which it is never able to fully assimilate. Even the scientist, Soloveitchik writes, recognizes the gap between scientific concept or paradigm and "event" ("Catharsis," 52). The incommensurability between language and object can never be overcome. Not only does cognition fail in specific contexts, but the contexts in which it has mastery become more and more limited: "the cognitive and technological gestures . . . have a chance to succeed only in small sectors of reality" ("Confrontation," 11n5). Not only does knowledge fail to penetrate the given as in the earlier works, but the "reality" to which cognition directs itself goes far beyond the latter's capacity to understand it.

Central to the essays of this period is a terminology appropriated from Rudolf Otto's *Idea of the Holy*. In a footnote to *Halakhic Man*, Soloveitchik employs Otto as a means of countering the simplistic conception of religious experience prevalent in liberal theologies (*Man*, 139–140n4). Otto had sought to set the grounds for a more profound Christianity by reinstating "the non-rational element" into an experience that had become "one-sidedly intellectualistic."[12] For Otto, that goal could be achieved by cultivating the "creature feeling," that is, man's "submergence into nothingness before an overpowering absolute might of some kind," which he dubbed, alternatively, the *mysterium tremendum*, or more simply, the "numinous."[13] Soloveitchik foregrounds this "creature feeling" and defines the "apocalyptic experience of God" as a "leap outside of oneself in a journey from a here-and-now reality to the numinous" (*Whirl*, 172, 121). Beyond the level of what Soloveitchik calls, following Otto, the "rationalization and categorization" of cognitive man is a "numinous awareness" that threatens to render the former irrelevant (*Whirl*, 127). The awareness of the "numen" entails a crisis that manifests itself in suffering, for God "reveals Himself" through a "whirlwind" of "pain and sorrow," appearing to "man through the violent shock of encountering infinity." Through the "apocalyptic trauma of revelation," "finite-conditioned man," confronted by the "numinous, all-powerful and all-negating" God, "becomes aware of the suspension of his own selfhood" (*Whirl*, 128).

For Soloveitchik, the apocalyptic trauma of revelation is not limited to sacred history but becomes part of the personally sanctified history of each individual. The prophet Ezekiel's "distressing encounter with nihility," presented through the lens of Otto's "numen," serves as a paradigm for the "existential" experience of modern man. Ezekiel experienced the "historical cataclysm" and entered into a great dialogue "with the hidden, numinous, mysterious God" (*Whirl*, 147). The message of the experience of cognitive inadequacy—the awareness of suffering that transcends the rationalist grasp—is transferred from the historical experience of the prophet to modern man in his experience of existentialist "anxiety." For the prophet as well as for contemporary man, the "catastrophic disclosure" instigated through the experience of the "numinous" must be assimilated into the "all-embracing existential awareness" of the spiritual personality (*Whirl*, 140–41).[14] Indeed, the "shock" of the encounter with nonbeing, of "peeping into the abyss of nihility," must leave a mark on the existential consciousness. The "heart engages in a dialogue with nihility," and this dialogue, Soloveitchik affirms, "should never be terminated" (*Whirl*, 130–31). Soloveitchik's insistence on suffering as imposing an imperative on man is not only a call to activity, an ethical imperative; before that, it is an existential imperative, a demand on the psyche.

Where in the earlier work the gap between concept and reality was a source of anxiety and despair, in Soloveitchik's post-Holocaust writings, despair is actively appropriated as a sign of existential authenticity, transmuted into a new conception of the subject. For Soloveitchik, paradoxically, the "submergence into nothingness" serves as the basis for a new conception of self. Through the subjectivity that comes into being through the experience of the *numen*, Soloveitchik develops a perspective to critique the impoverished utilitarian and rationalist theology, associated for him with both the biblical figure of Job and the American experience. More than that, however, the "I am lonely" of the *Lonely Man of Faith*, finding philosophical expression in the essays of *Out of the Whirlwind*, now transforms the memory of his existential anxiety and isolation of his youthful self in Pruzhna into a mark of distinctiveness, and even of chosenness, decisively distancing him from his Brisk ancestry. That is, with the crisis of human finitude emerges a new consciousness of both self and heroism that distinguishes him from the typological figure of the halakhic man. Crisis, embodied as an epistemological humility that emerges in confrontation with the *numen*, leads Soloveitchik to develop a conception of "Halakhic heroism" in which defeat and loneliness are signs of existential authenticity and election ("Catharsis," 43).

Rejecting "clear-cut logical processes and utilitarian approaches," Soloveitchik advocates instead "the spontaneous leap into the absurd"—a Kierkegaardian leap that "may save man when he finds himself in utter distress" ("Catharsis," 40). Against the classical heroism of Achilles, Soloveitchik advocates a heroism based on defeat, where the heroic "leap" is enacted in "humility and in the hush of a dark night of loneliness" ("Catharsis," 50). The "absurd" figure of loneliness who stands against both the utilitarian rationalism of modern man and the heroism of the ancients has biblical antecedents. The patriarch Jacob, after his battle with the angel of Esau, is represented by Soloveitchik as the "helpless, lonely non-logical Jacob" who unexpectedly finds himself "the victor, the hero" ("Catharsis," 41). Soloveitchik's interpretation reads not only as innovative biblical homiletics but also as a belated autobiographical reframing in which his own existential loneliness is projected onto the biblical patriarch.

Here, the loneliness suffered as a child emerges retroactively as a sign of chosenness; it is a loneliness that the elder Joseph is now finally in a position to choose. Despite the confidence of his appearance, the classical heroic figure, Soloveitchik writes, remains "frightened" and "disenchanted"; he only theatrically plays the figure of the "heroic figure on the stage." Those who play a public role—and the explicit attack is on the rational man of the American context—is, in fact, Soloveitchik writes in a Freudian vain, sublimating an unacknowledged existential anxiety. Jacob's heroism was different: "he was not out to impress anybody." The patriarch's heroism, Soloveitchik affirms, will last "as long as man is aware of himself as a singular being" ("Catharsis," 42). Soloveitchik is careful not to associate this public persona with the majestic public figure of halakhic man, but the lonely man in defeat—the one who realizes the imperative for individuation—nonetheless represents a qualification of the celebrated precedent of the earlier work. The singularity, once the burdensome given of Soloveitchik's life, alone on the bed in his grandfather's living room, is now represented as a form of election through an insight only available and developed in hindsight.

The singular "halakhic hero" of Soloveitchik's present is not only defeated, he actually elects defeat: "he foregoes the ecstasy of victory" to "take defeat at his own hands" ("Catharsis," 43). "The pointing out of one in the crowd," Soloveitchik writes, "is a traumatic experience," but it is also a "great experience" (*Whirl*, 43). Soloveitchik, after the Holocaust, now chooses the defeat that distinguishes him and shows him to be singular, distinct from those who pursue the theatrical spectacle of conquest. Soloveitchik's heroism of repentance is one he himself enacts by remaking his past, with the appropriation and recasting of his antecedent sense of melancholy loss. The singularity that had once characterized his shame and his traumatic private life, now transformed, becomes in this implicit autobiography the necessary precedent for divine service. Trauma and the recurring term "catastrophe" have become normative after the Holocaust. For Soloveitchik, the recognition, and even the conscious choosing of that trauma—both historical and personal—become necessary prerequisites for both cognition and ethics.

Confronting catastrophe, he learns "to stop short, turn around, and retreat." Although the catastrophic expresses itself as "pure negation" (the Hebrew word finds an equivalent in the Greek *katastrophein*, "to turn down or turn over"), Soloveitchik embraces, even chooses the defeat that catastrophe bears (*Whirl*, 136). The pathos of loneliness is transformed into the heroism of both defeat and what he calls "recoil." The figure, "engaged" in "recoil" from the experience of "being confronted by God," emerges as a new subject, born out of "withdrawal" and epistemological humility (*Whirl*, 107). Soloveitchik develops a form of agency that, already inchoate in the discussion of repentance in *Halakhic Man*, further distances him from his father and his Brisk inheritance.

In Soloveitchik's representation of the typological father, the attitude that the latter manifests toward his son is one of "recoil," a withdrawal that nurtures the autonomy of the son, the means through which he can attain "independence and maturity" (*Family*, 162). In Soloveitchik's definition of "halakhic heroism," with which he reframes the subject, it is not the father who recoils from the son in that ambivalent gesture nurturing independence but the son who recoils from the cognitive conquest bequeathed by the father. Where the father had, in Soloveitchik's typology, recoiled from the son to encourage independence, it is now the recoil enacted by the son—turning away from the cognitive mastery associated with the father—that allows for a different kind of independence, an individuation in relation to his predecessors. Indeed, for Soloveitchik, as he writes in "Majesty and Humility," "victory" may be found only "in retreat"; "the movement of recoil redeems the forward movement" (37). The son pursues that redemption, a heroism characterized by what Soloveitchik calls an "antithetical movement," which allows for the emergence of a new halakhic hero: Soloveitchik himself.

From a psychoanalytic perspective, Soloveitchik enacts what Leo Bersani calls the foundational motive of Oedipal rivalry, the achievement of "autonomy of consciousness." "Only after the father has been deposed," Bersani writes, can the son be born again, but "this time as the father."[15] Soloveitchik's "recoil" is part of a movement that associates him with the father even at the same time that the embrace of loss and despair distinguishes him from his forbearer. In Soloveitchik's constructions of childhood, it was the father whose recoil from the son had made the latter lonely; now it is the son, dramatically reclaiming his loneliness, recoiling from the father's cognitive excesses. Even as Soloveitchik aggressively foregrounds himself as a figure of loss—akin to the blessing and curse of the memory he associates with the feminine—there is the pathos of attempting to stave off the trauma associated with loss. The "Halakha," Soloveitchik writes, "wants man to be defeated by himself, to take defeat at his own hands." Yet the strange "technology of mental health" by which man will be trained gradually "to take defeat at his own hands in small matters, in his daily routine, in his habits of eating, in his sex life" reveals a persistent and acute fear of loss. Soloveitchik may celebrate loss and the persona of his works depends on its conscious appropriation, but his proposed mental health intervention betrays a continued fear and vulnerability to a loss, imagined as overwhelming, and finally, defeating (*Whirl*, 114).

After the catastrophe of Holocaust and his experience of personal loss, defeat figures centrally for Soloveitchik in the realm of cognition. But the antithetic sensibility spurred on by the experience of human finitude, in Soloveitchik's later work also plays out only in relationship to moral discourses and ethics. In Soloveitchik's terms, there are "two moralities"—"one of victory and triumph, one of withdrawal and retreat" ("Majesty," 35). To critique the absolutizing tendencies of cognition and the first 'morality' in relationship to the second, he turns to the figure of Job. The focus on Job and his moral absolutism becomes a counter-type for the second morality, accommodating loss and otherness, Soloveitchik's antithetic ethics.

One-Dimensional Man

Job appears in the essay "The Voice of My Beloved That Knocketh" as a type of the philosopher and a slave of fate, eschewing ethical engagement for metaphysical speculation ("Voice," 54). In contrast to the "man of destiny" as figure of creative engagement, Job eschews autonomous activity for philosophical speculation—stuck, as Soloveitchik writes, on the "why question," the perspective that commits him, parallel to the Newtonian scientist, to an external perspective.[16] In *Out of the Whirlwind*, Job is not so much the philosopher but the type of the cosmic man, addressed by the divine through abundance and wealth—the plenty of the "ontic revelation." When Job fails to heed that call, having "missed the message," he is visited by the catastrophic revelation of suffering and nihility (*Whirl*, 139).[17] The poles of experience that Job endures before and after the catastrophic revelation of his own suffering come to inform, for Soloveitchik, the experience of post-Holocaust man. Like Job, modern man oscillates between the natural revelation, which addresses itself to the "joyous ontic consciousness"—both the plenty and the forgetting it induces—and the "catastrophic revelation," which addresses itself to a "tormented nihilistic consciousness" (*Whirl*, 137).

In "The Crisis of Human Finitude," Job is represented simply as the "philistine." His philistine tendencies manifest themselves in a desire for "conquest and security," and he therefore "leads a narrow, shut-in-existence" where all of his efforts are aimed to maintain the status quo, to secure "safety for himself and his family." The "religious act" becomes "the expression of a utilitarian, economy-minded individual" (*Whirl*, 152). Akin to the "one-dimensional man" of Herbert Marcuse's nearly contemporary study, Job, the philistine, in the terms of the

Frankfurt School, "reifies" his spiritual service. Religion is merely "a business venture, a pragmatic affair" through which he "hopes to appease his Creator" (*Whirl*, 152). Marcuse, a Marxist Freudian, understands the individual as "introjecting" the commands of a postindustrial society, thereby repressing himself.[18] In Soloveitchik's parallel theological terms, the individual embraces a utilitarian service, and thus occludes both the spiritual and "the mystery." For both Soloveitchik and Marcuse, the self is reified through having been subjected, that is dominated by the instrumentalism of an impoverished contemporary culture. As Soloveitchik relates, Job brings his "bourgeois notions" even to his "ostensibly spiritual *avodah*," domesticating "the mystery" by subordinating it to his utilitarian schemes (*Whirl*, 152).

Job's desire to be "the first to attain and the last to lose" manifests itself as much in the epistemological realm as it does in the material one (*Whirl*, 151). As a cognitive "absolutist," Job insulates himself from a reality he refuses to acknowledge. In this sense, the perspectives of the "philosopher Job" of "The Voice of My Beloved That Knocketh" and the philistine Job of "The Crisis of Human Finitude" dovetail—they are both fundamentalists. The tendencies of the "philosophico-speculative thought" led the philosopher Job of the earlier essay to employ his capacities for "intellectual abstraction" to develop what Soloveitchik calls a "metaphysics of evil" in which evil is assimilated within a theological scheme. Yet a metaphysics determined to accommodate evil through the powers of a philosophical ideal is presupposed, for Soloveitchik, upon deception and denial. Job as philosopher uses the cognitive tools at his disposal to domesticate evil, to simply "cover it up."[19] Job the philistine clings to "a definitive pattern of existence" and is never willing to relinquish his cognitive mastery (*Whirl*, 153). Unmindful of the "dialectics of being," Job makes himself prone to the "absolutization and hypostatization of experiences," projecting his cognitive schemes on a world that resists them (*Whirl*, 138). Job attributed to his own "desires, dreams, ambitions and visions" an "absolute significance," an act described by Soloveitchik as an "an idolatrous performance" (*Whirl*, 138). Subjecting the divine to human paradigms constitutes an idolatry of placing the "numinous" fully within man's cognitive grasp. Soloveitchik understands conventional theological narratives as mere projections, akin to what Adam Phillips describes from a psychoanalytic perspective as mechanisms of "enchantment," teleological stories that lead away from the world rather than toward it.[20] The excesses of the world that appear in the works of the 1940s only to be subordinated to halakhic constructs now return in full force in the theological category of the numinous, that "trace" that resists objectification.

Job's absolutist tendencies and his desire for conquest define the personality of modern man. For contemporary man, Soloveitchik writes, "is axiologically minded"—satisfied as "long as he thinks that he is in the service of a value or system of values" (*Whirl*, 177). Modern anxiety, Soloveitchik observes, emerges when there is the perception that the "axiological order"—whether founded on political, social, intellectual, or even materialistic values—may collapse. Predisposed toward structuring his life axiologically, contemporary man fails to realize that "values" are themselves contingent human projections. The God–man relationship, forged at the moment of "numinous awareness" entails the acknowledgment that although the soul may have momentarily "befriended some value," that bond must always be considered dissoluble (*Whirl*, 178). Failing to show an awareness of the necessary dissolubility of axiological commitments, whether pragmatic or philosophical, invites, for Soloveitchik, catastrophe. In this sense, Job and his contemporary American counterpart, Soloveitchik suggests, share a similar fate.

For Job, the "catastrophic disclosure" is the inevitable (and unwanted) antidote for idolatrous tendencies (*Whirl*, 146). The closed world of idolatry opens only after the disclosure of nihility that eventually leads Job, as it does in the account "The Voice of My Beloved That Knocketh" out of the circumscribed bounds of his ego to community and prayer, representing a responsiveness to the human and divine, respectively. Mistaking "a fantasy for a fact, a mirage for a reality," Job had rendered himself unable to see beyond the limits of his own limited epistemological horizon. Living at the "majestic plane," complacent in "adopting a false sense of happiness and perfection" and content to only live "in triumph and victory," ends, Soloveitchik writes, "in eternal failure and Holocaust" (*Whirl*, 165).

During the 1940s, facing the chaos and disaster inflicted by the Nazis, Soloveitchik stressed the need for objectification. In the United States of the 1950s, where the "myopic" and "insensitive" modern Jew "shuts out the spiritual values of Judaism," Soloveitchik emphasizes the experience of infinitude, mystery, and emotion bracketed in the earlier works.[21] In his reading, the axiological drive, embodied even in the apparently noble undertaking of living in the "service of a . . . system of values," only manifests modern man's "neurotic" strategies—again Soloveitchik embraces a Freudian register—to insulate himself from the call of the infinite (*Whirl*, 177). Catastrophe and Holocaust were wrought during the 1940s through the apotheosis of the will and the "unbridled tide of the affective stream" (*Whirl*, 53). Amidst the "ontic plenty" of the United States in the 1950s, however, catastrophe, and even Holocaust, remains a possibility for those who, Job-like, turn away from the experience of mystery.

The catastrophic disclosure that Job eventually faces permits him, in Soloveitchik's reading, to transcend his self-centered life and to reach beyond the circumscribed goals formed by his idolatrous tendencies. This self-transcendence is presupposed upon the embrace of defeat and humility, and the consecration of "human incompleteness as an offering to God" in the "giving up" of "illusions of grandeur and glory, of success and conquest" (*Whirl*, 158). Soloveitchik relates in a confessional mode that on the eve of his operation in 1959, "the fantastic flights of human foolishness and egocentrism were distant from me" (*Whirl*, 131).[22] Here, through a personal account, the cognitive assuredness of the halakhic man is most aggressively qualified:

> The more knowledge I accumulate, the more the mystery deepens, the more complex is the problem, the more fascinating is the unknown. I shall restlessly explore, investigate, search and try to comprehend, but know that the radius of the scientifically charted sectors will grow one-dimensionally, while the area of the problem will expand two dimensionally (*Whirl*, 158).

The passage stands as a rejection of the "method of quantification"—the "difficult calculations" and "mathematical functions"—elaborated by the halakhic man (*Man*, 55, 83). As Soloveitchik writes in the later work: "I am not regretting my search for knowledge, but I am renouncing my arrogant desire for a complete cognitive experience, for conquest which is not followed by defeat" (*Whirl*, 158). Soloveitchik here becomes a figure of Job (in some partial ways, he may be all of the types he describes in his works), renouncing the assuredness of the halakhic man, the once "majestic" figure who now, after suffering, yields to the necessity of defeat. The defeat and loneliness that the young Joseph as a passive child of "fate" once perceived as regrettable, even victimizing, are now, by the Soloveitchik of the late writings, aggressively embraced, both as the man of suffering and the man of "destiny." Indeed, in the later work, the experience of suffering and the embrace of trauma emerge as the conditions for becoming the "man of destiny."

The cognizance of finitude and an "existence" acknowledged to be withdrawn from the realm of one's own influence leads to both "creative performance" and "service" (*Whirl*, 149). Accordingly, Soloveitchik locates creativity in the experiential realm of service, not the cognitive realm of knowing. Eschewing the axiological frames that impose values onto the world, the man of service stands before a world to whose call he is responsive. In this way, Soloveitchik's later work parallels that of not only Bergson, who inspires the man of repentance to embrace "the fleeting moment," but also Emanuel Levinas, for whom attention to the call of "the Other" is primary. For the later Soloveitchik, only one willing to abandon the metaphysical crutches of axiology can comprehend the responsibility that "time experience" necessarily entails. By living in the moment of time—outside of "an illusory eternity"—he can hear God's call, the "summons" to "service" (*Whirl*, 147). This is the type associated with Job, who is responsive to a call he can finally hear and ready for a creative engagement with a present moment defined in Bergsonian terms: "For this moment I am alive and capable of action; what will happen the next minute I do not know" (*Whirl*, 149). By eschewing the totalizing gestures of cognition, the "definitive patterns of existence" in which he took solace, and by thus evidencing an awareness of the contingency of metaphysics, axiology, and values, Soloveitchik's Job, embracing the moment, emerges as free to act.

Ethics and the Psyche

In the post-Holocaust writings, the "raging turbulence" of emotions associated with the *homo religiosus* in *Halakhic Man* are subject to reinterpretation; his energies and "his power to create" are appropriated for the "halakhic hero," willing to embrace man's "full adventure"—the project of individuation (*Man*, 113). Soloveitchik's arguments anticipate Lionel Trilling's *Sincerity and Authenticity* (1971), which critiqued unassimilated forms of emotion associated with modern conceptions of authenticity. These decadent forms of authenticity have their origins, for Trilling, in a conception of "personal integrity" that inverts all of the avowed principles of an "inauthentic" civilization. Tracing the authentic individual from the romantic poets, later to be refined in Freudian psychoanalysis and Sartrean existentialism, Trilling shows how this now-decadent figure reached its apotheosis in a contemporary culture that celebrates an "authenticity of personal being" achieved through an "ultimate isolateness."[23] The nearly pathological contemporary obsession with "authenticity," as Trilling diagnoses it, tends away from a conception of a self based on communal forms of obligations toward an isolated subject defined by the emotions, the "natural," and the Freudian subconscious.

Soloveitchik shares Trilling's antipathy to unmediated and uninterpreted emotions, but also accommodates the contemporary existentialist emphasis on the authentic, demanding expression of unchecked emotional experience. For Judaism, Soloveitchik writes, "does not tolerate hypocrisy and unnatural behavior which is contrary to human sensitivity." The confrontation with death entails suffering and an imperative of expression—"moaning, sudden fear and shrieking." Suffering implies a demand; it "must precipitate a show of protest, a bitter complaint, a sense of existential nausea and complete confusion." The demand for existential honesty is figured as a divine command: "I want the sufferer to act as a human being, God says. Let him not suppress his humanity in order to please Me" (*Whirl*, 12). The subject here is not only given unlimited range to pursue the authenticity of an emotional response; he is commanded to express himself independently of the constraining powers of logos, law, and reason. A long way from the stoic figure of his grandfather who was "strong like flint," attending to the obligations imposed by halakha before that of tending to his dying daughter, the figure emerging in the later works, Soloveitchik's new halakhic hero, shows his existential authenticity through grief and the experience of suffering (*Man*, 78).

In the dialectical ethics of Soloveitchik, the authenticity of the existential moment and the "pure emotion" that it engenders are prerequisites for the interpretive emotional experience. That is, these subjective emotions, corresponding to the emotional "hyle," or the given, are taken into the objective or interpretive realm. As discussed in chapter 3, the psychic realm for both Freud and Soloveitchik is the interpretive realm—in which the emotional given is transmuted through psychoanalytic sublimation and Jewish repentance, respectively. In respect to pure emotion, it is only in the exceptional circumstance of *aninut*, before the codified strictures of mourning come into effect that the individual is permitted, even commanded, to dwell in the (as of yet) uninterpreted realm of emotional anguish. The laws of *aninut* provide a legal context that licenses the individual to express unmediated emotions outside of the frame of legal obligation. "Let him tear his clothes in frustrating anger and stop observing *mitzvoth*," Soloveitchik's God intones, "because his whole personality is enveloped by dark despair" (*Whirl*, 12). When a man remains "emotionally neutral"—when he does not give voice to *bekhi*, or the crying "indicative of a spontaneous, overwhelming and uncontrollable grief"—he demonstrates his lack of *humanitas* (*Whirl*, 31, 34). In contrast to stoic "neutrality," Soloveitchik emphasizes the human capacity to acknowledge the experience of despair and to be immersed in the spontaneous moment of emotion. The halakha, as Soloveitchik reads it, therefore demands that man experiences the "worthlessness and absurdity of life." *Aninut* thus becomes a kind of microcosm for the catastrophic overturning of the norm, the individual laboratory environment in which unmediated emotions are expressed.

The psychic processes of the individual psyche demand the raw material produced by suffering. In this state, "he is not free to act," but that lack of freedom paradoxically emerges as the necessary condition for the eventual exercise of freedom (*Whirl*, 194). Indeed, Soloveitchik coins the term "man of destiny" in the meditation on the Holocaust and evil in "The Voice of My Beloved That Knocketh." Only the man who first feels himself as a passive "man of fate," immersed in suffering, can eventually become the "man of destiny." In Soloveitchik's hermeneutics of the psyche, the "bitter consciousness of catastrophe" is eventually to be transformed, that is, "redeemed" to a "higher consciousness" (*Whirl*, 13). As he explains in "Abraham Mourns Sarah," the emotional resources associated with *bekhi*—authentic cries—are transmuted into the developed language of *hesped*, or eulogy. Paralleling the process of repentance, unmediated emotions are transformed into discourse (*Whirl*, 32), in Freudian terms, primary process into secondary process languages. In Soloveitchik's later works, trauma, suffering, and pain are the necessary conditions for transformation and eventual redemption.

Soloveitchik provides his philosophical gloss on the verse from Ezekiel, "In your blood you shall live!" (16:6): through the "depths of inner contradiction and negation . . . find life" (*Whirl*, 177). In the antithetic life presupposed upon suffering, the experience of negation is preserved, transformed, and in the end, redeemed. Similarly, in the corresponding realm of repentance in *Halakhic Man* and in the citing of the Talmudic sage Reish Lakish, the psychic hermeneutics of mourning relies on a parallel verse in Ezekiel (33:19): "through them shall you live." Where in relation to the emotional life, Soloveitchik recalls blood—for him, contradiction and negation—in relation to repentance, he recalls the antecedents of Ezekiel's "them"—wickedness and willful transgression—as the necessary life forces of the penitent. In both these emotive realms, although there is an emphasis on the interpretive, the given, in its otherness, remains the necessary source for the more developed ethical stance.

In "A Theory of Emotions," the "pure emotion," for which the experience of the *onen* is paradigmatic is preserved and then contextualized within both the totality of emotional life and the continuity of emotional experience (*Whirl*, 179–80).[24] The "feeling-in-itself" described in "The Crisis of Human Finitude" as a mood, or an "unrestrained emotional response," is simply "degrading" (*Whirl*, 168).[25] The mood, as an "uncontemplative" reaction to "environmental events," entails an excess of unassimilated feeling that creates inertia and promotes passivity (*Whirl*, 167). The transition from mood to emotion, that is, from "pure emotion" to an "emotional awareness," parallels the move in "The Voice of My Beloved That Knocketh" from the "man of fate" to the "man of destiny"—from passivity to activity ("Voice," 51, 55).

In "the sphere of the mood," Soloveitchik writes, "we are bondsmen, enslaved to our compulsory responses to a variety of phenomena," thus paralleling what Freud understands as a psychic life compelled by repetition. Only when these abstract, amorphous, and as-yet uncultivated feelings are raised to the "level of experience," by which Soloveitchik means the interpretive realm, does one gain "the upper hand or control over our emotions" (*Whirl*, 168). Moods are transformed into complex emotions through a process of objectification, enabled through a "feeling awareness" (*Whirl*, 190). Beginning as moods, or mere emotional data, they require distancing and cognition to be properly contextualized into the "all embracing existential awareness" (*Whirl*, 140). Only through this process, entailing engagement with the "primordial" mood does one discover the "freedom of self-formation and self-actualization" (*Whirl*, 188). Acquiescing to a mood entails the passivity of the "man of fate"; interpretive engagement with that mood is the beginning of the freedom of the "man of destiny." Creativity, for Soloveitchik, as for Freud, entails the move away from compulsive repetition understood as passivity, and the adoption of an interpretive stance that allows for creative action. For both, knowledge of the primordial experience stands as the basis for knowledge, creativity, and freedom.

To further clarify the differences between mood and emotion, Soloveitchik elaborates the Aristotelian distinction between intuitive and discursive forms of knowledge. The first form of cognition is immediate, an "almost compulsive" response to a "challenge from outside." This form of experience is not yet "knowledge" but rather what Soloveitchik calls, following the phenomenologist Edmund Husserl, "a source of authority for knowledge." What presents itself to the intuition only emerges as genuine knowledge once it has been subordinate to the "logos awareness." Hylic matter—the "primordial emotional datum"—is transformed through an act of interpretation by which the raw material of the mood is transformed. The "hyle" of the past—the given—is also a critical part of Soloveitchik's elaboration of *teshuva*, transformed into a vision of futurity. The "dialectics of the emotional experience belongs to the interpretive, not the primordial intuitive sphere" (*Whirl*, 189), for, as Soloveitchik writes, there can be "no dialectical mood." Moods are the raw material awaiting critical transformation through objectification by means of cognition and interpretation (*Whirl*, 172). But that raw material—the hyle—of the mood, which Soloveitchik describes in *Halakhic Man* as having its own resources, is in the end present, preserved in its transformation. The given, though transformed by interpretation, remains the source and origin of emotional awareness.

Job's experience, however, was singular and one-dimensional, leading to an emotional outlook that contributed to a tendency toward "absolutizing." "He did not," Soloveitchik writes, "understand the possibility of emotional polarity, when contrasting states of mind . . . are interwoven into one fabric" (*Whirl*, 176). The type of Job does not understand that "the experience of life is ambivalent because existence itself abounds in dichotomies and contradictions" (*Whirl*, 193). Whether it is the complacent post-Holocaust American, or perhaps even a veiled reference to his Brisk ancestors of the first part of *Halakhic Man*, Job shows an inability to accommodate anything more than the singularity of simple moods. The pure emotion is local to the "present moment" and focused only on the "primordial data"; nevertheless, it is the immediacy of that experience that renders it indispensable.

What Soloveitchik calls "emotional awareness" is contingent upon placing the "uncritical emotion" in the context of a "total-life experience." The latter encompasses a stream of events that cannot be exhausted by "one state of mind" but rather a "full spectrum of feelings." From that perspective, the emotional experience at any particular instance is a "microcosm," partaking not only of the "dominant emotion, but also by its antithesis at its periphery" (*Whirl*, 193). This conception of an emotional continuum is very close to the one that Freud appropriates from Karl Abel in which "man is not able to acquire any conceptions otherwise than in contrast with their opposite" (*SE*, 11:155–57). For Freud, in addition to concepts, emotions are also built on their opposites, for every emotion is informed by an opposition it encompasses and upon which it is presupposed. For Soloveitchik, the narcissistic personality denies the complexity of human emotions, repressing the opposite on which any singular emotion is based. That single-mindedness—the inability to accommodate complexity—lends itself to what Soloveitchik calls "religious fanaticism," for which the only antidote is the cultivation of an antithetic temperament, that is a developed or interpretive emotional life ("Catharsis," 52).

For Soloveitchik, the joy, for example, associated with *simchat ha-regel*, the festival joy described in Deuteronomy, might reinforce the self-satisfied contentedness of a Job-like figure: "He is contented with himself; he has been successful, he rejoices at his own great achievements, and he is ready to shut out the whole world in his exultation over his marvelous self." The repression of the oppositions of emotional life defines the experience of the narcissist. But the obligation of *ma'aser sheni*, or the second tithe to the poor, ensures that the "joy aroused by man by the feeling of security" is tempered by an "apprehension of misery, destitution and want" (*Whirl*, 206).[26] This apprehension—the "redirection" of an emotion "towards its antithesis"—moves him out of the narcissism, thus tempering the tendency of "self-righteousness" and "fanaticism" by eliciting contraries (*Whirl*, 203). Moods are simple and self-contained, shutting out the presence of the other; emotions, however, are, for Soloveitchik, complex, for they always entail a consciousness of their antithesis.

The halakhic man, or man of "service," may take conceptual precedence in *Out of the Whirlwind*, but the *homo religiosus* who had been relegated to the margins in *Halakhic Man* takes temporal precedence, precisely because of his capacity for emotional receptivity. "Feeling," as e. e. cummings wrote, "is first." But the feeling awareness advocated in *Out of the Whirlwind* begins with the emotional authenticity celebrated by cummings. Indeed, the "ethico-moral inquiry"—Soloveitchik's ethically inflected hermeneutics of the psyche—saves contemporary man from the "nauseating experience of absurdity" commonly experienced "among existentialists" in pursuit of "pure emotion" (*Whirl*, 207). Emotional *awareness* takes precedence, not, however, what Soloveitchik defines as indulgence in the unassimilated and absolute emotions of self-satisfaction manifested in the figure of Job. In Soloveitchik's dialectical consciousness of the antithetic psyche, authentic emotions always need to be cultivated but only insofar as they serve as a prelude to ethical consciousness.

This critical emotional awareness, beginning with emotional life, informs the cognitive humility demanded in "A Crisis of Human Finitude," for the mystery of the divine, like the Kantian sublime, always shows the cognitive gesture coming up short. The complexity of a dialectical emotion, refined through its consciousness of time, reveals itself to already contain an awareness of its opposite. Such emotional awareness, for the later Soloveitchik, is the precondition for the actualization of the ethical: "Through the emotional thrust into the antithesis which the individual experiences, he frees himself from self-absorption, and he begins to see the other fellow" (*Whirl*, 207). The psychic acknowledgment of complexity (the multiplicity of internal psychic agencies) leads to an ethical moment: the acknowledgment of other agents. This conception of the ethical is a continuation of the conception of *teshuva* developed in *Halakhic Man*, but now moves out of the bounds of the single psyche into a social realm.

The understanding that any emotional experience must always be qualified by an awareness of its antithetical correlate enables the realization that an emotion (or a "value" that emerges from it) created through "partial vision" is an "absurdity" (*Whirl*, 190). Emotions may be subsumed under values (within the framework of what Soloveitchik calls "noetico-axiological judgments"), but values informed by pure moods only masquerade as benevolence, and are, in fact, as Freud would put it, mere self-serving projections, psychic mechanisms designed to cover up "inner crisis" (*Whirl*, 181, 176). Complex emotional awareness, by contrast, always holds out the possibility of an experience or perspective, that is, a "rival antithetic emotion," which, if not immediately present, is always lurking in the shadows of an emotional continuum (*Whirl*, 197).[27] What T. S. Eliot attributed to the seventeenth-century poet Andrew Marvell—the "recognition, implicit in the expression of every experience, of other kinds of experience which are possible"— marks the beginning, for Soloveitchik, of an antithetic ethical consciousness.[28] The experience of "dialectical nature of the emotions," writes Soloveitchik, is "the pre-requisite of ethics" (*Whirl*, 197). Out of this awareness, made possible through the dialectic, Soloveitchik writes, "the feeling of sympathy emerges" (*Whirl*, 206). Freed from narcissistic absorption, the self opens and awareness expands to include the "other," in whom he finds the "personification of a contradiction, of the inverted experience." Through this antithetic experience or "encountering" (Soloveitchik's nod to Buber), "the negation in the thou," a "community of existence is formed" (*Whirl*, 207). Through the internal and external oppositions, nurtured through the ethical life, Soloveitchik affirms, the possibility of community emerges.

Just as Freud saw the analytic process as leading to cultural transformation (it is "a work of culture"), for Soloveitchik, whose analytic treatment of emotions emphasizes the ethical, acknowledgment of psychic complexity leads to a possibility of community. The possibility for "community" and "friendship"—one, to adopt Wolosky's term, that is "feminized"—is already anticipated, albeit in microcosm, in Pruzhna in both the sympathy and community of Soloveitchik's mother, born out of the shared experience of defeat, adumbrating the possibility of an antithetic consciousness (*LMF*, 34, 53).[29] Oppositions, contradictions, and difference make up the processes of Talmudic dispute and legal hermeneutics, but for Soloveitchik, the antithetic—also nurtured by a consciousness of death— exists only in the realm of the psyche. That masculine realm of halakha and legal hermeneutics, insulated from the realm of death and loss (or the province of what Phillips calls "enchantment") remains, for Soloveitchik, a realm of singularity, knowledge always, still in his late works, a form of conquest.

Brisk Masculinity

Even as Soloveitchik cultivates a new persona through the figures of Job and Jacob, the realms of ethics and legal hermeneutics remain distinct. During the same period that Soloveitchik writes of ethics, he returns to the figure of the halakhic man in the *hesped*, or eulogy, given for his uncle, Velvel, the "Brisker Rav" in 1959. The eulogy stands as both a continuation and corrective to the image of the halakhic man related in the work of the 1940s. But even as Soloveitchik distances himself from some of the characteristics of the halakhic man, the eulogy goes on to restate the hermeneutic principles elaborated in the earlier work. Although Velvel, a new type, represents, in part, a concession to the sensibility implicit in Soloveitchik's antithetic ethics, the cognition and the legal hermeneutics with which is he is associated are also based on metaphors of conquest and possession.

The eulogy attempts to redefine the figure of "halakhic man," incorporating the emotional resources elaborated in his contemporary works. For Soloveitchik, Velvel stands as a new model for a generation of "orthodox youth" that formally had only "discovered the Torah through scholastic forms of thought, intellectual contact and cold logic." They may "know" the Torah as an idea, but do not, Soloveitchik laments, directly encounter "her reality," perceptible to "taste, sight and touch"; they do not know that feminine aspect of the tradition, Soloveitchik implicitly argues, associated for him, with the "Torah of the heart" ("Brisker," 52). The eulogy may, ironically, diagnose a symptom for which his "halakhic man," or the Soloveitchik family inheritance, may have been the cause—the advocacy of a masculine and super-rationalist legal system understood in terms of mathematical equations and principles of physics. In the eulogy, Velvel, now the genuine scion of Brisk, by contrast, knows that the "Halakha is two-sided," "intellectual" but also "ultimately . . . experiential" ("Brisker," 52). Soloveitchik advocates an ideal of halakha based on the "bold and lofty dialectic" between the intellectual and the experiential embodied in the figure of his uncle. The latter, the affective life, Soloveitchik writes, is the prerequisite for the former; the great figures of Brisk were all, in this representation, emotionally "enthralled" to the Torah. Soloveitchik, with this new and aggressive cultivation of affective and emotional realms, now projects backward onto the Brisk tradition, eliciting those integrated virtues in the figure of his uncle as well.

Yet Velvel also represents a figure of learning continuous with that elaborated in *Halakhic Man*, pursuing a singular and certain truth. In Soloveitchik's eulogy, its governing trope from Psalms 19:9—"the commandment of the Lord is lucid, enlightening the eyes"—is filtered through enlightenment conceptions of a perspicuous and immediate apprehension of an objective truth. The agents of that enlightenment are the figures in the Brisk school initiated by Soloveitchik's grandfather, R. Hayyim, who was able, with his effortless hermeneutics, to "cast a bright light on each and every subject." The divine command itself is "lucid" ("enlightening the eyes"), but in Soloveitchik's representation, his family inheritance—the Brisk method of learning—makes that light visible. By means of Brisk learning, truth, represented in the eulogy as the withholding and "reticent" feminine, finally yields and reveals "her face unto man" ("Brisker," 53). Indeed, the "face" of the feminine Torah is revealed through the illuminating agency of the halakhic men of Brisk.

In a further characterization of not only Velvel but the Brisk school in general, Soloveitchik writes that before their "innovations," students were simply "perplexed . . . not knowing where to turn or what to seek." However, "when R. Hayyim or his sons would conclude their *shiurim* or lectures, the situation had entirely changed," for "suddenly great light shone forth." In repetition of the scene of enlightenment Soloveitchik had described in his grandfather's living room, students find themselves in the presence of a mastery—a light revealed—they are unable to fathom. Though once the interpretive mystery had been solved through one of the privileged agents of Brisk, the students "wondered" why they themselves had not been able to explain the uncertainties they had encountered. In Soloveitchik's presentation, the hermeneutics of Brisk are effortless, and, accordingly, its agents can behave as if they had not actually "innovated anything at all." "They merely removed the veil from the pretty face of the halakha," Soloveitchik writes, "and all became enchanted by her beauty" ("Brisker," 53). With barely perceptible effort, the (feminine) truth is unmasked with—to adopt Levinas—feminine ontology subordinated to masculine law.

The simplicity of the encounter between the masculine interpreter and feminine truth is rendered more extensively through a parable of man and wife. While "the betrothed sends gift-bearing messengers," man and wife, Soloveitchik asserts, "need no messengers, intermediaries, interpreters or outsiders." The intimacy between the married couple is expressed in terms of immediacy, as the absence of intermediaries attests to an interpretation that is transparent to itself. The "contact and dealings" with his beloved occurs with no "side-stepping." The scholar, accordingly, does not indulge in the Talmudic corollary of foreplay: "there is no need for elongated *shiurim*." The method he advocates shuns "verbosity"; indeed, there are no "prefaces" and no need to "dally about the subject at hand." Instead, he "strikes right to the matter at hand." The language of *akifa* suggests resoluteness and toughness—a kind of attack, or, to continue the metaphor of marriage, there is easy penetration here, in Soloveitchik's phrasing, to "the root of the matter" ("Brisker," 55). Soloveitchik's metaphor combines registers of romance, marital love, and war. By means of all three, the masculine hermeneut, who is "madly in love," senses in his betrothed's "very being . . . the very depths of her heart" ("Brisker," 56).

In the eulogy, as in *Halakhic Man*, knowledge, though qualified in the gendered terms of both romance and married love, is still achieved through aggression, the "conquest of content and new ideas" ("Brisker," 53). The halakhic man, the inheritor of Brisk, extends "his control over both language and form." The act of understanding is stressed even more strongly here than it was in *Halakhic Man* as not just an act of conquest but of "enslavement," as the Brisker becomes "possessor of the Torah, doing with it as he wills" ("Brisker," 56). He enslaves, he conquers, he possesses—he is the masterful figure who penetrates to the depths and reveals the truth.[30]

Soloveitchik writes, in parallel terms, about the mechanisms of cognition in the essay "Confrontation," employing the same language of aggression. The "subject-knower," with his "great endowment," his "intellect," endeavors to "gain supremacy over the objective order" (10). The performance of knowledge, however, remains "fraught with difficulty," because it is always an activity based on "conflict," which sometimes renders the "act of conquest" ineffective ("Confrontation," 10, 11). The objective order resists knowledge, as Soloveitchik writes, rejecting "all pleas for a cooperative relationship" ("Confrontation," 11). The "attitude of man is one of dominion," while that "on the part of objective order" is one of "irresponsiveness" ("Confrontation," 11n5). Indeed, anxiety about the efficacy of knowledge is based, as in the 1940s, on the unavailability or "indifference" of an otherness that cannot be assimilated to categorical principles—the "and so on" of *And from There Shall You Seek* becoming even more resistant and threatening. Soloveitchik goes so far as to associate the pains that go along with the creative act, that is, the ambivalent act of conquest, as a kind of "agony" ("Majesty," 25). The Hebrew term *hafetz*, Soloveitchik explains, has "the connotation of something intensely desired, but not always attainable" ("Confrontation," 11n4). The object desired, in the terms of the parable of the eulogy, the feminine lover, is even less accessible than imagined. Indeed, through the later works, there is a continued sense of the inadequacy of the interpretive gesture, as well as the corresponding resistance of the world, now marked off as "indifferent." The desolation that haunted the young Joseph comes back in the later works, now a mark of chosenness, but characterized by a consciousness of the inadequacy of cognition and the law now circumscribed to just "small sectors of reality." The halakhic man may still be a figure of "majesty," but his dominion has radically contracted (*Man*, 70).

Adorno wrote famously "No poetry after Auschwitz," stressing the inadequacy of language, especially aesthetic languages, after the catastrophe of the Shoah. Soloveitchik entertains, however implicitly, the modified "No knowledge—even no halakha—after Auschwitz." A reality no longer able to be cognitively known leads to the imperative of silence: "Man may despair, succumb to the overpowering pressure of the objective outside and end in mute resignation." As a result, however, Soloveitchik adds, he would fail "to discharge his duty as an intellectual being," his intelligence "dissolving into an absurd nightmare." Heeding the command—again the emphasis on the law as *hok* or decree to be obeyed—the "lonely man" engages, however reluctantly, the "objective order in a cognitive conquest" ("Confrontation," 11). In the paradox of Soloveitchik's self-creation, the lonely man transforms into a different version of the halakhic man, the new, however reticent, halakhic hero.

The halakhic man of the 1959 eulogy continues to master the "objective outside" in that legal framework where cognitive mastery remains possible ("Confrontation," 11). Even here, however, the particular registers its resistance to those cognitive schemes, evident in halakhic man's need to harmonize "details," evincing his anxiety about the efficacy of the cognitive gesture even in this realm. Akin to nineteenth-century philosophical models devolving from Hegel, the particular is acknowledged, but with the goal of assimilating it within the conceptual whole. Similarly, parallel to the mathematician of *Halakhic Man*, Velvel of the eulogy is figured as restless until he assimilates the "most miniscule detail" into the "general conceptual framework" ("Catharsis," 54). In the nineteenth-century enlightenment notions of truth informing the Brisk method, the detail is subsumed by a hermeneutic gesture that produces interpretive harmony by means of what Adorno calls the "tyranny of the concept." In the figuration of Soloveitchik's uncle, the possibly errant detail, the persistence of the particular, is a source of continued apprehension—the "smallest iota can stymie and invalidate the whole" ("Catharsis," 54).[31] The Brisk concern for the appropriation of the particular in the system—the desire to assert cognitive mastery in the realm of law—is motivated by a concern for the integrity and harmony of the system, but not the detail in its specificity. Unlike the *discordia concors* of midrash, the Brisk "whole" does not sustain the discordant particular.

Daniel Boyarin argues that the rabbis of the Babylonian Talmud were actively fashioning a new notion of the masculine.[32] Soloveitchik's implicit historiography of Brisk also provides a new rabbinic concept of the masculine—"brave" and "bold"—wielding its interpretive powers of conquest in the service of the truth, with the paradigmatic figure Rabbi Moses, who is "hard like flint," in the living room of his father-in-law. While others present in that primal scene are represented in restless and unproductive activity, Rabbi Moses himself sits in the center masterfully providing the solution none of his students anticipate. So also, his Brisk ancestors would apprehend the truth, Soloveitchik writes, in an instant: "Many times, while they would be walking on their way, speaking with acquaintances, resting on the couch or eating—they would suddenly cry out in excitement: 'Our master's words are resolved.' The light had flashed" ("Brisker," 55). The casual mastery implied in the Brisker method is distilled in the figure of R. Hayyim, who is able, with a simple "wave of a hand" to illuminate the eyes of his students, revealing the truth ("Brisker," 55). Despite the apparent ease, he is nonetheless rendered as a powerful agent, with his interpretive efforts bearing "the impression of the noetic creation of the thinker" ("Brisker," 53). The powers of the Kantian "genius" are so great that R. Hayyim's interpretive innovations, though bearing his individual stamp, emerge as self-evident, objectively true.

In another parable from the eulogy, Soloveitchik represents the enlightened revelation within the context of an implicit historiography of Jewish learning. Soloveitchik imagines a figure "suddenly awoken in the middle of the night, unable to grasp his surroundings." Like the precedent scene in Pruzhna, the cognitive mastery eventually affirmed is preceded by confusion, but here the confusion is internal to the interpreter himself:

> For a brief moment he has lost his bearings. It seems as if the bed is askew, and he is spread across its width, grasping hither and non in the dark as if the door, which has always been just on the other side of the bed, is now right on top of him. All of the furnishings in the room have become distorted and unreal! ("Brisker," 53).

Both disoriented and incapacitated, the figure prone on the bed gropes in the Kafkaesque setting, a Brisker version of Gregor Samson. In the scene in Pruzhna, the restless nonproductive movement is attributed to the gathered students; here it is attributed to the singular figure "grasping hither and non." For him, there is no center or stability—he is without "bearings"—in a vertiginous state without stable references. The world outside reflects his internal state; the bed is "askew" and the door "now right on top of him," the furnishings "distorted and unreal." Although this door is proximate, it provides no means of escape. The figure in the parable, however, needs to marshal neither strength nor physical bearing to overcome his disorientation, just a simple action: "Suddenly, he finds the light switch, flicks it, and bright light floods the room" ("Brisker," 53). Soloveitchik's version of Gregor transforms himself and his environment immediately; similarly, for the practitioner of the Brisker method, the revelation of truth is sudden and immediate.

Soloveitchik's extended metaphor suggests that the tradition had been foundering and grasping—looking to open a door—when the simple flick of a light switch was all that was needed. In that instant, the metaphor continues, "all becomes normal." At the moment of revelation, the metaphor's protagonist thinks back, wondering "why he had been unable to picture the room and its furnishings," and further, why the "picture" had "become distorted" when "now all" was "so clear and simple" ("Brisker," 53). Before the realization—the enlightened revelations of Brisk learning—others had gone about the search for truth with their older impoverished methodologies, attempting to "open doors," forgetting the straightforward solution of just "switching on the light." That the Brisker hermeneut does so—employing a newer technology—underlines the radical innovations of Soloveitchik's halakhic men. There is no need to escape to another methodological context. Brisk enlightenment illuminates the "room"—that is, the tradition—in which the figure is already placed. Once perplexed, he is now enlightened.

As in the parable of the married couple, the aggressive reframing of the tradition takes place abruptly and decisively. With a minimum of words, "all questions evaporate, difficulties are solved and doubts resolved." Brisker study extrapolates "from particularities"; through "pure and pristine" study, "deficiencies" are rendered "invalid" and "excess removed." The abstraction from particularity and precedent traditions informs the affirmation of Soloveitchik's model interpreter that "there is no need for a library," only a simple bookshelf with "the basics and no more" ("Brisker," 55). Like his father in his grandfather's study, the triumphant Brisker renders the confusion of precedent traditions clear, rejecting the excrescences of impoverished interpretive modes. Briskers, as Sergey Dolgopolsky argues, adopted a historiography in which the "construction" of "a fantastic 'ancient' as well as a fantastic 'medieval' epoch" become the means through which their own more genuine critical—and modern—thought defines itself. The eschewing of libraries in the parable becomes a way of emphasizing the critical thinking that takes place, in Dolgopolsky's terms, independently of discourses of degraded and still linguistic "rhetoric."[33] In this sense, Brisk represents itself as a reform, entailing a return to original sources, and the rejection of decayed antecedent and multiple traditions. The figure represented in the eulogy, however, is tied not only to religious reform but also to enlightenment paradigms of knowledge that seek conceptual truth as a refuge from degraded forms of rhetorical disputation, thus moving away from an earlier conception of tradition where question and answer—dispute—were still part of a dialectical process.[34]

Mosheh Lichtenstein, grandson to Soloveitchik, and a contemporary inheritor of Brisk, knowingly reading against the grain of his grandfather's arguments in *Halakhic Mind*, sees a parallel between the method of his ancestors and those of early modern science in the shared emphasis on the possibility of the system to produce unambiguous statements of truth about a world of fact. Following Lichtenstein, one might argue further, as Norman Solomon has suggested, that the avatars of Brisk sought credibility for their truth-claims from their borrowings from contemporary enlightenment contexts, and further, that the claims for a singular truth grounded in halakha emerge as much from the coordinates of an enlightenment tradition as from a rabbinic one.[35] Indeed, from Lichtenstein's perspective, the Brisk method of learning, informing the halakhic man, actually participates in the enlightenment project of producing an objective conceptual truth, distanced from disputation and older interpretive methods.[36] Lichtenstein himself suggests a return to "question-and-answer, point-and-counterpoint" that are not reduced as mere "technicalities of practical problems" but are rather "the result of different conceptual points of view reflected in a dialogue." For Lichtenstein, Briskers often begin with their conceptual schemes, relegating details to the priority of system, leaving out what he calls "the *gemara*'s dialogue." He himself advocates return to the acknowledgment of independent and separate agencies, that is, return to the analysis of *gemara* as a form of rhetorical disputation.[37] By contrast, for Soloveitchik and the idealized figure of Velvel, the halakhic man, debate and disputation are pursued only for the purpose of leading to a telos of simplicity and clarity, a solution that appears as suddenly self-evident, and not subject to further analysis.

Soloveitchik's practice as halakhist and *lamdan* predictably both fulfill and undermine his representations of halakhic man. The *shiurim*, or lectures, delivered in memory of his father, according to the model forwarded in the *hesped*, proceed by raising a number of questions, which are then resolved through the invocation of a single overarching principle or concept.[38] A former student who remembered the form of such discourse reflected on Soloveitchik's rhetoric in the *hesped* for his uncle, recalling that once Soloveitchik clarified a problematic text, "it became so simple that we wondered . . . what was so difficult?"[39] Yet these polished public lectures commemorating and inflected by the methods of his father—often informed by meta-halakhic considerations—were by all reports different from the lectures he offered to his rabbinical students at Yeshiva University.[40] Norman Lamm recounts that, unlike the public lectures fashioned in the style of his ancestors, the lectures to students were "dynamic and stormy" and that Soloveitchik was, in this context, always "experimenting with a variety of arguments, testing, advocating and discarding, proving and disproving."[41] He was engaged, Lamm remembers, in "a no-holds-barred contest, a halakhic free for all, an open-ended process," not "a pre-determined lecture." Lamm is one of Soloveitchik's many students who, in the collection of published *hespedim*, praises the "astounding intellectual honesty" of his teacher (the worst insult Soloveitchik could offer, according to Abba Bronspiegel, was "you are intellectually dishonest"). As Lamm recalls, Soloveitchik constantly placed his own thought under revision, writ large in an anecdote appearing several times in the volume of eulogies. "The Rav," Lamm writes, "had been developing one line of thought for two or three weeks" when a student pointed out a contradiction from an earlier source:

> The Rav was stunned, held his head in his hands for three agonizingly long minutes while all of us were silent, then pulled out a sheaf of papers from his breast pocket, crossed out page after page, said that we should forget everything he had said, and announced that the *shi'ur* was over and that he would see us the next day.

Soloveitchik's theatrical self-revision does end, perhaps tellingly, with the student's acknowledgment that, in Lamm's account, "the Rav had been right all along."[42] Yet Soloveitchik's legal hermeneutics in practice, as reported by his students, remains at odds with the representations of the ideal halakhic man. When commemorating his father, his lectures share the contours and strategies of his Brisk ancestors. As a teacher, however, Soloveitchik's intellectual honesty and his frenetic theatrical energies, moving between different positions and perspectives, show a self-presentation self-consciously distinct from the steely hard countenance of his Brisk predecessors, testifying to another means of self-construction by which he differentiated himself from his ancestors.[43]

In the idealized rhetoric of the eulogy commemorating his ancestor Velvel, however, when Soloveitchik cites the story from the Talmud of the oven of *Achnai*, one of Steven Fraade's "poster children" for rabbinic pluralism, he does not do so to emphasize multiple perspectives or agencies but rather the verse from Deuteronomy at the end of the account, "it is not in heaven," that is, to affirm the halakhic man's power of conquest—that he "rules and reigns in the kingdom of the halakha" ("Brisker," 56). Although the Talmudic representation relates to questions about the nature of dispute, proof, and truth—thematizing pluralism—Soloveitchik emphasizes, in the idealized representation, the "power and will of the halakhic man," still conceived of as a man of conquest.[44]

Although Soloveitchik fully elaborates the antithetic temperament in the realm of the psyche, in the eulogy the powers of conquest of the halakhic man are reasserted more emphatically than in the works of the 1940s, as if in the realization of the problems of cognition, the mechanisms of cognitive conquest are in need of even more aggressive affirmation. That is, the epistemological gesture—notwithstanding the recurrent threat of melancholy and silence—remains associated in the legal realm with conquest: the domination of the abstract concept over the particular. The halakhic man, like the biblical man before him, remains "a conqueror" (*Whirl*, 107). Although the Soloveitchik of the later years cultivates loss, desolation, and defeat, as well as the epistemological humility that follows from them, when the halakhic man engages in the process of cognition, he remains a figure of mastery. The idealization of a tradition as outside of the realm of death is the only place where such cognitive mastery can be sustained, a tradition insulated from loss. Soloveitchik may cultivate the realm of "pure negation," but that negation does not impact the realm of legal hermeneutics, which is still represented, though with continued anxiety, through the figure of Velvel as the realm of conquest and singular truth.

In the hermeneutics of mourning, loss is internal to the processes of tradition—indeed constitutive of it, producing partiality, incomplete knowledge, and, necessarily, dispute. Soloveitchik, however, maintains a conception of cognition with its provenance in Kant and the Cartesian *cogito* as well. The Cartesian knower, as Bersani argues, exercises "fully and confidently" a "militant will to know," and "through science," acquires "power over the world."[45] Soloveitchik may affirm, in *Lonely Man of Faith*, the naiveté implicit in the "Age of Reason's" belief in the individual as "ontologically perfect" and "existentially adequate" (*LMF*, 30). Notwithstanding the epistemological humility that he enjoins and the radical consequences of that humility in the realm of ethics, in his representations of the realm of legal hermeneutics, he remains committed to the Cartesian ego and its will to know, assimilating halakha to scientific models—to the demands of "mastery," "dignity," and "fame" (*LMF*, 26). Hilary Putnam's dictum that "enough," though not "everything," is "enough" may be true for the rabbis of the Talmud, but for Soloveitchik, in the privileged realm of legal hermeneutics, there is only "all" or "nothing," the majestic and mastering subject either triumphant or experiencing catastrophic loss. Beneath the guise of equanimity of Soloveitchik's interpreting subject lies the conflict wrought through the melancholy oscillation between defeated desolation and the triumphant conquest achieved through the cognitive act.

Tradition for Soloveitchik, figured in the eulogy for Velvel, does not entail an encounter with loss—Lear's "ripped fabric of life"—but its negation, producing a version of tradition as idealized, ahistorical, and deathless, an escape from disappointment, doubt, and loss. The subject who avoids death and the mourning it demands, Abraham Drassinower, writes, "takes refuge in an illusory universe," insulating himself from "the possibility of loss that has been banished." The willed alienation from "mortality" and the pursuit of "an imaginary fullness" remove the subject from the struggle, Drassinhower continues, "that forms the substance of mortal life."[46] For Soloveitchik, it is the "man of destiny" who realizes himself as a creative and free individual, through an embrace of the "given," whatever its manifestation. Soloveitchik, the self-constructed "man of destiny," pursues that realization, both philosophically and personally, in a world outside of the one dominated by the masculine practitioners of Brisk hermeneutics. Indeed, the demands imposed by a consciousness of otherness are central to Soloveitchik's ethics as well as his conception of repentance. Ironically, the figure behind Modern Orthodoxy refuses, in the realm of legal hermeneutics, both history and modernity. Soloveitchik does show his sensitivity to loss and otherness early in his life—paradigmatically so in Pruzhna. In his later works, he finds that encounter in ethics, outside of the purview of legal hermeneutics.

Although Soloveitchik confronts death in his post-Holocaust writings, and even immerses himself in defeat, loss, and mortality, the continued emphasis on cognition as mastery, with the "fullness" it seeks and claims to produce, involves the refusal of loss that the Talmudic rabbis imagined as intrinsic to the processes of interpretation. Soloveitchik renders this tradition as singular, immortal, and timeless—refusing mortality—while that produced through the embrace of mortality, perpetuates itself only in the recognition of loss, thus producing difference. In conclusion, I return to that hermeneutics of mourning, elaborating the construction of Soloveitchik's "antithetical" subject not only in the realm of ethics but in the realm of legal interpretation as well.

Conclusion

The Last Rabbi and Talmudic Irony

Mourning can make fundamentalists of us all.
—Adam Phillips, *Promises, Promises*

For both the hermeneutics of mourning and melancholy, death figures centrally, though for the latter, more in repression than recognition. The former, the hermeneutics of mourning, presupposes the belief in the "good enough" interpretation, or rather "good enough" interpretations, mutually informing and complementary. In Soloveitchik's legal hermeneutics of melancholy, however, there is only the partial compensation for loss, that is, the cognitive and hermeneutic conquest that attempts to eradicate loss, though never fully succeeds in doing so. The absence of dispute and multiplicity as hermeneutic principles (except in justifying a place for "religious philosophy" against the stronger truth claims of the sciences) can be traced to his Brisk ancestors, perhaps even back to Hayyim of Volozhin and the *Nefesh Ha-Hayyim*. But Soloveitchik's work, inflected by historical and personal loss, gives philosophical articulation to the principles that remained only implicit in the works of his predecessors, and continue, in the present, to remain normative—and not just for Soloveitchik's former students and followers. The distance traveled between the hermeneutics of mourning and melancholy—between Soloveitchik and his Talmudic antecedents—can be traced in the varying responses to death, but also in the emphasis on love as part of the interpretive process.

Death experienced as untranscendable trauma leads to the melancholic construction of an idealized and authoritative law, sabotaging the possibilities for conversation in exchange for a fantasy of certainty and stability founded in singular truth. Death transformed into loss, and the subsequent mourning of that loss in an activity of hermeneutic engagement, presupposes, on the other hand, the possibility of innovation and multiplicity. This is not just a question of liberal tolerance before the letter, but a function of the limits of epistemology. More than just a tolerance of difference, these limits then produce as a necessary consequence a Talmudic *love* of difference. This love does not manifests itself on the psychic level, as in the interpsychic dialogue presupposed in Soloveitchik's *te-shuva*, but rather in the communal realm of interpretation in the multiplicity that follows the Masoretic act—indeed, upon which that act is based. My conclusion addresses some possibilities anticipated by Soloveitchik's antithetic ethics but occluded by his melancholy hermeneutics—a contemporary rearticulation of the hermeneutics of mourning.

I begin with Soloveitchik as "the last rabbi"—again finding an antecedent in Moses, the latter's breaking of the Tablets of the Law, and the ethical inflection of a moment that, in Talmudic renderings, revolves around transmission. The conclusion continues with another odd pairing, John Milton and R. Yohanan ben Zakkai, and their corresponding conceptions of difference and the public sphere. I close by providing an anatomy of irony. From the liberal irony of Richard Rorty to the psychoanalytic irony of Jonathan Lear, I offer a third term—Talmudic irony, inflected as it is here by Soloveitchik's ethical embrace of multiplicity.

The Last Rabbi

The death of Moses, central for the rabbis in their understanding of tradition, as I have argued, is the traumatic moment of death, transforming it into a loss redeemed through interpretation and producing multiplicity. This confrontation with death is thematized not only in the meta-halakhic representations of dispute but in the formal processes of dispute themselves. Further, "these and these are the words of the living God" emerges, as I have argued, as an acknowledgment of loss, in narrative terms, caused by the shattering of the tablets, which marks the entrance into a history characterized by difference.

In Soloveitchik's representation of the breaking of the tablets, however, the death of Moses does not serve as the beginning of an antithetical tradition of disputative inquiry. Moreover, Moses is not seen in his hermeneutic capacity, but rather as a lone figure enduring existential crises. That is, the focus is not on historical transmission, but rather on the great and even singular individual, and the ethical challenges he confronts. Soloveitchik does not associate loss with interpretive activity, the process of *mesora*, of loss and memory—"sometimes the Torah has to be negated before it can come into being"—but with the existential burdens endured by the singular individual. The experience of Otto's sublime, now turned toward what Kant calls the "humiliation of self-conceit," progresses toward a refinement enabled through suffering—an appreciation of the sublime catastrophe as a prerequisite for moral feeling.[1] Soloveitchik's hero emerges after the turns inward toward the psyche, his Moses ironically akin to the lawgiver in *Moses and Monotheism*, distinguished by his ethical characteristics and nurtured by his suffering.[2]

"Only after Moses had lost everything he was questing for," Soloveitchik writes, "did he ascend Mount Sinai." The halakhic man that emerges from the post-Holocaust writings is one who has reached the "absurd stage" at which he finds himself "bankrupt and forlorn" ("Catharsis," 53). This form of desolation is central to Soloveitchik's developing figure of the "halakhic man," who unlike the version of the 1940s, is refined, and indeed distinguished, by means of his suffering. The halakhic man, appropriated and transformed in Soloveitchik's work, has become the ethical man. Soloveitchik's Moses, an unmistakable type for Soloveitchik himself, is fit for ascent to leadership only after the acknowledgment and experience of loss. More than that, the ethical perspective that comes from suffering makes Moses the adequate vehicle to receive the law; indeed, the ascent to the mountain has suffering as its prerequisite. Both the trauma of the Holocaust and Soloveitchik's own family history inflect his affirmation that the experience of loss necessarily transforms the halakhic man. As I argued earlier, not only is there for Soloveitchik an ethic independent of halakha, but that ethic, derived from loss, becomes a precondition for ascent—for the receiving of the law at Sinai.

In this reading, Soloveitchik emphasizes the humility of the halakhic man but also his singularity, an isolated figure who suffers and becomes self-aware through his suffering. As we have seen, for Soloveitchik, Moses's life reflects his own, embodying "the tragedy" of the teacher who is "too great for his disciples . . . too exalted for his generations" (*Vision*, 212). Instead of seeing Moses as the narratives in Temurah figure him, in the context of the beginnings of tradition in a fallen world, Soloveitchik sees Moses as the lonely ethically-superior figure outside of tradition. His followers "could not follow him," and further, they were unwilling "to become his disciples" (*Vision*, 214). In rabbinic representations, Moses is figured as accommodating the perspectives and sensibilities of all of the people of Israel; for Soloveitchik, he is lonely, ineffective.[3]

As Soloveitchik writes in *Lonely Man of Faith*, though Moses, bearer of the "two tablets," does remain part of the community of "majesty," "bent on conquest," in the end, he returns to "his solitary hiding and to the abode of loneliness." Soloveitchik, like Moses, is also like Elisha, with whom the 1965 essay ends, finding solace in identification with "the Lonely One" who abides in the recesses of transcendental solitude, but also feels "disenchanted and frustrated because his words were scornfully rejected" (*LMF*, 112). Soloveitchik, like Elisha, remains committed to the "majestic community," though at the time resigned to "defeat and humiliation" (*LMF*, 111). Soloveitchik's loneliness surpasses that of his biblical, and by implication, his familial predecessors, for, as he writes, "the loneliness of contemporary man of faith is of a special kind." Soloveitchik sense of "social isolation" is sui generis—acute, idiosyncratic, and unprecedented (*LMF*, 106).

There is a particular pathos here, not just in the identification with Moses, the leader without disciples. But having, in Leo Bersani's terms, "killed off the Father" in order to become him, Soloveitchik leaves himself, in his role as "self-fashioner," as a father who disavows his sons, a leader without a sphere of influence (*Man*, 113). The individuation—the importing of halakhic creativity, the *hiddush* into the realm of the psyche—characteristic of so much of Soloveitchik's thought has its cost. Having transformed the paradigm leader into an isolated figure of ethics, Soloveitchik implicitly acknowledges, compromises that leader as an agent of tradition. The act of individuation, Soloveitchik's realization of the species imperative in decidedly non-Aristotelian terms, makes him a singular figure like his Moses, a leader who sees himself with no genuine followers. Soloveitchik represents himself as having transformed the legacy of halakhic man, with ethical and existential demands that make him not only a figure of Freudian melancholy, but the singular and lonely man at the end of the tradition of "halakhic men." Soloveitchik becomes his father, however, even as he transcends him to become himself, turning him into the last rabbi of the Brisk tradition—a tradition in which, by his own lights there are no genuine inheritors.

In Soloveitchik's melancholy sensibility, loss remains extrinsic to the processes of interpretation, centered instead on the ethical figure, the individual, transformed through his humility but isolated from history. By contrast, the rabbinic recognition of the untranscendable nature of epistemological pluralism is figured in Moses's breaking of the tablets, the entrance into history, and the beginning of a tradition based on loss. The tradition that follows from this founding act informs the constitution of a particular kind of subject—for whom dispute is the means through which knowledge is produced. The emphasis on a hermeneutics of mourning focuses on the antithetical and communal activity of interpretation, and the subject presumed in that interpretive engagement. In turning to competing conceptions of contemporary irony, moving on from Soloveitchik but incorporating his antithetic ethical sensibility, the chapter elicits the ironic perspective that Talmudic argument presupposes, as well as the form of subjectivity it produces.

Talmudic Irony

Between conceptions of psychoanalytic irony and liberal irony—one emphasizing the subject, the other, the social—the contours of what I am calling Talmudic irony more clearly emerge. To return to Jonathan Lear, his psychoanalytic irony functions as a corrective psychic mechanism enabled primarily through "therapeutic action" in the clinical framework of psychoanalysis, the discovery and recovery of multiple psychic agencies. That is, therapeutic action, local to the psychoanalytic situation and engendering irony, entails what Lear calls "the sympathetic subversion of a pretense"—a way for the subject of that process, the analysand, to discover and undermine behavioral single-mindedness (*Action*, 104). The psychoanalytic process—presupposed on the discovery of repressed agencies—provides an antidote for the strident attachment to a single perspective.

Therapeutic irony, from Lear's psychoanalytic perspective, is a subtle way of undoing defensive stances, the opening of a psychic space within which the certainty of perceptions and even commitments look different than first perceived. Such irony depends, for Lear, on the intrapsychic love about which I wrote in chapter 3, allowing for an appreciation of parts of the self as well as the multiple psychic agencies and the different perspectives such acknowledgment yields. This form of irony does not abolish belief (or a framework in which belief is possible), but sustains a sensibility allowing for both skepticism and commitment. Irony, for Lear, is not a form of detachment in which different "vocabularies" are treated "as though they were objects of disinterested choice," but remains subordinate to belief.[4] That is, skepticism, in this reading, becomes a built-in part of the ironic self, not a corrosive external irony, as it is for Adam Phillips, putting all beliefs and commitments in question.[5] Irony, for Lear, does not obviate striving, or what might better be called engagement, but reveals what unselfconscious earnestness, naive enthusiasm, and unbridled idealism may leave out or repress.

Psychoanalytic irony revolves, of course, around the individual analysand, though Lear's later work suggests that a Freudian-inflected version of Socratic irony may have implications for the polis. The carefully cultivated "ignorance" of Socrates, he argues, is not a way of "withdrawing from battle on behalf of the polis but a way of participating in it."[6] In this sense, the not-knowing that leads toward eliciting a perspective of "human openness" has a potentially transformative social function, as for Freud, the process leading to a better relationship between psychic agencies can also be part of a "work of culture." Whether cultivated philosophically or psychoanalytically, however, Lear's delineation of irony revolves around the relationship between individual psychic agencies.

Talmudic irony, in my reading, produces a similar skepticism toward singularity, cultivating an acknowledgment of complexity but one produced through the communal activity of Talmudic engagement, the relationship between different social, not psychic agencies. The subject's participation in the intergenerational conversation enacts Talmudic irony, formed through the hermeneutic engagement with different interpretive agents. This irony, raised to a hermeneutic cultural principle, is presupposed, as is Lear's Freudian irony and Soloveitchik's ethics, on Abel's insight about the antithetical meaning of primal words—that every experience contains its opposite, and that every rendering of that experience will necessarily be partial. "These and these are the words of the living God" is a Talmudic rendering of that insight and hermeneutic accommodation to its consequences. Not merely a fanciful approbation of difference, or a political (or editorial, as in Daniel Boyarin's reading) strategy of inclusion, "these and these" accommodates the epistemological limitations of man, thus affirming a non-Aristotelian perspective of the authority of competing and contradictory perspectives. This is not to make the claim that Talmudic discourse articulates a

Freudian conception of psychic agency, or any analytic framework comparable to the Freudian. Talmudic disputation does, however, presuppose a conception of interpretive antagonism that leads to an acknowledgment of different agencies, and furthermore, a community of subjects that are able to entertain the multiplicity, even the *discordia concors*, that this acknowledgment entails.

Not only Aristotle but analytic philosophers in general have been hostile to irony so defined—certainly to the Freudian enterprise that presupposes contradiction and paradox. For Lear, Willard Quine's observations on anthropology represent a tendency evidenced by analytic philosophers to reject apparently contradictory utterances or practices as incoherent. Quine (who in other contexts shows himself to be a relativist regarding conceptual schemes) argues in the passage Lear quotes that anthropological findings proving the existence of "prelogicality" (that is, contradiction) in non-Western rituals are simply, indeed must be, a function of "bad translation." Human societies, even putatively prelogical ones, Quine assumes, operate according to strictly logical principles. The assertion that "x" and "not x" are both true is not and never can be viable, and must, in Quine's reading, be a result of mistranslation. Lear takes Quine here to be paradigmatic of analytic philosophy's refusal to entertain contradiction, to limit mental activity to a realm of what he calls, following Freud, "secondary processes thinking"—that is, the "articulate and conscious realm of conceptualized judgment." For Lear, taking up what he calls the "challenge" of psychoanalysis to "redraw the boundaries of the mental" leads to the recognition of those "intelligible actions and utterances which, from a rigidly secondary-process perspective" are considered irrational (*Love*, 190–92). Although the Aristotelian law of noncontradiction may maintain for the developed languages of secondary process thought, archaic mental activity, as in the natives of Quine's study, operates, for Lear, according to other laws.

Lear affirms that in the realm of the archaic, antithetical meanings are retained, as in Freud's affirmation that the unconscious does not know negation. The "other mindedness" of the archaic, Lear asserts, "continues to live on in . . . as part of a higher psychic organization" (*Love*, 195). For Freud, there are linguistic markers of this archaic duality in "primal words"; they also persist in dreams and poetry, and for Lear, in the ritual practices that remain unassimilable to the rigors of certain kinds of philosophical discourse. Lear prescribes cultivating a "developmental relation to a more archaic preconceptualized form of activity that is genuinely unconscious" (*Love*, 9). That is, for Lear, part of the psychoanalytic project is to solicit archaic paradox within the language of secondary process thought—in not only personal but cultural spheres.

Lear faults Quine not just for misreading his natives and producing a species of bad anthropology but for ignoring the antithetical possibilities inherent and informing more articulated secondary process languages. Lear's critique of Quine might be further translated as the philosophical failure to accommodate love. Indeed, the failure to acknowledge primary processes and render them intelligible is in Lear's own terms a failure of acknowledgment based on the absence of love. Only with love, starting for Lear at the intrapsychic level, does the principle of interpretive charity emerge, a love that renders, in his framework, the unconscious as a possible object of knowledge. Without cultivating the developmental relationship between primary and secondary processes, a loving relationship between intrapsychic agencies, "rational thought" itself becomes, as Lear's teacher Hans Loewald writes, "sterile and destructive of life, as it denies or ignores its own living source" (*Loewald*, 566). This may be to restate the old argument between the disciplines, with psychoanalysis taking the part of poetry, combating the at once more rigorous but in Lear's reading, more sterile and schematic, disciplines of philosophical thought.

For Lear, the contradictions inherent in primary processes elaborate themselves in dreams, mystical religious experience, and poetry, but also, against the more rationalizing and dismissive tendencies of Freud, religious ritual. Lear affirms the salutary aspects of ritual and, primarily, mystical religious experience as a means through which the "infantile dimensions of psychic life" are accessed and affirmed.[7] For Lear, however, the religious experiences to which he refers are themselves associated with primary process—the overlap, for example, between the experience of the Eucharist and the orality of infantile life. That is, Lear recapitulates the Freudian emphasis on religious life understood in primarily mystical terms (again, Rolland's "oceanic feeling"), with the erasure rather than affirmation of differentiation.

However, in the hermeneutics of mourning—brought on, in the rabbis' figuration, by the breaking of the tablets and the death of Moses—the antithetic characteristic of primary discourse is rendered in developed secondary process languages of differentiation. Contradictions coincide not only in dreams, mystical religious expression, or ritual, but in the discursive realm of dispute. What seem to be incommensurable opposites are affirmed at once, for Freud a characteristic of primary process only, maintained within Talmudic argument in the articulated languages of secondary process thought. This, then, is to dignify the Talmud and its legal discourses as a special form of discourse similar to poetry— the poetry of dispute—sharing its associative, nonanalytic tendencies. What Quine sees as the violation of the Aristotelian principle of noncontradiction in "native" ritual is characteristic of the articulated secondary process form of the Talmud. Indeed, the poetics of Talmudic dispute, with the assertion and maintenance of opposites, hypothesizes a subject, akin to Soloveitchik's ethical subject, that may become attuned to the complexities that inform both paradox and poetry.

In the *Birth of Tragedy*, Nietzsche laments the death of not only tragedy but also poetry, as it became subordinated to rational categories, becoming a kind of impoverished philosophy. Talmudic dispute, in this reading, emerges not as a hypostatized set of scholarly discourses but as a set of intergenerational performances, a generic hybrid, neither law nor poetry, what Nietzsche might have described as one of the "realms of wisdom" where the strictures of the logician are "exiled."[8] Of course, the Talmud is nothing if not logical, but the presence of contradiction or paradox within the strictures of legal and logical dispute requires an epistemological humility, the defining characteristic of the subject of Talmudic irony.

Soloveitchik emphasis on existential humility, as much as it informs his ethics, focuses on the individual. Talmudic irony, by contrast, both imposes and, in my reading, produces, an epistemological humility in a community of readers through which the limitations of knowledge and the single interpretive gesture are always in the foreground, not only on the intrapsychic level but on the interpsychic one as well. "These and these are the words of the living God" consecrates the resultant contradiction or allows for antithetical perspectives to coexist, simultaneously affirmed. In this sense, what would later become part of the Freudian project of acknowledging multiple agencies in the realm of the psyche is affirmed in the privileged secondary process discourse of the rabbis, the Talmud. Talmudic irony both presupposes and performs Eliot's insight that in every experience, there are other experiences that are possible, while at the same time elaborating normative teachings. Love is at the center of Soloveitchik's ethical thought, defining his conception of *teshuva*; Talmudic irony presupposes love, as I argue below, as part of the processes of interpretation and transmission.

Liberal Irony and the Avoidance of Love

The understanding, presented thus far, of Talmudic irony relies on Lear's psychoanalytic correlate, though the former emphasizes hermeneutics, not the psyche. In the pragmatist philosopher Richard Rorty's work, irony is raised to a social principle, a liberal irony put to clearly articulated social and political ends. What follows constitutes a further anatomy of irony, through the lens of Rorty's more political perspective, with the conception of Talmudic irony refined in relation to Rorty's liberal counterpart. I continue complicating the story by elaborating Talmudic irony in relationship to the disagreement among pragmatists—that is, through Stanley Fish's critique of Rorty's model, eliciting the consequences of their disagreement for the understanding of rabbinic dispute. I conclude by discussing Fish's reading of my representation of Soloveitchik and rabbinic dispute, and his dismissal of that model as recapitulating what he calls the "theory mistake" that characterizes Rorty's liberal irony.

For Rorty, the principle of "liberal irony" is an antidote to fundamentalism and the metaphysical perspectives that nurture it. Anyone "who thinks that there are well-grounded theoretical answers . . . algorithms for resolving moral dilemmas," Rorty writes, is "still, in his heart, a theologian or a metaphysician." Against those explicit or merely residual metaphysicians, however, Rorty posits a vision of a "liberal utopia: one in which ironism in the relevant sense is universal." The ironists "who face up to the contingency of [their] most central beliefs and desires" become candidates for Rorty's "post-metaphysical culture"—a culture, Rorty adds, "no more impossible than a post-religious one, and equally desirable."[9] For Rorty, the ironic stance of liberals has the salvific capacity to rescue culture from the metaphysical and theological commitments that lead to fundamentalism.

Stanley Fish's critique of this form of irony, which is part of a sustained engagement with Rorty, serves, in the current argument, as a means to distinguish Talmudic irony from contemporary or "liberal" counterparts. Indeed, Fish's resistance to metadiscursive claims can be read retrospectively to inform Talmudic argument. Fish dismisses liberal irony as a nonposition, and its advocates (especially Rorty) as masking their real agenda—the pursuit of a particularism pretending to be a universalism, a form of engagement masquerading as neutrality. Fish identifies not only theologians or politicians who make such moves—adopting the "view from nowhere" or occupying "the God's Eye position"—but also a class of legal, literary, and cultural critics of whom Rorty is the paradigm example.[10] Fish, with his pragmatic assault on "neutrality," akin to Soloveitchik's critique of Newtonian science, insists that Rorty's dismissal of metaphysical thinking itself entails a species of unacknowledged metaphysics. In the name of the persistence of language games and the contexts from which they emerge, Fish places himself as a kind of pharisaic skeptic in relation to Rorty's celebration of the "spirit," with Rorty champion of a liberalism that dispenses with those antecedent contexts still tainted by the particularity of their commitments.

Those whom Rorty valorizes as liberal ironists "begin by acknowledging and celebrating difference," but in the end, Fish claims, they are, in an irony that escapes them, not able to tolerate it.[11] Similarly, Rorty may start by asserting the "irreducibility of difference and the concomitant unavailability of overarching principles," but then "go on unaccountably," according to Fish, "to the proclamation of an overarching principle." The advocacy of the "heterogeneity" of "contingent" beliefs is the vehicle through which the liberal ironist erases "contingency" under its own sign. For Rorty, the "awareness of contingency" transforms its adherents "into something new": a utopian enclave of liberal ironists who unite together over the dead letter of outmoded and still-metaphysical particularisms.[12] The culture of liberal irony, Fish asserts, involves Rorty's self-proclaimed "millenarian gospel," a transcendence of the particularities of individual commitments. For

Fish, Rorty's desire for "postmetaphysical" and "postreligious" culture is founded, paradoxically, on the exclusion of that which informs it—the contingency of interpretation.

Fish, by contrast, against those advocating for a space, a metaposition outside of the constraints imposed by interpretation, continues to argue that interpretive practices never transcend the contingency of their utterance. For Fish, as in Soloveitchik, whose pragmatic bent makes his work a genuine precursor to that of Fish, the critique of forms of objectivity or neutrality emerges from an abiding sense of the centrality of the relationship between subject and object, and what follows for Fish, interpretation understood as an always-contingent activity.[13] Liberal ironists make what Fish called, writing at the height of High Theory, "the central theory mistake" founded on "anti-foundationalist theory hope" and the claim that theoretical insights themselves alter the conditions for the interpretive act.[14] That is, Fish protests against the assertion of a liberal metaperspective, the assumption that belief in pluralism or irony—or any theoretical principle— makes a significant difference to the act of interpretation.

At a 2011 panel on the relationship between his work and that of Soloveitchik, Fish continued to affirm his conception of the contingency of interpretation in relationship to Soloveitchik's works and rabbinic dispute.[15] There are, he argued in that context, no "ultimate epistemological reference points," but only "local and revisable contexts"—affirming that the constraints of interpretation make "change, revision and pluralism inevitable." Never a "theoretical activity," interpretation moves from "partial perspective to partial perspective." For Fish, any account of truth and the conditions of its emergence is irrelevant to the "consideration of the truth of a particular matter." Theoretical languages do not change the "subjective" conditions under which truth is produced, and conceptions of pluralism do not change the irreducible nature of the interpretive act as one participating in the creation of meaning.

Fish's rehearsing of his oft-iterated account of the nature of interpretation, as well as the pluralism that necessarily follows, is significant for both the way he relates it to Soloveitchik, and further, to the account I gave (on the same panel) of rabbinic dispute. Fish attributes to my explanation of the principle of "these and these" a version of the "theory mistake" he finds in the works of Rorty and other "utopian" liberal thinkers, namely, a belief that an "awareness of the contingency of interpretation has an effect on interpretation." In particular, he is troubled by the assertion that Beit Hillel's "forbearing attitude" toward Beit Shammai in their dispute in Eruvin 13b should lead to a more "charitable view of the interpretation of others." Consistent with his role as pharisaic gadfly, he turns my reading of the rabbis into a Christian one based on an abstract ideal of charity. In the attribution of a Rortian "spirit" of liberalism to my account, he turns the dispute between *tannaim* into a study in liberalism, an antecedent representation of contemporary toleration. The Rortian reading of Fish's construction would indeed suggest that Beit Hillel are somehow not fully committed to their interpretation, and that their generosity is presupposed on a lack of conviction, providing the necessary distance from the impoverishment of commitment. Indeed, this is how Rorty might read the passage, converting the text into an enactment of toleration only, positing Beit Hillel as ironists, "detached from the (vulgarity) of commitment," merely investigating "the myriad cultural forms in which others have found a path to commitment."[16] To Fish, such a representation of the Talmudic principle is another way of putting contingency under erasure, an implicit advocacy of a perspective of liberal irony that betrays the conception of contingency while celebrating it.[17] That is, in the raising of "these and these" to an interpretive principle (with Beit Hillel's interpretive charity informing it), Fish senses rabbinic pluralism transforming into a metaphysical position.

For Fish, as he reiterated on the Soloveitchik panel, pluralism cannot be a program and "acknowledgment of pluralism" is no more than "a nice social gesture," and only then "on some occasions." Pluralism "won't," he affirms, "get you anywhere"; neither, he adds, "will it prevent you from getting anywhere." Ideas about interpretation are simply irrelevant to the practice of interpretation. The suggestion that extrainterpretive criteria—the interpretive charity manifested in Beit Hillel's forbearing stance—"makes a difference" is simply another example of a metaposition advocated by liberal ironists. It is equivalent, Fish argues, to telling a physicist about the contingency of his practice as a scientist, situated as he is in institutional contexts that constrain him. Such an insight will not change the way he practices science, but rather, he will just continue "to be either a good or a bad scientist." The experiments of a particle physicist will not change with his evolving theoretical sophistication; he will carry on, as Fish puts it, "doing what comes naturally," that is, engaging in the processes of interpretation local to his discipline. That Beit Hillel foregrounds the perspective of Beit Shammai is only then, from Fish's perspective, a question of manners without consequences. Just as there are no consequences of pragmatism, against Rorty's contrary claim, there are no consequences to rabbinic pluralism, certainly not to the forbearing attitude informing it.

Fish's pragmatic localism does help elaborate a parallel rabbinic suspicion of transcendence. In his observations on Talmudic dispute, however—on the disagreement between the Houses of Hillel and Shammai—his model shows itself to be insufficient for describing the contours of Talmudic irony in the nonacknowledgment of love as a philosophical and hermeneutic category. For Fish, paradigms are incommensurable, languages and discourse always excluding one from the other, indeed impervious one to the other. Although Fish's early work enjoined readers to "be part of the conversation" within larger "interpretive communities," his later works have focused on agents in a decidedly liberal public sphere. Indeed,

Fish was the foremost Milton scholar of his generation, but his own conception of the public sphere is more Hobbesian than Miltonic.[18] For where the latter allows for the possibility of reasonable conversations within a mediated public sphere, Hobbes eviscerates that sphere, leaving isolated individuals defined only by power, interest, and desire. Fish's understanding of dispute is governed by a conception of a public sphere defined through a Hobbesian conflict of individuals in which there is no *discordia concors*, that is, no public or textual mediation to overcome different perspectives.

For Beit Hillel and Beit Shammai, however, the construction of truth is a collaborative enterprise between agents participating in tradition as a common activity, the shared recovery and transmission of sacred texts. The sacred status of texts as authoritative and the common acknowledgment of their origin in divine revelation produces what Frank Kermode calls a particular "form of attention," rendering Beit Hillel's acknowledgment of the perspective of Beit Shammai as a matter of more than just etiquette.[19] Talmudic discourse, the continued participation in the process of truth finding and dispute, presupposes a sensibility informed by Wittgenstein—that the hybrid reality of the duck/rabbit picture can only be accessed from complementary perspectives, and then only one at a time. "Now I see it as a rabbit," Wittgenstein writes. "Now, I see it as a duck."[20] Beit Hillel enacts a process by which he sees that which he knows to be true, but is also, and will always be, a truth only partially rendered. Their convictions are such—or their perspectives are such—that they will see their version of the rabbit, and only the rabbit, even as they acknowledge a competing, even contrary, account of that reality.

Hillel's affirmation "if I am not for myself, who will be for me?" emphasizes the imperative of engaged interpretation against the Rortian ideal of detachment. That Hillel continues, "if I am only for myself," however, "then what am I?" reads as an antecedent explaining the forbearance evidenced by the school that bears his name (Avot 1.4). In this rhetorical question, Hillel does not erase his own commitment, nor does he advocate an attention to the other to be understood as only "etiquette." Understanding the lost traditional text, that is, a text rendered sacred through the process of interpretation (as in R. Elazar's reading of the verse from Ecclesiastes, by which the words of the sages become words of Torah) entails the acknowledgment and embrace of alternative perspectives. Talmudic dispute enacts a process that leads to an epistemological humility based on the conviction that no single perspective exhausts the meaning of the traditional text and is thus presupposed on commitment to multiplicity and difference. In Wittgensteinian terms, one is always only seeing either the rabbit or the duck, never both simultaneously.

Fish, however, sees the assertion of rabbinic pluralism through Rorty's liberal lens, and therefore as yet another advocacy of an impossible metaperspective.

In my reading, acknowledgment of the other as a form of love is an intrinsic, albeit unstated aspect, of the hermeneutic act. Hillel's forbearance is symptomatic of that love, with interpretation understood always as a necessarily collaborative activity. For Fish, the rabbinic gesture of interpretive charity erases difference, where the principle of love informing the hermeneutic activity of Beit Hillel sustains such difference—"if I am only for myself, what am I?" Talmudic irony resists the claims of the nonsituated metaperspective, affirming differentiation as a function of love. That is, what Soloveitchik calls "the bonds of love" are not only internal to the epistemological act, but are a social principle, based on love for the other, itself a mediated love for the divine.

Fish's universe, in the end, is one of autonomous and independent subjects, and his model, even for conversation, is agonistic, a Hobbesian realm of conflicting agents, devolving into a public sphere where conversation may be reduced, as Alisdair MacIntyre suggests, to "shrillness."[21] The pluralism and interpretive community presupposed by Talmudic irony, however, is based on love, a form of interpretive activity not as a means of eventual unification, but first and primarily, differentiation. The love of the other emerges out of the love enacted through tradition and the knowledge that the beloved lost object—figured in the first tablets—can only be rendered whole through dispute and the acknowledgment of the lost and partial "splinters." Maharal, within the rabbinic tradition, provides a gloss on "dispute for the sake of heaven"—particularly that between Beit Hillel and Shammai—in which both perspectives are "beloved" by God and sustained "forever." They are words of the living God, but also amenable in the Hebrew to a different translation: "the living words of a living God" (Avot 5.17).[22] The divine love in this reading is the precedent for the love between interpreters. God sanctifies the dispute with his love, providing a human imperative for a parallel love.[23]

For Fish, by contrast, different conversations are finally incommensurable one to another and disagreement is even impossible, with change described either in the language of religious conversion or Thomas Kuhn's secular version of the religious experience, paradigm shifts. In the framework of rabbinic hermeneutics, however, the perspectives of Beit Hillel and Beit Shammai are mediated, and the two schools have the ability to disagree through their participation in the common activity of tradition, the hermeneutic activity of recovery. For a community of interpreters—of Talmudic ironists—the object of love, the lost or forgotten law, can only be represented through multiple perspectives but never fully recovered. The rabbinic conceptions of love I am suggesting to be defining of the hermeneutic act do not require a disavowal of the self but rather the assertion that the love for truth—the "words of Torah"—and its recovery can only be fully realized through the acknowledgment of the other. The enterprise of interpretation may, in rabbinic figurations, start as an activity based on animus but translate into one of love, but only through the mediated third term, the common object of love of the divine text (Kiddushin 30b). Fish's account, in its avoidance of love, disavows a conception of community other than one of conflict always defined as unmediated differentiation. In this sense, Talmudic discourse anticipates Rorty's affirmation of a political irony and Fish's pragmatist suspicion of transcendence, but also Lear's Freudian irony founded on love.

Talmud encompasses an activity that unifies the community that it constitutes, with the reader/interpreter as the agent of tradition encountering for herself the possibility of difference, despite the inclination to deny it. "If I am only for myself, then what am I?" reads in psychoanalytic terms as an acknowledgment of the subject's antecedent desire for primacy, and the desire to overcome it. A reading of Eruvin 13b on this basis foregrounds Beit Hillel's awareness of the tendency to disavow complexity. Their forbearance represents a deliberate attempt to militate against the propensity for single-minded thinking, or the absolutizing desire to see a singular unqualified truth. As Fish might say to Rorty, Hillel, like all interpreters, is decisively for himself. But so much so, and self-consciously so, that he guards against a question that Fish's interpreter does not consider: "if I am only for myself, what am I?" In this reading, Hillel and later his followers not only tolerate difference but grant differences a reality through those "bonds of love." For Soloveitchik, psychic unity is presupposed upon differentiation; the process of hermeneutic unification, for the rabbis, enacted through tradition, is also presupposed upon the acceptance of differentiation. The Talmud constitutes itself, or rather the activity that it presupposes, as the locus for disagreement as a unifying activity. Through dispute, the Talmudic ironist constitutes Jewish community and continuity through the shared activities of interpretation and transmission.

Mourning Jerusalem

The reopening of the Jewish mind as not only a cognitive but psychic achievement might entail the embrace of Talmudic irony as a personal as well as cultural sensibility, cultivating a different response to loss. Such a response would entail a renewed openness to difference, of love as not only a psychic but cultural principle. The return to the model of Talmudic irony and participation in many conversations may be an antidote to the defeat of melancholy desolation—the Talmud refers to the learning of Torah as a "cure"—as well as the unwarranted optimism and perfectionism (and consequent fundamentalism) born out of melancholy conquest (Kiddushin 30b). Talmudic irony entails accommodating the possibility of more than one perspective, of hesitating before providing hasty—and always already complete—syntheses, of cultivating a community that foregrounds its lack. A community embracing such irony would have to outgrow the melancholy desire for the always-insufficient compensations of Kristeva's imaginary father, and accept uncertainty and difference.

The Talmud founds its practices on a community that advertises its failure to manifest the ideal—the founding of Yavne. After the catastrophe for the destruction of the Temple, the end of Jewish life centered on sacrifice, R. Yohanan ben Zakkai remakes Jewish community, not through the city or the land, or even through the Book, but through the interpretive experience—Talmudic irony—that informs it.[24] After destruction, it is the subjects constituted through dispute who maintain Judaism in exile. To make that transition, the Talmud figures R. Yohanan enacting his own death, smuggling himself out of the soon-to-be destroyed city in a coffin. There are those who wish to die with the city—for whom there will be no mourning of the destroyed Temple, but only a final and definitive death. For them, death is the preferable alternative to the continued experience of loss; they are not willing to take up the task of mourning. But R. Yohanan urges: "find me a way to get out of Jerusalem; for perhaps there will be a small measure of salvation" (Gittin 56a). Once R. Yohanan escapes the imminent destruction, bound to found the academy at Yavne, taking rabbinic Judaism into the post-Temple era, his ambition is modest—for a "small measure of salvation." R. Yohanan persists in the act of mourning for destruction, through the establishment of Yavne, the beginnings of a recovery rendered possible through engagement and interpretation. R. Yohanan does not die with the city, but through his symbolic enactment of his own death, he commits himself to both loss and mourning.

For R. Yohanan, any eventual unification must first accede to the reality of differentiation. In a different but nonetheless parallel context, John Milton imagines a public sphere of print as an idealized realization of commonwealth. Responding to early modern trauma, culminating in revolution, Milton, in his prose tract against licensing of 1644 *Areopagitica*, celebrates print as the utopian sphere of commonwealth, a place where "there of necessity will be much arguing, much writing, many opinions." In the experience of the modern, Milton also emphasizes epistemological limitations, advocating the multiplying of perspectives, and a truth based on diverse and contingent interpretations, but unified through the interpretive activities that for him define commonwealth. Milton argues, however, in a trope revolving around the Temple in Jerusalem that for those who desire a coerced "uniformity" of belief, there can be no "continuity in this world," only "contiguity."[25] In a fallen world—a world of mourning—difference can never yield to a single encompassing truth. When it does, it becomes only a "rigid external formality," a "gross conforming stupidity, a stark and dead congealment . . . forced and frozen together." "He who thinks we are to pitch our tent here," Milton writes of the one who believes in the possibility of the "face to face" in this world, shows "that he is yet far short of truth."[26]

After the catastrophe of the destruction of the Temple, R. Yohanan ben Zakkai, in his own practice, revives Judaism by creating an interpretive sphere, what

Charlotte Fonrobert calls "the utopian *beit midrash*."[27] He also commits himself to finding truth in various places. The Talmud relates that R. Yohanan studies "constellations and calculations, the sayings of launderers and the sayings of fox-keepers, the conversation of demons and the conversation of palm-trees, the conversation of the ministering angels, the great things and the little things" (Sukka 28a). He not only studies law and science—constellations and calculations—but is also attuned to the nondiscursive, whispers among the palm trees, as well as conversations of ministering angels. For R. Yohanan, after exile, and as part of the process of mourning, there are a multiplicity of natural and supernatural conversations in the universe. They are not held together—"synthetized"—as in the parlance of some students of Soloveitchik, through an act of cognitive conquest, but retain their independence and multiplicity. This is, to adopt Boyarin's phrase, a form of "disputation without telos," a soteriology deferred—certainly not just subordinated to the governing mandate of Halakha.[28] Instead, the Talmud represents R. Yohanan as interested in the encounter with otherness in all of its varieties. For all the conversations in which he participated, the Talmud says, R. Yohanan, "never engaged in frivolous conversations." After destruction, truth has many locales, with differentiation taking priority.

In the face of trauma, having gone so far as to "experience" death himself, R. Yohanan begins the cultural project of mourning, not aiming to experience unity, but to find knowledge in difference. As Milton, in his analogous context writes, aspirations for anything more than disagreement masks a fundamentalist agenda, the desire for what he calls pejoratively "a fine conformity," an "obedient unanimity." For Milton as well, the fallen world is defined by differentiation; a premature proclamation of "continuity" will always be misleadingly false, producing only a "forced and outward union of cold and neutral and inwardly divided minds." Milton, like R. Yohanan, finds solace in the multiplicity of discourses in a community, for him, enabled by the innovations of a new print culture where there is "much writing, much arguing," and consequently, "knowledge in the making."[29] The irony which the Talmud fosters, a function of the hermeneutics of dispute cultivated and refined at Yavne, depends on a similar consciousness of differentiation, also enacting "knowledge in the making."

Soloveitchik's work cultivates differentiation but in the realm of the psyche, not in the realm of *mesora*, thus occluding the subject of Talmudic irony. His response to trauma—the *hurban* of Europe, not Jerusalem—differs from that of R. Yohanan ben Zakkai. Soloveitchik's representation of hermeneutics—and the privileged interpretive figure of halakhic man—remains tied to a singular notion of truth and the melancholy vacillation between the despair of loss and the triumph of conquest. Although it is precisely "dissonance," in Adorno's phrase, which is the "truth about harmony," a *discordia concors* of Talmudic perspectives remains exiled from Soloveitchik's hermeneutic realm of singular truth. With its attachment to nineteenth-century conceptions of genius and enlightenment notions of truth, the halakhic man's hermeneutics, adopting the truth criteria of modernity, distances itself from the differences cultivated in the hermeneutics of mourning.

For us, Soloveitchik's works may raise the question of how loss can be faced, that is, whether the traumas of the twentieth century can ever lead beyond the anxious vacillation between hermeneutic despair and conquest. As Adam Phillips writes, the melancholy figure can turn easily into a fundamentalist, with the shattering of belief a prelude to a "kind of triumphalism."[30] The persistent and melancholy desire for certainty represents a failure of mourning, with Soloveitchik, as perhaps Freud himself (another melancholy modern), finally unable to mourn. Haunted by a fantasy of both historical and personal perfection, Soloveitchik reveals both his idealism and the despair engendered by it. The pessimism born out of melancholy—what Bersani calls the presumed incommensurability between "language" and "authentic being"—leaves Soloveitchik, the individual, isolated and singular: the lonely "last rabbi of Brisk."[31] While the inverse, an optimism no less a function of melancholy, with a confidence in knowledge as a form of conquest, sustains a conception of tradition inured to loss and death that, in its pursuit of certainty, allows no accommodation of difference.

Perhaps the hermeneutics of mourning—and the multiplicity it cultivates—can survive the catastrophe and traumas of contemporary life, allowing for a rebirth of a Talmudic culture of irony, the revitalization of the activity of tradition, and the difference it cultivates. For Soloveitchik, however, only in his reminiscences does he allow for the presence of such uncertainty, in the figure of the feminine, his mother. She is the one who tells the heartbroken Joseph that one can live with loss; that solutions do not have to be ready at hand; that one can live in a state of not-knowing; that the "main thing is to learn Torah with joy and excitement" (*Seek*, 145). She comforts the young Joseph, disconsolate at the hermeneutic failure of his father, initiating him into a "Torah of the heart," telling him that if he doesn't find a solution for the Rambam, "then maybe when you grow up you'll resolve his words." Here the feminine, not as the lost ideal and fantastic remnant of psychic wholeness as in the eulogy for the Talne Rebbetzin, but of genuine sympathy, advises the young Joseph to live with loss, to look into an unknown future where he may himself answer the questions that perplexed his father and where he may (further) narrate the story of his own self-creation. The feminine here, associated with Bergsonian memory and the historicity implied in the conception of repentance—where the future represents both radical break and continuity—allows for a new (but also older) conception of tradition. Negation and loss sustain this tradition, not just *teshuva* and the ethical life. Forgetting brings the possibility of remembrance and acknowledged loss becomes a prerequisite for continuity and innovation. The antithetical nature of Soloveitchik's ethical awareness, the great achievement of his work for the current generation, may help inform attempts to revive the hermeneutics of mourning, which remained for Soloveitchik only a fantasy, shared with his mother, away from his grandfather's living room and the normative hermeneutics of halakhic men.

Notes

Unless otherwise noted, all English translations of quotations are my own—with the exception of Biblical translations which are adaptations of the King James version.

Introduction

1. For a biography of Soloveitchik that presents his life in the context of both his Brisk inheritance and the shaping of Modern Orthodoxy, see Aaaron Rakeffet-Rothkoff, *The Rav: The World of Rabbi Joseph B. Soloveitchik* (New York: Ktav, 1999), 2 vols.

2. On self-fashioning as a trope, see Stephen Greenblatt, *Renaissance Self-Fashioning* (Chicago: University of Chicago Press, 1980), 1–9.

3. Adam Phillips, *Becoming Freud: The Making of a Psychoanalyst* (New Haven, CT: Yale University Press, 2014).

4. Phillips, *Becoming Freud*, 9.

5. Jonathan Sacks, "A Hesped in Honor of Rav Yosef Soloveitchik," in *Memories of a Giant: Reflections on Dr. Joseph B. Soloveitchik*, ed. Michael A. Bierman (New York: Urim, 2003), 290–92.

6. For the act of cultural transmission as a form of "translation," see Thomas Greene, *The Light in Troy* (New Haven, CT: Yale University Press, 1982), 72–80.

7. From Soloveitchik's "Al Ahavat Ha-Torah ve-Geulat Nefesh Ha-Dor," translated in Aharon Lichtenstein, *Leaves of Faith* (Jersey City: Ktav, 2003), 202.

8. For the rabbinic conception of synecdoche, see *Midrash Tanhuma, Bamidbar* 23; lecture cited by Yair Kahn, "Vezeh Lekha Ha'Ot Ki Anochi Shlachticha," in *Memories of a Giant*, 204 (recording of original lecture at http://www.yutorah.org/lectures/lecture.cfm/767912/Rabbi_Joseph_B_Soloveitchik/Megillas_Esther).

9. Thomas Hobbes, *Leviathan*, ed. Richard Tuck (Cambridge: Cambridge University Press, 1996), 120.

10. See Walter Wurzburger, "Rav Joseph B. Soloveitchik as Posek of Post-Modern Orthodoxy," *Tradition* 29, no. 1 (1994): 5–20.

11. William Kolbrener, "'No Elsewhere': Fish, Soloveitchik and the Unavoidability of Interpretation," *Journal of Literature and Theology* 10, no. 2 (1996): 177–78.

12. For an account explaining this disjunction and Max Scheler's largely unacknowledged influence in Soloveitchik's articulation of pluralism (and the latter's assertion of the autonomy of religion, and "metaphysical realism"), see Yonatan Brafman, "Critical Philosophy of Halakha (Jewish Law): The Justification of Halakhic Norms and Authority" (Ph.D. dissertation, Columbia University, 2012), 162–68.

13. See Daniel Rynhold, "The Philosophical Foundations of Soloveitchik's Critique of Interfaith Dialogue," *Harvard Theological Review* 96, no. 1 (2003): 101–20.

14. Kolbrener, "No Elsewhere," 174.

15. Ibid., 174.

16. See Christine Hayes, '"In the West, They Laughed at Him': The Mocking Realists of the Babylonian Talmud," *Journal of Law, Religion & State* 2 (2013): 167.

17. Steven Marcus and Charles Taylor, "Calls for Papers," *Common Knowledge* 1, no. 1 (1992).

18. For a similar response to reading (and rereading) Soloveitchik's work, see Daniel Rynhold, "Letting the Facts Get in the Way of a Good Thesis: On Interpreting R. Soloveitchik's Philosophical Method," *Torah u-Madda Journal* 16 (2012–2013): 52–77.

19. "Catastrophe and Halakhic Creativity: Ashkenaz—1096, 1242, 1306 and 1298," *Jewish History* 12, no. 1 (1998): 71.

20. Albert I. Baumgarten and Marina Rustow, "Judaism and Tradition: Continuity, Change and Innovation," *Jewish Studies at the Crossroads of Anthropology and History*, ed. Ra'anan S. Boustan, Oren Kosansky, and Marina Rustow (Philadelphia: University of Pennsylvania Press, 2011), 229.

21. Sigmund Freud, *SE*, 14:243–58; *SE*, 23:7–137.

22. Dominick Lacapra, *History and Memory after Auschwitz* (Ithaca, NY: Cornell University Press, 1998), 144–45.

23. For more on Geertz's "thick description" and contemporary method, see Jeffrey Perl, "Fuzzy Studies," *Common Knowledge* 17, no. 3 (2011): 441–49.

24. Such a rupture, named in different ways, has been noted in Soloveitchik's reception history since 1973. See Lawrence Kaplan, "The Religious Philosophy of Joseph Soloveitchik," *Tradition* 14, no. 2 (1973): 43–64. For a fuller account of the ruptures internal to Soloveitchik's work, see the historiography of *Halakhic Man* in chapter 5.

1. Hermeneutics of Rabbinic Mourning

1. For how the revelation at Sinai undid the original transgression of Adam and Eve, see Shabbat 108a.

2. Jean-Luc Nancy, *The Inoperative Community*, ed. Peter Connor (Minneapolis, MN: University of Minnesota Press, 1992), 17; Harold Fisch, "Revelation and Concealment: A Note on 'Another Tallit' by S. Y. Agnon," in *Ocular Desire*, ed. Aharon R. E. Agus and Jan Assman (Berlin: Akademie Verlag, 1994), 172.

3. Fisch, "Revelation," 171–72. Augustine's *De Doctrina* echoes and refines Pauline hermeneutics: "It is, then," Augustine writes, "a miserable kind of spiritual slavery to interpret signs as things, and to be incapable of raising the mind's eye above the physical creation so as to absorb the eternal light." See Augustine, *De Doctrina*, trans. R. P. H. Green (Oxford: Oxford University Press, 1995), 141.

4. Plato, *The Republic*, ed. Desmond Lee (London: Penguin Books, 1987), 364.

5. Spinoza, *Tractatus Theologico-Politicus*, trans. Samuel Shirley (Leiden: Brill, 1989), 65.

6. For John Milton and the older poetic culture he represents, Jesus is himself a "mediator" characterized by the linguistic, while the angels are defined by their capacities for both discursive and intuitive forms of knowledge. See my *Milton's Warring Angels* (Cambridge: Cambridge University Press, 1996), 147–51, and *Paradise Lost* (5:488–89) in William Kerrigan, John Rumrich, and Stephen M. Fallon, eds., *The Complete Poetry and Essential Prose of John Milton* (New York: Modern Library, 2007).

7. On the emergence of these scientific methodologies from an earlier "poetic" culture, see Steven Fallon, *Milton among the Philosophers* (Ithaca, NY: Cornell University Press, 2007), 19–49.

8. On Thomas Hobbes's rejection of the poetic culture embodied in John Milton's works, see my introduction to Milton's *Areopagitica* (Jerusalem: Shalem, 2013); for the eventual shift from a poetic culture to a philosophical one, with the Cambridge Platonists as transitional fig-

ures, see Aharon Lichtenstein, *Henry More: The Rational Theology of a Cambridge Platonist* (Cambridge, MA: Harvard University Press, 1962).

9. Thomas Nagel, *The View from Nowhere* (Oxford: Oxford University Press, 1989).

10. Robert A. Paul, *Moses and Civilization* (New Haven, CT: Yale University Press, 1996), 189.

11. In the Freudian historiography of Judeao-Christianity, psychoanalysis emerges as the privileged means of remembrance by which enlightened Jews, to use Jonathan Lear's term, "leapfrog" over both their Jewish and Christian antecedents. For Freud, it is psychoanalysis that offers "soul transforming ways of remembrance and acknowledging guilt," but without the retrograde and illusory connection to theological traditions and the divine. See Lear, *Happiness, Death and the Remainder of Life* (Cambridge, MA: Harvard University Press, 2002), 151. For a different psychoanalytic approach on the "defensive dimensions of the Christian posture towards Judaism," see José Faur, "De-Authorization of the Law: Paul and the Oedipal Model," in *Psychoanalysis and Religion*, ed. Joseph Smith and Susan Handelman (Baltimore, MD: Johns Hopkins University Press, 1990), 222–43. See also Jan Assman, *Moses the Egyptian: The Memory of Egypt in Western Monotheism* (Cambridge: Cambridge University Press, 1997).

12. Richard J. Bernstein, *Freud and the Legacy of Moses* (Cambridge: Cambridge University Press, 1998), 61. See also Michel de Certeau, "The Fiction of History: The Writing of Moses and Monotheism," *The Writing of History* (New York: Columbia University Press, 1988), 308–54.

13. Lear, *Happiness*, 91.

14. On Freud's Moses, see Harold P. Blum, "Freud and the Figure of Moses: The Moses of Freud," *Journal of the American Psychoanalytic Association* 39 (1991): 513–36.

15. Rashi on Exodus 33:34.

16. Hilary Putnam, *Realism with a Human Face* (Cambridge, MA: Harvard University Press, 1990), 177, 120.

17. Cited in *Mishnayot Zekher Hinukh* (Jerusalem: H. Vagshal, 1999), 499–500.

18. For discussion of a different set of views on this matter, pluralism as a literary artifact performing ideological work in Daniel Boyarin and David Stern, see chapter 2.

19. Dominick LaCapra, *History and Memory after Auschwitz* (Ithaca, NY: Cornell University Press, 1998), 144–45.

20. On rabbinic representations of the death of Moses, see Rella Kushelevsky, *Moses and the Angel of Death* (New York: Peter Lang, 1995), and Gerald J. Blidstein, *The Death of Moses: Readings in Midrash* (Alon Shvut: Tevunot, 2008).

21. See *Loewald*, 100.

22. For the development of Rose's argument and her suggestive reading of Poussin's "Landscape with the Ashes of Phocion," see *Mourning Becomes the Law: Philosophy and Representation* (Cambridge: Cambridge University Press, 1996), 20–39.

23. For Lear, Freud's description of a child's conversion of his mother's absence into a "game of loss"—the *fort - o-o-o-o game*—is "a profile in the development of courage," opening the possibility for the creation of meaning (*Happiness*, 94, 96).

24. On divine "mourning" in rabbinic representations, see David Stern, *Parables in Midrash* (Cambridge, MA: Harvard University Press, 1991), 126–30.

25. On the decline of the generations, see Menachem Kellner, *Maimonides on the Decline of the Generations and the Nature of Rabbinic Authority* (Albany, NY: SUNY Press, 1996), 7–26.

26. Putnam, *Realism*, 170.

27. Mark Edmundson, *The Death of Sigmund Freud* (London: Bloomsbury, 2007), 232.

28. In the same way that the sages focus on Joshua as a figure of transmission, T. S. Eliot, in his *What Is a Classic?* (London: Faber and Faber, 1944), focuses on the "universal classic," Virgil (11). Classicism, like the tradition figured in *Temurah*, relies on a historical movement both

backward and forward. Homer is the Western originary text, and therefore, in Eliot's estimation it is not a "universal classic," certainly not the paradigm for it. In this view, Virgil, the true classic, follows Homer, as both imitator and innovator; Joshua, in relationship to Moses, occupies a parallel place in the Jewish tradition, the first agent of transmission.

29. Dominick LaCapra, *History and Memory*, 144–45. LaCapra's point of departure is the Freud of "Mourning and Melancholy": "Reality-testing has shown that the loved object no longer exists, and it proceeds to demand that all libido shall be withdrawn from its attachment to that object. This demand arouses understandable opposition—it is a matter of general observation that people never willingly abandon a libidinal position, not even, indeed, when a substitute is already beckoning to them. This opposition can be so intense that a turning away from reality takes place and a clinging to the object through the medium of a hallucinatory wishful psychosis" (*SE*, 14:244).

30. *Loewald*, 94, 99.

31. Adam Phillips, *On Flirtation* (Cambridge, MA: Harvard University Press, 1994), 24.

32. On the "two deaths of Moses" and the Israelites' imagining of Moses's death as a projection of their desire to murder him, see Betty Rojtman, "The Double Death of Moses," in *New Perspectives on Freud's Moses and Monotheism*, ed. Ruth Ginsburg and Ilana Pardes (Tubingen: De Gruyter, 2006), 108–9.

33. Rashi on Hagiga 16a.

34. For more on this, see Yitzchak Hutner, *Pachad Yitzchak: Hanuka* (New York: Gur Aryeh, 1998), 35–37.

35. See Gedalyahu Shor, *Ohr Gadalyahu* (New York: Keren Zichron Gadalyahu, 2000), 3:159.

36. As David Weiss Halivni writes, "the Rabbis say 'if the tablets had not been broken, Torah would not have been forgotten in Israel.'" For him, the corollary principle is: "if the tablets had not been broken, the Oral Torah would not exist." See his *Breaking the Tablets: Jewish Theology after the Shoah* (New York: Rowman and Littlefield, 2007), 88.

37. Phillips, *Flirtation*, 31.

38. Yehuda Loew, *Derekh Ha-Hayyim* (Tel Aviv: Yad Morechai, 1975), 604.

39. As David Kraemer, in *Responses to Suffering in Classical Rabbinic Literature* (Oxford: Oxford University Press, 1994), writes, "the Bavlie prefers to support these opposing views, side by side, rather than deciding definitively in favor of one or another." "The posture of the Bavlie," he continues, "is due to the recognition on the part of its authorship that divine will, preserved in Torah, is accessibly only through the acutely human act of interpretation." In light of this condition, Kraemer concludes, "the authorship of the Bavlie recognized the need to learn from multiple, equally imperfect opinions" (220). See also his *Mind of the Talmud* (Oxford: Oxford University Press, 1990), esp. pp. 139–70, and chapter 2 in the present work.

40. Lear, *Happiness*, 96.

41. Hilary Putnam, *Realism*, 120.

2. Pluralism, Rabbinic Poetry, and Dispute

1. Daniel Boyarin, *Border Lines: The Partition of Judaeo-Christianity* (Philadelphia: University of Pennsylvania Press, 2004), 153. In *Dispute for the Sake of Heaven: Legal Pluralism in the Talmud* (Providence, RI: Brown University Press, 2010), Richard Hidary, following Steven Fraade, calls such programmatic texts the "poster children" for rabbinic pluralism in opinions (27).

2. Samuel Johnson, "Cowley,"' in *Lives of the Poets* (London, 1896), 1:13.

3. See, for example, David Kraemer, *The Mind of the Talmud* (Oxford: Oxford University Press, 1990), 99–138; Michael Rosensweig, "*Elu Va-Elu Divre Elokim Hayyim*: Halakhic Pluralism and Theories of Controversy," *Tradition* 26, no. 3 (1992): 4–23; Eli Turkel, "The Nature and Limitations of Rabbinic Authority," *Tradition* 27, no. 4 (1993): 80–99; Shalom Carmy, "Pluralism and the Category of the Ethical," *Tradition* 30, no. 4 (1996): 145–63; Avi Sagi, " 'Both Are the Words of the Living God': A Typological Analysis of Halakhic Pluralism," *Hebrew Union College Annual* 65 (1994): 105–36; Marc-Alan Ouaknin, *The Burnt Book: Reading the Talmud* (Princeton, NJ: Princeton University Press, 1998), 59–163; Christine Hayes, "Theoretical Pluralism in the Talmud: A Response to Richard Hidary," *Dine Israel: Studies in Halakhah and Jewish Law* 26/27 (2009–2010): 257–307; Steven D. Fraade, "Rabbinic Polysemy and Pluralism Revisited: Between Praxis and Thematization," *AJS Review* 31, no. 1 (2007): 1–40, and " 'A Heart of Many Chambers': The Theological Hermeneutics of Legal Multivocality," *Harvard Theological Review* 108, no. 1 (2015): 113–27; Azzan Yadin-Israel, "Rabbinic Polysemy: A Response to Steven Fraade," *AJS Review* 38, no. 1 (2014): 129–41; and Richard Hidary's comprehensive *Dispute* (esp. pp. 17–39; 369–93).

4. Ludwig Wittgenstein, *Culture and Value*, trans. Peter Winch (Oxford: Oxford University Press, 1980), 24e. As Adin Steinsaltz has remarked, in the Talmud "there is a deliberate evasion of abstract thinking based on abstract concepts" (cited in Susan Handelman, *Slayers of Moses: The Emergence of Rabbinic Interpretation in Modern Literary Theory* [Albany, NY: SUNY Press, 1983], 61).

5. Daniel Boyarin, *Intertextuality and the Reading of Midrash* (Bloomington: Indiana University Press, 1990), xi; David Stern, *Parables in Midrash* (Cambridge, MA: Harvard University Press, 1991), 1.

6. Geoffrey Hartman, "Midrash as Law and Literature," *Journal of Religion* 74 (1994): 338.

7. Hartman, "Midrash as Law and Literature," 342, 358.

8. Sanford Budick and Geoffrey Hartman, eds., *Midrash and Literature* (New Haven, CT: Yale University Press, 1986), xi.

9. Budick and Hartman, *Midrash and Literature*, xi. In this light, see also Susan Handelman, " 'Everything Is In It': Rabbinic Interpretation and Modern Literary Theory," *Judaism* 35 (1986): 429–40, and her "Fragments of the Rock: Contemporary Literary Theory and the Study of Rabbinic Texts: A Response to David Stern," *Prooftexts* 5 (1985): 75–95, where she argues that "midrash takes delight in precisely those aspects of language to which poststructuralist criticism has alerted us," thus rendering the text as "a field of play" (86).

10. Hartman, "Midrash as Law and Literature," 354.

11. Betty Rojtman, "Sacred Language and Open Text," in *Midrash and Literature*, 159; Myrna Solotorevsky, "The Model of Midrash and Borges's Interpretative Tales and Essays," in *Midrash and Literature*, 255.

12. Edith Wyschogrod, "Trends in Postmodern Jewish Philosophy," *Soundings* 76 (1994): 129–37.

13. For the problems of employing poststructuralist theory as a lens for understanding the rabbis, see David Stern's review of Handelman's *Slayers of Moses*, "Moses-cide: Midrash and Contemporary Literary Criticism," in *Prooftexts* 4 (1984): 193–213, as well as the subsequent exchange of letters in *Prooftexts* 5 (1985): 75–103.

14. Stern's assertion that editorial pluralism has become "a condition of meaning" is informed by the assumptions about Talmudic redaction in David Weiss Halivni's work; see Halivni's *The Formation of the Babylonian Talmud*, trans. Jeffrey Rubenstein (Oxford: Oxford University Press, 2013).

15. *Border*, 176, 173.

16. See also Robert Cover, "The Supreme Court, 1982 Term—Foreword: Nomos and Narrative," *Faculty Scholarship Series*, paper no. 2705.55-63, accessed March 15, 2016 http://digitalcommons.law.yale.edu/fss_papers/2705. For Cover, "the multiplicity of meaning" leads "at once to the imperial virtues and the imperial mode of world maintenance," placing the "contraints of peace on the void at which strong bonds cease" (16).

17. *Border*, 180. See also Fraade, "Rabbinic Polysemy and Pluralism Revisited": "we cannot presume that the multivocal textual practices of such texts reflect a 'pluralistic' rabbinic social reality that lies *behind* them (indeed they may mask the very opposite)" (12). Yaakov Elman, in his "Arguments for the Sake of Heaven: The Mind of the Talmud: A Review Essay," *Jewish Quarterly Review* 84, nos. 2/3 (1993–1994), also affirms that the society reflected in the Babylonian Talmud is "authoritarian rather than pluralistic, a conclusion which," he adds, "is historically highly probable" (269).

18. Stephen Greenblatt, *Shakespearean Negotiations: The Circulation of Social Energy in Renaissance England* (Berkeley, CA: University of California Press, 1988), 21–65.

19. *Border*, 182.

20. *Border*, 189, 199.

21. In his response to Handelman (*Prooftexts* 5), Stern asserts that in "historical fact," midrash "has been the neglected stepchild of rabbinic literature, ignored and subordinated to the more practical serious rigors of halakha" (97). In contemporary literary circles, however, the hierarchy has been reversed.

22. Rojtman, "Sacred Language," 159; see also Edith Wyschograd, "Trends in Postmodern Jewish Philosophy; Afterword" *Soundings* 76 (1994): 129–37; 191–96, who writes that since "law is governed by an arche outside of itself," rabbinic legal exegisis is "Platonic" (195). In addition, see José Faur, "The Limits of Readerly Collusion in Rabbinic Tradition," *Soundings* 76 (1994): 153–61, which contrasts the interpretive freedom of midrash with the limitations imposed by the law.

23. Johnson, "Cowley," 13; see my "Discordia Concors," *Common Knowledge* 11, no. 1 (2005): 111–21.

24. For the worldview, or "episteme," that underlies the Donnean aesthetic, see Michel Foucault, *The Order of Things: An Archaeology of the Human Sciences* (London: Vintage, 1970), 60–61.

25. See, for example, Donne's "Canonization" and Holy Sonnet 14 in Herbert Grierson, ed., *The Poems of John Donne* (Oxford: Oxford University Press, 1968), 14, 49, 328. Thomas Hobbes, *Leviathan*, ed. Richard Tuck (Cambridge: Cambridge University Press, 1996), in his attempt to kill off the culture of poetry represented in figures such as Donne and Milton, similarly dispensed with the merely fanciful "ornamentation" of the poet for the more rigorous "wit" of men of "judgment" (20–22). On this history of wit in the seventeenth century, see Edward Tayler, *Literary Criticism of Seventeenth-Century England* (New York: Knopf, 1967), esp. pp. 30–31.

26. *Border*, 178.

27. Yadin-Israel, "Rabbinic Polysemy," 130.

28. On the passage as providing evidence for the relative consistency between Talmudic and *tannaitic* conceptions of "legal multivocality," see Fraade, "Many Chambers," 125–27. Yadin-Israel, by contrast, limits multivocality to the post-*tannaitic* period: in his view, there is no "valorized legal pluralism . . . until a significantly later stratum of the rabbinic corpus" ("Rabbinic Polysemy,"139).

29. Cited by Stern, *Midrash*, 26.

30. Rashi on Deuteronomy 1:13, and his citation of *Sifre*.

31. Cited by Edward Tayler, *Donne's Idea of a Woman: Structure and Meaning in the Anniversaries* (New York: Columbia University Press, 1991), 4.

32. For a different elaboration of the subject–object dichotomy, see *"Torat Hesed* and *Torah Emet,"* in Aharon Lichtenstein, *Leaves of Faith* (Jersey City, NJ: Ktav, 2003), 1:61–87.

33. For the attack on Gadamerian "anarchy" in interpretation, see E. D. Hirsch, *Validity in Interpretation* (New Haven, CT: Yale University Press, 1967), 31; for attacks on Skinnerian intentionalism, see the essays collected in *Meaning and Context*, ed. James Tully (Cambridge: Cambridge University Press, 1988), especially articles by Keith Graham and John Keane, both invoking the name of Gadamer. See also John Hall, "Illiberal Liberalism," *British Journal of Sociology* 31 (1980): 297–99.

34. Quentin Skinner, ed., *The Return of Grand Theory* (Cambridge: Cambridge University Press, 2000), 7.

35. See also Skinner's "A Reply to My Critics," in *Meaning and Context*, esp. pp. 276–81. For the canonical essay "The Intentional Fallacy," see W. K. Wimsatt and Monroe C. Beardsley, *The Verbal Icon: Studies in the Meaning of Poetry* (Lexington, KY: University Press of Kentucky, 1954): 468–88.

36. See Skinner's "Motives, intentions, and the interpretation of texts" in *Meaning and Context*, 68–78, esp. pp. 70–72.

37. *Meaning and Context*, 260, 279; for Skinner's confrontation with more contemporary figures (Barthes, Foucault, and Derrida), see 272–81.

38. Nancy S. Streuver, *Theory as Practice: Ethical Inquiry in the Renaissance* (Chicago: University of Chicago Press, 1992), x.

39. For a notable exception, see *Meaning and Context*, 338n172.

40. *Meaning and Context*, 257. For an earlier acknowledgement of the influence of Kuhn on the Cambridge School of history, see J. G. A. Pocock, *Virtue, Commerce and History* (Cambridge: Cambridge University Press, 1985), 3, 61.

41. Quentin Skinner's *Visions of Politics* (Cambridge: Cambridge University Press, 2002) also asserts an affinity with Gadamer. Gadamer's arguments, writes Skinner, embody "a salutary reminder about the need to be aware of our inevitable tendency towards pre-judgment and the fitting of evidence into pre-existing patterns of interpretation and explanation" (1:15).

42. Skinner, *Visions*, 1:15.

43. Hans George Gadamer, *Truth and Method* (New York: Continuum, 1963), 297, 300, 120.

44. Gadamer, *Truth*, 118, 298, 269; emphasis added.

45. For a discussion of the episode, see Boyarin, *Intertextuality*, 34. However, Menachem Fisch, *Rational Rabbis: Science and Talmudic Culture* (Bloomington: Indiana University Press, 1997), takes exception to Boyarin's reading, which Fisch claims goes to "the point of interpretive anarchy" (85). See also David Kraemer, *Mind of the Talmud*, 122–23.

46. *Hiddushie Ha-Ritba al Ha-Shas* (Jerusalem: Mossad Ha-Rav Kook, 1974), 3.107.

47. Cited in Rosensweig, *"Elu Va-Elu,"* 13.

48. Rashi (Ketuvot 57b) explains amoraic dispute: "when two *amoraim* argue in a legal dispute [*din*], or in the case of prohibition or permission, each one saying that their reasoning is more logical, there is no falsehood. Each one is presenting his own conclusions: this one compares the matter to this; this one compares the matter to this."

49. Daniel Boyarin, "Pilpul: The Logic of Commentary," *Dor le-dor* 3 (1986): 1–25.

50. R. Hayyim Friedlander, *Siftie Hayyim* (B'nai Brak: Friedlander, 1996), *Moadim* 3:171.

51. R. Hayyim Volozhin, *Nefesh Ha-Hayyim* (Jerusalem: Issakhar Dov Ruvin, 1989), 217.

52. See Harold Fisch, *Divine Contradictions: Judaism and the Language of Paradox* (Ramat Gan: Bar Ilan University Press, 2001), 124–33.

53. Moshe Halbertal, *People of the Book* (Cambridge, MA: Cambridge University Press, 1997), 27.

54. Gadamer, *Truth*, 105–9.

55. In *Rational Rabbis*, Fisch sees his advocacy of what he calls "the anti-traditionalist" and pluralist voice of the Babylonian Talmud as an attempt "to retrieve, isolate, and amplify one voice in a Talmudic polyphony" (44).

56. The traditional rabbinic historiographical designations employed here have been complicated in contemporary scholarship, primarily by David Weiss Halivni; see his *The Formation of the Babylonian Talmud*.

57. Halivni and subsequent scholars refer to this anonymous voice as the "stam"; for simplicity's sake, I refer to this voice as the "Talmud."

58. Ludwig Wittgenstein, *The Blue and Brown Books* (Oxford: Blackwell, 1958), 5.

59. For a corresponding reading of *amoraim* through the lens of *rishonim*, see my "The Hermeneutics of Mourning: Multiplicity and Authority in Jewish Law," *College Literature* 30, no. 4 (2003): 114–39.

60. Adam Phillips, *Terrors and Experts* (Cambridge, MA: Harvard University Press, 1997), 84.

61. *Nefesh Ha-Hayyim*, 225.

62. Betzalel Ashkenazi, *Shita Mekubzet* on Nedarim (Jerusalem: Brochman, 1997), 154.

63. Bernard Williams, "Wittgenstein and Idealism," in *Understanding Wittgenstein*, ed. George Vesey (Ithaca, NY: Cornell University Press, 1974), 87. For a further commentary on the duck-rabbit, see Thomas Kuhn, *Structure of Scientific Revolutions* (Chicago: University of Chicago Press, 2012): "The duck-rabbit shows that two men with the same retinal impressions can see different things. No language," Kuhn writes, "thus restricted to reporting a world fully known in advance can produce mere neutral and objective reports on the 'given'" (127).

64. *Bamidbar Rabba*, 13.15. See also Berakhot 58a: "Just as each face is different, so the knowledge (or sensibility) of each person is different."

Interlude

1. In a rabbinic representation of Moses ascending to the heavens to receive the Torah, the leader of Israel is given a vision of the sage who will live hundreds of years after his death, Rabbi Akiva (Menakhot 29b). In this depiction, Moses is transported to the back of R. Akiva's classroom: "Moses went and sat at the end of the eight rows of students." But in listening to R. Akiva, Moses, unable to understand him or his students, is disheartened and his "strength wanes." When one of R. Akiva's students inquires, "Teacher, from where do you know this?," the latter responds, "It is a law received from Moses from Sinai"—to Moses's surprise and relief. The Talmud depicts R. Akiva expounding "heaps and heaps of laws"—multiplicity and differentiation, with their origin in Mosaic prophesy.

2. David Singer and Moshe Sokol, "Joseph Soloveitchik: Lonely Man of Faith," *Modern Judaism* 2 (1982): 229.

3. Christopher Bollas, *Cracking Up: The Work of Unconscious Experience* (New York: Hill and Wang, 1996), 139.

3. Love, Repentance, Sublimation

1. Jonathan Lear, *Freud* (London: Routledge, 2005), 207.

2. On the phylogenetic inheritance in Freud, see Lear, *Freud*, 145.

3. Yonathan Brafman, "Critical Philosophy of Halakha (Jewish Law): The Justification of Halakhic Norms and Authority" (Columbia University dissertation, 2012) argues for the "cogency" of Soloveitchik's approach, explaining the difference between the disciplinary defense of pluralism and the resistance to a pluralism that is internal to Jewish frameworks. For Brafman, although Soloveitchik acknowledges that "being" is not homogenous and calls for different disciplinary responses, what he calls Soloveitchik's "metaphysical realism," (derived from Max Scheler and resulting in a "realist philosophical account of halakha"), justifies the account of Jewish law as normative (173, 171; and see 162–68).

4. In their introduction to *Seek*, David Schatz and Reuven Ziegler affirm that the three texts of the 1940s "are parts of an ambitious intellectual program and are related to one another in various ways, involving both comparisons and contrasts" (xxxv–xxxvi).

5. See Aviezer Ravitzky, "Rabbi J. B. Soloveitchik on Human Knowledge: Between Maimonidean and Neo-Kantian Philosophy," *Modern Judaism* 6, no. 2 (1986): 157–88.

6. In another context showing the reciprocity of subject and object, "the ancient dichotomy of freedom and determinism," is understood by Soloveitchik as "nurtured on the paradoxical character of objectivity which rest upon subjective premises" (*Mind*, 127n81).

7. Clifford Geertz, *The Interpretation of Cultures* (New York: Basic Books, 1973), 17.

8. For etiological readings of the Bible, see James L. Kugel, *How to Read the Bible: A Guide to Scripture, Then and Now* (New York: Free Press, 2007), and my review, " 'The Real Thing': How to Read the Bible," *Jewish Quarterly Review* 100, no. 1 (2010): 183–89.

9. Lear provides a reworking of the precedent essay by Loewald, "On the Therapeutic Action of Psychoanalysis," *Loewald*, 221–56.

10. See Sigmund Freud, "Recommendation on Analytic Technique," *SE*, 12:111–12.

11. For Lear, psychoanalysis need not apologize for its methods, but given what Lear identifies as Freud's "postulation of love," science itself must re-elaborate its methodology to incorporate love. "If science is to capture human reality, its bounds and methods must be redrawn"; science itself is, after all, an act of unification, "a development of higher complexity, an act of love" (*Love*, 220–21).

12. See "Sublimation: Inquiries in the Theoretical Psychoanalysis," in *Loewald*, 435–517, as well as "Psychoanalysis and the History of the Individual," in ibid., 529–79.

13. Jessica Benjamin, *The Bonds of Love: Psychoanalysis, Feminism, and the Problem of Domination* (New York: Pantheon, 1988), 12.

14. On Lear's implicit reference to Aeschylus's *Oresteia* as a model for psychic health, see my "Irony at the Crossroads," *Free Associations* 6 (2014): 88–97.

15. In *Whirl*, Soloveitchik forcefully distinguishes his conception of internal life—"emotional experience"—from that of Freud, which he claims does not belong to the realm of "the interpretive" (188–89). For more on Soloveitchik's conceptions of emotions, see chapter 6.

16. Sigmund Freud, "An Outline of Psycho-Analysis," *SE*, 23:206.

17. The Freudian concept of *nachtraglich* may be a precursor to the "interpenetration" of temporal modes described by Loewald. According to Laplanche and Pontalis in *The Language of Psychoanalysis* (New York: W. W. Norton, 1973), the term that Freud used "repeatedly and constantly" challenges the "linear determinism" of the past's influence on the present. *Nachtraglich* suggests "a conception of temporality" in which "consciousness constitutes its own past, constantly subjecting its meaning to revision in conformity with its 'project' " (111–12).

18. Frank Kermode, *The Sense of an Ending: Studies in the Theory of Fiction* (Oxford: Oxford University Press, 1967), 46.

19. See my "Towards a Genuine Jewish Philosophy: *Halakhic Mind*'s New Philosophy of Religion," *Tradition* 30, no. 3 (1996): 36–39.

4. Joseph Soloveitchik

1. Shaul Magid, "Deconstructing the Mystical: The Anti-Mystical Kabbalism in Rabbi Hayyim of Volozhin's Nefesh Ha-Hayyim," *Journal of Jewish Thought and Philosophy* 9, no. 1 (1999): 27, 27n20.

2. Cited by Magid, ibid., 30n29.

3. Ibid., 62.

4. Aviezer Ravitzky, "Rabbi J. B. Soloveitchik on Human Knowledge: Between Maimonidean and Neo-Kantian Philosophy," *Modern Judaism* 6, no. 2 (May 1986): 165, 166, 170.

5. John Searle, *The Construction of Social Reality* (New York: Free Press, 1995), 74.

6. Emanuel Levinas, *Totality and Infinity* (Pittsburgh, PA: Duquesne University Press, 1969), 304.

7. On the relationship for Soloveitchik between "natural consciousness" and "revelational consciousness," see David Shatz and Reuven Ziegler's introduction to *Seek*, xiii–xvii.

8. Jonathan Lear, *Happiness, Death, and the Remainder of Life* (Cambridge, MA: Harvard University Press, 2000), 94.

9. See also Christopher Bollas, *The Shadow of the Object* (New York: Columbia University Press, 1989).

10. Sara Beardsworth, *Julia Kristeva: Psychoanalysis and Modernity* (Albany, NY: SUNY Press, 2004), 98–99.

11. Walter Benjamin, *The Origin of German Tragic Drama* (London: Verso, 2003), 226–35. See also Terry Eagleton, *Walter Benjamin: Or Towards a Revolutionary Criticism* (London: Verso 1981), 3–24.

12. Marcus Bullock, "Bad Company: On the Theory of Literary Modernity and Melancholy in Walter Benjamin and Julia Kristeva," *boundary 2* 22, no. 3 (1995): 61.

13. Beardsworth, *Kristeva*, 107–8.

14. Cited in Tammy Clewell, "Mourning Beyond Melancholia: Freud's Psychoanalysis of Loss," *Journal of the American Psychoanalytic Association* 52, no. 1 (2004): 58.

15. Cited in Clewell, ibid., 61.

16. For Soloveitchik on mourning, see his "*Aveilut*," in *Shiurim*, 2:197–212, and Alex Sztuden, "Grief and Joy in the Writings of Rabbi Soloveitchik," *Tradition* 43, no. 4 (2010): 37–55; 44 no. 3 (2011): 9–32; 45 no. 2 (2012): 67–79.

17. See Ari Ackerman, "Rabbi Joseph Dov Soloveitchik on Gender Difference," *Jewish Women: A Comprehensive Historical Encyclopedia*, ed. Paula Hyman and Dalia Ofer, http://jwa .org/encyclopedia/article/soloveitchik-rabbi-joseph-dov - consulted March 15, 2016.

18. See Soloveitchik's Hebrew essay, "*Ha-Barakhot be-Yehadut*," in *Yemei Zikaron* (Jerusalem: Eliner Library, 1986), 29–57, esp. pp. 31–37, as well as the further discussion in chapter 6.

19. Jacques Lacan, *On the Names-of-the-Father* (Cambridge: Polity, 2013).

20. On Soloveitchik's assertion of the idealized unity between masculine and feminine, and the possibility of a "quest" that will result in finally encountering "Her," see *Family* 178–79.

21. See, for example, D. W. Winnicott, *The Child, the Family, and the Outside World* (Middlesex: Penguin, 1973), 11.

22. Evelyn Scott Keller, *Reflections on Gender and Science* (New Haven, CT: Yale University Press, 1988), 86.

23. Cited in Keller, ibid., 87.

24. Ibid., 88.

25. Ibid., 88.

26. Shira Wolosky, "The Lonely Woman of Faith," *Judaism* 52, nos. 1/2 (2008): 12. Wolosky suggests further that Soloveitchik's works have "surprising implications for feminist theory" and that the notions of "selfhood and community" can be brought "into suggestive proximity with feminist ethical and political theory" (3, 8). For a further discussion of Soloveitchik's gendered nature of the self, see chapter 6.

27. In "'What' Hath Brisk Wrought: The Brisker Derekh Revisited," *Torah u-Madda Journal* 9 (2000), Mosheh Soloveitchik writes that the "metaphysic of awe is the control element beyond the ideal of *devekut* developed by R. Hayyim of Volozhin in the fourth chapter of *Nefesh Ha-Hayyim* and the key to the spiritual world of the ideal halakhic personality that the Rav presented in *Halakhic Man*, the two major philosophical works written in defense of Lithuanian '*Torah lishmah*'" (5–6).

5. Beyond the Law

1. On *Halakhic Man* as memorial, see *Religion*, 13.

2. Shalom Carmy, "Pluralism and the Category of the Ethical," in *Exploring the Thought of Rabbi Joseph B. Soloveitchik*, ed. Marc Angel (Jersey City, NJ: Ktav, 1996), 343.

3. Lawrence Kaplan, "Revisionism and the Rav: The Struggle for the Soul of Modern Orthodoxy," *Judaism* 48, no. 3 (1999): 290, 291.

4. Alan J. Yuter, "The Nuanced Ambiguities of Rabbi Joseph B. Soloveitchik's Thought," *Review of Rabbinic Judaism* 12, no. 2 (2009): 1.

5. Kaplan, "Revisionism," 291, 306. See also Marc B. Shapiro, *Changing the Immutable: How Orthodox Judaism Rewrites Its History* (Oxford: Littman Library, 2015), 28–30. In another context, in "Letting the Facts Get in the Way of a Good Thesis: On Interpreting R. Soloveitchik's Philosophical Method," *Torah u-Madda Journal* 16 (2012–2013), Daniel Rynhold writes that while R. Soloveitchik's "more liberal interpreters" might prefer to emphasize the methodological discussion leading to "potentially radical implications," those of a more "conservative disposition can apparently emphasize R. Soloveitchik's actual practice and its seeming independence from these methodological strictures" (67).

6. David V. Erdman, ed., *The Complete Poetry and Prose of William Blake* (Garden City, NY: Doubleday, 1982), 35.

7. For the former, see Moshe Meiselman, "The Rav, Feminism and Public Policy: An Insider's Overview," *Tradition* 33, no. 1 (1998): 5–30, and Mayer Twersky, "A Glimpse of the Rav," *Tradition* 30, no. 4 (1996): 79–114. For a similar dynamic in Milton studies (over many centuries), see my *Milton's Warring Angels* (Cambridge: Cambridge University Press, 1996).

8. David Hartman, *Conflicting Visions: Spiritual Possibilities in Modern Israel* (New York: Schocken, 1990), 160, 163.

9. David Hartman, *The God Who Hates Lies: Confronting and Rethinking Jewish Tradition* (New York: Jewish Lights, 2011), 134, 135.

10. Alex Sztuden, "Hermann Cohen in Disguise: Review of Dov Schwartz, 'Religion or Halakha; the Philosophy of Rabbi Joseph B. Soloveitchik,'" *Modern Judaism* 33, no. 1 (2013): 91.

11. David Singer and Moshe Sokol, "Joseph Soloveitchik: The Lonely Man of Faith," *Modern Judaism* 2, no. 3 (1982): 258, 229. See also Morris Sosevsky, "The Lonely Man of Faith Confronts the Ish ha-Halakhah," in *Exploring the Thought of Rabbi Joseph B. Soloveitchik*, 89–106.

12. Marvin Fox, "The Unity and Structure of Rabbi Joseph B. Soloveitchik's Thought," in *Exploring the Thought of Rabbi Joseph B. Soloveitchik*, 25–48.

13. Allan Nadler, "Soloveitchik's Halakhic Man: Not a 'Mithnagged,'" *Modern Judaism* 13, no. 2 (1993): 120, 126.

14. Against the majority of students who claimed Soloveitchik's immersion in and allegiance to philosophical discourse, Martin Meiselman, also accounting for the contradictions in Soloveitchik's work, claims Soloveitchik only turned to secular knowledge to "show the general American public the intellectual responsibility and sophistication of halakha" (cited in Kaplan, "Revisionism," 297).

15. In Nadler's words, "Soloveitchik's spiritual expression is monistic, integrative, and comfortable with the world." Nadler continues: "His soul is at peace with his body. . . . He knows no wrenching religious alienation, and no deeper existential sickness" (*"Mithnagged,"* 126).

16. Schwartz argues that Soloveitchik may have consciously appropriated Straussian method (*Religion,* 33). Sztuden suggests, without mentioning Strauss, that the reading suggested by Schwartz would only be relevant in a premodern context. "There is no genuine need to read a work of modernity," he suggests, "written by a dialectical thinker, as an esoteric text, even if that text is mired in 'inconsistencies'" ("Herman Cohen," 92). For Milton, see William Kerrigan, John Rumrich, Stephen M. Fallon, eds., *The Complete Poetry and Essential Prose of John Milton* (New York: Modern Library, 2007), *Paradise Lost* 7.31.

17. Eliciting a parallel between *Halakhic Man* and Yehuda HaLevi's *Kuzari,* Schwartz writes that like the "Rabbi" in the latter work, the halakhic man, not just as a persona but as the work that bears his name, does not "represent R. Soloveitchik's authentic views about the religious person" (*Religion,* 33).

18. Sztuden, "Hermann Cohen," 92.

19. For a detailed division of the parts of *Halakhic Man,* see Lawrence J. Kaplan, "Joseph Soloveitchik and Halakhic Man," *Cambridge Companion to Modern Jewish Philosophy,* ed. Michael L. Morgan and Peter Eli Gordon (Cambridge: Cambridge University Press, 2007), 216. Kaplan, however, sees the shift in the essay from "man as creator of worlds" to "man as creator of himself" only in the second of the six sections internal to part 2 of *Halakhic Man* (on page 109).

20. On the importance of creativity to Soloveitchik's work, see Walter Wurzburger, "The Centrality of Creativity in the Thought of Rabbi Joseph B. Solovetichik," in *Exploring the Thought of Rabbi Joseph B. Soloveitchik,* 277–89.

21. Ken Kulton-Fromm, *Material Culture and Jewish Thought in America* (Bloomington, IN: Indiana University Press, 2010), 110, 115, 122.

22. See Singer and Sokol, "Lonely Man," 257.

23. *Bereishit Rabba,* 84.8.

24. See Kant's "Critique of Aesthetic Power of Judgment," in *The Cambridge Edition of the Works of Emanuel Kant,* ed. Paul Guyer and Allen W. Wood (Cambridge: Cambridge University Press, 2000), 1:99–101.

25. On this inconsistency, see Lawrence Kaplan, "The Religious Philosophy of Joseph Soloveitchik," *Tradition* 14, no. 2 (1973): 52.

26. Harold Bloom, *The Anxiety of Influence* (Oxford: Oxford University Press, 1973), xxiii.

27. On Soloveitchik's supervision of the translation process of *Halakhic Man,* see http://admin2.collegepublisher.com/preview/mobile/2.2469/2.2836/1.298176 (accessed March 15, 2016).

28. Kulton-Fromm, *Material Culture,* 123.

29. *Paradise Lost* (1.26), in *Complete Poetry.*

30. In "The Voice of My Beloved That Knocketh," Soloveitchik explicitly pushes off the question of traditional theodicy (the "why?"), preferring instead the question, "what?" (98–99). See my "Towards a Genuine Jewish Philosophy: *Halakhic Mind*'s New Philosophy of Religion," *Tradition* 30, no. 3 (1996): 35–38.

31. Kulton-Fromm, following the religious historian Robert Orsi, *Material Culture*, 109.

32. Friedrich Nietzsche, *The Birth of Tragedy* and *The Case of Wagner*, trans. Walter Kaufmann (New York: Viking, 1967), 33.

33. Singer and Sokol see a radical discontinuity between what they refer to as the introduction of *Halakhic Man* and the rest of the work, pointing also to a "vast gulf in outlook" that separates the earlier text and *The Lonely Man of Faith* ("Lonely Man," 244).

34. See Yitzchak Blau, "Creative Repentance: On Rabbi Joseph B. Soloveitchik's Concept of Teshuva," in *Exploring the Thought of Rabbi Joseph B. Soloveitchik*, 268.

35. See Blau, "Creative Repentance," 267–72.

36. See also *Repentance*, 248–54.

37. In "'What' Hath Brisk Wrought: The Brisker Derekh Revisited," *The Torah u-Madda Journal* 9 (2000), Mosheh Lichtenstein advocates a change in emphasis in Brisk learning, from one that only considers the quantitative question "what?" to the deeper question "why?" The former emphasis is based on what he calls the metaphysic of Brisk predicated on *yir'ah*, or fear. The quest for the "why" should be associated, Lichtenstein suggests, with *ahavah*, or love, an attempt to "fathom the idea" (10). Although Lichtenstein makes no explicit connection with *teshuva*, the fathoming of antecedent history with the question of the penitent—"*why* did I perform these acts?"—would be related to love, not fear.

38. Henri Bergson, *Matter and Memory* (New York: Zone Books, 1988), 83, 33, 84, 88.

39. Adam Phillips, *On Flirtation* (Cambridge, MA: Harvard University Press, 1996), 24.

40. Shira Wolosky, "The Lonely Woman of Faith," *Judaism* 52, nos. 1/2 (2008): 8.

41. Soloveitchik distills this notion in an idealized version of history: "The Rambam is at my right, Rabbenu Tam at my left, Rashi sits up front and interprets, Rabbenu Tam disputes him; the Rambam issues a ruling, and the Rabad objects. They are all in my little room, sitting around my table. They look at me affectionately, enjoy arguing and studying the Talmud with me, encourage and support me the way a father does." The fantastic association with the company of fathers provides the realization of this idealized community, "the joining of one spirit with another, the union of souls" (*Seek*, 145). For another idealized (and gendered) account of tradition, see "Uniting of Generations-Pidyon Haben," cited by Tzvi Pittinsky, "The Role of Teacher and Student in Jewish Education According to Rabbi Joseph B. Soloveitchik," *Ten Dat* 18 (2006): 95–96.

6. From Interpretive Conquest to Antithetic Ethics

1. Aharon Lichtenstein, *Leaves of Faith: The World of Jewish Learning* (Jersey City, NJ: Ktav, 2003), 201. See also David Shatz, who writes in "A Reader's Companion to Ish Ha-Halakhah: Introductory Section," Rabbi Joseph B. Soloveitchik Institute (2002), that Soloveitchik "displays a keen sense for the contradictions, tensions, and, to use another philosophical term for the same notion, antinomies of existence." Soloveitchik's stress, Shatz continues, is on "understanding the inner reality of human life, and especially religious life, as a dialectic" (18). See also Shatz's "The Traveler's Route Home: Rabbi Joseph B. Soloveitchik and the Unending Dialectic," *Jewish Action* 57, no. 1 (1996): 16–19.

2. Shira Wolosky, "The Lonely Woman of Faith," *Judaism* 52, no. 1/2 (2008): 10.

3. On Kaplan, see Alex Sztuden, "Hermann Cohen in Disguise: Review of Dov Schwartz, 'Religion or Halakha; the Philosophy of Rabbi Joseph B. Soloveitchik,'" *Modern Judaism* 33, no. 1 (2013): 91, and Wolosky, "Lonely Woman," 10.

4. For Kaplan's reading, based on Soloveitchik's "Ha-Barakhot be-Yehadut," in *Yemei Zikaron* (Jerusalem: Elinor Library, 1986), and his reading of *Bereshit Rabba* 8.1, see his

Hebrew essay, "Rav Soloveitchik's *The Lonely Man of Faith* in Contemporary Modern Ortho-dox Jewish Thought," in *Rabbi in the New World: The Influence of Rabbi J.B. Soloveitchik on Culture, Education and Jewish Thought,* ed. Avinoam Rosenak and Naftali Rothenberg (Jeru-salem: Magnes, 2011), 153.

5. Wolosky, "Lonely Woman," 4. See also my earlier, "Into the Whirlwind: The Persistence of the Dialectic in the works of Rabbi Joseph B. Soloveitchik," *Tradition* 40, no. 2 (2007), 78–95.

6. Aharon Lichtenstein, "Does Jewish Tradition Recognize an Ethic Independent of Halakha?" *Modern Jewish Ethics,* ed. Marvin Fox (Columbus, OH: Ohio State University Press, 1975): 62–88. For another response to this question, see Shalom Carmy, "Pluralism and the Category of the Ethical," in *Exploring the Thought of Rabbi Joseph B. Soloveitchik,* ed. Marc Angel (New Jersey, 1996): 325–46.

7. Mayer Twersky in "Counterpoint: On the Rav's Philosophy of Halakha," *Jewish Action* (Summer 2004).

8. See Zachary Braiterman, *(God) after Auschwitz* (Princeton, NJ: Princeton University Press 1998), 72–77.

9. David Weiss Halivni, *Breaking the Tablets: Jewish Theology after the Shoah* (New York: Rowman and Littlefield, 2007), 99, 114.

10. T. S. Eliot, "Tradition and the Individual Talent," *Selected Essays* (New York: Faber and Faber, 1950), 7.

11. Eliot, "Tradition," 11. The subjectivity of the *homo religiosus* is associated with not only an excess of emotion as the "raging turbulence," but the simultaneous experience of antitheti-cal emotional extremes—the characteristic of the Freudian melancholic. The contradic-tory emotions threatening to sweep away the "entire being" of the *homo religiosus* leave him suspended between the contradictory magnets of "love and fear," "desire and dread," and "longing and anxiety" (*Man,* 66–67). For Soloveitchik of *Halakhic Man,* the objectifications of halakha prevent the downward spiral into the contradictions of an antithetical emotional life.

12. Rudolf Otto, *The Idea of the Holy* (New York: Oxford University Press, 1970), 3.

13. Otto writes further: The "numen," overpoweringly experienced as the "all-in-all," leads to a concomitant feeling in the creature of "submergence and prostration and of the diminu-tion of the self into nothingness" (*Holy,* 12, 50).

14. "The notion of 'revelation through the catastrophic' may be part of a philosophical ar-gument that leads back to Kant" (*Whirl,* 129). As Gene Ray writes in his "Reading the Lisbon Earthquake: Adorno, Lyotard, and the Contemporary Sublime," *Yale Journal of Criticism* 17, no. 1 (2004): 1–18, there is a connection between the notion of catastrophe employed by Kant in three short tracts on earthquakes (following the Lisbon earthquake in 1755) and his concep-tion of the sublime. Since, as Otto remarks, there "exists a hidden connection between the numinous and the sublime which is something more than a merely accidental analogy" (*Holy,* 63), Soloveitchik's appeal in *Whirl* to both the "numinous" and to "catastrophe" may point back to Kant.

15. Leo Bersani and Adam Phillips, *Intimacies* (Chicago: University of Chicago Press, 2008), 15.

16. See my "Towards a Genuine Jewish Philosophy: *Halakhic Mind*'s New Philosophy of Religion," *Tradition* 30, no. 3 (1996), 26–28, 35–38.

17. On "missing the moment," see "Voice," 62–68.

18. Herbert Marcuse, *One-Dimensional Man* (Boston: Beacon Press, 1964), 18.

19. "Voice," 54. Regarding the metaphysics of evil in "A Halakhic Approach to Suffering" associated with "thematic Halakha," Soloveitchik confides his own sense of the inefficacy of its message. "We know," he writes, "that the friends of Job were not that successful in convincing

Job about the nonexistence of evil. Can a rabbi be more successful? . . . I will be frank with you; I do not know" (*Whirl*, 99).

20. Adam Phillips, *On Balance* (London: Farrar, Straus and Giroux, 2012), 144.

21. See Aaron Rakefett-Rothkoff, *The Rav: The World of Rabbi Joseph B. Soloveitchik* (Hoboken, NJ: Ktav, 1999), 2:16–17.

22. Rakefett-Rothkoff writes, "the Rav's mellowing was described and analyzed by his son Professor Haym Soloveithik in his eulogy for his father held at Yeshiva University on April 15, 1993" (*The Rav*, 1:74n43).

23. Lionel Trilling, *Sincerity and Authenticity* (Cambridge, MA: Harvard University Press, 1971), 110, 171.

24. The "totality" of emotional life places individual emotions in a synchronic context, while the "continuity" of emotional experience focuses on the diachronic element; the first is perhaps best categorized as spatial, the latter, temporal. See *Whirl*, 179–94, and the editors' *Introduction*, xliv–xlvii.

25. On the distance between Soloveitchik's and Hermann Cohen's conception of the "thing-in-itself" (with the latter's provenance in neo-Kantianism), see Yonatan Brafman, "Critical Philosophy of Halakha (Jewish Law): The Justification of Halakhic Norms and Authority" (Ph.D. dissertation, Columbia University, 2012), 163.

26. On the relationship, for Soloveitchik, between the commandments and the particular emotional experiences they are meant to elicit, how "halakha becomes expression," see Brafman, "Critical Philosophy of Halakha," 180–88.

27. "What Judaism wants to attain with its principle of the dialectical emotion," Soloveitchik writes, is "not a restrained emotional experience, but a critical one." Indeed, the "creative emotion" must "possess a boundless energy and dynamic qualities; it must be overpowering, shattering all artificial hedges and fences which convention erects around it" (*Whirl*, 196). For the distinction between the emotions elicited by Judaism and the Aristotelian mean, see *Whirl*, 195–97.

28. T. S. Eliot, "Andrew Marvell," *Selected Essays*, 262.

29. Lawrence Kaplan, "The Religious Philosophy of Joseph Soloveitchik," *Tradition* 14, no. 2 (1973), writes suggestively that "Adam the second meets God not as 'father, brother and friend' but rather 'as mother'" (46).

30. On metaphors of enslavement and possession in scientific discourse, beginning with Francis Bacon, see Evelyn Scott Keller, *Gender and Science* (New Haven, CT: Yale University Press, 1985), 33–42. See also, Kaplan, "Religious Philosophy," who links Soloveitchik's "intellectual mastery" with Baconian knowledge (53).

31. On the failure of what Normal Solomon calls the "Analytic Movement" to live up to the "Grand Illusion" of a truth that would be "coherent" and "comprehensive," see his *The Analytic Movement: Hayyim Soloveitchik and his Circle* (Atlanta, GA: Scholar's Press, 1996), xi.

32. Daniel Boyarin, *Unheroic Conduct: The Rise of Heterosexuality and the Invention of the Jewish Man* (Berkeley, CA: University of California Press, 1997), 127–50.

33. Sergey Dolgopolski, "Constructed and Denied: 'The Talmud' from the Brisker Rav to the *Mishneh Torah*," in *Encountering the Medieval in Modern Jewish Thought*, ed. Aaron W. Hughes and James A. Diamond (Leiden: Brill, 2012), 179. As Dolgopolsky argues, "Who Thinks in the Talmud?," *Journal of Jewish Thought and Philosophy* 20, no. 1 (2012), Brisk methodology carries with it an implicit view of the Talmud as a downgraded realm of "rhetorical disputations," a view abstracted from earlier Maimonidean conceptions, with their assumption of the inferiority of rhetoric to philosophy: "Thus for Maimonides, the style of refutations and counter-refutations signifies philosophical disarray and an unnecessarily chaotic plurality of

opinions that can be replaced with an exposition from one philosophically sound point of view" (16).

34. Marc Shapiro, "The Brisker Method Reconsidered," *Tradition* 31, no. 3 (1997), recounts a conversation between R. Hayyim and his father, showing the extent to which the persistence of the antithesis of dispute, so much a part of Talmudic argument, is absent in the methodology of Brisk. The father says to the son: "When people point out a difficulty to me and I answer it, the questioner is happy because he asked well, and I am happy because I succeeded in formulating an answer. However, when they ask you a question and you answer it, no one is happy, because you show the questioner that there was never a difficulty in the first place" (81–82).

35. For the suggestion that the "Analytic Movement" of Brisk, "wishing to appear intellectual," adopted the languages of *haskala*, or enlightenment, particularly the languages of "scientific research," see Solomon, *Analytic Movement*, 119–20.

36. For the relationship of Brisker thought to "nineteenth century legal scientism," see Chaim Saiman, "Legal Theology: The Turn to Conceptualism in Nineteenth-Century Jewish Law," *Journal of Law and Religion* 21, no. 1 (2005–2006): 39–100. On "Analytical Positivism" and the "Soloveitchik School," see Solomon, *Analytic Movement*, 86–89.

37. Mosheh Lichtenstein, "'What' Hath Brisk Wrought: The Brisker Derekh Revisited," *The Torah u-Madda Journal* 9 (2000): 13, 12.

38. Abba Bronspiegel, "Memories of My Rebbe, the Rav," in *Memories of a Giant*, ed. Michael A. Beirman (Brookline, MA: Urim, 2003) remembers, "The Rav used to begin either with a difficult Rambam or a difficult *Gemara*, ask four, five, six questions, then introduce a new *Gemara*, develop a certain principle, and then show how all the questions automatically fell away with this one principle" (141).

39. Saul Weiss, "In Memory of Hagaon Yosef Dov Soloveitchik," *Memories of a Giant*, 343.

40. In the former category, "Kavod ve-Oneg Shabbat," for example, Soloveitchik considers the way in which rabbinic traditions intersect with prophetic ones (the difference between *divrei soferim and divrei kabbala*); in "Shnei Sugei Masorat," Soloveitchik elaborates on forms of tradition that rely either on rationality or authority (*Shiurim*, 1.50–68, 241–61).

41. Hershel Reichman's collections on various Talmudic tractates provide testimony to Soloveitchik's constant revisiting and revision of the themes and arguments of his lecture. See for example *Sefer Reshimot Shiurim al Massekhet Babba Kamah* (New York: self-published, 2005).

42. Norman Lamm, "Hesped Mar: A Eulogy for the Rav," *Memories of a Giant*, 217–18, and Bronspiegel, "Memories," 136.

43. On Soloveitchik's innovations as a *posek* or legal authority, see Walter Wurzburger, "Rav Joseph B. Soloveitchik as *Posek* of Post-Modern Orthodoxy," *Tradition* 29, no. 1 (1994): 5–20. Wurzburger notes that Soloveitchik's legal decisions were always informed by halakha conceived as "an autonomous set of *a priori* categories . . . completely independent of historical factors" (18). In *The God Who Hates Lies* (New York: Jewish Lights, 2011), David Hartman rejects the ahistorical conservatism of what he calls this "theology of halakhic permanence," which manifested itself most fully in the debate with Emanuel Rackman on the "aguna problem." In this context, Hartman writes, Soloveitchik takes a Talmudic social presumption (*hazaka*) and transforms it into a "permanent ontological principle" (149–50), abandoning concrete historical circumstances for the a priori categories. For more on Soloveitchik's having endowed "legal presumptions" with "the highest form of certain and immutability," see Christine Hayes, *What's Divine about the Divine Law?* (Princeton, NJ: Princeton University Press, 2015), 373.

44. See also *Shiurim*, 1.250.

45. Bersani, *Intimacies*, 2.

46. Abraham Drassinower, *Freud's Theory of Culture: Eros, Loss, and Politics* (London: Rowman and Littlefield, 2003), 89.

Conclusion

1. Cited in Sanford Budick, *Milton and Kant* (Princeton, NJ: Princeton University Press, 2010), 226.

2. On Freud's version of the Mosaic ethical hero, see Mark Edmundson, *The Death of Sigmund Freud* (London: Bloomsbury, 2007), 232–33.

3. On Moses reaching adulthood, see Rashi on Exodus 2:11, in which Moses is understood to possess the characteristic of understanding the different perspectives of all the people of Israel; on his passing on the mantle of leadership to Joshua, see Numbers 27:12–23; on Moses imploring God to appoint a leader who is able to "suffer" the different perspectives and sensibilities of all Israel, see Rashi on 27:16.

4. Jonathan Lear, *A Case for Irony* (Cambridge: Harvard University Press, 2010), 38.

5. For a review of Lear's *Case* and Adam Phillips's *Missing Out* (London: Penguin, 2013), and their competing senses of irony, see my "Irony at the Crossroads," *Free Associations* 66 (2014): 88–97.

6. Jonathan Lear, *Case*, 36.

7. Jonathan Lear, *Freud* (London: Routledge, 2005), 207. "Even if one accepts Freud's analysis," Lear writes, "that there is an infantile dimension embedded in religious conviction, from a religious point of view, that can be a source of genuine solace, and may serve to enhance rather than impugn religious conviction" (218).

8. Friedrich Nietzsche, *The Birth of Tragedy*, trans. Walter Kaufman (New York: Vintage, 1967), 93.

9. Richard Rorty, *Contingency, Irony, and Solidarity* (Cambridge: Cambridge University Press, 1989), xv–xvi.

10. For the "God trick," see Donna Haraway, "Situated Knowledges: The Science Question in Feminism and the Privilege of Partial Perspective," *Feminist Studies* 14 (1988): 578–80. For the "view from nowhere," see Thomas Nagel, *The View from Nowhere* (Oxford: Oxford University Press, 1989).

11. Stanley Fish, *There's No Such Thing as Free Speech* (Oxford: Oxford University Press, 1993), 174.

12. Fish, *No Such Thing*, 218.

13. Stanley Fish, in *Is There a Text in This Class?* (Cambridge, MA: Harvard University Press, 1982), writes that the opposition between objectivity and subjectivity is a false one because "neither exists in the pure form that would give the opposition its pointing" (332).

14. Fish, *No Such Thing*, 135.

15. For Fish's untranscribed lecture, see https://www.youtube.com/watch?v=IkwBIPWr-Us (accessed March 15, 2016).

16. Lear, *Case*, 119.

17. Ammiel Hirsch, in his debate with Yosef Reinman in *One People, Two Worlds: A Reform Rabbi and an Orthodox Rabbi Explore the Issues That Divide Them* (New York: Schocken, 2002), reads the principle of "these and these"—an "imperative" for liberal "democracy, pluralism, tolerance, and theological humility" (51). See my review, "Reflections on the Reinman-Hirsch Exchange," *Torah u-Madda Journal* 12 (2004): 208–23.

18. For the distinction between the Hobbesian and Milton public sphere, see my introduction to the Hebrew translation of Milton's *Areopagitica* (Jerusalem: Shalem, 2013): 7–60.

19. Frank Kermode, *Forms of Attention* (Chicago: University of Chicago Press, 1985), 90–93.

20. Ludwig Wittgenstein, *Philosophical Investigations* (Oxford: Oxford University Press, 1953), 194. Wittgenstein writes in the first person: "I should not have answered the question 'What do you see here?' by saying: 'Now I am seeing it as a picture-rabbit.' I should simply have described my perception: just as if I had said: 'I see a red circle over there.' Though an outsider to the situation of perception might be able to say: 'He is seeing the figure as a picture rabbit'" (198).

21. Alasdair MacIntyre, *After Virtue: A Study in Moral Theory* (South Bend, IN: University of Notre Dame Press, 2007), 9–10.

22. Yehuda Loew, *Derekh Ha-Hayyim* (Tel Aviv: Yad Morechai, 1975), 604.

23. See my *Open Minded Torah: Of Irony, Fundamentalism and Love* (London: Continuum, 2011), 156–59.

24. See Jonathan Rosen, *The Talmud and the Internet* (New York: Farar, Straus and Giroux, 2000), 14–17.

25. William Kerrigan, John Rumrich, and Stephen M. Fallon, eds., *The Complete Poetry and Essential Prose of John Milton* (New York: Modern Library, 2007), 958.

26. Milton, *Complete Poetry*, 962, 955. Milton alludes to 1 Corinthians 13:12: "Now we see through a glass darkly, but then face to face."

27. Cited by Boyarin, *Border,* 154. See also David Stern, *Midrash* and his conception of the "idealized academy of Rabbinic tradition" (164). Moshe Halbertal, in *People of the Book* (Cambridge, MA: Harvard University Press, 1997), considers the legacy of the Talmud in the modern Jewish curriculum after having lost its canonical and "normative status": "the question now is whether it can still serve a formative role and become an integral part of the language associations, concerns, and mode of thought of present-day Jewish culture" (134).

28. Boyarin, *Border,* 161.

29. Milton, *Complete Poetry*, 953, 956.

30. Adam Phillips, *Side Effects* (New York: Harper Perennial, 2007), 177.

31. Leo Bersani and Adam Phillips, *Intimacies* (Chicago: University of Chicago Press, 2008), 77.

Index

Abel, Karl, 171, 188
Achilles, 162
Adorno, T. W., 15, 38, 176, 177, 199
Aeneas, 70
Aeschylus, 211n14
Akiva ben Joseph, 4, 69, 150, 210n1
America, 1, 3, 130, 135, 152, 155, 159, 161, 162, 166, 171, 214n14
Aristotle, 9, 11, 77–100, 187, 188, 217n27; abandonment of particular in, 98–100; conception of soul for, 46; contemplation in, 84, 88–89, 93, 98–99; and courage, 26, 46; discursive and intuitive knowledge in, 19, 170; and hyle, 98, 140; Maimonidean appropriation of, 79–80, 84, 87, 89–90, 91; and non-contradiction, 52, 54, 188–190; rejected by Joseph Soloveitchik, 77, 79, 87–91, 98–100; unity of knower and known in, 78, 79, 80–81, 84–87, 89. *See also* cognition; epistemology
Augustine, 204n3
Auschwitz, 38, 176
Austin, J. L., 23, 48, 59
autobiography, xi, 4, 162. *See also* self-creation; self-fashioning
axiology, 165–168, 173

Bacon, Francis, 49, 217n30
Barthes, Roland, 209n37
Baumgarten, Albert and Marina Rustow, 7
Beardsworth, Sara, 109
Beit Hillel and Beit Shammai, 33–34, 193–197
Benjamin, Jessica, 92
Benjamin, Walter, 110
Bergson, Henri, 132, 146–150, 167, 200
Bernstein, Richard, 21
Bersani, Leo, 11, 163, 182, 186, 200
Blake, William, 128, 131
Blau, Yitzchak, 144
Bloom, Harold, 12, 138
Bollas, Christopher, 74, 111
Boyarin, Daniel, 8, 36, 37, 40, 41, 43, 52, 58, 61, 177, 188, 199
Brafman, Yonatan, 203n12, 211n3, 217nn25, 26

breaking of tablets, 8, 31–34, 185, 187, 190, 206n36; and "through negating the law . . ." [Menachot 99b], 32, 34; and "well done . . ." [Menakhot 99b], 31–33
Brisk, 10, 104, 141, 174–181, 187, 200, 215n37, 217n33, 218nn34–36; ancestry, xi, 2, 3–6, 12, 124, 127–132, 135, 151–152, 157, 161, 163, 171, 182; and hermeneutics, 72, 74, 133, 217n33; *hiddush*, 132, 143; and *hukkim*, 126, 155; last rabbi of, 1, 75, 200; masculinity, 11, 13, 133, 153, 174–177; and Modern Orthodoxy, 1, 203n1; and neo-Kantians, 107; Rabbi of (Brisker Rav), 174–175; theodicy, 141
Bronspiegel, Abba, 180, 218n3
Buber, Martin, 173
Budick, Sanford, 37–38
Bullock, Marcus, 110
Butterfield, Herbert, 48

Cambridge history, 9, 41. *See also* Quentin Skinner
Cambridge Platonists, 204n8
Carmy, Shalom, 127
Cavell, Stanley, 17, 22
cognition, 104, 105, 135, 138, 170–172, 184; and conquest, 13, 74, 121, 131–134, 138, 152–155, 157–160, 163–165, 167, 174, 176–178, 181–182, 199; and defeat, 10, 164, 181–182; and divine, 79–80, 89–90, 159–161, 165, 172; and humility, 166–167, 172; inadequacy of, 158–160, 166–167, 172, 176, 184; and love, 78–79, 90, 98–99; and masculine, 124, 150; of moods, 170–171; pluralistic conception of, 83, 95; and psyche, 11, 95, 134, 197; rabbinic model of, 62; Spinozan model of, 19. *See also* Aristotle; epistemology
Cohen, Hermann, 217n25
Collingwood, R. G., 48
Cover, Robert, 208n16
cummings, e. e., 172

David, 140–143, 145
deconstruction, xiii, 38–39, 40, 60–61

defeat, 1, 197; and cognition, 10, 12, 154, 158, 164, 181–182; embrace of, 158–164, 166–167, 182, 186; of father, 10, 72–73, 159; and feminine, 173; and heroism, 161–163; and triumph (conquest) 12, 74, 154, 167, 182

Derrida, Jacques, 38, 43, 61, 209n37

Descartes, Rene, 182

dialectic, 179; of emotions, 111–113, 171–173, 217n27; and ethics, 154, 168, 172; of experiential and intellectual, 174; of masculine and feminine, 153; and midrash, 36; opposed to mastery, 152, 165; of Otniel, 24, 30; as *pilpul*, 24, 30, 61, 168; as principle of reception, 127, 129–131, 142, 153, 214n16, 215n1; of psyche, 4, 172; of subject and object, 152

disciplines, 7, 36, 76, 77–78, 79, 105, 125, 190, 195; hierarchy of, 19, 81–83, 85; humanities, 81–83, 150; and interdisciplinary, xi–xiv, 5–7, 9; and pluralism, 5, 9, 78, 81–83, 85, 86–87, 211n3

discordia concors: and "blooming nails," 62–63, 138; and John Donne, 8, 37, 41–42, 46; of legal multiplicity, 46, 58–59, 62, 189, 195, 199; of midrash, 37, 42, 44–46, 53, 58, 177; of the psyche, 97; repression of in Joseph Soloveitchik, 62–63, 142

Dolgopolsky, Sergey, 179, 217n33

Donne, John, xii, 8, 36–37, 42–44, 46, 62, 208nn24, 25

Drassinhower, Abraham, 182

Eddington, A. S., 105

Edmundson, Mark, 29

Elazar ben Azariah, 41–47, 51, 52, 55, 59, 61, 62, 138–139, 142, 195

Eliade, Mircea, 21, 25, 28

Elijah, 73

Eliot, T. S., 143, 157, 173, 191, 205n28

Elisha, 186

Elman, Yaakov, 208n17

emotions, 3, 166, 217nn14, 26; antithethical (dialectical) 10, 111–113, 171–173, 217n27; associated with feminine, 2, 71, 72; authentic (unmediated), 168–170; and Brisk, 174; distinct from Freudian, 111–112, 211n15, 216n11; and ethics, 112, 168, 170, 172–173; and *homo religiosus*, 130, 157, 168; in Lionel Trilling, 168; and moods, 112, 170–173; as non-ambivalent, 111–112; rejection by halakhic man, 143–144, 156–158; split with intellect (knowledge), 18, 81, 89, 129

enlightenment, 23; and Brisk, 13, 174, 177–179, 200, 218n35; knowledge, 154, 179; rejection of in *Halakhic Mind*, 6; universalism, 6

epistemology, 17, 20, 23, 45–47, 74–75, 80–91, 193, 196; and Aristotle, 78, 81–82, 84, 87, 90–91; in early modern science, 20, 83–85, 97, 99, 100; and Hans-Georg Gadamer, 49; and humility, 8, 12, 13, 74, 106, 124, 152, 155, 158, 163, 181–182, 191, 195; and John Milton, 198; and Kant and neo-Kantians, 10, 101; limitations of, 184, 188, 198; and love, 11, 12, 75, 78–79, 84–85, 87, 90–91, 99–100, 127, 196; Maimonidean, 79–80, 87, 91; and mastery (or conquest), 13, 123, 126, 152–155, 157, 165–166, 181; and "mill-hopper," 45–47, 51, 53, 55, 61, 62; and monism, 5; and *Nefesh Ha-Hayyim*, 10; and ontology, 5, 18, 82–83, 102–104, 106; and pluralism, 5–6, 35, 154, 187; and postmodern relativism, 41, 60; and Talmudic hermeneutics, xiii, 6, 7, 8–9, 36–37, 40, 42; and unity, 76–78, 81, 84–87, 89–90, 127. *See also* cognition

ethics, 5, 100, 106, 126, 137, 157, 159, 163, 188, 190–191, 200–201; antithetic, 13, 151, 154, 164, 173–174, 183, 185; independent of hermeneutic realm, 12, 13, 35, 74, 100, 151, 153–155, 174, 182–183, 185; of love, 131, 191; and Moses, 185–187, 219n2; and multiple agencies, 2, 12, 153–154, 185; and psychic realm, 2, 4, 11, 12, 17, 35, 74–75, 90, 100, 132, 147, 161, 168–173; relation to moods and emotions, 170–173; and repentance, 2, 75, 152–154, 173, 182, 191, 200; suffering as pre-condition for, 161, 185

etiology, 82–83, 86

existential authenticity: defeat as sign of, 161; and emotional response, 168–169; in Lionel Trilling, 168; as means of distinction from ancestors, 4, 5, 124, 126; and service, 124

Ezekiel, 161, 169–170

Feinstein, Elijah, 10, 67, 70, 133, 144

Fisch, Harold, 18, 23

Fisch, Menachem, 54, 209n45, 210n55

Fish, Stanley, 191–197, 219n13

Fonrobert, Charlotte, 199

Foucault, Michel, 37, 209n37

Fox, Marvin, 129–130

Fraade, Steven, 37, 48, 181, 206n1, 208n17

Freud, Sigmund, 12, 34, 67, 79, 84, 87, 92, 97, 125, 127, 131, 132, 142, 168–170, 188–189, 190, 191,

197, 205n23, 211n11; as antecedent for (and influence on) Joseph Soloveitchik, 2–3, 10–11, 12, 76–77, 112, 120, 122, 136–137, 147, 149, 154–155, 162, 166, 169, 211n15; and conception of mourning and melancholy, 7–9, 24, 35, 101–102, 107–114, 120, 154, 187, 206n29, 216n11; and creative memory, 148–148; and culture, 76, 110–111, 173, 188; Jonathan Lear's appropriation of, 79, 84, 88–90, 95, 99–100; Joseph Soloveitchik's rejection of, 111–112, 125; as melancholy modern, 3, 11, 200; Moses of, 17, 20–22, 26–28, 31, 33, 185, 219n2; Oedipus complex in, 116–117, 119–120; oppositions in, 171, 188; phylogenetic inheritance of, 77, 100; primal scene of, 10, 69; primary and secondary process thought in, 169; religion for, 76–77, 118–119, 189–190, 205n11, 219n7; on sexuality, 10, 12, 113, 122, 125, 136–137; and sublimation, 11, 75, 91, 94; temporality for, 94, 211n17. *See also* gender; sexuality
Friedlander, Hayyim, 53
fundamentalism, 8, 29, 165, 184, 192, 197, 199

Gadamer, Hans-Georg, 9, 37, 41, 47–51, 54, 55, 60, 61, 209nn33, 41
Gay, Peter, 111
Geertz, Clifford, 9, 82
gender, xii, 2, 9–10, 11, 101–102, 109, 112–126, 153, 176, 212n20, 213n26, 215n41; Adam as ambivalent figure of, 149, 153; and archetypal Mother and Father, 10, 113–121, 126, 148–149, 163, 173, 217n29; equality, 5; and family history, 71–75; feminine, 6, 10–12, 71–75, 102–103, 109, 111, 113–115, 118–126, 132, 136, 138, 148–150, 153, 163, 173–176, 200; masculine, 12, 13, 68, 70–73, 75, 102, 103, 109, 111, 113–116, 118–124, 133, 138, 148–151, 153, 173–177, 182; and memory, 12, 74, 132, 143, 146–151, 163; and repentance, 12, 132, 143, 146–151; studies, xii. *See also* sexuality
Greenblatt, Steven, 40

Halbertal, Moshe, 55, 220n27
HaLevi, Yehuda, 214n27
Halivni, David Weiss, 156, 206n36, 210nn56, 57
Handelman, Susan, 207n9, 13, 209n21
Haraway, Donna, 192
Hartman, David, 128, 218n43
Hartman, Geoffrey, 37–38, 62
Hasidism, 103–104, 106
Hayes, Christine, 6, 37, 218n43

Hegel, G. W., 177
Heidegger, Martin, 155
hermeneutics, xii, 75, 100, 127, 132, 156, 188, 191, 194–195, 204n3; of Hans-Georg Gadamer, 37, 41, 47, 48, 49–55; Joseph Soloveitchik's representation of, 6–7, 10, 12, 55, 62–63, 67, 70–75, 100–101, 143, 150–151, 152, 153–155, 157, 169, 172, 173–175, 177, 181–182, 184–185, 199–200; melancholy, 12, 63, 74, 75, 100, 184–185; midrashic, 40; rabbinic, of mourning, xiii, 1–2, 5, 7–9, 13, 17, 22–23, 26, 28–33, 35, 37, 41, 42, 47, 50, 54, 60–62, 74, 77, 101, 108, 150–151, 170, 181, 183–185, 187, 190, 196–197, 199–201; rabbinic praxis of, 55–60. *See also* pluralism
heroism: of Brisk, 69–70, 72; and the feminine, 120, 177, 185; Freudian ethical, 219n2; halakhic, 161–163, 168, 177, 185; of quantum physicists, 5, 82
Hidary, Richard, 37, 46, 206n1
Hirsch, Ammiel, 219n17
Hobbes, Thomas, 5, 103, 106, 195, 196, 204n8, 208n25, 220n18
Holocaust, xii, 38, 155, 156, 158, 166, 168, 169, 171, 176; impact on Joseph Soloveitchik, 1, 3, 111, 152, 156, 162, 164, 166; writings of post-, 2, 11, 12, 75, 132, 158, 161, 168, 182, 186
Homer, 205–206n8
hukkim, 126, 131, 139–141, 177. *See also* Brisk
Husserl, Edmund, 155, 171
hyle, 98, 140, 144, 149, 169, 171
Hyppolite, Jean, 127

imitation Deo, 107, 124
individuation, 76–78, 91, 125–126, 162, 163, 168; and autonomy, 78, 88, 163; of developing child, 118, 119; loneliness of, 4, 120, 187; and love, 92, 94, 99–100; as rejection of Aristotelian ideal, 98–100; in relation to predecessors, 11, 101, 123, 163
interdisciplinarity, xii, xiii, xiv, 5, 6. *See also* disciplines
irony, 184, 185, 187–198, 199, 219n5; liberal, 13, 185, 187, 191–192, 194; Socratic, 188; Talmudic, 13, 184–185, 187, 188, 190–192, 194, 196–200; therapeutic, 188

Jacob, 162, 175; and Esau, 162
James, William, 5, 130
Jerusalem, 128, 132, 140; and Athens, 91, 143; mourning of, 197–199

Jesus, 17, 19–20, 23, 204n6
Jewish studies, xiii, xiv, 9
Job, 161, 164–168, 171, 172, 174, 216–217n19
Johnson, Samuel, 8, 37, 42, 62
Jonson, Ben, xii
Joseph, 135–136
Joshua, 25, 26–30, 32, 33, 205n28, 219n3

Kabbalah, 104
Kafka, Franz, 178
Kant, Immanuel, 101, 105, 126, 133, 156, 178, 182;
    and beautiful, 137–138; and genius, 178; and
    sublime, 172, 185, 216n1. *See also*
    neo-Kantianism
Kaplan, Lawrence, 127–131, 139, 153, 214n19,
    217n29
Keane, John, 48
kedusha, 102
Keller, Evelyn Fox, 118–119, 120–121, 138
Kermode, Frank, 95, 147, 195
Kierkegaard, Soren, 162
Koltun-Fromm, Ken, 134, 140, 143
Kraemer, David, 37, 206n39
Kristeva, Julia, 2, 11, 75, 101, 109–111, 113, 114,
    120–122, 125–126, 133, 154
Kuhn, Thomas, 49, 83, 196, 209n40, 210n63

Lacan, Jacques, 11–12, 115, 116, 136
LaCapra, Dominick, 8, 9, 24, 28, 32, 108,
    206n29
Lamm, Norman, 180–181
Lear, Jonathan, 30, 75–100, 182; appropriation
    of Freud in, 79, 84, 88–90, 95, 99–100; and
    Aristotle, 26, 77–81, 84, 87–93, 95, 98–100;
    and courage, 26–27; and early modern
    neutrality, 20, 86; love in, 75, 77–79, 84–94,
    97–100, 188–190, 197, 211n11; and melancholy,
    102, 108, 182, 185, 205nn11, 23, 211n11, 219n7;
    and Moses, 22, 31; and Plato, 34, 51; and
    subject-object relation, 84–87, 92;
    sublimation in, 11, 76–78, 84, 91–94, 98, 100;
    and therapeutic irony, 13, 185, 187–191, 197.
    See also Sigmund Freud
Levinas, Emanuel, xiii, 36, 106, 167, 175
Lichtenstein, Aharon, 152, 154
Lichtenstein, Mosheh, 179–180, 215n37
Litvak, 104, 129
Loew, Yehuda [Maharal], 33, 196
Loewald, Hans, 11, 85, 102; and childhood
    development, 119–120; and modernity, 33;
    primary and secondary process thought in,

76, 190; sublimation for, 91–93; and
    temporality, 21, 30, 33, 94–95, 97, 211n17
loneliness: childhood, 67, 74–75, 101, 111, 162,
    167; and chosenness, 148, 161–162; and divine,
    124, 186; and feminine, 123, 149, 153; and
    halakhic heroism, 161–163; and halakhic
    man, 177; of Jacob, 162; and man of destiny,
    167; as means of autonomy from father (and
    Brisk ancestry), 12, 122–124, 148, 161, 163,
    186–187, 200; and melancholy, 2, 4, 102, 107,
    108, 111, 120, 187; of Moses, 4, 185–187; and
    shame, 122–124; as sign of authenticity, 161
love, 197; and ambivalence, 11, 107, 112, 127; and
    Brisk, 175–176; and epistemology, 11, 12, 75,
    78–79, 84–85, 87, 90–91, 99–100, 127, 196; and
    ethics, 13, 191; of father, 118; and feminine, 75;
    in John Donne, 42; in Jonathan Lear, 75,
    77–79, 84–94, 97–100, 188–190, 197, 211n11;
    and law, 11; as metaphysical principle, 77,
    88–91; prophet as object of divine, 99;
    rabbinic disputes as object of divine, 33–34,
    186; and repentance, 11, 75, 78–80, 89, 94–100,
    127, 144–146, 149, 215n37; and Talmudic irony,
    184–185, 194, 196, 197
Luria, Solomon [Maharshal], 52

MacIntyre, Alisdair, 196
Magid, Shaul, 196
Maimonides [Rambam], 150, 215n41, 217n33,
    218n38; and Aristotle, 79–80, 84, 87, 90–91,
    123–124, 150; in Joseph Soloveitchik's family
    drama, 67–72, 123–124, 200; reciprocal
    love in, 90
Marcus, Steven and Charles Taylor, 6, 128
Marcuse, Herbert, 164–165
Marvell, Andrew, 173
Meiselman, Martin, 214n14
melancholy, xiv, 24, 197; ambivalence towards
    law, 11, 75, 101, 111, 131, 154; and certainty, 8–9,
    35, 184, 200; contrast to hermeneutics of
    mourning, 7, 113, 184–185, 187; and cultural
    loss, 110–111; defined in Freudian terms,
    107–111; and ethics, 12, 126, 151; and gender,
    73–74, 102, 107–111, 120–121, 126;
    hermeneutics of, 12, 63, 74, 75, 100, 184–185;
    and identity, 11–12, 101, 120–121, 126, 162, 187;
    Joseph Soloveitchik as modern figure of, 2, 3,
    7, 9, 11, 13, 102, 110–111, 200; and Joseph
    Soloveitchik's family history, 67, 72–74;
    Joseph Soloveitchik's rejection of Freudian,
    111–112; and loneliness, 2, 4, 102, 107, 108, 111,

120, 187; and Moses, 4; opposition between extremes, 154, 158, 181–182, 199, 216n11; as repetition, 8. *See also* Sigmund Freud

memory, 185; as forgetting, 33, 34, 107, 149, 200; Freudian conception of, 20–22, 28–30, 74, 109–110, 118, 147; and gender, 12, 74, 132, 143, 146–151, 163; Henri Bergson's conception of, 146–150, 200; and humility, 8; rabbinic conception of, 29–33; and repentance, 12, 132, 143, 146–151

mesora. *See* tradition

metaphysical poetry, 8, 36, 42–43, 44

midrash, 36, 136; Christian, 18; and death of Moses, 24–32; "face to face" in, 17, 19, 21–23, 34; and halakha, 9, 17, 40–41, 208n21; Joseph Soloveitchik's contemporary, 69–70, 72, 139–140, 177; and legal pluralism, 37, 39–40, 46, 54–55, 58, 61; and literary theory, 8, 36–39, 207n9; and metaphysical poetry, 36; and multiplicity (indeterminacy), 8, 28, 36–40, 45–46, 53, 54, 59; poetry of, 41–47, 54; subject-object relation in, 36–37, 46, 51–54, 61

Milton, John, xii, 130–131, 185, 195, 204nn6, 8, 208n25; *Areopagitica*, 198–199, 220nn18, 26; *Paradise Lost*, xi, 128, 141

Modern Orthodoxy, 1, 2, 7, 127, 182, 203n1

Mordechai, 4

Moses: Freudian figure of, 17, 20–22, 26–28, 31, 33, 185, 219n2; as lonely figure, 4, 185–187; Pauline representation of, 18–20; rabbinic representations of, 17, 22–34, 61, 190, 206n32, 210n1 (Interlude), 219n3; representation of in Spinoza, 19–20; as shepherd, 45; and Sinai, 52–53, 69–70, 135, 185–187, 190, 206n32, 210n1, 219n3; suffering of, 4, 30, 186

mourning, 26, 212n16; and *aninut*, 169; for death of Moses, 24–27; as defined by Freud, 7–8, 107–111, 113; divine, 205n24; failure of, 28, 30, 154, 182, 200; of Jerusalem, 197–199; and John Donne, 43; loss of feminine, 114; rabbis, 2, 7, 11, 22. *See also* hermeneutics; Sigmund Freud

mysticism, 76, 77, 80, 81, 86, 104–105, 118, 190

Nadler, Allan, 104, 129–131, 132, 214n15

Nagel, Thomas, 20, 23, 192

Nancy, Jean-Luc, 17

Nazism, 38, 155–156, 166

Nefesh Ha-Hayyim, 6, 53, 61, 184; and *Halakhic Man*, 10, 103–104, 107, 134, 136, 213n27; and

Kant, 105, 134, 184, 213n27. *See also* Hayyim Volozhin

neo-Kantianism, 9, 10, 11, 79, 105, 149, 155. *See also* Immanuel Kant

New Criticism, 48

New Historicism, xiii, 37, 40

Newton, Isaac, 81–83, 85, 105, 164, 192

New World. *See* America

Nietzsche, Frederick, 65, 143, 152, 156, 191

Nissim ben Jacob [Rabbenu Nissim], 51

objectification, 156–157, 165, 166, 170–171, 216n11

Oedipus, 11, 93, 98

Oedipus complex, 101, 117, 119, 163

Onkelos, 23

Orsi, Robert, 215n31

ontology, 18, 62, 82–83, 99, 125, 144, 145, 182, 218n43; and the divine, 19, 22; and epistemology, 5, 18, 82–83, 102–104, 106; and the feminine, 111, 124, 175. See also *Shekhina*

Otniel, 24, 26, 29–30, 32, 33, 61, 62

Otto, Rudolf, 160–161, 185, 216nn13, 14

Paul, 17–20, 22–23, 204n3

Paul, Robert C., 20–21

Phillips, Adam, 2–3, 30, 33, 61, 75, 165, 173, 184, 188, 200

Picasso, Pablo, 136, 172

pilpul, 24, 30, 61

Plank, Max, 105

Plato, 4, 18–19, 34, 39, 41, 54, 94, 208n22

pluralism, xiv; epistemological, 5, 6, 35, 154, 187; expressed in "these and these" [Eruvin 13b], 7, 33, 40, 51–54, 60, 96, 144–145, 150, 185, 188, 191, 193–195; and John Milton, xii, Joseph Soloveitchik's disciplinary, 2–3, 5–7, 75, 78, 81–83, 85–87, 105, 203n12, 211n3; literary theory and, xiii, 40, 193–194; psychoanalytic, 84–87; rabbinic legal, 8–9, 12–13, 22, 28, 30, 35, 36–37, 39–41, 42, 46, 54, 61, 105, 181, 193–195, 205n18, 208nn17, 28, 210n55; rabbinic praxis of, 55–60; and Talmudic irony, 196. *See also* epistemology; hermeneutics

polysemy, 36–37, 39–41, 44–46, 52, 54, 61

poststructuralism, xiii, 39–40, 41, 207nn9, 13

primary and secondary process thought, 169, 189–190, 191

Pruzhna, 10, 13, 67, 70, 101, 120, 123, 149, 153, 161, 173, 178, 182

Putnam, Hilary, 23, 26, 28, 34–35, 74, 182

quantum physics, 82–83, 85, 86, 101, 105–107, 125
Quine, Willard, 54, 58, 189–190

Rabad [Abraham ben David], 69, 71
Rabbenu Tam [Jacob ben Meir], 215n41
Rakeffet-Rothkoff, Aaron, 217n22
Rashi, 46, 68, 209n48, 215n41, 219n3
Ravitzky, Aviezer, 105
Ray, Gene, 216n14
reception history, 2, 98, 204n24; of *Halakhic Man*, 6, 12, 126, 127–132; of John Milton, 1, 128
Reichman, Hershel, 218n41
Reinman, Yosef, 219n17
religious philosophy, 81; autonomy of, 5, 6, 81; disciplinary apology for, 77
repentance, 5, 79, 94–100, 113, 143, 169–170; in contrast to atonement, 94, 96; and ethics, 2, 75, 152–154, 173, 182, 191, 200; and gendered memory, 12, 146–151, 200; and love, 11, 75, 78–80, 89, 94–100, 127, 144–146, 149, 215n37; Reish Lakish's conception of, 96, 145–146, 170; and sublimation, 11, 76–78, 91, 113, 169; and time, 94–98, 132, 146–151, 171, 200
Rojtman, Betty, 38–39, 40–41, 45
Rolland, Romain, 119, 125, 190
Rolling Stones, 17
Rorty, Richard, 13, 185, 192–194, 195, 197
Rose, Gillian, 25–26, 205n22
Rynhold, Daniel, 204n17, 213n5

Sacks, Jonathan, 3–4
Sartre, Jean Paul, 168
Schopenhauer, Arthur, 156
Schwartz, Dov, 129–131, 135, 142, 214nn16, 17
Searle, John, 106
Seder *MeKabblie Ha-Torah*, 23, 33
self-creation, 10–11, 63, 73, 75, 91, 91, 107, 11, 124, 125, 152, 177, 200; and repentance, 76, 95–97, 99, 149, 151. *See also* autobiography; self-fashioning
self-fashioning, 1–3, 76, 94, 112, 151, 186. *See also* autobiography; self-creation
sexuality, 10, 11, 12, 42, 101, 112–113, 120, 122, 125, 136–138, 164. *See also* gender
Shakespeare, William, 1, 97, 112
Shapiro, Marc, 218n34
Shatz, David, 121n7, 215n1
Shekhina, 102–103, 113–114, 137
Shoah. *See* Holocaust
Singer, David and Moshe Sokol, 74, 129, 131, 135, 215n33

Skinner, Quentin, 9, 37, 41, 47–51, 54–55, 57, 59–61, 209nn33, 37, 209n41. *See also* Cambridge history
Socrates, 18, 34, 188
Solomon, Norman, 179, 217n31, 218n35
Solotorevsky, Myrna, 39
Soloveitchik, Haym, 7, 217n22
Soloveitchik, Hayyim, 156, 157, 175, 177–178
Soloveitchik, Joseph: *Types in works of:* cleaving man, 102, 106; cognitive man, 105, 134, 159–160; cosmic man, 159, 164; covenantal man, 15, 159; halakhic man, xiv, 1, 11, 12, 70, 73, 74, 75, 98, 99, 100, 101, 112, 113, 120, 121, 123, 130–138, 140–141, 142–146, 149–155, 156–158, 161, 162, 167, 172, 174, 176–177, 179–181, 185–187, 199–200, 214n17; *homo religiosus*, 86, 94, 96, 130–131, 133, 156–158, 168, 172, 216n11; majestic man, 124, 137, 150, 153; man of fate and man of destiny, 98, 147, 164, 167, 169, 170, 182; man of service, 172.
Works by: And from There Shall You Seek, 67–74, 79–81, 89–90, 96, 102–107, 113–114, 121–122, 125–126, 131, 133–135, 136–137, 150, 176, 200, 211n4, 215n41; "Brisker Method," 174–179, 181; "Catharsis," 153, 154, 160, 161–162, 172, 177, 186; "Confrontation," 153, 160, 176–177; *Family Redeemed*, 11, 112, 115–118, 120, 122–124, 125, 137, 148–149, 163, 212n20; *Halakhic Man*, 3, 6, 10, 12, 62, 68, 75, 76, 78, 79, 86, 90, 94–100, 103–104, 117, 126, 127, 129–151; *Halakhic Mind*, xiii, 2, 5, 6, 9, 79, 81–83, 103, 105, 155–156, 179; "It is the Voice of My Beloved That Knocketh," 98, 164–166, 169–170, 214n30, 216n17; *Lonely Man of Faith*, 67, 124, 137, 149, 150, 173, 182, 186; "Majesty and Humility," 62, 113, 154, 163–164, 176; *On Repentance*, 96, 144–145, 150; *Out of the Whirlwind*, 12, 137, 153, 155, 158–173, 181, 211n15, 216–217n14, 217nn24, 27; "Sacred and Profane," 147; *Shiurim*, 180, 212n16, 218nn40, 44; "A Tribute to the Rebbetzin of Talne," 113–115, 119, 200; *Vision and Leadership*, 4, 120, 186
Soloveitchik, Velvel, 135, 174–175, 177, 180, 181, 198. *See also* Brisk
Soloveitchik Moshe [Rabbi Moses], 67–73, 101, 106, 154, 177
Spinoza, Benedict, 17, 19–20, 22–24, 26, 89
Steinsaltz, Adin, 207n4
Stern, David, 8, 28, 37, 39–43, 45–46, 58, 60, 207n14, 208n21

Stevens, Wallace, 69

Strauss, Leo, 130–131, 142, 214n16

Streuver, Nancy, 48

subject-object relation, xi, 75, 77–87, 152, 197, 209n32, 211n6; Aristotelian unity of, 77–87; and conquest, 134, 176; for David Weiss Halivni, 156; for D. W. Winnicott, 118; and early modern epistemology, 20, 78, 81–82, 83, 95, 105; for Hans-Georg Gadamer and Quentin Skinner, 9, 47–51; for Jonathan Lear, 84–87, 92; and midrash, 36–37, 46, 51–54, 61; in *Nefesh Ha-Hayyim*, 61, 134; and neo-Kantianism, 155; for Stanley Fish, 193, 219n13

sublimation, 11, 75, 76–78, 84, 91, 93, 94, 98, 113, 162, 169

sublime, 172, 185, 216n14

suffering, 98; and authenticity, 168; childhood, 133, 162; and freedom, 93–94, 169; and man of destiny, 167, 169; and melancholy, 4, 110, 154; of Moses, 4, 30, 186; of Oedipus, 93–94; pre-condition for ethics, 161, 185; pre-condition for revelation, 161, 164; of Rabbi Moses (Moshe Soloveitchik), 73, 154; and "why" question, 141

Sztuden, Alex, 129, 131, 214n16

Temple, 132, 140–143, 198

teshuva. See repentance

theodicy, 12, 132, 138–141, 143, 144, 145, 214n30

tradition, 7, 26, 27, 38, 39, 199; atemporal conception of, 4, 8, 12–13, 35, 63, 128, 150–151, 179, 181–182, 200, 215n41, 218n43; conception of in Spinoza, 19–20; and family history, 68–75, 123; Freudian conception of, 21–22;

Pauline conception of, 18, 20; Talmudic, xiii, 1–8, 17, 23–34, 42, 60–61, 185, 187, 195–197, 200; T. S. Eliot's conception of, 157, 205–206n28; without inheritors, 186–187

trauma, 2, 13, 25, 26, 32, 74–75, 106, 109–111, 112, 144, 184, 199–200; and chosenness, 159, 161–163, 167, 169

Trilling, Lionel, 168

Twersky, Mayer, 155

Virgil, 205–206n28

Volozhin, Hayyim, 103–104, 106, 110, 184, 213n27. See also *Nefesh Ha-Hayyim*

"why" question, 141, 164, 214n30, 215n37

Wilde, Oscar, xi

Williams, Bernard, 62

Wimsatt, W. K., 48

Winnicott, D. W., 11, 30, 92, 117–119

Wittgenstein, Ludwig, 7, 37, 48, 57, 62, 195, 220n20

Wolosky, Shira, 124–125, 153, 173, 213n26

Wurzburger, Walter, 218n43

Wyschograd, Edith, 39

Yadin-Israel, Azzan, 44, 208n28

Yavne, 198–199

Yehuda Na-Nasi [Rebbe], 55

Yeshiva University, 3, 129, 180

Yohanan ben Zakkai, 185, 198–199

Yom Tov ibn Asevilli [Ritba], 52–53

Yuter, Alan, 128, 131

Zionism, 5

WILLIAM KOLBRENER is a Professor of English at Bar Ilan University in Israel. With degrees from Oxford and Columbia, Kolbrener has written extensively on the literature, philosophy, and theology of early modern England, with his *Milton's Warring Angels* published in 1996 and his edited edition, *Mary Astell: Reason, Gender, Faith* published in 2008. Kolbrener also writes on psychoanalysis, culture, and contemporary religion; his *Open Minded Torah: Of Irony, Fundamentalism and Love* was published in 2011.